DON'T KNOW MUCH ABOUT® HISTORY

Other Books by
Kenneth C. Davis

DON'T KNOW MUCH ABOUT® GEOGRAPHY
DON'T KNOW MUCH ABOUT® THE CIVIL WAR

*And coming soon in hardcover from
Eagle Brook, an imprint of William Morrow and Company*

DON'T KNOW MUCH ABOUT® THE BIBLE

DON'T KNOW MUCH ABOUT® HISTORY

Everything You Need to Know about American History but Never Learned

KENNETH C. DAVIS

AVON BOOKS ◆ NEW YORK

**To Jenny and Colin,
with the hope that their history
will know only peace.**

AVON BOOKS, INC.
1350 Avenue of the Americas
New York, New York 10019

Copyright © 1990, 1995 by Kenneth C. Davis
Excerpt from *Don't Know Much*® *About the Bible* copyright © 1998 by Kenneth C. Davis
"Don't Know Much About"® is a registered trademark of Kenneth C. Davis
Published by arrangement with Crown Publishers, Inc.
Visit our website at **http://www.AvonBooks.com**
ISBN: 0-380-71252-0

The Crown Publishers, Inc. edition contains the following Library of Congress Cataloging in Publication Data:

Davis, Kenneth C.
    Don't know much about® history: everything you need to know about American history (but never learned) / Kenneth C. Davis.
    p.   cm.
    Includes bibliographical references.
    1. United States—History—Miscellanea. 2. Questions and answers. I. Title
E178.25.D37   1990   89-25215
973—dc20   CIP

First Avon Books Revised Trade Printing: August 1995
First Avon Books Trade Printing: June 1991

AVON TRADEMARK REG. U.S. PAT. OFF. AND IN OTHER COUNTRIES, MARCA REGISTRADA, HECHO EN U.S.A.

Printed in the U.S.A.

OPM 50

Contents

Acknowledgments

I would first like to thank my parents for those many trips to Fort Ticonderoga, Gettysburg, Freedomland, and all the other places that gave me a taste for the romance of history. I guess they paid off.

To New York City, a debt of gratitude for all the museums and public libraries that enabled me to write this book.

I would also like to thank Mark Levine and Steve Boldt for their insights and provocative comments on the manuscript. I am also grateful to Michael Dorris for his special insights into the American Indian.

My editor at Crown, Mark Gompertz, has been a model of patience, and his steady encouragement and friendship are of great value to me. Thanks also to Crown's James Wade and Kate Towson for their help in stepping in to pinch hit.

I am also grateful to Wallis Cooper of the Bookstore for her assistance in having all the books I needed. I also thank Marga Enoch for her friendship and for the steady support and encouragement she has given to my career.

My greatest thanks go to my wife, Joann, and my children, Jenny and Colin, for their long-suffering patience, support, and love. And yes, Jenny. The book is finished.

Introduction

Back in the early 1960s, when I was growing up, there was a silly pop song called *What Did Washington Say When He Crossed the Delaware?* Sung to a tarantella beat, the answer was something like "Martha, Martha, there'll be no pizza tonight." Of course, these lyrics were absurd; everybody knew Washington only ate cherry pie.

On that December night in 1776, George may have told himself that if this raid on an enemy camp in Trenton, New Jersey, didn't work, he might be ordering a last meal before the British strung him up. But as the general rallied his ragged, barefoot troops across the icy Delaware, one of his actual comments was far more amusing than those lyrics. Stepping into his boat, Washington—the plainspoken frontiersman, not the marbleized demigod—nudged 280-pound General Henry "Ox" Knox with the tip of his boot and said, "Shift that fat ass, Harry. But slowly, or you'll swamp the damned boat."

According to A. J. Langguth's fascinating history of the Revolution, *Patriots,* that is how Knox himself reported the story after the war. I certainly never heard that version of the crossing when I was in school. And that's too bad, because it reveals more of Washington's true, earthy nature than all the hokey tales about cherry trees and nonexistent prayer vigils in Valley Forge. And that's the point of this book: much of what we remember about our history is either mistaken or fabricated. That is, if we remember it at all.

For all too many Americans who dozed through American History 101, the Mayflower Compact might as well be a small car. Reconstruction has something to do with silicone implants. And the Louisiana Purchase means eating out at a Cajun restaurant. In recent years, several writers have enjoyed remarkable success by lambasting Americans' failure to know our past. Americans were shown to be know-nothings in the books *Cultural Literacy* and *The Closing of the American Mind.*

Well, we're probably not as dumb as these books would have us. But the sad truth is clear: we are no nation of scholars when it comes to history. On the 1988 hustings, for instance, vice-presidential candidate Dan Quayle had trouble fielding a question about the Holocaust—fumbling the facts as to when and to whom it happened.

Another highly publicized example of our "historical illiteracy" was the 1987 survey of high school juniors that exposed astonishing gaps in what these seventeen-year-olds knew about American history and literature. A third of the students couldn't identify the Declaration of Independence as the document that marked the formal separation of the thirteen colonies from Great Britain. Only 32 percent of the students surveyed could place the American Civil War in the correct half century.

But why dump on the kids? While there are constant warnings issued about the yawning gaps in the education of American students, another question looms larger. Would their parents score any higher? Most thirty-seven-year-olds or forty-seven-year-olds might not do any better on a similar pop quiz. Don't ask for whom the gap yawns. The gap yawns for thee.

The reason for these common historical shortcomings is simple. Most of us learned history from textbooks that served up the past as if it were a Hollywood costume drama. In schoolbooks of an earlier era, the warts on our Founding Fathers' noses were neatly retouched. Slavery also got the glossy make-over—it was merely the misguided practice of the rebellious folks down South until the "progressives" of the North showed them the light. American Indians got the same portrayal in textbooks that you saw in B-movies.

Truth isn't so cosmetically perfect. Our historical sense is frequently skewed, skewered, or plain screwed up by myths and misconceptions. Schools that packaged a tidy set of simplistic historical images are largely responsible for fostering these American myths. There was a tendency to hide the less savory moments from our past, the way a mad aunt's photo gets pulled from the family album. If anyone thinks it only happens in George Orwell's *1984*, take a look at the official Chinese version of the June 1989 massacre in Tiananmen Square. How will Chinese history books tell that in ten or twenty years?

The gaping chasms in our historical literacy have been reinforced by images from pop culture. Books, movies, and television have magnified the myths and make-overs. But looking past these myths is revealing. The real picture is far more interesting than the historical tummy-tuck.

This book's intent is to bridge those chasms with some simple, accessible answers to basic questions about American history. This single volume is obviously not an encyclopedic history of America. For simplicity, I have used a question-and-answer approach, and there are literally shelves of books about each of the questions I have included. My intent is to refresh the shaky recollection or reshape the misconception with some simple answers. Or, in some cases, to point the way to longer answers.

The book is organized along chronological lines, moving from America's "discovery" by Europe to more recent events, including the Bill Clinton administration. I have attempted to focus on the sort of basic questions that the average person might have, emphasizing names, places, and events that we vaguely recall as being important, but forget exactly why. The reader is welcome to read the book straight through as a narrative history, or to use it as a reference book by dipping into a particular question or period. Because wars have been central, shaping events in our history, and because many people lack a sense of what actually happened during these wars, I have included a series of chronologies that condense the events of the major conflicts in American history. Also scattered throughout the book are "American Voices," which are selected quotes, passages from books, speeches, and court decisions that reflect the spirit of the times.

Following the seeming ambivalence of the American public about the 1988 election, it also seemed appropriate to include an election primer that explains some of the more mysterious elements of the process, from caucuses and delegate counts to the nearly mystical electoral college. A second appendix presents a quick guide to the American presidents. An annotated list of sources for each chapter offers a selective rather than an exhaustive bibliography. The books cited are either widely accepted standards or recent works that offer fresh insights or update accepted wisdom. I have also tried to single out those critically well-received books written for the general reader rather than the specialist, such as James M. McPherson's *Battle Cry of Freedom,* a masterful single-volume history of the Civil War. A general bibliography lists books that cover broader periods and themes.

In some cases, these sources take very specific political viewpoints. While I have attempted to present a spectrum of opinions on those issues where there is no broad consensus, I have tried to avoid any particular stance. If there is an underlying theme here, it is that the struggle for power is the essence of history. The battle between those holding power—whether it be the power of land, money, church, or votes—and the have-nots—the poor, the weak, the disenfranchised, the rebellious—is the main thread in the drama of history.

A second thread is one that our schools sadly bury, either out of laziness or owing to a shortfall in imaginative teaching. This is the impact of personality in history. At many turning points, it was the commanding presence of an individual—Washington, Lincoln, Frederick Douglass, the Roosevelts, and Susan B. Anthony, to name a few—that determined events, rather than the force of any idea or movement. Great ideals and noble causes have died for lack of a champion. At other times, the absence of a strong personality has had the reverse effect. For example, if a dominant president had emerged in the years before the Civil War, instead of a string of mediocrities, Lincoln's emergence might have been stillborn.

I came to this project with the same misconceptions many people may have about our past. I have learned a great deal about the Americans who shaped the country, and it hasn't always been a pleasant discovery. The simple view of men like Washington, Lincoln, and Roosevelt as beatified heroes of the American epic doesn't always stand up to scrutiny. The American story is not that simple. There are moments in our past that can breed feelings of cynicism and disgust. Yet there are other moments that evoke pride and admiration.

Generally speaking, Americans have behaved worse than our proudest boosters proclaim. On the other hand, Americans have also shown a capacity to be better than the worst claims of their detractors. Barely two hundred years old, America is still young in the broad sense of history, even though the pace of history has accelerated radically as the twentieth-century techno-revolution has transformed media, travel, and communications. The history of this country is not necessarily a continuum moving toward a perfectly realized republic. More accurately, history has acted like a pendulum with long swings creating a flux in one direction or another. America remains shockingly divided along racial and economic lines. One can look at that rift and feel pessimism. But the optimist points to the distance America has come in a relatively brief time. Of course, that is small consolation to those who have always received the short end of the stick.

Perhaps what is more important is the commitment to an acknowledgment of the true American dream. Not the one about the house with two cars in the driveway and a barbecue in the backyard, but the dream Jefferson voiced two hundred years ago. Even though his vision of "all men created equal" was probably different from our modern understanding, it remains the noblest of dreams and the greatest of aspirations. The struggle to fulfill that dream has been a long, strange trip. And it is never over.

Brave New World

- Who really "discovered" America?

- If he wasn't interested in the Bahamas, what was Columbus looking for in the first place?

- So if Columbus didn't really discover America, who did?

- Okay, the Indians really discovered America. Who were they, and how did they get here?

- If Columbus was so important, how come we don't live in the United States of Columbus?

- Where were the first European settlements in the New World?

- If the Spanish were here first, what was so important about Jamestown?

- What was the Northwest Passage?

• What was the Lost Colony?

• When and how did Jamestown get started?

• Did Pocahontas really save John Smith's life?

• What was the House of Burgesses?

• Who started the slave trade?

• Who were the Pilgrims, and what did they want?

• What was the Mayflower Compact?

• Did the Pilgrims really land at Plymouth Rock?

• Highlights in the development of New England

• Who started New York?

• Did the Indians really sell Manhattan for $24?

• How did New Amsterdam become New York?

• When did the French reach the New World?

• Why is Pennsylvania the Quaker State?

• What were the thirteen original colonies?

Few eras in American history are shrouded in as much myth and mystery as the long period covering America's discovery and settlement. Perhaps this is because there were few objective observers on hand to record so many of these events. There was no "film at eleven" when primitive people crossed into Alaska. No correspondents were on board when Columbus's ships reached land. Historians have been forced instead to rely upon accounts written by participants in the events, witnesses whose views can politely be called jaundiced. This chapter covers some of the key events during several thousand years of history.

However, the spotlight is on the development of what would become the United States, and the chapter ends with the thirteen original colonies in place.

Who really "discovered" America?

"In fourteen hundred and ninety-two, Columbus sailed the ocean blue." We all know that. But did he really discover America? The best answer is, "Sort of."

A national holiday and two centuries of schoolbooks have left the impression of Christopher Columbus as the intrepid sailor and man of God (his given name means "Christ-bearer") who was the first to reach America, disproving the notion of a flat world while he was at it. Italian-Americans who claim the sailor as their own treat Columbus Day as a special holiday, as do Hispanic Americans who celebrate *El Día de la Raza* as their discovery day. It would be unthinkable to downplay the importance of Columbus's voyage, or the incredible heroism and tenacity of character his quest demanded. Even the astronauts who flew to the moon had a pretty good idea of what to expect; Columbus was sailing, as "Star Trek" puts it, "where no man has gone before."

However, rude facts do suggest a few different angles to his story.

After trying to sell his plan to the kings of Portugal, England, and France, Columbus doggedly returned to Isabella and Ferdinand of Spain, who had already said no once. Convinced by one of their ministers that the risks were small and the potential return great, and fueled by an appetite for gold and fear of Portugal's lead in exploration, the Spanish monarchs later agreed. Contrary to myth, Queen Isabella did not have to pawn any of the crown jewels to finance the trip.

Columbus set sail on August 3, 1492, from Palos, Spain, aboard three ships, *Niña, Pinta,* and *Santa María,* the last being his flagship. Columbus (christened Cristoforo Colombo) had been promised a ten-percent share of profits, governorship of new-found lands, and an impressive title—Admiral of the Ocean Sea.

On October 12 at 2:00 A.M., just as his crews were threatening to mutiny and force a return to Spain, a lookout named Rodrigo aboard the *Pinta* sighted moonlight shimmering on some cliffs or sand. Having promised a large reward to the first man to spot land, Columbus claimed that he had seen the light the night before, and kept the reward for himself. Columbus named the landfall—*Guanahani* to the natives—San Salvador. While it was long held that Columbus's San Salvador was Watling Island in the Bahamas, recent computer-assisted theories point to Samana Cay. Later on that first voyage, Columbus reached Cuba and a large island he called Hispaniola (presently Haiti and the Dominican Republic).

Although he found some naked natives whom he christened *indios* in the mistaken belief that he had reached the so-called Indies or Indonesian Islands, the only gold he found was in the earrings worn by the Indians. As for spices, he did find a local plant called *tobacos,* which was rolled into cigars and smoked by the local Arawaks. It was not long before all Europe was savoring pipefuls of the evil weed. (Tobacco was brought to Spain for the first time in 1555. Three years later, the Portuguese introduced Europe to the habit of taking snuff. The economic importance of tobacco to the early history of America cannot be understated, especially with respect to the later English colonies, where it literally kept the settlers alive. Powerful tobacco lobbies that influence government decisions practically arrived with the first European settlers.)

Still believing that he had reached some island outposts of China, Columbus left some volunteers on Hispaniola in a fort called Natividad, built of timbers from the wrecked *Santa María,* and returned to Spain. While Columbus never reached the mainland of the present United States of America on any of his three subsequent voyages, his arrival in the Caribbean signaled the dawn of an astonishing and unequaled era of discovery, conquest, and colonization in the Americas. Although his bravery, persistence, and seamanship have rightfully earned Columbus a place in history, what the schoolbooks gloss over is that Columbus's arrival also marked the beginning of one of the cruelest episodes in human history.

Driven by an obsessive quest for gold, Columbus quickly enslaved the local population. Under Columbus and other Spanish adventurers, as well as later European colonizers, an era of genocide was opened that ravaged the native American population through warfare, forced labor, draconian punishments, and European diseases to which the Indians had no natural immunities.

If he wasn't interested in the Bahamas, what was Columbus looking for in the first place?

The arrival of the three ships at their Caribbean landfall marks what is probably the biggest and luckiest blooper in the history of the world. Rather than a new world, Columbus was actually searching for a direct sea route to China and the Indies. Ever since Marco Polo had journeyed back from the Orient loaded with spices, gold, and fantastic tales of the strange and mysterious East, Europeans had lusted after the riches of Polo's Cathay (China). This appetite grew ravenous when the returning Crusaders opened up overland trade routes between Europe and the Orient. However, when Constantinople fell to the Turks in 1453, it meant an end to the spice route that served as the economic lifeline for Mediterranean Europe.

Emerging from the Middle Ages, Europe was quickly shifting from an agrarian, barter economy to a new age of capitalism in which gold was the coin of the realm. The medieval Yeppies (Young European Princes) acquired a taste for the finer things such as gold and precious jewels, as well as the new taste sensations called spices, and these were literally worth their weight in gold. After a few centuries of home-cooked venison, there was an enormous clamor for the new Oriental take-out spices: cinnamon from Ceylon, pepper from India and Indonesia, nutmeg from Celebes, and cloves from the Moluccas. The new merchant princes had also acquired a taste for Japanese silks and Indian cottons, dyes, and precious stones.

Led by Prince Henry the Navigator, founder of a great scholarly seaport on coastal Portugal, Portugese sea captains like Bartholomeu Dias (who reached the Cape of Good Hope in 1488) and Vasco da Gama (who sailed all the way to India in 1495) had taken the lead in exploiting Africa and navigating a sea route to the Indies. Like others of his day, Columbus believed that a direct westward passage to the Orient was not only possible, but would be faster and easier. In spite of what Columbus's public-relations people later said, the flat-earth idea was pretty much finished by the time Chris sailed. In fact, an accepted theory of a round earth had been held as far back as the days of the ancient Greeks. In the year Columbus sailed, a Nuremberg geographer constructed the first globe. The physical proof of the Earth's roundness came when eighteen survivors of Magellan's crew of 266 completed a circumnavigation in 1522.

Columbus believed a course due west along latitude twenty-eight degrees North would take him to Marco Polo's fabled Cipangu (Japan). Knowing that no one was crazy enough to sponsor a voyage of more than 3,000 miles, Columbus based his guess of the distance on ancient Greek theories, some highly speculative maps drawn after Marco Polo's return, and some figure-fudging of his own. He arrived at the convenient estimate of 2,400 miles.

In fact, the distance Columbus was planning to cover was 10,600 miles by air!

So if Columbus didn't really discover America, who did?

The debate over who reached America before Columbus goes back almost as far as Columbus's voyage. Enough books have been written on the subject of earlier "discoverers" to fill a small library. There is plenty of evidence to bolster the claims made on behalf of a number of voyagers who may have reached the Americas, either by accident or design, well before Columbus reached the Bahamas.

Among these, the one best supported by archaeological evidence is the theory that holds that the Norse captain Leif Eriksson not only reached North America but established a colony, called Vinland, in present-day Newfoundland around 1000 A.D., five hundred years before Columbus. Most of what is guessed about the Norse colony in North America is derived from two Icelandic epics called *The Vinland Sagas*.

While "Leif the Lucky" gets the credit in history and the

roads and festivals named after him, it was another Norseman, Bjarni Herjolfsson, who was the first European to sight North America, in 985 or 986. But it was Leif who supposedly built some huts and spent one winter in this land where wild grapes—more likely berries—grew before returning to Greenland. A few years later, another Greenlander named Thorfinn Karlsefni set up housekeeping in Eriksson's spot, passing two years there. Among the problems they faced were unfriendly local Eskimo tribes, whom the Norsemen called *skrelings* (a contemptuous term translated as "wretch" or "dwarf"). During one attack, a pregnant Norse woman frightened the *skrelings* off by slapping a sword against her bare breast. Terrified at this sight, the *skrelings* fled back to their boats.

Then there are those who hold out for the Irish voyagers who supposedly reached America in the ninth or tenth century, sailing in small boats called *curraghs*. However, there is no archaeological or other evidence to support this. Another popular myth, completely unfounded, regards a Welshman named Modoc who established a colony and taught the local Indians to speak Welsh. More recent evidence, including an Oriental ship's bell found off the coast of California, suggests an ironic twist on the idea of Europeans sailing to China; fishermen from Japan and China may have sailed as far as the Pacific coast of North America.

If we are talking about North America, a significant discovery belongs to another of Columbus's countrymen, Giovanni Caboto (John Cabot), who was sailing for the British. In 1496, Cabot (and his son, Sebastian) received a commission from England's King Henry VII to find a new trade route to Asia. Sailing out of Bristol aboard the *Matthew*, it is known only that Cabot reached present-day Newfoundland, laying a claim that would eventually provide the English with their foothold in the New World. Sailing with five ships on a subsequent voyage in 1498, Cabot ran into bad weather. One of the vessels returned to an Irish port, but Cabot disappeared with the four other ships.

The distinction of being the first European to set foot on what would become United States soil rightfully belongs to Juan Ponce de León, the Spanish adventurer who conquered Puerto Rico. Investigating rumors of a large island north of Cuba that contained a "fountain of youth" whose waters could restore youth and vigor, Ponce de León found and named Florida in 1513 and "discovered" Mexico on that same trip.

Finally there is the 1524 voyage of still another Italian, Giovanni de Verrazano, who sailed in the employ of the French. Verrazano was searching for a strait through the New World that would take him westward to the Orient. He reached land at Cape Fear in the Carolinas, and sailed up the Atlantic coast until he reached Newfoundland and then returned to France. Along the way, he failed to stop in either Chesapeake or Delaware Bay. Verrazano reached New York Bay (where he only went as far as the narrows and the site of the bridge that bear his name), and Narragansett Bay, but he also missed the Bay of Fundy.

But all these European seamen were no more than Johnny-come-latelies in the Americas. In fact, America had been "discovered" long before any of these voyages. The true "discoverers" of America were the people whose culture and societies were well established here while Europe was still in the Dark Ages, the so-called Indians.

Okay, the Indians really discovered America. Who were they and how did they get here?

Until recently, it was generally believed that humans first lived in the Americas approximately 12,000 years ago. However, new evidence suggests that the people who would eventually come to be called Indians arrived in America some thirty to forty thousand years ago. Radiocarbon dating of charcoal found in southern Chile has bolstered the argument that humans lived in America much earlier than had been widely accepted.

The version of events suggested by archaeological finds and highly accurate carbon testing is that the prehistoric people who populated the Americas were hunters following the great herds of woolly mammoths. They walked from Siberia across a land bridge into Alaska, and then began heading south toward warmer climates, slaughtering the mammoth as they went. Eventually as the glaciers melted, the oceans rose and covered this land bridge, creating the present-day Bering Strait and separating Alaska from Russia.

By the time Columbus arrived, there were millions of what might be called First Americans or Amerindians occupying the two continents of the Americas. These were divided into hundreds of tribal societies, the most advanced of which were the Mayas and later the Aztecs in Mexico and the Incas of Peru, all of whom became fodder for the Spanish under the reign of terror wrought by the *conquistadores*. Many history books present Amerindians as either a collection of nearly savage civilizations or as groups of people living in harmony with themselves and nature. Neither view is realistic.

There were, first of all, many cultures spread over the two Americas, from the Eskimo and Inuit of the North down to the advanced South American societies. While none of these developed along the lines of the European world, substantial achievements were made in agriculture, architecture, mathematics, and other fields. On the other hand, some basic developments were lacking. Nor were these Indians free from savagery, as best witnessed by the Aztec human sacrifice that claimed as many as 1,000 victims a day in Tenochtitlán (the site of present-day Mexico City) or the Iroquois who had raised torture of captured opponents to a sophisticated but ghastly art.

Estimates of the Indian population at the time of Columbus vary, ranging from 8 million to 16 million people, spread over two continents. Although Hitler's attempted extermination of the Jews of Europe was a calculated, methodical genocidal plan, the European destruction of the Indians was just as ruthlessly efficient, killing off perhaps 90 percent of the native population it found, all in the name of progress, civilization, and Christianity.

If Columbus was so important, how come we don't live in the United States of Columbus?

The naming of America was one of the cruel tricks of history and about as accurate as calling Indians "Indians." Amerigo Vespucci was another Italian who found his way to Spain and, as a ship chandler, actually helped outfit Columbus's voyages. In 1499 he sailed to South America with Alonso de Hojeda, one of Columbus's captains, reaching the mouth of the Amazon. He made three more voyages along the coast of Brazil. In 1504 letters supposedly written by Vespucci appeared in Italy in which he claimed to be captain of the four voyages and in which the words *Mundus Novus*, or "New World," were first used to describe the lands that had been found. Some years later, in a new edition of Ptolemy, this new land, still believed to be attached to Asia, was labeled "America" in Vespucci's honor.

Where were the first European settlements in the New World?

While we make a great fuss over the Pilgrims and Jamestown, the Spanish had roamed over much of the Americas by the time the English arrived. In fact, if the Spanish Armada launched to assault Queen Elizabeth's England hadn't been blown to bits by storms and the English "sea dogs" in 1588, this might be *Los Estados Unidos*, and we'd be eating tacos at bullfights.

Following Columbus's bold lead, the Spanish (and, to a lesser extent, the Portugese) began a century of exploration, colonization, and subjugation with the primary aim of providing more gold for the Spanish crown. Among the highlights of Spanish exploration:

1499 Amerigo Vespucci and Alonso de Hojeda (or Ojeda) sail for South America and reach mouth of Amazon.

1502 Vespucci, after second voyage, concludes South America is not part of India and names it *Mundus Novus*.

1505 Juan Bermudez discovers the island that bears his name, Bermuda.

1513 Balboa crosses Isthmus of Panama and reaches Pacific for the first time, but believes it to be part of the Indian Ocean.

1513 Ponce de León, searching for the "fountain of youth," reaches and names Florida.

1519 Cortés enters Tenochtitlán (Mexico City); Domenico de Piñeda explores Gulf of Mexico from Florida to Vera Cruz.

1522 Andagoya discovers Peru.

1523 Jamaica founded.
1531 Pizarro invades Peru, conquers Incas.
1535 Lima founded.
1536 Buenos Aires founded.
1538 Bogota founded.
1539 De Soto explores Florida.
1539 First printing press in New World set up in Mexico City.
1540 Grand Canyon discovered.
1541 De Soto discovers Mississippi River; Coronado explores from New Mexico across Texas, Oklahoma, and eastern Kansas.
1549 Jesuit missionaries arrive in South America.
1551 Universities founded in Lima and Mexico City;
1565 St. Augustine founded (razed by Francis Drake in 1586).
1567 Rio de Janeiro founded.
1605 Santa Fe, New Mexico, founded (date in dispute; some say 1609).

If the Spanish were there first, what was so important about Jamestown?

Winners write the history books, so, even though the Spanish dominated the New World for almost a century before the English settlers arrived in Jamestown, the Spanish were eventually supplanted in North America and the new era of English supremacy began.

Just as modern American life is shaped by global happenings, international events had begun to play an important role even at this stage in world history. By the mid-sixteenth century, Spain had grown corrupt and lazy, the Spanish king living off the spoils of the gold mines of the Americas, with a resultant lack of enterprise at home. With gold pouring in, there was little inducement or incentive to push advances in the areas of commerce or invention. Perhaps even more significant was the revolution that became known as the Protestant Reformation. A zealous Catholic, Spain's King Philip II saw England's Protestant Queen Elizabeth not only as a political and military rival, but as a heretic as well. His desire to defend Roman Catholicism dictated his policies, including his support of the Catholic Mary Queen of Scots against Elizabeth. For her part, Elizabeth saw the religious conflict as the excuse to build English power at Spain's expense. And she turned her notorious "sea dogs," or gentlemen pirates, loose on Spanish treasure ships while also aiding the Dutch in their fight with Spain. The Dutch, meanwhile, were building the largest merchant marine fleet in Europe.

When the English repulsed the Spanish Armada in 1588, the proverbial handwriting was on the wall. It was a blow from which Spain never fully recovered, and it marked the beginning of England's rise to global sea power, enabling that nation to embark more aggressively on a course of colonization.

What was the Northwest Passage?

If you answer, "A movie by Alfred Hitchcock," Go Directly to Jail. Do Not Pass Go.

Almost a century after Columbus's first voyage, Europeans remained convinced that a faster route to China was waiting to be found and that the New World was just an annoying roadblock—although Spain was proving it to be a profitable one—that could be detoured. Some tried to go around the top of Russia, the "northeast passage." Sebastian Cabot organized an expedition in search of such a passage in 1553. Cabot had also tried going the other way back in 1509, but the voyage failed when his crew mutinied.

In 1576, Sir Humphrey (or Humfrey) Gilbert first used the phrase "North West passage," to describe a sea route around North America, and he continued to search for such a route to China. An Oxford-educated soldier, courtier, and businessman, Gilbert also played a hand in the earliest English attempts at colonization. In 1578 another Englishman, Martin Frobisher, set off for the fabled route and reached the northeast coast of Canada, exploring Baffin Island.

Among the others who searched for the route through the Arctic from Europe to Asia was Henry Hudson, an Englishman sailing for the Dutch, who embarked on his voyage aboard the

Half Moon to North America in 1609, the voyage on which he discovered the bay, river, and strait later named after him.

While a northwest passage to the East does exist, it requires sailing through far northern waters that are icebound much of the year.

What was the Lost Colony?

In 1578 and again in 1583, Humphrey Gilbert set sail with a group of colonists and Queen Elizabeth's blessings. The first expedition accomplished little, and the second, after landing in Newfoundland, was lost in a storm, and Sir Humphrey with it.

But Gilbert's half-brother, Sir Walter Raleigh (or "Ralegh" as other historians spell it), the thirty-one-year-old favorite of Queen Elizabeth, inherited Gilbert's royal patent and continued the quest. He dispatched ships to explore North America and named the land there "Virginia" in honor of Queen Elizabeth, "the virgin queen." In 1585 he was behind a short-lived attempt to form a colony on Roanoke Island on present-day North Carolina's Outer Banks. In 1586 Sir Francis Drake found the colonists hungry and ready to return to England. In the following year, Raleigh sent another group of 107 men, women, and children to Roanoke. It was an ill-planned and ill-fated expedition. The swampy island was inhospitable, and so were the local Indians. Supply ships, delayed by the attack of the Spanish Armada, failed to reach the colony in 1588, and when ships finally did arrive in 1590, the pioneers left by Raleigh had disappeared without a trace.

All that was found was some rusted debris and the word CROATOAN, the Indian name for the nearby island on which Cape Hatteras is located, carved on a tree. Over the years there has been much speculation about what happened to the so-called Lost Colony, but its exact fate remains a mystery. Starvation and Indian raids probably killed off most of the unlucky colonists, with any survivors being adopted by the Indians, the descendants of whom still claim Raleigh's colonists as their ancestral kin. In his book *Set Fair for Roanoke*, the historian David Beers Quinn produces a more interesting bit of historical detection. Quinn suggests that the Lost Colonists weren't lost at all; instead, they made their way north toward Virginia, settled among peaceable Indians, and were surviving at nearly the time Jamestown was planted but were slaughtered in a massacre by Powhatan, an Indian chief whose name becomes prominent in the annals of Jamestown.

When and how did Jamestown get started?

It took another fifteen years and a new monarch in England to attempt colonization once again. But this time there would be a big difference: private enterprise had entered the picture. The costs of sponsoring a colony were too high for any individual, even royalty, to take on alone. In 1605, two groups of merchants, who had formed joint stock companies that combined the investments of small shareholders, petitioned King James I for the right to colonize Virginia. The first of these, the Virginia Company of London, was given a grant to southern Virginia; the second, the Plymouth Company, was granted northern Virginia. At this time, however, the name "Virginia" encompassed the entire North American continent from sea to sea. While these charters spoke loftily of spreading Christianity, the real goal remained the quest for treasure, and the charter spoke of the right to "dig, mine, and search for all Manner of Mines of Gold, Silver, and Copper."

On December 20, 1606, 104 colonists left port aboard three ships, *Susan Constant, Goodspeed,* and *Discovery,* under Captain John Newport. They reached Chesapeake Bay in May 1607 and founded Jamestown, the first permanent English settlement in the New World.

Here again, rude facts intrude on the neat version of life in Jamestown that the schoolbooks gave us. While the difficulties faced by the first men of Jamestown were real, many of the problems were self-induced. The choice of location, for instance, was a bad one. Jamestown lay in the midst of a malarial swamp. The settlers had arrived too late to get crops planted. Many in the group were gentlemen unused to work, or their menservants, equally unaccustomed to the hard labor demanded by the harsh task of carving out a viable colony. In a few months, fifty-one of the party were dead; some of the survivors were deserting to the Indians whose land they had invaded. In the "starving time" of 1609–10, the Jamestown settlers were in even worse straits. Crazed for food, the settlers were reduced to cannibalism, and one contemporary account tells of men "driven through insufferable hunger to eat those things which nature abhorred," raiding both English and Indian graves. In one extreme case, a man killed his wife as she slept and "fed upon her till he had clean devoured all parts saving her head."

Did Pocahontas really save John Smith's life?

This is how you learned it in school: Captain John Smith, the fearless leader of the Jamestown colony, was captured by Powhatan's Indians. Smith's head was on a stone, ready to be bashed by an Indian war ax, when Pocahontas (a nickname loosely translated as "frisky"—her real name was Matowaka), the eleven-year-old daughter of Chief Powhatan, "took his head in her arms" and begged for Smith's life. The basis for that legend is Smith's own version of events, and he was not exactly an impartial witness to history. David Beers Quinn speculates that Smith learned of Powhatan's massacre of the Lost Colonists from the chief himself, but kept this news secret in order to keep the peace with the Indians. This "execution" was actually an initiation ceremony in which Smith was received by the Indians.

One of those larger-than-life characters with mythic stature, Captain John Smith was an English adventurer whose life before Jamestown was an extraordinary one. As a soldier of fortune in the wars between the Holy Roman Empire and the Turks, he rose to captain's rank and had supposedly been held prisoner by the Turkish Pasha and sold as a slave to a young, handsome woman. After escaping, he was rewarded for his services in the war and made a "gentleman." He later became a Mediterranean privateer, returning to London in 1605 to join Bartholomew Gosnold in a new venture into Virginia.

While some large questions exist about Smith's colorful past (documented largely in his own somewhat unreliable writings), there is no doubt that he was instrumental in saving Jamestown from an early extinction. When the Jamestown party fell on hard times, Smith became a virtual military dictator, instituting a brand of martial law that helped save the colony. He became an expert forager, and was a successful Indian trader. Without the help of Powhatan's Indians, who shared food with the Englishmen, showed them how to plant local corn and yams, and introduced them to the ways of the forest, the Jamestown colonists would have perished. Yet, in a pattern that would be repeated elsewhere, the settlers eventually turned on the Indians, and fighting between the groups was frequent and fierce. Once respected by the Indians, Smith became feared by them. While he stayed in Jamestown for only two years before setting off on a voyage of exploration that provided valuable maps of the American coast as far north as New England, Smith's mark on the colony was indelible. A hero of the American past? Yes, but, like most heroes, not without flaws.

After Smith's departure, his supposed savior, Pocahontas, continued to play a role in the life of the colony. During the sporadic battles between settlers and Indians, Pocahontas, now seventeen years old, was kidnapped and held hostage by the colonists. While a prisoner, she caught the attention of the settler John Rolfe, who married the Indian princess, as one account put it, "for the good of the plantation," cementing a temporary peace with the Indians. Rolfe later took the Indian princess to London, where she was a sensation, even earning a royal audience. Renamed "Lady Rebecca" after her baptism, she died of smallpox in England.

Besides this notable marriage, Rolfe's other distinction was his role in the event that truly saved Jamestown and changed the course of American history. In 1612 he crossed Virginia tobacco with seed from a milder Jamaican leaf, and Virginia had its first viable cash crop. London soon went tobacco-mad, and in a very short space of time, tobacco was sown on every available square foot of plantable land in Virginia.

American Voices

Powhatan to John Smith, 1607:

Why will you take by force what you may have quietly by love?
Why will you destroy us who supply you with food? What can
you get by war? . . . In these wars, my men must sit up
watching, and if a twig breaks, they all cry out 'Here comes
Captain Smith!' So I must end my miserable life. Take away
your guns and swords, the cause of all our jealousy, or you may
all die in the same manner.

What was the House of Burgesses?

Despite the tobacco profits, controlled in London by a
monopoly, Jamestown limped along near extinction. Survival
remained a day-to-day affair while political intrigues back in London reshaped the colony's destiny. Virginia Company shareholders were angry that their investment was turning out to be a bust,
and believed that the "Magazine," a small group of Virginia Company members who exclusively supplied the colony's provisions,
were draining off profits. A series of reforms was instituted, the
most important of which meant settlers could own their land,
rather than just working for the Company. And the arbitrary rule
of the governor was replaced by English common law.

In 1619, new management was brought to the Virginia Company, and Governor Yeardley of Virginia summoned an elected
legislative assembly—the House of Burgesses—which met in
Jamestown that year. (A *burgess* is a person invested with all the
privileges of a citizen, and comes from the same root as the
French bourgeois.) Besides the governor, there were six counci-
lors appointed by the governor, and two elected representatives
from each private estate and two from each of the Company's
four estates or tracts. (Landowning males over seventeen years
old were eligible to vote.) Their first meeting was cut short by an
onslaught of malaria and July heat. While any decisions they
made required approval of the Company in London, this was
clearly the seed from which American representative government
would grow.

The little assembly had a shaky beginning, from its initial malarial summer. In the first place, the House of Burgesses was not an instant solution to the serious problems still faced by the Jamestown settlers. Despite years of immigration to the new colony, Jamestown's rate of attrition during those first years was horrific. Lured by the prospect of owning land, some 6,000 settlers had been transported to Virginia by 1624. However, a census that year showed only 1,277 colonists alive. A Royal Council asked, "What has become of the five thousand missing subjects of His Majesty?"

Many of them had starved. Others had died in fierce Indian fighting, including some 350 colonists who were killed in a 1622 massacre when the Indians, fearful at the disappearance of their lands, nearly pushed the colony back into the Chesapeake Bay. Responding to the troubles at Jamestown and the mismanagement of the colony, the King revoked the Virginia Company's charter in 1624, and Virginia became a royal colony. Under the new Royal Governor, Thomas Wyatt, however, the House of Burgesses survived on an extralegal basis and would have much influence in the years ahead.

Exactly how representative that House was in those days is another question. Certainly women didn't vote. Before 1619 there were few women in Jamestown, and in that year a shipload of "ninety maidens" arrived to be presented as wives to the settlers. The going price for one of the brides: 120 pounds of tobacco as payment for their transport from England.

Ironically, in the same year that representative government took root in America, another ominous cargo of people arrived in the port of Jamestown. Like the women, these new arrivals couldn't vote, and also like the women, they brought a price. These were the first African slaves to be sold in the American colonies.

Who started the slave trade?

While everyone wants a piece of the claim to the discovery of America, there are fewer arguments over who started the slave trade. The unhappy distinction probably belongs to Portugal, where ten black Africans were taken about fifty years before

Columbus sailed. But by no means did the Portuguese enjoy a monopoly. The Spanish quickly began to import this cheap human labor to its American lands. In 1562 the English seaman John Hawkins began a direct slave trade between Guinea and the West Indies. By 1600 the Dutch and French were also caught up in the "traffick in men," and by the time those first twenty Africans arrived in Jamestown aboard a Dutch slaver, a million or more black slaves had already been brought to the Spanish and Portuguese colonies in the Caribbean and South America.

Who were the Pilgrims, and what did they want?

The year after the House of Burgesses met for the first time, the Pilgrims of the *Mayflower* founded the second permanent English settlement in America. Their arrival in 1620 has always been presented as another of history's lucky accidents. But was it?

Had Christopher Jones, captain of the *Mayflower,* turned the ship when he was supposed to, the little band would have gone to its intended destination, the mouth of the Hudson, future site of New York, and a settlement within the bounds of the Virginia Company's charter and authority. Instead, the ship kept a westerly route—the result of a bribe to the captain, as London gossip had it—and in November 1620, the band of pioneers found safe harbor in Cape Cod Bay, coming ashore at the site of present-day Provincetown. Of the 102 men, women, and children aboard the small ship, fifty were so-called Pilgrims.

Here again, as it had in Queen Elizabeth's time, the Protestant Reformation played a crucial role in events. After the great split from Roman Catholicism that created the Church of England, the question of religious reform continued heatedly in England. Many English remained Catholic. Others felt that the Church of England was too "popish" and wished to push it further away from Rome—to "purify" it—so they were called Puritans. But even among Puritans strong differences existed, and there were those who thought the Church of England too corrupt. They wanted autonomy for their congregations, and wished to separate from the Anglican church. This sect of Separatists— viewed in its day the same way extremist religious cults are thought of in our time—went too far for the taste of the authorities, and they were either forced underground or out of England.

A small band of Separatists, now called Pilgrims, went to Leyden, Holland, where their reformist ideas were accepted. But cut off from their English traditions, the group decided on another course, a fresh start in the English lands in America. With the permission of the Virginia Company and the backing of London merchants who charged handsome interest on the loans they made, the Pilgrims sailed from Plymouth in 1620. Among their number were the Pilgrim families of William Brewster, John Carver, Edward Winslow, and William Bradford. The "strangers," or non-Pilgrim voyagers (men faithful to the Church of England, but who had signed on for the passage in the hope of owning property in the New World), included ship's cooper John Alden and army captain Miles Standish.

What was the Mayflower Compact?

When the rough seas around Nantucket forced the ship back to Cape Cod and the group decided to land outside the bounds of the Virginia Company, the "strangers" declared that they would be free from any commands. Responding quickly to this threat of mutiny, the Pilgrim leaders composed a short statement of self-government, signed by almost all of the adult men.

This agreement, the Mayflower Compact, is rightly considered the first written constitution in North America. Cynicism about its creation, or for that matter about the House of Burgesses, is easy in hindsight. Yes, these noble-minded pioneers slaughtered Indians with little remorse, kept servants and slaves, and treated women no differently from cattle. They were imperfect men whose failings must be regarded alongside their astonishing attempt to create in America a place like none in Europe. As the historian Samuel Eliot Morison put it in *The Oxford History of the American People,* "This compact is an almost startling revelation of the capacity of Englishmen in that era for self-government. Moreover, it was a second instance of the Englishmen's determination to live in the colonies under a rule of law."

Despite their flaws, the early colonists taking their toddling steps toward self-rule must be contrasted with other colonies, including English colonies, in various parts of the world where the law was simply the will of the King or the church.

American Voices

From the Mayflower Compact (signed December 1620):

> We whose names are under-written . . . doe by these presents solemnly and mutually in the presence of God, and one of another, covenant and combine our selves togeather into a civil body politick, for our better ordering and preservation and furtherance of the ends aforesaid; and by vertue hearof to enacte, constitute, and frame such just and equal lawes, ordinances, acts, constitutions, and offices, from time to time, as shall be thought most meete for the generall good of the Colonie, unto which we promise all due submission and obedience. . . .

Did the Pilgrims really land at Plymouth Rock?

After a brief exploration of Cape Cod, the *Mayflower* group sailed on and found a broad, round harbor that they recognized from Captain John Smith's maps as Plimoth (Plymouth). The Indians called it Patuxet. On December 16, the *Mayflower*'s passengers reached their new home. There is no mention in any historical account of Plymouth Rock, the large stone that can be seen in Plymouth today, into which the year 1620 is carved. The notion that the Pilgrims landed near the rock and carved the date is a tradition that was created at least a hundred years later, probably by some smart member of the first Plymouth Chamber of Commerce.

Like the first arrivals at Jamestown, the Pilgrims and "strangers" had come to Plymouth at a bad time to start planting a colony. By spring, pneumonia and the privations of a hard winter had cost the lives of fifty-two of the 102 immigrants. But in March, salvation came, much as it had in Virginia, in the form of Indians, including one named Squanto, who could speak English. Who Squanto was, and how he came to speak English, are among history's unsolved mysteries. One claim is made for an Indian named Tisquantum who had been captured by an English slaver in 1615. A second is made for an Indian named Tasquantum, brought to England in 1605. Whichever he was, he moved into the house of William Bradford, governor of the Plymouth colony, and was the means of survival for the Pilgrims until his death from fever in 1622. Another Indian of great value to the Pilgrim Fathers was Samoset, a local chief who also spoke English and introduced the settlers to the grand chief of the Wampanoags, Wasamegin, better known by his title Massasoit. Under the rule of Massasoit, the Indians became loyal friends to the Pilgrims, and it was Massasoit's braves who were the invited guests to the October feast at which the Pilgrims celebrated their first harvest. For three days the colonists and their Indian allies feasted on turkey and venison, pumpkin and corn. It was the first Thanksgiving. (Thanksgiving was first officially celebrated during the Presidency of Abraham Lincoln in 1864. It became a national holiday and was moved to its November date by President Franklin D. Roosevelt.)

While life did not magically improve after that first year, the Pilgrims carved out a decent existence and, through trade with the Indians, were able to repay their debts to the London backers and even to buy out the shares that these London merchants held. Their success helped inspire an entire wave of immigration to New England that came to be known as the Great Puritan migration. From 1629 to 1642, between 14,000 and 20,000 settlers left England for the West Indies and New England, and most of these were Anglican Puritans brought over by a new joint stock company called the Massachusetts Bay Company. They came because life in England under King Charles I had grown intolerable for Puritans. Though the newcomers demonstrated a startling capacity for fighting among themselves, usually over church matters, these squabbles led to the settlement and development of early New England.

Highlights in the development of New England

1629 Naumkeag, later called Salem, is founded to accept first wave of 1,000 Puritan settlers.

1630 John Winthrop, carrying the Massachusetts Bay Charter, arrives at Naumkeag and later establishes Boston, named after England's great Puritan city. (In 1635, English High and Latin School, the first secondary school in America, is founded. The following year a college for the training of clergymen is founded at Cambridge and named Harvard after a benefactor in 1639.)

1634 Two hundred settlers, half of them Protestant, arrive at Chesapeake Bay and found St. Mary's, in the new colony of Maryland, granted to Cecil Calvert, Lord Baltimore, who instructs his brother, the colony's leader, to tolerate the Puritans. The so-called Catholic colony, ostensibly named for Charles I's Queen Henrietta Maria, but in fact named to honor the Virgin Mary, will have a Protestant majority from the beginning.

1636 Reverend Thomas Hooker leads a group into Connecticut and founds Hartford; other Connecticut towns are soon founded.

1636 Roger Williams, a religious zealot banished from Boston by Governor Winthrop, founds Providence, Rhode Island, preaching radical notions of separation of church and state and paying Indians for land.

1638 Anne Hutchinson, banished from Boston for her heretical interpretations of sermons, which drew large, enthusiastic crowds, settles near Providence and starts Portsmouth. (Newport is founded about the same time.) In 1644, Rhode Island receives a royal colonial charter.

1638 New Haven founded.

1643 New England Confederation, a loose union to settle border disputes, is formed by Connecticut, New Haven, Plymouth, and Massachusetts Bay Colony.

Who started New York?

The Englishmen who were quickly populating the Atlantic seaboard from the Carolinas to New England had no monopoly on the New World. French and Dutch explorers had also been busy, and both nations were carving out separate territories in North America. The Dutch founded New Netherland in the Hudson Valley of present-day New York State, basing their claims upon the explorations of Henry Hudson in 1609.

An Englishman, Hudson was hired by a Dutch company that wanted to find the Northeast Passage, the sea route to China along the northern rim of Asia. In 1609, Hudson set off instead, aboard the *Half Moon,* for the northwest alternative. Sailing down the Atlantic coast, he entered Chesapeake Bay before making a U-turn and heading back north to explore the Hudson River as far upriver as Albany. Noting the absence of tides, he correctly assumed that this route did not lead to the Pacific. While we are left with reminders of Hudson's intrepid seamanship in the river, strait, and bay that bear his name, his life ended with little glory. During another voyage in search of the Northwest Passage, Hudson's crew mutinied in 1611 and put their captain into an open boat in Hudson Bay. While the mutineers returned to England, no trace of their captain was ever discovered.

England was flexing its new muscles in the early 1600s, but it was the Dutch who had become the true world power in maritime matters by building the world's largest merchant marine fleet. There was literally not a place in the known world of that day in which the Dutch did not have a hand in matters. Amsterdam had become the busiest and richest city in the European world. In 1621 the Dutch West India Company was formed with the aim of taking over trade between Europe and the New World, and the Dutch soon took from the Portuguese control of the lucrative slave and sugar trades. Fort Orange, the site of Albany, took hold as a fur-trading outpost in 1624. Two years later the trading village of New Amsterdam, soon to be renamed New York, was established at the mouth of the Hudson. The Dutch West India Company did more than trade and set up colonies. In 1628 the Dutch admiral Piet Hein captured a Spanish treasure fleet, pirating away enough silver to provide company shareholders with a 75-percent dividend.

Did the Indians really sell Manhattan for $24?

The first Dutch settlers to arrive on the narrow, twelve-mile-long island of Manhattan didn't bother to pay the Indians for the land they chose for their settlement. But when Peter Minuit arrived in the spring of 1624 and was chosen as leader of the settlement, he quickly met with the local Indian chiefs. Before them he set a sales agreement for all of Manhattan Island and two boxes of trade goods—probably hatchets, cloth, metal pots, and bright beads—worth sixty Dutch guilders. At the time, that equaled 2,400 English cents, which has come down in history as the famous twenty-four-dollar figure.

From its inception Dutch New Amsterdam was far less pious and more rowdy than Puritan New England. As a trading outpost it attracted a different breed of settler, and unlike Boston, taverns in New Amsterdam quickly outnumbered churches. As few Dutch settlers were lured to the new colony by the promise of low pay to work on West India Company farms, the company welcomed settlers from any nation and by 1640, at least eighteen languages were spoken in New York, a polyglot tradition that was to continue throughout the city's history.

How did New Amsterdam become New York?

The Dutch got New York cheap. The English went them one better. They simply took it for nothing. Why pay for what you can steal?

Dutch rule in America was not long-lived, but it was certainly influential in the stamp it put on the future New York. It was the Dutch who erected, as a defense against Indians, the wall in lower Manhattan from which Wall Street takes its name. And what would some Dutch burgher think of finding today's Bowery instead of the tidy *bouweries,* or farms, that had been neatly laid out in accordance with a plan drawn up in Amsterdam. Besides the settlement on Manhattan island, the Dutch had also established villages, such as Breukelen and Haarlem. And early Dutch and Walloon (Belgian Protestant) settlers included the ancestors of the Roosevelt clan.

New Amsterdam developed far differently from the English colonies, which held out the promise of land ownership for at least some of its settlers. Promising to bring over fifty settlers to work the land, a few wealthy Dutch landholders, or *patroons,* were able to secure huge tracts along the Hudson in a system that more closely resembled medieval European feudalism than anything else, a system that continued well after the Revolution and that contributed to New York's reputation as an aristocratic (and, during the Revolution, Loyalist) stronghold.

New Amsterdam became New York in one of the only truly bloodless battles in American history. As the two principal competing nations of the early seventeenth century, England and Holland sporadically came to war, and when Charles II reclaimed the throne in 1661 after the period of Oliver Cromwell's Protectorate, he asserted English rights to North America. Charles II granted his brother, the Duke of York, the largest and richest territorial grant ever made by an English monarch. It included all of present New York, the entire region from the Connecticut to Delaware rivers, Long Island, Nantucket, Martha's Vineyard, and the present state of Maine. In 1664, four English frigates carrying 1,000 soldiers sailed into New York Harbor. The Dutch and other settlers there, unhappy with the administration of the West India Company, gladly accepted English terms despite Peter Stuyvesant's blustery call to resist. Without a shot fired, New Amsterdam became New York.

The Duke of York in turn generously created a new colony when he split off two large tracts of land and gave one each to two friends, Sir George Carteret and Lord John Berkeley, an area that would become New Jersey. Also gained as part of this annexation was a settlement known as New Sweden. Established in 1638 by Peter Minuit (dismissed earlier as governor of New Amsterdam and now in Swedish employ), and centered on the site of Wilmington, Delaware, New Sweden had fallen to the Dutch under Stuyvesant in 1655. (Although this Swedish colony had little lasting impact on American history, the Swedes did make one enormous contribution. They brought with them the log cabin, the construction destined to become the chief form of pioneer housing in the spreading American frontier of the eighteenth century.)

The English exercised a surprisingly tolerant hands-off policy in ruling the former New Amsterdam. Life as it had been under Dutch rule continued for many years.

When did the French reach the New World?

French attempts to gain a piece of the riches of the New World began in earnest with Jacques Cartier's voyage of 1534, another expedition in the ongoing search for a China route. Cartier's explorations took him to Newfoundland, discovered by Cabot almost forty years earlier, and up the Gulf of St. Lawrence, sailing as far as the Huron Indian villages of Stadacona (modern Quebec) and Hochelaga (Montreal). In 1541, Cartier's attempt to settle a colony failed and he returned to France. While cod fishermen from France, as well as England and Portugal, continued to make temporary settlements around Newfoundland, the French also began some early fur-trading with Indians that would provide France with the real economic impetus for its colonizing efforts. In 1600, Tadoussac, a French trading post on the St. Lawrence, was founded.

The key mover in the French era of exploration was Samuel de Champlain, who founded Quebec in 1608, the year after Jamestown was settled. Like the Dutch in New Amsterdam, the French explorers who started New France were primarily interested in trading, as opposed to the English settlers of New England and Virginia, who were planting farms and permanent communities.

An inevitable head-to-head confrontation between England and France, already the two great European powers, over sovereignty in the New World existed almost from the beginning of the colonial period. A Scots expedition took a French fort in Acadia, and it was renamed Nova Scotia (New Scotland). Then, in 1629, an English pirate briefly captured Quebec. While New England and the other English colonies were taking in thousands of new settlers during the massive immigration of the mid-seventeenth century, the French were slow to build a colonial presence, and settlers were slow to arrive in New France. Worse for France than the threat of English attack were the Iroquois, the powerful confederacy of five tribes of Indians in New York, and the best-organized and strongest tribal grouping in North America at the time. The Iroquois were sworn enemies of France's Indian trading partners, the Huron and Algonkian Indians, and a long series of devastating wars with the Iroquois preoccupied the French during much of their early colonial period.

But if the French failed as colony builders, they excelled as explorers. Led by the _coureurs de bois,_ the young French trappers and traders, Frenchmen were expanding their reach into the North American heartland. One of these, Medard Chouart, mapped the Lake Superior–Hudson Bay region and then sold the information to the English, who formed the Hudson Bay Company to exploit the knowledge. An even greater quest came in 1673, when Louis Joliet and the Jesuit priest Jacques Marquette set out from Lake Michigan and eventually reached the Mississippi, letting the current carry them down into the American South as far as the Arkansas River. Based on these expeditions, the French laid a claim in 1671 to all of western North America in the name of King Louis XIV, the Sun King, a claim re-exerted in 1682 by La Salle, a young French nobleman who named the province Louisiana in honor of his king. From the outset, the English would contest this claim. The stage was set for an epic contest over a very substantial prize—all of North America. La Salle, like Hudson, was another of history's glorious losers. In 1684, at the head of another expedition, La Salle mistook the entrance to Matagorda Bay, in Texas, for the mouth of the Mississippi. He spent two years in search of the great river, until, tired of the hardships they were forced to endure, La Salle's men mutinied and murdered him in 1687.

Why is Pennsylvania the Quaker State?

While the French were making their claims, the English carved out another major colonial territory in 1682, virtually completing the quilt that would become the original thirteen colonies. This was the "holy experiment" of William Penn, one of the most fascinating characters in America's early history. Although the colony, which was named for its founder's father, and its chief city, Philadelphia ("City of Brotherly Love") quickly became vibrant centers of commerce and culture, it was primarily founded to allow the Society of Friends, or Quakers, a place to worship, and to permit religious tolerance for all.

A highly individualistic left-wing Protestant sect founded in England by George Fox around 1650, the Friends had an impact on America far greater than their numbers would suggest. But life was never simple for them, in England or the colonies. Fox believed that no ministry or clergy was necessary for worship, and that the word of God was found in the human soul, not necessarily in the Bible, eliminating almost all vestiges of organized religion, including church buildings and formal liturgy. In a Friends meeting, members sat in silent meditation until the "inward light," a direct spiritual communication from God, caused a believer to physically tremble or quake, the source of the group's commonly used name. Fox also took literally the commandment "Thou shalt not kill," beginning a long tradition of Quaker pacifism.

Of course, these notions did not sit well with either the religious or the political authorities, and the Quakers were vigorously persecuted from the beginning. Three thousand English Quakers were imprisoned under Charles II. In America, where freedom to worship had been the ostensible motivating force for many colonists, every colony but Roger Williams's Rhode Island passed strident anti-Quaker laws. The worst of these was in Puritan Massachusetts, where a number of Quakers were hanged when they returned to Boston after having been banished.

Back in England, William Penn, the son of a prominent and powerful admiral, became a zealous follower of Fox in 1667, and his devotion, expressed in a tract entitled *The Sandy Foundation Shaken,* earned Penn a stint in the Tower of London. Released through his father's influence, Penn became a trustee of the Quaker community in West Jersey and later, with an inheritance and a proprietary grant from the Duke of York (in payment of debts owed Penn's father), Penn took possession of the territory that would become Pennsylvania.

As with other proprietary grants of colonial territory, Pennsylvania already belonged to somebody, namely the Indians who lived there. But Penn, unlike many other early founders, believed in the rights of the Indians, and on a journey to America in 1682 he negotiated a price for Pennsylvania. Like many colonial chapters, Penn's Indian dealings are obscured by mythology. In a famous painting, Penn is depicted making a treaty under the elm tree at Shackamaxon, a treaty that didn't exist. Part of the deal was known as the "Walking Purchase" in which Penn vowed to take only as much land as a man could walk in three days. Penn took a leisurely stroll. (Penn's successors were not as charitable. His son hired three runners to head off at a good pace, and the Indians were forced to relinquish a good bit more of their hunting grounds.)

The new colony faced few of the privations that the first generation of colonists had suffered. In the first place, the territory was already settled by the Swedes who had begun New Sweden, and food was plentiful. Besides the English Quakers, the colony attracted many Dutch and German Quakers and other sects lured by Penn's promise of religious tolerance and the generous terms offered by Penn for buying the new colony's extensive lands. In 1683, for instance, a group of Mennonite families from the Rhineland founded the settlement of Germantown. By 1685 the colony's population numbered nearly 9,000.

Penn's liberal religious views were mirrored in his political beliefs. He developed a plan for a colonial union, and his Frame of Government provided a remarkably progressive constitution for the colony, which included selection of a governor (at first, Penn himself) by ballot. By 1700, Philadelphia trailed only Boston as an American cultural center, possessing the second colonial printing press, the third colonial newspaper, the Penn Charter school, and the colony's best hospital and charitable institutions, all a legacy of Penn's Quaker conscience.

Penn himself fared not nearly as well. He became embroiled in political and financial feuds, even being accused of treason by William and Mary. He lost possession of the colony for a period, but regained it in 1694. Money problems landed him in debtors' prison and a stroke left him incapacitated. But his legacy of practical idealism marks Penn as one of America's early heroes. And the Quaker traditions of nonviolence and social justice that he established left indelible marks on American history as Quakers stood in the forefront of such movements as Abolitionism, Prohibition, universal suffrage, and pacifism.

What were the thirteen original colonies?

With Pennsylvania quickly established, all but one of the thirteen furture states were in place by the end of the seventeenth century. In order of settlement, they were as follows:

1607 Virginia (Jamestown)
1620 Massachusetts (Plymouth and Massachusetts Bay Colony)
1626 New York (originally New Amsterdam; annexed by the English)
1633 Maryland
1636 Rhode Island
1636 Connecticut
1638 Delaware (originally New Sweden; annexed by the Dutch and later the English)
1638 New Hampshire
1653 North Carolina
1663 South Carolina
1664 New Jersey
1682 Pennsylvania

In 1732, Georgia, the last of the original thirteen, was founded by James Oglethorpe, a humanitarian interested in recruiting settlers from English debtors' prisons. The colony, which became another haven for persecuted Protestants, was of special strategic importance, standing as a buffer between South Carolina and possible attacks from Spanish Florida and French Louisiana.

Two

Say You Want
a Revolution

- What was King Philip's War?

- What was Nat Bacon's Rebellion?

- Who were the witches of Salem?

- What was the Great Awakening?

- What was John Peter Zenger on trial for?

- Who fought the French and Indian War?

- What do sugar and stamps have to do with revolutions?

- What was the Boston Massacre?

- What was the Boston Tea Party about?

- What was the First Continental Congress? Who chose its members, who were they, and what did they do?

• Milestones in the American Revolution

• The patriots

• The soldiers

• What was "the shot heard 'round the world"?

• What was *Common Sense?*

• What exactly does the Declaration of Independence say? What did Congress leave out?

• What were the Articles of Confederation?

• How did the colonies win the war?

• What did America win?

Somebody dumped some tea into Boston Harbor. Somebody else hung some lights in a church steeple. Paul Revere went riding around the countryside at midnight. Jefferson penned the Declaration. There were a few battles and a rough winter at Valley Forge. But George Washington kicked out the British.

That's the sum of the impression many people keep of the American Revolution. It was not that simple or easy.

This chapter highlights some of the major events in the colonial period leading up to the War of Independence, along with the milestones in the political and military victory over England.

What was King Philip's War?

We tend to think of the colonial period after the early "starving time" as a rather calm era in which Yankee resourcefulness and the Puritan work ethic came to the fore, forging a new American character that would burst forth into nationhood in 1776.

Overlooked in this view is the genocidal campaign carried out against the Indians by the Pilgrim fathers and other colonists. The English, French, and Dutch could be as ruthlessly cruel and deadly as the worst of the *conquistadores*. In 1643, for instance, following the murder of a Dutch farmer, the governor of New Amsterdam ordered the massacre of the Wappingers, a friendly tribe that had come to the Dutch seeking shelter. Eighty Indians were killed in their sleep, decapitated, and their heads displayed on poles in Manhattan. A Dutch lady kicked the heads down the street. One captive was castrated, skinned alive, and forced to eat his own flesh as the Dutch governor looked on and laughed.

In New England, the first of two Indian wars was fought against the Pequot, a powerful Mohegan clan treated by the English as a threat. Urged on by Boston preachers and using a trumped-up murder charge as a pretext, the Puritans declared all-out war on the Pequot in 1637.

It was not a war fought by the chivalrous standards of European engagement. The Puritans sacked and burned Indian villages by night. Aided by loyal Narragansett and Mohegan forces, the colonial equivalent of a search-and-destroy team entered a stockaded Pequot town near the Mystic River, slaughtered its 600 inhabitants, and burned the village. In the only other confrontation of the war, a group of Pequots was trapped. The men were killed, the boys sold to slavers, and the women and girls kept by the Puritans as slaves. As a tribe, the Pequot was practically exterminated.

The English maintained peace for nearly forty years thanks to their old allies, Massasoit's Wampanoag—saviors of the Pilgrims—and the Narragansett led by Canonicus (who had sheltered Roger Williams after he was banished from Boston). When these two chiefs died, the English were ready to complete the subjugation of the New England Indians. But Massasoit's son Metacom, called King Philip by the English for his adoption of European dress and customs, struck back.

The fighting took place in the summer of 1676, and for the colonists it wasn't as easy as the Pequot battles had been. The combat was the fiercest in New England history, and far bloodier than much of the fighting during the Revolution. Metacom's

Indians were equipped with guns and armor acquired through trade, and he was an aggressive leader. The outcome of this war was not assured, particularly in the early going. But the colonists had too much on their side: superior numbers—including 500 Mohegan gunmen, blood rivals of the Wampanoag—and devastating battle tactics, including a return to the wholesale massacre of noncombatants.

King Philip was ultimately killed, his head displayed on a pole. His wife and son, the grandson of the chief who had saved the Pilgrims, was sold into slavery in the West Indies, an act of mercy according to the leading Puritan clerics.

American Voices

An account of the battle against the Pequot, from Governor William Bradford's *History of the Plymouth Plantation:*

> It was a fearful sight to see them thus frying in the fyer, and the streams of blood quenching the same, and horrible was the stincke and sente there of, but the victory seemed a sweet sacrifice, and they gave the prayers thereof to God, who had wrought so wonderfully for them. . . .

What was Nat Bacon's Rebellion?

As the New England colonists learned at great cost from Metacom, the "Indian problem" was not a simple matter. Massed confrontations were risky, so new tactics emerged. The colonists found an effective measure in the "scalp bounty," a Dutch innovation in which a fee was paid for Indian scalps. The common conception is of Indians as scalp-takers, but it was the colonists who adopted the tactic as a means of Indian control, and it even became a profitable enterprise. In the Bay Colony in 1703, a scalp brought twelve pounds sterling, a price inflated to one hundred pounds by 1722. Even in Pennsylvania, the most tolerant and progressive of the colonies, scalps brought a handsome price, and Benjamin Franklin, in a move to avoid a rebellion by the backwoods "Paxton Boys" in 1763, pushed the Pennsylvania legislature to approve a bounty on Indian scalps.

In 1676, while New England struggled against King Philip, the Indian issue boiled over into something different in Virginia. This overlooked episode, known as Nat Bacon's Rebellion, can be seen as another in a series of wrongs committed against the Indians. But it was also a demonstration of a new anti-authority sentiment in America, a foreshadowing of the Revolutionary spirit.

A cousin to the scientist and philosopher, Sir Francis Bacon, Nathaniel Bacon was a young planter and an up-and-coming member of Virginia's ruling elite. At the time, Virginians were fighting sporadic battles with the Susquehannock, the result of treaties broken by the English. When his plantation overseer was killed, Bacon grew angry at what he thought was the docile Indian policy of Virginia's Governor Berkeley. Without the governor's permission, Bacon raised a militia force of 500 men and vented his rage on the Indians. When his little army attacked the peaceful Occaneechee (instead of the more warlike Susquehannock), Bacon became an immediate local hero, especially among the Indian-hating frontier colonists who favored pushing farther west. In his *Declaration of the People,* written exactly one hundred years before another Virginian wrote another Declaration, Bacon criticized the Berkeley administration for levying unfair taxes, placing favorites in high positions, and not protecting the western farmers from Indians. Governor Berkeley branded Bacon a traitor, but granted some of the reforms he demanded, and Bacon was later pardoned, having apologized.

When Bacon felt that the governor had reneged on his pledge to pursue the Indians, the fiery rebel focused his anger toward the colonial government. In the first popular rebellion in colonial America, Bacon led troops of lower-class planters, servants, and some free and slave blacks to Jamestown and burned it. Faced with a true rebellion, Governor Berkeley fled. An English naval squadron was sent to capture Bacon, who died of dysentery before they reached him, and the remnants of his backwoods army were rounded up, with two dozen of them ending up on the gallows.

Nat Bacon's Rebellion was the first of almost twenty minor uprisings against colonial governments, including the Paxton uprising in Pennsylvania mentioned above, Leisler's Rebellion in New York in 1689, and the Regulator Rebellion in South Carolina in 1771. All of these were revolts against the colonial "haves," those wealthy colonists who owned the bulk of America's land and controlled its prosperity, and the "have-nots," often backwoodsmen or lower-class farmers struggling for survival. By adding these bloody outbreaks of popular resentment against the colonial "establishment" to the numerous riots and slave revolts of the pre-Revolutionary period, the picture of colonial gentility is destroyed. Instead we get a clouded image of unsettled grievances waiting to boil over.

Who were the witches of Salem?

Modern-day Salem does a good business in lightheartedly promoting its Halloween-capital image. But for the twenty people who died there in 1692, there was little humor in the affair. The hysteria developed, as many New England disputes had, out of religious infighting. New England was a theocracy, a Puritan church-state in which church and government were closely connected. And since Puritanism then controlled the politics and economy of most of New England, such a controversy among churchmen was no small matter.

Salem Village was created in 1672 by a group of rural families who wanted their own church instead of going to church in the larger town of nearby Salem. Several years of haggling over ministers followed until Samuel Parris, a former merchant and Harvard dropout, was called. No peacemaker, Parris failed to calm his troubled parish, and in two years' time things went haywire. The minister's daughter Betty and niece Abigail, aged nine and eleven, and twelve-year-old Ann Putnam, daughter of one of the town's most powerful men, began to act strangely, and a doctor diagnosed them as bewitched and under the influence of an "Evil Hand." Suspicion immediately fell on Tituba, the Parris family's West Indian slave, who had been teaching the girls sorcery and fortune-telling games.

At first, the slave Tituba and two local women were accused of witchery, and a general court jailed them on suspicion of witchcraft. But their trial triggered an astonishing wave of accusations, and the three young girls, basking in their sudden notoriety, ignited a storm of witchcraft hysteria. The charge of witchery soon became a means to settle village feuds. Fanned by a book by the powerful cleric Cotton Mather (1662–1727), entitled *Memorable Providences Relating to Witchcraft and Possessions,* the frenzy spread to the rest of Massachusetts, with charges reaching as high as the wife of Governor William Phips, who convened a special court that formally charged more than 150 people.

The three Salem Village girls were the chief witnesses, and even though they said they had concocted the whole affair for "sport," the trials continued. Reason was turned upside-down and the court was right out of *Alice's Adventures in Wonderland.* To escape the hangman's noose, the panic-stricken accused often "confessed" to anything, including broomstick rides and sex with the Devil. Professions of innocence or criticism of the proceedings were tantamount to guilt. Refusal to implicate a neighbor meant a death sentence.

Eventually twenty-eight suspected witches, mostly women, were convicted. Five of them "confessed" and were spared, two escaped, and a pregnant woman was pardoned. But in the end, nineteen "witches" were hanged, and the husband of one convicted witch was suffocated under a pile of stones for refusing to plead. At the belated urging of Cotton Mather's father Increase Mather (1639–1723), the president of Harvard, and other Puritan ministers, Governor Phips called off the trials that were literally ripping the colony apart.

While the incident at Salem had no lasting impact on the course of American history, it certainly demonstrated the intolerance and stiff-necked sanctimoniousness of the New England Puritan spirit. It also proved the real danger of a church-state, an institution vigorously avoided by the framers of the Constitution. The failure of an entire community to prevent the madness was a sad tribute to moral cowardice, a trait not limited in American history to either New England or the colonial period. (Another "witch hunt" with eerie parallels to the Salem affair but far more damaging was carried out by Senator Joseph McCarthy against alleged Communists in government in the 1950s, and is covered in Chapter 7. Arthur Miller's play *The Crucible* is a compelling dramatic treatment of the Salem incident, written in response to the McCarthy Red Scare.)

What was the Great Awakening?

Another, more benevolent outpouring of religious fervor swept the Middle Colonies, New England, and the rest of the colonies in the 1740s. A wave of fundamental, orthodox Protestantism that touched every colony, the Great Awakening was largely created by two powerful, charismatic evangelists who—without benefit of television crusades and religious theme parks—would have put the likes of Pat Robertson, Jim and Tammy Bakker, and Oral Roberts to shame.

American-born Jonathan Edwards, pastor of a church in Northampton, Massachusetts, became famous for his fire-and-brimstone, pit-of-hell sermons, which provoked near hysteria in his listeners. Edwards was responding to a softening of religious attitudes that had been occurring throughout the colonies. As the colonies prospered, attention had turned from observing the Sabbath to such earthly pursuits as real estate, slave trading, the rum business, and other profitable worldly enterprises. In the most famous of his sermons, "Sinners in the Hands of an Angry God," Edwards likened his sinning listeners to a spider hung over a flame. When his popularity and influence later waned, Edwards became a missionary to the Indians and was later appointed president of Princeton, but died before taking office.

George Whitefield, an Oxford-trained Anglican minister, was one of those influenced by Edwards. An orator of legendary ability, Whitefield attracted thousands to his outdoor meetings. His emotionally charged sermons chastised his listeners and then brought the promise of salvation. Even Benjamin Franklin, no model of piety, was moved by Whitefield and commented on how he transformed all who heard him. But Edwards and Whitefield's influence went beyond religion. Their ardent followers tended to be lower or middle class, with little education or influence. The wealthy, powerful elite of America, its new ruling class, preferred traditional worship, and the differences between these factions threatened to turn radical.

Although the Awakening eventually ran its course, it did have considerable long-term impact on America. In a practical sense, the split among the various factions encouraged the founding of several new colleges, including Princeton, Brown, Rutgers, and Dartmouth. In political terms, the divisions the Awakening had created contributed to a new spirit of toleration and secularism. The old-guard Puritans no longer held complete control over church and political matters. New .religious forces forced the loosening of ties between church and state throughout the colonies, a new secular spirit that would become embedded in the Constitution.

American Voices

"An Elegiac Poem" on the death of George Whitefield by Phyllis Wheatley, a seventeen-year-old black slave and one of America's first poets (1770):

> Thou didst, in strains of eloquence refin'd,
> Inflame the soul, and captivate the mind.

What was John Peter Zenger on trial for?

In 1732 a wealthy landowner, Lewis Morris, founded the *New York Weekly Journal*. Like others before and since, the *Journal* contributed to a grand American newspaper tradition, not by reporting the news, but by ax-grinding and mudslinging at a political opponent. In this case the target was New York Governor William Cosby and his allies, among them the prominent merchant James DeLancey.

A German-born printer, John Peter Zenger was hired to edit and produce the paper, but editorial policy was in the hands of a Morris ally, attorney James Alexander. The *Journal*'s front page usually offered a polemic on the right of the people to be critical of rulers. But what Governor Cosby found intolerable were the back-page "advertisements," thinly veiled attacks in which the governor was likened to a monkey and his supporters to spaniels. Cosby shut down the paper, charged Zenger with seditious libel, and had him jailed for ten months.

In the trial that followed, Zenger's attorney, the Philadelphia lawyer Andrew Hamilton, contended that the articles in question were truthful and therefore not libelous. Although the judges ruled Hamilton's argument out of order, the jury was swayed. Hamilton's defense carried the day and Zenger was acquitted. Of the jury, Hamilton later said, "You have laid a noble foundation for securing to ourselves that to which Nature and the Laws of our country have given us a Right—The Liberty—both of exposing and opposing arbitrary Power by speaking and writing Truth."

For a royal colony still forty years away from independence, that was pretty heady stuff. Though subjects of the English Crown, an American jury had demonstrated a stiff resolve that they did not feel duty-bound by English civil law. Just as important, Zenger's trial and acquittal marked the first landmark in the tradition of a free press, a somewhat radical notion that became the law of the land as the First Amendment in the Bill of Rights. There was a practical effect as well. In the immediate years ahead, that freedom would become an important weapon in the war of words that preceded the War for Independence.

Who fought the French and Indian War?

No. It was not the French against the Indians.

At the end of the seventeenth century, North America was an extremely valuable piece of real estate, teeming with the beavers so prized by the hatmakers of Europe and claimed in part by the Dutch, the French, and the Spanish, as well as by the King of England. The people in Canada and America were pawns in a larger chess game. Between 1689 and the War for Independence, the major European powers engaged in a series of wars, usually fought under the guise of disputes over royal succession. In fact, they were wars of colonial expansion, fought for territory, raw materials, and new markets for exports.

European Wars Fought in the Colonies

Date	European Name	Colonial Name
1689–97	War of the League of Augsburg	King William's War
1702–13	War of the Spanish Succession	Queen Anne's War
1740–48	War of the Austrian Succession	King George's War
1756–63	Seven Years War	French and Indian War

In the first three of these, the colonists played supporting roles. Most of the fighting was limited to sporadic surprise attacks by one side or another, usually joined by their respective Indian allies. Colonial losses, especially in New England and Canada, were still heavy, and the costs of these wars created a serious inflation problem, particularly in Massachusetts, where paper money was printed for the first time to finance the fighting. By the time the first three wars had been played out, England and France were left standing as the two major contenders, and England had acquired a good portion of Canada from France. In the last of the four wars, however, these two rivals fought for absolute dominion over North America. And it was the French and Indian War that most shaped America's destiny.

The conflict started inauspiciously enough for the Anglo-American cause when a young Virginian was dispatched to the Pennsylvania backwoods in 1753 to tell the French that they were trespassing on Virginia's territory. The French politely informed the messenger that it was their design to take Ohio. On his return, the inexperienced twenty-two-year-old son of a planter was made an officer and sent back with a militia force of 150 men. To his dismay, the new lieutenant colonel found the French already occupying a fort, called Duquesne (on the site of Pittsburgh). Though badly outnumbered, the young commander fired on a French party, took some prisoners, and hastily constructed a fort that was aptly named Necessity. Surrounded by French forces, he surrendered and the French sent him packing back to Virginia, where he was still hailed a hero for taking on the sworn enemies of England.

How differently world history might have turned out had the French decided to do away with this green soldier when they had cause and opportunity! Instead, twenty-two years later, the French would again come to the aid of George Washington in his war of revolution against England.

Bad went to worse for the English and their colonial allies in the war's early years. The 90,000 French in America, vastly out-numbered by 1.5 million English colonials, were better organized, more experienced fighters and had the most Indian allies. To the Indians, the French were the lesser of two evils; there were fewer French than English, and they seemed more interested in trading for beaver pelts than did the English, who were pushing the Indians off their lands. For many Indians, the war also provided an opportunity to repay years of English treachery. The Indians' rage exploded in the viciousness of their attacks, which were met with equal savagery by the British. Scalp-taking was a popular British tactic, and the British commander, General Edward Brad-dock, offered his Indian allies five pounds sterling for the scalp of a French soldier, one hundred pounds for that of a Jesuit mission-ary, and a grand prize of two hundred pounds for the hair of the powerful Delaware chieftain Shinngass.

For the English side, the Dunkirk of this war came in 1755, when 1,400 redcoats, under General Braddock, marched on Fort Duquesne in a poorly planned mission. A much smaller force of French slaughtered the English, leaving George Washington, Braddock's aide-de-camp, to straggle home with 500 survivors. The English suffered similar defeats in New York.

This colonial war became linked to a global clash that com-menced in 1756, the first true world war. Things went badly everywhere for the English until there was a change of leadership in London, with William Pitt taking over the war effort in 1758. His strategy emphasized naval warfare and the conquest of North America, which Pitt viewed as the key to overall victory. He poured in troops and found talented new commanders in James Wolfe and Jeffrey Amherst. One of Amherst's novel tactics, when negotiating with some attacking Indians, was to give them blankets from the smallpox hospital. A string of victories between 1758 and 1760 gave the English control over the American colonies and, with the fall of Montreal in 1760, all of Canada.

In 1763 the Treaty of Paris brought peace and, with it, a complete British triumph. The English now owned all of Canada, America east of the Mississippi Valley, Florida, and a number of Caribbean islands. Colonial Americans, now fully blooded in a major armed conflict, took pride and rejoiced at the victory they had helped win for their new king, George III, who had taken the throne in 1760.

What do sugar and stamps have to do with revolutions?

In the short space of thirteen years, how did the colonies go from being loyal subjects of King George III, flush in their victory over the French, to becoming rebels capable of overthrowing the most powerful nation on earth?

Obviously, no single factor changes the course of history. And different historians point to different reasons for the Revolution. The established traditionalist view is that the American Revolution was fought for liberties that Americans believed they already possessed as British citizens. The more radical political and economic viewpoint holds that the Revolution was simply a transfer of power from a distant British elite to a home-grown American power class that wanted to consolidate its hold over the wealth of the continent.

History is a boat big enough to carry both views comfortably, and a mingling of these perspectives brings an approximation of truth. It is safe to say that British bungling, economic realities, a profound philosophical revolution called the Enlightenment, and historical inevitability all played roles in the birth of the American nation.

As for the British bungling: In the immediate aftermath of the Seven Years War, England had an enormous wartime debt to pay. In London, it was naturally assumed that the colonies should chip in for some of the costs of the defense of America as well as the yearly cost of administering the colonies. To do this, Parliament enacted what it thought an entirely reasonable tax, the so-called Sugar Act of 1764, which placed tariffs on sugar, coffee, wines, and other products imported into America in substantial quantities. A postwar colonial depression—economic doldrums typically following the free spending that accompanies wartime—sharpened the act's pain for American merchants and consumers. Almost immediately, negative reaction to the tax set in, an economic dissent that was summed up in a new political slogan, "No taxation without representation." James Otis, one of the most vocal and radical leaders in Massachusetts, wrote that everyone should be "free from all taxes but what he consents to in person or by his representative."

In real terms, the representation issue was a smokescreen—a useful phrase, but not what the new breed of colonial leaders wanted. They had the wisdom to see that getting a handful of seats in Parliament for the colonies would be politically meaningless. Growing numbers of American politicians saw a wedge being driven between colony and Mother England, and they had their eyes on a larger prize.

Resistance to the sugar tax, in the form of drafted protests from colonial legislatures and halfhearted boycotts, failed to materialize. Until, that is, Parliament tightened the screws with a second tax. The Stamp Act of 1765 set stiff tariffs on virtually every kind of printed matter from newspapers and legal documents to playing cards. One member of Parliament, protesting the new tax plan, used the phrase "Sons of Liberty" to describe the colonists, and it was quickly adopted by men in every colony. While the Sugar Act reflected Parliament's power to tax trade, the Stamp Act was different. It was a direct tax, and the protests from America grew louder, stronger, and more violent. Riots broke out, the most violent of which were in Boston, where the house of Governor Thomas Hutchinson was destroyed by an angry mob. In New York, the home of the officer in charge of the stamps was also ransacked. A boycott of the stamps, widely joined throughout the colonies, was followed by a general boycott of English goods. Hit hard by the economic warfare, London's merchants screamed and the law was repealed in 1766.

But it was a case of closing the barn door after the horses had scattered. In America, forces were gathering that most London politicos, ignorant of American ways, were too smug or superior to acknowledge.

What was the Boston Massacre?

Having been kicked once by the colonial mule, Parliament failed to grasp the message of the Stamp Act boycott, and in 1767 thought up a new set of incendiary taxes called the Townshend Acts, once again placing itself directly behind the mule's hind legs. Once again, an American boycott cut imports from England in half. The British answer to the Americans' protest was a typical superpower response—they sent in troops.

Soon there were 4,000 British redcoats in Boston, a city of 16,000 and a hotbed of colonial protest. These troops, however, did not just idly stand guard over the populace. In a town already hard-pressed for jobs, the British soldiers competed for work with the laborers of Boston's waterfront. Early in March 1770, a group of ropemakers fought with a detachment of soldiers who were taking their jobs, and all around Boston, angry encounters between soldiers and citizens became more frequent. Tensions mounted until March 5, when a mob, many of them hard-drinking waterfront workers, confronted a detachment of nine British soldiers. The scene turned ugly as snow and ice, mixed with stones, began to fly in the direction of the soldiers. Confronted by a taunting mob calling for their blood, the soldiers grew understandably nervous. It only took the word "Fire," most likely yelled by one of the crowd, to ignite the situation. The soldiers shot, and five bodies fell. The first to die was a fifty-year-old former slave, either a black or Indian mulatto sailor named Crispus Attucks.

It did not take long for the propagandists, Samuel Adams chief among them, to seize the moment. Within days the incident had become the "Boston Massacre," and the dead were martyred. An engraving of the shootings made by Henry Pelham, a half-brother of the painter John Copley, was "borrowed" by silversmith Paul Revere, whose own engraving of the incident got to the printer's first and soon became a patriotic icon. As many as ten thousand marched at the funeral procession (out of Boston's population of 16,000).

In the wake of the killings, British troops were withdrawn from the city. With the Townshend Acts repealed (coincidentally on the day of the Massacre), a period of relative calm followed the massacre and the trial of the soldiers—defended by John Adams, who wanted to ensure fairness—most were acquitted and two were branded and discharged—but it was an uneasy truce at best.

What was the Boston Tea Party about?

In the thick of the 1988 presidential election campaign, candidate George Bush made Boston Harbor an issue that badly hurt his opponent, Michael Dukakis. Bush made political hay out of the fact that the harbor was an ecological disaster zone, and placed the blame squarely in the lap of Dukakis, the Massachusetts governor. Once before, the mess in that harbor played a role in history, and back then the results were quite extraordinary. If George Bush thought Boston Harbor was a mess in 1988, he should have seen it in 1773.

The post-Massacre peace and the end of the non-importation boycott brought renewed prosperity to the colonies and with it a respite from the bickering with London. Fearing this calm would soften resistance, Samuel Adams and his allies tried to fan the embers over such local issues as moving the Massachusetts assembly out of Boston and who should pay the governor's salary. These were important legal questions, but not the sort of outrages that inspire violent overthrow of the government. Things heated up considerably when a party of patriots in Rhode Island boarded and burned the *Gaspee*, a grounded Royal Navy boat intensely disliked for its anti-smuggling patrols.

While the *Gaspee* arsonists avoided arrest, the British Crown threatened to bring the guilty to England for trial, rebuffing the English tradition of right to trial by a community jury. It was the bit of tinder that Samuel Adams needed to stoke the flames a little higher. In Virginia the House of Burgesses appointed Patrick Henry, Thomas Jefferson, and Richard Henry Lee as a Committee of Correspondence, and by 1774, twelve of the colonies had such committees to maintain a flow of information between like-minded colonists.

But a burning—or boiling—issue was still lacking until Samuel Adams found one in tea. In 1773, Parliament had granted a legal monopoly on tea shipment to America to the nearly bankrupt East India Company. The injury was made worse by the insult of funneling the tea business through selected loyalist merchants, including the sons of Governor Hutchinson of Massachusetts. The East India Company could now undercut American merchants, even those using smugglers, on the sale of tea. Tea first, thought the colonists, what will be next?

In November 1773, three tea-laden cargo ships reached Boston. Led by Samuel Adams and a powerful ally, John Hancock, one of the richest men in America and one of those most threatened by the possibility of London-granted trade monopolies, the patriots vowed that the tea would not be landed. Governor Hutchinson, whose sons stood to profit by its landing, put his back up. After two months of haggling, the Boston patriots made up their minds to turn Boston Harbor into a teapot.

On the night of December 16, 1773, about 150 men from all layers of Boston's economy, masters and apprentices side by side, blackened their faces with burnt cork, dressed as Mohawk Indians, and boarded the three ships. Once aboard, they requested and received the keys to the ships' holds, as their target was the tea alone and not the ships or any other cargo aboard. Watched by a large crowd, as well as the Royal Navy, the men worked for nearly three hours, hatcheting open the cases of tea and dumping it into the harbor. So much was dumped that the tea soon piled up in the waters and spilled back onto the decks, where it was shoveled back into the water.

The Boston Tea Party, as it was quickly annointed, was soon followed by similar tea parties in other colonies and served to harden lines, both in America and England. Patriots became more daring; Loyalist Tories became more loyal; Parliament stiffened its back.

The Sons of Liberty had slapped London's face with a kid glove. The King responded with an iron fist. "The die is now cast," King George told his Prime Minister, Lord North. "The colonies must either submit or triumph."

What was the First Continental Congress? Who chose its members, who were they, and what did they do?

From the moment the tea was dumped, the road to revolution was a short one. In a post–Tea Party fervor, Parliament passed a series of bills, called the Coercive Acts, the first of which was the Port Bill, aimed at closing down Boston until the dumped tea was paid for. It was followed by the Administration of Justice Act, the Massachusetts Regulating Act (which virtually nullified the colony's charter), and the Quebec Act, establishing a centralized system of government in Canada and extending the borders of Canada south to the Ohio River. Parliament backed up these acts by sending General Thomas Gage to Boston as the new governor, along with 4,000 troops. In addition, it reinforced provisions of the Quartering Act, which gave the army the right to demand food and shelter from colonists.

In response to these "Intolerable Acts," as the colonists called them, the colonial assemblies agreed to an intercolonial meeting, and each assembly selected a group of delegates. Gathering in Philadelphia from September 5 to October 26, 1774, the First Continental Congress was made up of fifty-six delegates from every colony but Georgia. They represented the full spectrum of thought in the colonies, from moderates and conservatives like New York's John Jay or Pennsylvania's Joseph Galloway, who were searching for a compromise that would maintain ties with England, to fiery rebels like Samuel Adams and Patrick Henry of Virginia (Thomas Jefferson was not selected to make the trip). As they gathered, John Adams privately worried, "We have not men fit for the times. We are deficient in genius, in education, in travel, in fortune—in everything."

But his opinion would soon change as the debate began, and Adams became aware that he was indeed in remarkable company. The first Congress moved cautiously, but ultimately adopted a resolution that opposed the Coercive Acts, created an Association to boycott British goods, and passed ten resolutions enumerating the rights of the colonists and their assemblies. Before adjourning, they provided for a second session to meet if their grievances had not been corrected by the British. While they had not yet declared for independence, the First Congress had taken a more or less unalterable step in that direction. In a very real sense, the Revolution had begun. It needed only for the shooting to start.

What was "the shot heard 'round the world"?

Now governor of Massachusetts, General Gage wanted to cut off the rebellion before it got started. His first move was to try to capture hidden stores of patriot guns and powder and arrest John Hancock and Sam Adams, the patriot ringleaders in British eyes. The Sons of Liberty had been expecting this move, and across Massachusetts the patriot farmers and townspeople had begun to drill with muskets, ready to pick up their guns on a minute's notice, giving them their name "Minutemen."

In an increasingly deserted Boston, Paul Revere, silversmith and maker of false teeth, waited and watched the British movements. To sound an early warning to Concord, Revere set up a system of signals with a sexton at Christ Church in Boston. One lantern in the belfry meant Gage's troops were coming by land; two lanterns meant they were crossing the Charles River in boats. Late on the night of April 18, 1775, as expected, it was two lanterns. Revere and another rider, Billy Dawes, started off to Lexington to warn Hancock and Adams and alert the Lexington Minutemen that the British regulars were coming. Continuing on to Concord, Revere and Dawes were joined by Samuel Prescott, a young patriot doctor. A few minutes later a British patrol stopped the three men. Revere and Dawes were arrested and briefly jailed, while Prescott was able to escape and warn Concord of the British advance.

Meanwhile, in Lexington, the group of seventy-seven Minutemen gathered on the green to confront the British army. The British tried to simply march past the ragtag band when an unordered shot rang out. Chaos ensued, and the British soldiers broke ranks and returned fire. When the volleying stopped, eight Minutemen lay dead.

Warned by Prescott, the Concord militia was ready. Farmers from the nearby countryside responded to the churchbells and streamed toward Concord. The resistance became more organized, and the Concord Minutemen attacked a troop of British holding a bridge leading into Concord, and later took up positions behind barns, houses, stone walls, and trees, pouring fire down on the British ranks. Unused to such unfair tactics as men firing from hiding, the British remained in their standard formations until they reached Lexington again and were met by reinforcements.

By the day's end, the British tallied seventy-three dead and 174 wounded.

The Second Continental Congress, meeting in Philadelphia on May 10, 1775, had come to the crisis point. The bloodshed at Lexington meant war. With swift action, the patriots could bottle up the whole of the British army in Boston. To John Adams, all that needed to be done was to solidify the ranks of Congress by winning the delegates of the South. The solution came in naming a Southerner as commander of the new Continental army. On June 15, 1775, George Washington, a delegate from Virginia who had hinted at his ambitions by wearing his old military uniform to the Philadelphia meetings, received that appointment.

Milestones in the American Revolution

1775

April 18–19 Seven hundred British troops march on Concord, Massachusetts, to secure a rebel arsenal. They are met on the Lexington village green by a small force of colonial Minutemen, and an unordered shot—the "shot heard 'round the world"—leads to the killing of eight Americans. During a pitched battle at Concord and on their return to Boston, the British are harassed constantly by colonial snipers and suffer heavy losses.

May 10 Under Ethan Allen and Benedict Arnold, a colonial militia force takes the British arsenal at Fort Ticonderoga, New York, capturing cannon and other supplies; in a separate attack, the British garrison at Crown Point on Lake Champlain is seized.

June 15 The Second Continental Congress decides to raise an army and appoints George Washington to lead it.

June 17 In the Battle of Bunker Hill (actually fought on Breed's Hill), the British sustain heavy losses, with more than 1,100 killed or wounded, before forcing a rebel retreat. Nathanael Greene, an American commander, comments, "I wish we could sell them another hill at the same price." In the wake of this costly victory, General Gage is replaced by Howe as the British commander in America.

1776

January Tom Paine publishes the pamphlet *Common Sense*, a persuasive and widely read argument for independence.

March 4–17 Rebel forces capture Dorchester Heights, overlooking Boston Harbor. Cannon captured by the Americans at Ticonderoga are brought in, forcing a British evacuation of Boston.

May King Louis XVI of France authorizes secret arms and munitions assistance for the Americans.

June 11 Congress appoints a committee to compose a declaration of independence.

June 28 Under General Charles Lee, American forces in Charleston, South Carolina, fend off British attack, damaging the British fleet. The British suspend operations in the South for another two years.

July 2 British General Sir William Howe lands an army at Staten Island, New York, eventually amassing 32,000 troops, including 9,000 German mercenaries.

July 4 The Declaration of Independence is formally adopted by Congress.

August 27–29 Battle of Long Island. Howe forces withdrawal of Washington's army from Brooklyn Heights to Manhattan. Before Howe can finish off the rebel army, a miraculous retreat saves Washington and the army. In September, Washington evacuates New York.

September 22 Nathan Hale, captured by the British in Long Island, is hanged, without trial, as a spy. He goes to his death bravely and is reported to have said, "I only regret that I have but one life to give for my country."

October–November Crushing American defeats at the battles of White Plains (New York) and Fort Lee (New Jersey) force Washington to move westward through New Jersey and into Pennsylvania. Again, Howe fails to pursue Washington vigorously, and the army is saved.

December 25 In a surprise Christmas Day attack, Washington leads troops across the Delaware River for a successful attack on British forces at Trenton, New Jersey. Although a small victory, it boosts American morale. It is followed by a second victory at Princeton.

1777

April 27 Benedict Arnold defeats the British at Ridgefield, Connecticut.

June The American seaman John Paul Jones is given command of the *Ranger* and begins raiding English shipping.

July 6 The British retake Fort Ticonderoga.

July 27 The Marquis de Lafayette, a twenty-year-old French nobleman, arrives in America to volunteer his services to the revolution.

August 16 Battle of Bennington (Vermont). Americans wipe out a column of General Burgoyne's men.

September 9–11 Battle of Brandywine (Pennsylvania). Howe drives Washington's army toward Philadelphia: Congress forced to flee.

September 19 First Battle of Saratoga. An American victory.

September 26 General Howe occupies Philadelphia.

October 4–5 Battle of Germantown (Pennsylvania). A costly American defeat, the battle is inconclusive as Howe fails again to finish Washington.

October 7–17 Second Battle of Saratoga. British are routed and 5,700 surrender. A major turning point for the American cause as Europe is encouraged to aid the revolution, including formal French recognition of American independence.

December 17 Washington's Continental Army enters winter quarters at Valley Forge, Pennsylvania.

1778

February Franco-American treaties of alliance and commerce are signed.

February 23 The Prussian Baron von Steuben arrives and assists Washington in drilling and training army at Valley Forge. By the end of the difficult winter, the Continental Army is a cohesive, disciplined fighting force.

May 8 Howe is replaced by Henry Clinton as the British commander in America.

July 8 Continental Army headquarters are established at West Point.

July 9 The Articles of Confederation are signed by Congress.

July 10 A French fleet arrives; France declares war against Britain.

December 29 The British capture Savannah, Georgia, from American General Robert Howe.

1779

January 10 The French give a dilapidated ship to John Paul Jones. It is refitted and renamed *Bonhomme Richard* in honor of Ben Franklin, internationally renowned as "Poor Richard" of *Almanac* fame.

January 29 British forces capture Augusta, Georgia.

February 25 Americans under George Rogers Clark defeat the British at Vincennes.

May 10 Portsmouth and Norfolk, Virginia, captured and burned by the British.

June 16 Spain declares war on England, but makes no American alliances.

July 15 American General Anthony Wayne recaptures Stony Point, New York, and takes some 700 prisoners while suffering fifteen casualties.

August 19 American General Henry Lee drives the British from Paulus Hook, New Jersey.

August 29 American generals John Sullivan and James Clinton defeat combined Loyalist and Indian forces at Newton (Elmira, New York).

September 3–October 28 An attempt to recapture Savannah results in a disastrous loss for the American-French combined forces.

September 23 In a naval battle off the coast of England, John Paul Jones captures the British warship *Serapis,* although he loses the *Bonhomme Richard.* A French vessel takes another British ship.

September 27 Congress appoints John Adams to negotiate peace with England.

October 17 The Continental Army returns to winter quarters at Morristown, New Jersey, where it will suffer a winter even worse than the year before at Valley Forge. Desertions and mutiny are commonplace.

1780

January 28 A fort is established on the Cumberland River to defend North Carolina from Indian attack. It is later named Nashville.

February 1 A British fleet carrying 8,000 men from New York and Newport, Rhode Island, reaches Charleston, South Carolina.

May 6 Fort Moultrie falls to British, and with it Charleston. In the heaviest single American defeat of the war, 5,400 Americans are captured along with ships, munitions, and food supplies.

May 25 A major mutiny in Morristown is put down by Pennsylvania troops, and two leaders of the mutiny are hanged.

June 22 Reinforcements sent by Washington join General Horatio Gates in North Carolina, as the focus of the war shifts to the South.

July 11 Five thousand French troops under Rochambeau arrive at Newport, Rhode Island, but are trapped by a British blockade

August 3 Benedict Arnold is appointed commander of W Point. He has been secretly communicating Washington's m ments to the British commander Henry Clinton.

August 16 At Camden, South Carolina, American forces under General Gates are overwhelmingly defeated by General Charles Cornwallis; Gates is relieved of command.

September 23 Carrying the plans for Benedict Arnold's surrender of West Point, British Major John André is captured and later hanged as a spy. Arnold flees to a British ship and is made a brigadier general in the British army.

October 7 A frontier militia force captures a Loyalist force of 1,100 at Kings Mountain, North Carolina, forcing General Cornwallis to abandon plans for an invasion of North Carolina.

October 14 General Nathanael Greene replaces General Gates as commander of the southern army. Greene begins a guerrilla war of harassment against the British.

1781

January 17 The Battle of Cowpens (South Carolina). American forces under General Daniel Morgan win a decisive victory.

March 15 Despite a victory at the Battle of Guilford Courthouse (North Carolina), Cornwallis suffers heavy losses, abandons plans to control the Carolinas, and retreats to await reinforcements.

June 10 American forces under Lafayette are reinforced by General Anthony Wayne in Virginia to combat Cornwallis.

August 14 Washington receives news that French Admiral de Grasse is sailing a fleet carrying 3,000 men to Chesapeake Bay. Washington secretly abandons plans to attack Clinton in New York and moves south instead.

August 31 French troops, under de Grasse, land at Yorktown, Virginia, and join American forces under Lafayette, blocking off retreat by Cornwallis.

⸱ember 5–8 In a naval battle off Yorktown, the French fleet is ⸱ and additional French troops arrive from Newport,

⸱ American troops under Washington are trans-
⸱g, Virginia, by de Grasse's ships.

⸱ined force of 9,000 Americans and 7,000
⸱ge of Yorktown.

⸱llis, with 8,000 troops, surrenders at Yorktown, effectively ending British hopes of victory in America. Aware of Cornwallis's predicament, Clinton fails to send British reinforcements in time. They sail back to New York.

1782

January 1 Loyalists in America, fearing confiscations and reprisals, begin to leave for Nova Scotia and New Brunswick.

February 27 The House of Commons votes against waging further war in America; the English Crown is empowered to seek peace negotiations. In March, Lord North resigns as Prime Minister and is replaced by Lord Rockingham, who seeks immediate negotiations with America.

April 19 The Netherlands recognizes the independence of the United States.

August 27 A skirmish in South Carolina is the last wartime engagement on the Eastern Seaboard.

November 30 A preliminary peace treaty is signed in Paris.

1783

January 20 Preliminary peace treaties are signed between England and France and England and Spain.

February 4 Great Britain officially declares an end to hostilities in America.

April 11 Congress declares a formal end to the Revolutionary War.

June 13 The main part of the Continental Army disbands.

September 3 The Treaty of Paris is signed, formally ending the war. The treaty is ratified by Congress in January 1784.

The Patriots

John Adams (1735–1826) Born in Braintree (Quincy), Massachusetts, a Harvard-educated lawyer, he was the cousin of Samuel Adams. A thorough but cautious patriot, Adams safely crossed political highwire in defending the British soldiers accused in Boston Massacre. A prominent member of the Continental gresses, Adams was among those named to draft the Declaration of Independence, which he later signed. As America's wartime envoy to France and Holland, he was instrumental in obtaining the foreign aid of both of those countries, and then joined in negotiating the Peace of Paris ending the war.

After the war he served as first U.S. minister to Great Britain and then returned home to serve as Washington's Vice-President for two terms. Adams succeeded Washington as the second President in 1796, but was defeated by Thomas Jefferson in 1800. Both Adams and Jefferson died on July 4, 1826, the fiftieth anniversary of the Declaration of Independence.

Samuel Adams (1722–1803) After squandering an inheritance, ruining his father's brewery business, and failing as a tax collector, this most fiery of Adamses found his calling as a rabble-rouser. Always a step ahead of arrest or debtor's prison, he was one of the most radical of the patriots, far better at brewing dissent than beer. Samuel Adams was the chief political architect behind the machinations that led to the Boston Tea Party, as well as tutor to his younger cousin, John Adams. A signer of the Declaration, he all but faded from the national picture after the war was over, holding a variety of state offices and leaving his more illustrious cousin to take a leading role.

Dr. Benjamin Church (1734–1778?) Although not as notorious as Benedict Arnold, Church earned the unpleasant distinction of being the first American caught spying for the British. A physician from Boston, Church had established powerful credentials as a patriot zealot, being the first on hand to treat the wounded after the Boston Massacre. But in 1775, coded documents he was ͏mitting to the British were intercepted and he was tried as a ͏d guilty, he was spared the hanging that George Wash-
͏ted.

͏706–1790) Of all the figures in the Revolu-
͏rhaps only Washington has inspired more
͏n. Printer. Writer. Philosopher. Scientist.
͏t. All of the labels fit, but none defines the man

who was, during his life, one of the most famous men in the world.

Born in Boston, he was the fifteenth of a candlemaker's seventeen children. His brief formal schooling ended when he was apprenticed to his older half-brother James, printer of the *New England Courant* and a member of the young radicals of Boston. Failing to get along with James, Ben moved to Philadelphia and found work as a printer, quickly gaining the confidence of the most powerful men in that cosmopolitan city. A trip to London followed in 1724, although financial support promised to Franklin by Pennsylvania's governor fell through and he was forced to find work as a printer.

Returning to Philadelphia in 1726, he began a rise that was professionally and financially astonishing. By 1748 he was able to retire, having started a newspaper; begun a tradesmen's club called the Junto; founded the first American subscription library; become clerk to the Pennsylvania legislature; established the first fire company; become postmaster of Philadelphia; established the American Philosophical Society; and launched *Poor Richard's Almanac,* the collection of wit, wisdom, and financial advice he produced for twenty-five years.

Franklin turned his attention to science and politics. He performed his electrical experiments—most famously the silken kite experiment, which proved that lightning and electricity were the same force of nature—and he invented the lightning rod. He added to his list of inventions with bifocal eyeglasses and the efficient Franklin stove. A key mover in the Pennsylvania legislature, he was sent to England as the colony's agent in 1764, emerging as the leading spokesman against the Stamp Act. (His illegitimate son William became colonial governor of New Jersey, but remained a Loyalist, a fracture of his relationship with his father that was never repaired.)

With war looming, Franklin returned to America a month before the battles at Lexington and Concord. During the war, he sat in the Second Continental Congress, was a member of the committee that formed to draft the Declaration, and soon afterward was sent to Paris to negotiate an alliance with the French, staying in Europe to make the terms of peace.

Nathan Hale (1755–1776) A Connecticut schoolteacher, Hale joined Washington's army but saw no action. When Washington called for volunteers to gather information on British troops, Hale stepped forward. Recognized and reported by a Tory relative, he was arrested by the British in civilian clothing with maps showing troop positions. After confessing, Hale was hanged. While his dignity and bravery were widely admired and he became an early martyr to the rebel cause, his famous last words of regret are most likely an invention that has become part of the Revolution's mythology. The words have never been documented.

John Hancock (1736–1793) The richest man in New England before the war, Hancock was a merchant who had inherited his wealth from an uncle who had acquired it through smuggling. As an ally of the Adamses, Hancock's purse assured him a prominent place among the patriots, and he bankrolled the rebel cause. Hancock attended the Continental Congresses and served as President of the Congress. Despite a total lack of military experience, Hancock hoped to command the Continental Army and was annoyed when Washington was named. He was the first and most visible signer of the Declaration, but his wartime service was undistinguished, and after the war he was elected governor of Massachusetts.

Patrick Henry (1736–1799) Far from being a member of the Virginia aristocracy, Henry was the son of a frontier farmer whose first attempts to earn a living met with failure. Through influential friends, he was licensed to practice law and made a name for himself, eventually winning a seat in the House of Burgesses. An early radical and an ambitious self-promoter, Henry represented frontier interests against the landed establishment and was known throughout the colonies for his fiery orations. He went to both Continental Congresses, and following the first, he returned to Virginia to make the March 20, 1755, speech for which he is most famous.

He was elected first governor of Virginia, and sent George Rogers Clark to expel the British. After the war he opposed the

Constitution, but later reversed himself. His poor health kept him from taking a position offered in Washington's administration.

American Voices

Patrick Henry to the House of Burgesses:

> Is life so dear or peace so sweet as to be purchased at the price of chains and slavery? . . . I know not what course others may take, but as for me, give me liberty or give me death!

Thomas Jefferson (1743–1826) Born into a well-off farming family in Virginia's Albemarle County, the Declaration's author distinguished himself early as a scholar, and gained admission to the Virginia bar in 1767. Although no great admirer of Patrick Henry's bombastic style, Jefferson was drawn to the patriot circle around Henry after his election to the House of Burgesses, having provided voters with the requisite quantities of rum punch. His literary prowess, demonstrated in political pamphlets, prompted John Adams to put Jefferson forward as the man to write the Declaration, a task he accepted with reluctance.

Most of his war years were spent in Virginia as a legislator and later as governor. After his wife's death, in 1783, he joined the Continental Congress and served as ambassador to France, where he could observe firsthand the French Revolution that he had helped inspire. Returning to America in 1789, Jefferson became Washington's Secretary of State and began to oppose what he saw as a too-powerful central government under the new Constitution, bringing him into a direct confrontation with his old colleague John Adams and, more dramatically, with the chief Federalist, Alexander Hamilton.

Running second to Adams in 1796, he became Vice-President, chafing at the largely ceremonial role. In 1800, Jefferson and fellow Democratic Republican Aaron Burr tied in the electoral vote and Jefferson took the Presidency in a House vote. After two terms, he returned to his Monticello home to complete his final endeavor, the University of Virginia, his architectural masterpiece. As he lay dying, Jefferson would ask what the date was, holding out, like John Adams, until July 4, 1826, the fiftieth anniversary of the Declaration.

Richard Henry Lee (1732–1794) A member of Virginia's most prominent family and the House of Burgesses, Lee was a valuable ally of Patrick Henry and Samuel Adams. Sent to the Continental Congress in 1776, he proposed the resolution on independence and was one of the signers of the Declaration.

James Otis (1725–1783) A descent into madness kept this Boston lawyer, a writer and speaker on a par with the greats of the era, from earning a greater place in Revolutionary history. Samuel Adams's first ally, Otis became one of the most fiery of the Boston radicals, his pamphlets declaring the rights of the colonists and introducing the phrase "no taxation without representation." Although he attended the 1765 Stamp Act Congress, by 1771 his behavior was increasingly erratic. Walking the streets of Boston, he fired pistols and broke windows until his family bound him and carted him off to a country farm. In and out of asylums, he died when his farmhouse was struck by lightning.

Thomas Paine (1737–1809) One of the Revolution's pure idealists, the English-born Paine lived up to his name in the eyes of those he attacked. Unsuccessful in London, where his radical notions got him into trouble, he came to America with the aid of Benjamin Franklin. At Franklin's urging, he wrote *Common Sense* and helped push the colonies toward independence.

With the Continental Army in retreat, he later wrote a series of pamphlets at Washington's request that became *The Crisis*. In 1781 he went to France and helped secure a large gold shipment for the rebel cause. After the war he returned to England and wrote *The Rights of Man,* which earned him a conviction on charges of treason. He took refuge in France, where his anti-monarchist ideas were welcomed as France went through the throes of its great Revolution. But as that Revolution began to eat its own, Paine was imprisoned and wrote *The Age of Reason* while awaiting the guillotine. Spared execution, he returned to America. The eternal gadfly, Paine alienated the new American powers-that-be with his *Letter to Washington,* and died a poor outcast.

American Voices

From *The Crisis* by Thomas Paine:
> These are the times that try men's souls. The summer soldier and the sunshine patriot will shrink from the service of his country. . . . Tyranny, like Hell, is not easily conquered.

Paul Revere (1735–1818) "Listen my children and you shall hear . . ."

It is perhaps the best-known bit of doggerel in American literature. But like most epic poems, Longfellow's tribute to the Boston silversmith fudges the facts. Boston-born, Revere was the son of a Huguenot, the French Protestants who had been driven from France. In America, he changed his name from Apollos Rivoire. A silversmith like his father, Paul Revere also went into the false-teeth business. A veteran of the French and Indian War, he was in the Samuel Adams circle of rebels, serving as a messenger. He took an active part in all the events leading up to the war, and his famous engraving of the Massacre, which had been lifted from the work of another artist, became an icon in every patriot home.

But it was the ride to Lexington that brought him immortality of sorts. In fact, he made two rides. The first was to warn the patriots to hide their ammunition in Concord, and the second was the famous "midnight ride." After receiving the signal from the South Church, Revere and two other riders set off. Although he was able to reach Lexington and warn John Hancock, Samuel Adams, and the Minutemen of the British approach, Revere was soon captured.

His wartime record was also slightly tarnished. Despite his services as a trusted courier, he had not received a commission from Congress and served out the war in a militia unit. In one of his few actions, Revere was ordered to lead troops against the British at Penobscot. Instead he marched his men back to Boston when American ships failed to engage the British. Relieved of command and accused of cowardice, Revere's honor was smudged until a court acquittal in 1782.

Joseph Warren (1741–1775) A Boston physician, Warren became one of Sam Adams's most devoted protégés. An active participant in the major prewar event in Boston, Warren became an instant hero when he charged into enemy fire at Lexington to treat the wounded. His fame was short-lived as he became one of the first patriot martyrs. Commissioned a general despite a lack of experience, he joined the ranks on Breed's Hill and was killed in the fighting there.

Mercy Otis Warren (1728–1814) Sister of the patriot leader James Otis, Mercy Warren surmounted the considerable odds placed before women in eighteenth-century America to become a writer of considerable influence. A dramatist, she was unable to see her plays performed because Puritan Boston did not permit theatrical works. An outspoken critic of the Constitution, she wrote widely to defeat its ratification. In 1805 she published the first history of the Revolution, the three-volume *Rise, Progress and Termination of the American Revolution*. While rich in anecdotal material and period detail, the book was colored by Warren's fierce anti-Federalist bias, and was written in the full fervor of postwar patriotic sentiment.

The Soldiers

Ethan Allen (1738–1789) A flamboyant veteran of the French and Indian War and a giant of a man, Allen raised a private army in Vermont called the Green Mountain Boys during an ongoing border dispute with Vermont's sister colony, New York. After Lexington, Allen and his men, joined by Benedict Arnold, captured the undermanned Fort Ticonderoga in upstate New York from the British. Captured during an assault on Montreal in 1775, Allen was thrown in irons and returned to England to stand trial. He was held prisoner for two years. Later he attempted to negotiate a separate peace treaty with the British. He took no further part in the war. He died of apoplexy.

Benedict Arnold (1741–1801) Perhaps the greatest villain in American history, Arnold might have been a great hero. An audacious, even reckless field commander, he fought with distinction in the early days of the Revolution. Raising his own militia force, Arnold joined Ethan Allen in the capture of Fort Ticonderoga and later attempted a brave but ill-fated assault on Quebec. Bitter at being passed over for promotion, he then played an important role in the crucial victory at Saratoga, where he was wounded. Belatedly promoted, Arnold was made commander of the Philadelphia garrison, where he was accused of improprieties and a shadow fell over his career. At about this time, Arnold began to supply the British with military information, culminating in the plan to surrender the strategic fort at West Point. When Arnold's contact, British Major John André, was captured with the plans in his boots, Arnold fled to a British ship. (André was hanged as a spy, partly in retaliation for the execution of Nathan Hale.) Given rank in the British army, Arnold conducted vicious raids on American forces in New England and Virginia. After the war, he and his family were granted a royal pension and given a tract of land in Canada.

George Rogers Clark (1752–1818) A surveyor and frontiersman, Clark led the successful military operations against the British and their Indian allies on the western frontier in what would later become Kentucky.

Horatio Gates (c. 1728–1806) A British-born soldier, he was badly wounded in his first action during the French and Indian War. Gates took up the patriot cause and led the American forces that won the key battle at Saratoga in 1777. But later that year he took part in an abortive attempt to wrest control of the army from George Washington. In 1780 he was given command of the army in the South, but was badly defeated at Camden, South Carolina, and lost his command. After the war, Gates was reinstated as the army's second-ranking officer.

Nathanael Greene (1724–1786) A Rhode Island Quaker with no military experience, Greene became a self-taught student of military history and emerged as one of the war's most successful tacticians, rising to the rank of general. At the war's outset, he commanded Rhode Island's three regiments but was picked by Washington for rapid advancement. With Washington at the defeats in Long Island and Manhattan as well as the victory at Trenton, his greatest contribution came as commander in the South. Utilizing a guerrilla strategy, he harassed Cornwallis from the Carolinas, forcing him back toward Virginia and the Yorktown showdown.

Alexander Hamilton (1757–1804) Born in the West Indies, Hamilton was proof that low birth need not be an impediment in early America. The illegitimate son of a shopkeeper mother whose father deserted them, Hamilton caught the attention of wealthy benefactors who sent him to King's College (now Columbia University) in New York. He became an ardent patriot and, at age nineteen, was leading a company of New York artillery.

At Trenton he caught Washington's eye and became a favorite, rising to the position of Washington's aide and private secretary, and later commanding in the field. A convenient marriage to the daughter of Philip Schuyler, a powerful New Yorker, gave him entrée to society and additional clout.

His career was even more significant after the war, when he established a law practice in New York and became a key figure in the Constitutional convention of 1787. Hamilton was one of the chief essayists behind *The Federalist Papers* arguing for the Constitution's ratification (see Chapter 3). He became Washington's Secretary of the Treasury, and was a crucial figure in the first two administrations, establishing the nation's economic policies. But he became involved in political and amorous intrigues that crippled his career.

He returned to private practice, remaining a central figure in the Federalist Party, and his views were the source of the feud that led to his fatal duel with Aaron Burr.

John Paul Jones (1747–1792) Essentially an adventurer who followed the action, America's first naval hero was born John Paul in Scotland and began his career on a slave ship. He came to

America under a dark cloud following the death of one of his crewmen, and added Jones to his name. When the Congress commissioned a small navy, Jones volunteered and was given the *Providence,* with which he raided English ships. With the *Ranger,* he sailed to France and continued his raids off the English coast. The French later gave him a refitted ship called the *Bonhomme Richard,* and with it he engaged the larger, British ship *Serapis* in a battle he won at the loss of *Bonhomme Richard.* A hero to the French, Jones was later sent there as an emissary, and received a congressional medal in 1787. He finished his sea career with the Russian navy of the Empress Catherine before his death in Paris. (In 1905, his supposed remaíns were returned to the U.S. and reburied at Annapolis, Maryland.)

American Voices

John Paul Jones during the battle against *Serapis:*

> I have not yet begun to fight.

Henry Knox (1750–1806) A Boston bookseller and a witness to the Boston massacre, Knox rose to become the general in charge of Washington's artillery and one of the commander-in-chief's most trusted aides. His nickname, "Ox," came from both his substantial girth—he stood six feet three inches and weighed some 280 pounds—and for the exploit in which, during the dead of winter in 1776, he transported the British cannons captured at Fort Ticonderoga by oxcart back to Boston. In Washington's first engagement as commander, these guns were placed on Dorchester Heights, forcing General Howe's army to evacuate the city without a shot being fired.

At Yorktown, Knox commanded the artillery bombardment of General Cornwallis's forces and after the war, he served in Congress. Following Washington's election, Knox became the first War Secretary.

Marquis de Lafayette (1757–1834) One of the Revolution's idealists, this young Frenchman came to America at age nineteen, wealthy enough to pay for his own ship to make the journey. Like other young European aristocrats for whom war was a matter of personal honor and social standing, Lafayette came in search of glory and adventure. In exchange for a major general's rank, he offered to serve without pay, and quickly earned Washington's affection. They developed an almost father-son relationship. Given a minor command, Lafayette proved to be an able and loyal commander.

During a trip back to France, he was instrumental in securing the French military assistance that was the key to the American victory at Yorktown. At the surrender, Lafayette's personal band proudly piped "Yankee Doodle Dandy," once a song mockingly sung by the British to taunt the Americans. After the war, Lafayette returned to France with enough American soil in which to be buried.

Charles Lee (1731–1782) A British-born soldier who rose to general in the patriot army, Lee had fought in the French and Indian War with Braddock, and had seen combat in Europe as well. A professional soldier, he was far more experienced than most of the American commanders, including Washington, whom he grew to disdain. Commissioned a major general, he justified the rank with his defense of Charleston early in the war. He was later captured and held by the British for fifteen months. Allegedly, he offered his captors a plan for defeating the Americans. At the Battle of Monmouth, Lee ordered a confused and nearly costly retreat, for which he was court-martialed and broken of command. He returned to Virginia, where he died in a tavern before the peace treaty was signed.

Francis Marion (1732?–1795) Best known as the "Swamp Fox," Marion led a successful guerrilla war against British and vicious Tory troops under General Cornwallis in the Carolinas. It was the efforts of Marion and other guerrillas, including Charles Sumter, in the southern colonies that frustrated the British strategy to control the South.

Daniel Morgan (1735–1789) A veteran of Braddock's French and Indian disaster, Morgan had driven supply trains, earning his nickname "Old Wagoner." Another of Washington's most valuable commanders, he led a troop of buckskinned frontier riflemen who played a crucial role in the victory at Saratoga. Elevated to general, he commanded half the southern army and led the key victory at Cowpens and was also instrumental in the bloody Battle of Guilford Court, where General Cornwallis's losses were so heavy that the British commander had to abandon his plans to hold the Carolinas and retreat to Virginia.

"Molly Pitcher" **(1754–1832)** During the exhausting summer heat of the Battle of Monmouth (1778), Mary McCauley Hays, the wife of Private John Hays, fetched water for her husband and his gun crew, earning her the sobriquet "Molly Pitcher." When her husband was wounded in the battle, she knew his job well enough to help the gun crew continue firing. An apocryphal story they perhaps didn't tell you in grade school was that a cannonball passed through "Molly's" legs and tore away her petticoats. "Molly" is said to have told the men that it was a good thing it hadn't been higher, or it would have carried away something else! After the war, Mary Hays became a scrubwoman and the Pennsylvania Assembly later granted her a yearly pension of $40.

Israel Putnam (1718–1790) A colonel in the Connecticut militia, "Old Put" left his plow, in the great tradition of civilian soldiers, and headed for Boston when the shooting started at Lexington. One of those in command on Breed's Hill, he achieved immortality of sorts with his order, "Don't fire until you see the whites of their eyes," a well-known piece of military advice of the day.

When the rebel troops started to break ranks after inflicting heavy losses on the British, Putnam unsuccessfully tried to keep his troops in place. But his failure to reinforce an American position was one reason the patriot army left off the battle when a victory might have been won, and Putnam was nearly court-martialed. Instead, Congress made him a general out of regional political considerations. Though never a great strategist or commander, he remained a loyal aide to Washington throughout the war.

Comte de Rochambeau (1725–1807) Commander of the 7,000 French troops sent to aid the rebels, Rochambeau had far more experience than Washington. Coordinating his movements with the French war fleet under Admiral de Grasse, Rochambeau deserves much of the credit for forcing the showdown at Yorktown at a time when Washington seemed to prefer an assault on New York.

Deborah Sampson (1760–1827) Assuming the name "Robert Shurtleff," this former indentured servant enlisted in the Continental Army in 1782 and became the only woman to serve formally in the Revolution. Fighting with the Fourth Massachusetts, she managed to maintain her disguise, although her fellow soldiers nicknamed her "Molly" because of her hairless face. A fever finally uncovered her true identity, and Sampson was discharged in 1783. She married the next year and received a small military pension. In 1802 she began a lecture tour, one of the first American women to do so, recounting her experiences as a soldier, a performance capped by her donning a soldier's uniform. Congress granted her heirs a full military pension in 1838.

George Washington (1732–1799) As for the "cherry tree" story, it was one of many fabrications created by Washington's "biographer," Parson Weems, who also fashioned the "fact" that he was rector of a nonexistent parish at Mount Vernon. The coin tossed across the Rappahannock—not the Potomac—was another of Weems's inventions. The legends began there, leaving "the father of our country" enshrouded in more layers of myth than any other figure in American history.

Washington was born into a modestly prosperous Virginia family. His father's death reduced his fortune, but with the help of relatives he did well, eventually inheriting the family estate at Mount Vernon. He spent about eight years in school, but never went to college. He set out to study law, but gave it up for his preference for the outdoors. Becoming a surveyor, he eventually bought some of the land he had been mapping. His early military career was mostly remarkable for the fact that he survived it. Yet when the French and Indian War was over, Washington was something of a military hero.

His wealth came from his marriage to the young widow, Martha Dandridge Custis, and by the time of the Revolution he was supposedly one of the richest men in America, although his holdings were in land and slaves rather than cash. As expected of men of his station, he ran for the House of Burgesses and was sent to the two Continental Congresses. After volunteering to serve without pay, he was unanimously chosen commander of the Continental Army when it became apparent that for political reasons a southerner had to fill the job.

There are conflicting views about his military leadership. Traditionalists say that he held together a ragged, ill-equipped army by sheer force of will, chose his commanders well, and had to spend too much time dickering with Congress for enough money to arm his men. This view also holds that he was a master of the strategic retreat, and tricked the British into believing his point of attack would be New York when it was actually Yorktown.

The revisionist view holds that Washington was an unduly harsh leader who maintained brutal discipline in the ranks, nearly lost the war several times, to be saved only by greater incompetence on the part of the British, was better at politicking than commanding, and had to be dragged against his will by the French to attack Yorktown. Several historians argue that Charles Lee or Horatio Gates would have been more daring commanders who might have ended the war sooner. It is an intriguing speculation that will remain unanswered, although Lee's actions in battle and assistance to the British while a captive do little to arouse confidence in his abilities.

The fact remains that Washington, dealt a weak hand, surmounted the odds of poorly outfitted troops, political intrigues, numerous betrayals, and a vastly better equipped opposition to sweep up the jackpot. If nothing else, he was a consummate survivor, and that may have been what America required at the time. That he was loved by his soldiers seems unlikely; there were frequent mutinies for the suppression of which Washington kept a well-fed and trained group of militia. He did inspire fierce loyalty among his officer corps, perhaps the true strength of a commander. For the American people, he was the first larger-than-life national hero, something a new nation arguably needs to survive.

After his emotional farewell at Fraunces Tavern in New York, he retired to Mount Vernon, until he was called back to serve as President at a time when probably no other man in America could have united the country behind the new government. The presidency was tailored with him in mind, and he led the nation through eight critical years during which the machinery of government was literally invented. He returned to the gentleman's life at Mount Vernon, where he caught a chill on a cold December day. Left alone, he might have survived. Instead his physicians bled him, standard medical procedure in the day, and the treatment probably doomed him.

What was Common Sense?

When the Continental Congress met for the second time, in May 1775, it was a very different group. The first Congress had been cautious and even conciliatory with conservative and moderate voices holding sway. But the pendulum was swinging to the radical position, and there were new faces among the delegates, Benjamin Franklin—once cautious, now rebellious—and Thomas Jefferson among them.

Events were also moving swiftly. The battles at Lexington and Concord, the easy victory at Fort Ticonderoga, the devastating casualties inflicted on the British army by the rebels at Breed's Hill, and the evacuation of British troops from Boston in March 1776 had all given hope to the Whig (patriot) cause. But the final break—independence—still seemed too extreme to some. It's important to remember that the vast majority of Americans at the time were first and second generation. Their family ties and their sense of culture and national identity were essentially English. Many Americans had friends and family in England. And the commercial ties between the two were obviously also powerful.

The forces pushing toward independence needed momentum, and they got it in several ways. The first factor was another round of heavy-handed British miscalculations. First the King issued a proclamation cutting off the colonies from trade. Then, unable to conscript sufficient troops, the British command decided to supplement its regulars with mercenaries, soldiers from the German principalities sold into King George's service by their princes. Most came from Hesse-Cassel, so the name "Hessian" became generic for all of these hired soldiers.

The Hessians accounted for as much as a third of the English forces fighting in the colonies. Their reputation as fierce fighters was linked to a frightening image—reinforced, no doubt, by the British command—as plundering rapists. (Ironically, many of them stayed on in America. Benjamin Franklin gave George Washington printed promises of free land to lure mercenaries away from English ranks.) When word of the coming of 12,000 Hessian troops reached America, it was a shock, and further narrowed chances for reconciliation. In response, a convention in Virginia instructed its delegates to Congress to declare the United Colonies free and independent.

The second factor was a literary one. In January 1776, an anonymous pamphlet entitled *Common Sense* came off the presses of a patriot printer. Its author, Thomas Paine, had simply, eloquently, and admittedly with some melodramatic prose, stated the reasons for independence. He reduced the hereditary succession of kings to an absurdity, slashed down all arguments for reconciliation with England, argued the economic benefits of independence, and even presented a cost analysis for creating an American navy.

With the assistance of Ben Franklin, Thomas Paine came to America from London and found work with a Philadelphia bookseller. In the colonies for only a few months, Paine wrote, at Franklin's suggestion, a brief history of the upheaval against England. It is impossible to understate the impact and importance of *Common Sense*. Paine's polemic was read by everyone in Congress, including General Washington, who commented on its effects on his men. Equally important, it was read by people everywhere. The pamphlet quickly sold 150,000 copies, going through numerous printings until it had reached half a million. (Approximating the American population at the time, including slaves, at 3 million, a current equivalent pamphlet would have to sell more than 35 million copies!) For the first time, mass public opinion had swung toward the cause of independence.

American Voices

From a letter written by Abigail Adams to her husband, John, who was attending the Continental Congress (March 31, 1776):

> In the new Code of Laws which I suppose it will be necessary for you to make I desire you would Remember the Ladies, and be more generous and favourable to them than your ancestors. Do not put such unlimited powers into the hands of the Husbands. Remember all men would be tyrants if they could. If particular care and attention is not paid to the Ladies, we are determined to forment a Rebellion, and will not hold ourselves bound by any laws in which we have no voice, or Representation.

Upon receipt of this directive from home, a bemused John Adams replied, in part, "Depend upon it. We know better than to repeal our Masculine systems."

What exactly does the Declaration of Independence say? What did Congress leave out?

On June 7, 1776, Richard Henry Lee, a delegate from Virginia and a member of one of that colony's leading families, rose in Philadelphia to propose a three-part resolution: (1) to declare the colonies independent; (2) to form foreign alliances; (3) to prepare a plan of confederation. After days of debate, Congress compromised. In that time-honored congressional tradition of putting off important decisions, this Congress decided to form committees, one for each of these points.

The committee selected to draw up some document declaring that America was free of England naturally included John Adams and Ben Franklin, already an internationally known writer.

Robert Livingston, a conservative from New York, was named along with Roger Sherman of Connecticut. A southerner was needed for political balance, and John Adams lobbied hard for the fifth member. His choice, Virginian Thomas Jefferson, was seen as a compromise. Jefferson had a reputation as a writer, and had already contributed one pamphlet to Congress, *A Summary View of the Rights of British America*. Although a bitter political rival in later years, Adams now deferred to Jefferson because, as he admitted, Jefferson could write ten times better than he.

Distracted by his wife's health and a preference to work on the new constitution of Virginia that was being written while he was in Philadelphia, Jefferson was a reluctant author. But closeting himself away, he set to work quickly, writing on a portable desk he had designed. He presented his draft to the committee, which recommended minor changes and forwarded it to Congress for debate.

Of course the delegates demanded changes, all of which Jefferson considered deplorable. The most debated was Jefferson's charge that the King was responsible for the slave trade. The southern delegates, joined by northerners who were known to have profited from, in Jefferson's own phrase, "this execrable commerce," deleted this section.

With the advantage of hindsight, cynicism about this Congress and Thomas Jefferson in particular is easy. But the baffling question remains: How could a man who embodied the Enlightenment—who wrote so eloquently that "all Men are created equal" and are endowed by the Creator with the right of liberty—how could such a man keep black slaves, of which Jefferson (like Washington and many others in Congress) possessed many? There is no truly satisfying answer. Earlier in his life, as a lawyer and member of the Burgesses, he had unsuccessfully argued against aspects of slavery. At worst, Jefferson may not have thought of slaves as men, not an unusual notion in his time. And he was a man of his times. Like other men, great and small, he was not perfect. This imperfection certainly seems glaring, but to dismiss his other accomplishments for this moral failure is unrealistic.

On July 2, Lee's resolution of independence was passed by

Congress. On the evening of July 4, the Declaration of Independence, which explained the act of independence, was adopted. At the signing, John Hancock reportedly urged unanimity. "There must be no pulling different ways. We must hang together," he said.

"Yes," said the inimitable Ben Franklin. "We must indeed all hang together, or most assuredly we shall all hang separately."

Although Jefferson suffered doubts because of the changes forced upon him, the finished document was cheered throughout the colonies. In his stirring prose, Jefferson had voiced all the pent-up anguish that the American rebels had been feeling for years.

What were the Articles of Confederation?

Congress had invented a wonderful new machine, with a flag and an army, but they didn't quite know how to work it. Ben Franklin, who knew a thing or two about inventing, had been tinkering with the idea of a colonial confederation as far back as 1754, but his attempts to create one had been in vain. Local colonial power brokers wanted to see that power stayed that way—local and in their hands, not in the hands of the rabble. But now, with independence declared, British warships floating off the coast, and the threat of the hangman's noose if they failed, a little machinery of government seemed a sensible idea.

In August the Congress began to debate what would become the Articles of Confederation, the first loosely organized federal government. Disagreement hinged on questions of representation and voting: should votes be apportioned on population, or should each state receive a single vote in Congress? Obviously, big states wanted population to determine votes; small states wanted one vote per state. The war diverted their attention to other matters—such as saving their own necks. It was 1777 before the Articles were submitted to the states for ratification, and 1781 before they were ratified. As foundations for national governments go, this was a rather shaky one. Under the Articles, the presidency was a powerless office and Congress lacked the power to tax. Owing to uncertainties about what kind of power the government should have, the Articles provided almost none. But Congress was able to sputter through the war until it could build itself a better mousetrap.

How did the colonies win the war?

Does this sound familiar? The world's most powerful nation is caught up in a war against a small guerrilla army. This superpower must resupply its troops from thousands of miles away, a costly endeavor, and support for the war at home is tentative, dividing the nation's people and leadership. The rebels also receive financial and military support from the superpower's chief military and political antagonist. As the war drags on and casualties mount, generals are disgraced and the rebels gain momentum, even in defeat.

The United States in Vietnam? It could be. But it is also the story of the British loss of the American colonies. There are numerous parallels between the two conflicts. For the United States, substitute England under George III, the dominant world power of the day, but caught up in a draining colonial conflict that stretches its resources. For the Vietcong, substitute the colonial army under Washington, a ragtag collection if ever there was one, who used such unheard-of tactics as disguising themselves in British uniforms and attacking from the rear. British generals, accustomed to precisely drawn battle formations, were completely taken aback, just as American commanders schooled in the tank warfare of World War II were unprepared for the jungles of Vietnam. For foreign support, substitute England's chief European adversary, France (as well as Spain and the Netherlands) for the Soviet (and Red Chinese) supplying of the Vietcong.

There can be no question that without France's armies, money, and supplies (as much as 90 percent of the American gunpowder used in the war came from France), the American forces could not have won. Why did the French do it? Certainly King Louis XVI and his charming wife, Marie Antoinette, had no particular sympathy for anti-monarchist, democratic rabble. Their motive, actually the strategy of a pro-American minister, the Comte de Vergennes, was simple: to bloody England's nose in any way they could and perhaps even win back some of the territory lost after the Seven Years War. Had the monarchy and aristocracy of France known that their own subjects would be greatly inspired by the American Revolution a few years later, the French royalty might have thought the matter over a bit longer. An American loss might have saved their necks. *C'est la vie!*

Equally important to America's victory was the consistent bungling of the British high command, which treated the war as an intolerable inconvenience. At any number of points in the fighting, particularly in the early years, before France was fully committed, aggressive generalship from various British commanders might have turned the tide.

If Washington's army had been destroyed after Long Island or Germantown . . .

If Congress had been captured and shipped off to England for trial—and most likely the noose . . .

And what if England had "won"? Could it possibly have maintained sovereignty over a large, prosperous, diverse, and expanding America, a vast territory far richer in resources than England? It is unlikely. Independence was a historical inevitability, in one form or another. It was simply an idea whose time had come, and America was not alone, as the revolutions that followed in Europe would prove.

The British had to weigh the costs of maintaining their dominance against its returns. They would have seen, as America did in Vietnam, and as the Soviets did more recently in Afghanistan, that the costs of such wars of colonial domination are usually more than a nation is willing or able to bear.

It's a pity that America's military and political leaders never learned a lesson from our own past, a fact that speaks volumes about the arrogance of power.

What did America win?

The Peace of Paris, negotiated for the United States by Benjamin Franklin, John Adams, and John Jay, was formally signed on February 3, 1783. At the same time, England signed treaties with America's allies, France, Spain, and the Netherlands.

The most important thing the treaty did was to recognize the independence of the United States of America. Beyond that, it marked the boundaries of the new nation.

The United States now meant everything from the Atlantic west to the Mississippi River, save New Orleans and the Floridas. This area was ceded by England back to Spain as part of New Spain, the massive empire that now stretched from South America north, well into coastal California, and including much of the American southwest, east to the Florida peninsula. The northern border was set at the Great Lakes and along the provincial frontiers of Quebec and Nova Scotia.

The victory also left America with a considerable foreign debt. In a report to Congress several years later, Alexander Hamilton would place this debt at $11,710,379 (in addition to domestic and state debts totaling more than $65 million). This enormous debt was just one of the problems that would threaten the new nation in its first years of independence.

Three

Growth of a Nation: From the Creation of the Constitution to Manifest Destiny

- What was Shays's Rebellion?

- What was the Constitutional Convention?

- What are "checks and balances?"

- Who were the Federalists, and what were the Federalist Papers?

- Who elected George Washington the first President?

- What was the Bill of Rights?

- Why didn't Jefferson like Hamilton?

- The 1790 Census

- What were the Whiskey Rebellion and the "Revolution of 1800"?

• What was *Marbury v. Madison?*

• How did America purchase Lousiana?

• Who were Lewis and Clark?

• Why did Aaron Burr shoot Alexander Hamilton?

• Thomas Jefferson and Sally Hemings: Did he or didn't he?

• What was "impressment"?

• Who were Tecumseh and the "Prophet"?

• What was the War of 1812 about?

• Milestones in the War of 1812

• What was the Monroe Doctrine?

• What was the Missouri Compromise?

• The Union in 1821

• What was the "corrupt bargain"?

• What were "Jacksonian Democracy" and the "spoils system"?

• What was the "Trail of Tears"?

• Who was Tocqueville, and why did he say all those things about America?

• What made the South fear a slave named Nat Turner?

• Who were the Whigs?

• Who fought at the Alamo?

• What was Manifest Destiny?

• Why did the Mormons move west?

After the shooting stopped, the United States of America was recognized by the major powers as independent. But this gangling new child was an ugly duckling among nations, a loose collection of states under the Articles of Confederation, not yet a sovereign nation. The big question was "Now what?" Following eight years of fighting, this new entity had to face the realities of governing. As might be expected, different people from different states had a lot of different ideas as to how that should be done.

During the next seventy-odd years, powered by dynamic forces, America would expand swiftly and aggressively. However, in that expansion, and in the way in which the new nation formed itself, the seeds of the next great American crisis were being sown. This chapter highlights the milestones in a developing America between the end of the Revolution and the prelude to the Civil War.

What was Shays's Rebellion?

Rebellion, as the Founding Fathers quickly discovered, is a catchy tune. Besides independence, the end of the war had brought economic chaos to America. As with most wars, the Revolution had been good for business. Everybody works, soldiers spend money, factories turn out ships and guns, armies buy supplies. That's the good news. The bad news is that after war comes inflation and depression. The years immediately following the Revolution were no different. America went through bad economic times. Established trading patterns were in disarray. Under the Articles of Confederation, Congress had no power to tax. In the thirteen states, where power was centered, the separate currencies were a shambles.

While the situation was bad almost everywhere, in Massachusetts, the home of the Adamses and birthplace of the patriot cause, the economic dislocation boiled over into bloodshed between Americans. Like the prewar Bacon's Rebellion, the Regulator Movement in the Carolinas, and the Paxton Boys of Pennsylvania (see pages 62–64), this "little rebellion" (Jefferson's phrase) was a sign of class conflict, a symptom of the economic tension that had always existed in America between, on one side, the working-class frontier farmers, inner-city laborers, the servant class, smaller merchants, and free blacks, and on the other side the bourgeoisie, the landed, slaveholding gentry, and international merchants of the larger cities.

When Massachusetts passed a state constitution in 1780, it found few friends among the poor and middle class, many of them veterans of the Continental Army still waiting for promised bonuses. When they learned that they were now barred from voting and holding office, they must have wondered what they had been fighting for. As the economy worsened, many farms were seized to pay off debts. When the local sheriffs looked to the militia to defend the debt courts against angry crowds, the militia sided with the farmers.

In the summer of 1786, an army veteran named Daniel Shays emerged on the scene. With 700 farmers and working-class people, Shays marched on Springfield and paraded around town. Onetime radical Sam Adams, now part of the Boston Establishment, drew up a Riot Act, allowing the authorities to jail anyone without a trial. Revolt against a monarch was one thing, said Adams, but against a republic it is a crime punishable by death.

Shays soon had a thousand men under arms and was marching on Boston, the seat of wealth and power. Then General Benjamin Lincoln, one of Washington's war commanders, brought out an army paid for by Boston's merchants. There was an exchange of artillery fire, leaving some casualties on both sides, and Shays's army scattered. Lincoln's army pursued the rebels, but refrained from attacking when the rout was assured. A harsh winter took its toll, and the army disintegrated. Some of the rebels were caught, tried, and hanged. Others were pardoned. Shays, on the run in Vermont, was pardoned, but died in poverty in 1788.

Writing from the safe distance of Paris, Thomas Jefferson said of the uprising, "A little rebellion now and then is a good thing. . . . God forbid that we should ever be twenty years without such a rebellion. . . . The tree of liberty must be refreshed from time to time with the blood of patriots and tyrants."

Lacking cohesion and stronger leadership, the Shaysites disintegrated. However, several of the reforms they had demanded were made, including the end of the state's direct taxation, lowered court costs, and the exemption of workmen's tools and household necessities from the debt process.

What was the Constitutional Convention?

While the Massachusetts uprising was a relatively minor affair that did not spread armed insurrection throughout the states, it shook up the new American ruling class. Something stronger than the Confederation was in order; the states had little ability to control local rebellion, let alone a foreign attack, a real threat as Spain and England kept troops in America. Equally pressing was the substantial threat posed by Indians on the western frontier who outnumbered the state militias. Nor could the states adequately handle the other two related crises facing America: the disruption of overseas trade and the postwar financial and currency collapse.

But the idea for a stronger central government did not spring out of the ashes of Shays's defeat. In 1785 a group in Virginia had already called for a meeting of the states, and again, in January 1786, the Virginia legislature called for a gathering at Annapolis, Maryland. Although only five states sent delegates to Annapolis in September 1786, they were able to persuade Congress to accept a plan for a meeting of delegates from the states "to devise such further provisions as shall appear to them necessary to render the constitution of the Federal Government adequate to the exigencies of the Union." This constitution would correct, in Alexander Hamilton's words, "such defects as may be discovered to exist" in the Articles of Confederation, an understatement if ever there was one.

On May 25, 1787, after a delay of ten days because too few delegates had arrived, the convention to draw up a new plan of government gathered in Philadelphia. Every state but Rhode Island sent delegates, and George Washington was unanimously selected to preside over the convention. In the course of the next four months, they would create the Constitution.

At various times during the four months, fifty-five delegates were present. In his book *The Vineyard of Liberty,* James McGregor Burns neatly encapsulated this group as "the well-bred, the well-fed, the well-read, and the well-wed." To other modern historians, they represented not the broad masses, but the wealthy merchants of the North and the wealthy, slaveholding plantation owners of the South.

Of them, the oldest was also perhaps the most famous, eighty-one-year-old Benjamin Franklin; Jonathan Dayton of New Jersey was youngest at twenty-seven. Their median age was forty-three. A little more than half (thirty-one) were college-educated, the same number as were lawyers. Seventeen of the delegates who were present to "establish justice . . . and secure the blessings of liberty to ourselves and our posterity . . ." (in the words of the Preamble), owned some 1,400 black slaves; three delegates, George Mason (Virginia), John Rutledge (South Carolina), and George Washington (Virginia), were the largest slaveholders in the country.

After two hundred years of rule under the Constitution, we have come to think of it as a perfect ideological and idealistic document created by a gathering of legislative geniuses. It has often been said that no new nation before or since has enjoyed a more politically experienced group than the men who wrote the Constitution. It might be useful to think of them as a collection of, in a modern phrase, "special interest groups" and regionally minded legislators, almost all of them admittedly brilliant politicians. And in politics, then as now, the art of compromise is the secret of success.

The Constitution was no different; it was a political creation, hammered together in a series of artfully negotiated compromises, balancing political idealism with political expediency. There were conflicts everywhere: between small states and large states, North and South, slave states and abolitionist states.

While there was near unanimity that a federal government was necessary, there was less agreement about the structure of such a government. The first broad scheme for the Constitution came from the Virginians, young James Madison chief among them, and came to be known as the Virginia Plan. Its key points were a bicameral (two-chamber) legislature; an executive chosen by the legislature; and a judiciary also named by the legislature. An alternate, known as the New Jersey Plan, was favored by smaller states. Through the heat of summer, debate dragged on, the convention facing a deadlock essentially over two key questions.

The first was representation. Should Congress be based on population, with larger states getting proportionately more votes, or should each state receive equal representation?

The second question was that of slavery. The southern states wanted to have their cake and eat it too. Faced with growing abolitionist sentiments, the southern delegates would not bend on questions affecting slavery, nor would they grant freed blacks the vote. On the other hand, they wanted slaves counted for the purpose of determining representation in Congress. In other words, it was "Now you see 'em, now you don't."

With an impasse near, Roger Sherman proposed what is called the Connecticut Compromise, or Great Compromise. Seen in retrospect, it seems an obvious solution to the representation issue, providing for equal representation in the upper house of Congress (the Senate) and proportional representation in the lower house (the House of Representatives).

Two more compromises "solved" the issue of slavery and slaves, words that appear nowhere in the Constitution. Instead, flowery euphemisms like "no person held in service," and "all other persons" were coined in accordance with the Constitution's flowing legal prose. Under these bargains, Congress was prohibited from taking any action to control slavery for a period of twenty years (until 1808), although the gentlemen did agree that the slave trade could be taxed. (Apparently the anti-slave forces thought, "We may not like it, but at least let's make some money out of it.") And for the purposes of determining representation, slaves ("all other persons") would be counted as three-fifths of their total population. In hindsight, it was a small step forward for blacks. At least they had gone from being ignored to being three-fifths human. If they could hold out for another seventy years, they would be free! In turn, the southern states agreed to allow a maximum of three new future states that would ban slavery.

And in the ultimate exercise of compromise, the men who put the Constitution together recognized that it might have to be changed, so they built in an acceptable form of amending their work. Change would not be easy, but it was possible.

As is true of other moments in American history, cynicism born of perfect hindsight is easy. On the other hand, credit should be given where it is due. The Framers were intelligent, even brilliant men; they knew their history and their law. The Constitution they forged was then the pinnacle of thousands of years of political development. They were familiar with, and could draw on, such sources and models as the Greek philosophers, the Roman Republic, and the evolution of the English democratic tradition running from the Magna Carta through Parliament and the English Bill of Rights of 1689. Above all, in the Constitution—and earlier, in the Declaration—they embodied the triumph of the Enlightenment, that glorious flowering of ideas in the seventeenth and eighteenth centuries that elevated the powers of human reason and strove for new forms of government, free of tyranny. The philosophies they were striving to fulfill had been expressed by such giants of the age as Hume, Locke, Rousseau, Voltaire, and Kant. They were all familiar to the Framers, and these ideas contributed to the heady debate, a debate that centered on the ongoing struggle between liberty and democracy, two ideas that often clash.

As for debate, there was plenty. Even with the broad outlines agreed upon, major differences cropped up at every turn. It took nearly six hundred separate votes to settle them all. These were not small matters of detail, either, but large questions that might have altered the course of the nation. For instance, New York's Alexander Hamilton, one of the staunchest advocates of powerful central government and the chief representative of northern commercial interests—he was one of the founders of the Bank of New York—wanted the President and the Senate appointed for life. He also argued for giving the "first class," the wealthy men of America, among whom he could certainly be counted, "a distinct permanent share of the government."

Hamilton's suggestion was turned down, but the Constitution did not provide for direct elections, except for the House of Representatives, where it was still left to the states to determine who voted. Property ownership was the key qualification in almost every state. And of course, women, Indians, and blacks—free or slave—had no vote. It is simple to dismiss even that basic decision as the result of sexism and racism. But, again, the temper of the times must be considered. In a period in which class differences were so clearly delineated, though less so in America than in Europe, it may have been inconceivable for these men to consider allowing just anyone to vote. They took as an article of faith that to participate responsibly in a democracy required education and the measure of property that would allow one the leisure to read and think. That said, however, they also did everything they could to make sure that women, Indians, blacks, and the white poor would be excluded from obtaining such education and property.

The final form of the Constitution, prepared by New York's Gouverneur Morris, was put to a vote on September 17, 1787. Thirty-nine of the delegates present voted in favor; three were opposed. Another thirteen of the principals were absent, but seven of these were believed to favor the Constitution. It was sent on to Congress, which decided to submit the document to the states for ratification, with the approval of nine states needed for passage.

What are "checks and balances"?

This has nothing to do with monthly bank statements. Whether out of wisdom or fear, the Constitution's architects created a fundamental principle underlying the strength and tension of the federal government. The fear was obvious: no one wanted anyone else to become too powerful. So for almost every power they granted to one branch of government, they created an equal power of control for the other two. The legislature could "check" the power of the President, the Supreme Court could "check" the power of Congress, and so on, maintaining a careful symmetry or "balance" among the three branches.

Basic Powers and Checks

Executive Powers (President)
• Approves or vetoes federal bills.
• Carries out federal laws.
• Appoints judges and other high officials.
• Makes foreign treaties.

- Can grant pardons and reprieves to federal offenders.
- Acts as commander-in-chief of armed forces.

Checks on Executive Powers
- Congress can override vetoes by two-thirds vote.
- Senate can refuse to confirm appointments or ratify treaties.
- Congress can impeach and remove the President.
- Congress can declare war.
- Supreme Court can declare executive acts unconstitutional.

Legislative Powers (Congress)
- Passes federal laws.
- Establishes lower federal courts and the number of federal judges.
- Can override the President's veto with two-thirds vote.

Checks on Legislative Powers
- Presidential veto of federal bills.
- Supreme Court can rule laws unconstitutional.
- Both houses of Congress must vote to pass laws, checking power within the Legislature.

Judicial Powers
- Interprets and applies the law by trying federal cases.
- Can declare laws passed by Congress and executive actions unconstitutional.

Checks on Judicial Powers
- Congress can propose constitutional amendments to overturn judicial decisions. (These require two-thirds majority in both houses, and ratification by three-quarters of states.)
- Congress can impeach and remove federal judges.
- The President appoints judges (who must be confirmed by Senate).

Who were the Federalists, and what were The Federalist Papers?

Two hundred years of miseducation have left an image of the Constitution as a sort of American Ten Commandments, divinely inspired and carved in stone. So it is hard to imagine that its ratification was not assured. Like an unsuccessful organ implant, it was nearly rejected by the body politic. When the Constitution left Philadelphia, the country was almost evenly split between those favoring the strong central government it promised, who came to be known as Federalists, and those for a weaker central government with stronger states' rights, a.k.a. the anti-Federalists.

Loyal Americans and staunch patriots—many of them were Revolutionary leaders and veterans—the anti-Federalists feared a new brand of elected monarchy at the expense of individual liberties. They were led by such major contemporary figures as Virginia's governor Patrick Henry, Boston's Samuel Adams of Revolution fame, and New York's longtime governor, George Clinton. Their disdain for the Constitution might best be summed up in the words of Thomas Paine: "Government, even in its best state, is but a necessary evil."

But no small part of their resistance was personal; many anti-Federalists simply didn't *like* their opposites among the Federalists. No better example of this could be found than in New York, where the anti-Federalists were led by George Clinton, who had only disdain for Alexander Hamilton, or in Virginia, where Patrick Henry kept James Madison, the chief architect of the Constitution, from being elected to the Senate.

Championing the Federalist cause, Hamilton, Madison, and John Jay—then serving as the head of the Confederation's state department—attempted to influence the ratification debate with a series of pseudonymous newspaper letters signed "Publius" and later collected as *The Federalist Papers*. Eighty-five of these essays were published, and while they are considered among the most significant political documents in American history, after the Declaration of Independence and the Constitution, their direct impact on the debate of the day is dubious. Probably most of the people who counted had already made up their minds.

Of far greater consequence than the *Papers* was the pro-ratification stance of America's two most prominent men, Franklin and Washington, the latter of whom everyone assumed would become the first President under the new Constitution. (Of Washington's impact on Virginia's ratification vote, James Monroe wrote to Jefferson, "Be assured his influence carried this government.") One by one, the state conventions voting on the question came to ratification—some unanimously; others, like Massachusetts, by the narrowest of margins. The oldest kind of "smoke-filled room" politicking was often required, and several states agreed only with the proviso that a bill of rights be added to the Constitution. Delaware, a small state happy with the representation it would receive, was first to ratify and was joined in succession by Pennsylvania, New Jersey, Georgia, Connecticut, Massachusetts, Maryland, South Carolina, and New Hampshire, the ninth ratifying state.

But even with the required nine states, there was uncertainty. Virginia and New York had not spoken, and rejection by either or both of these powerful, wealthy states might have rendered the Constitution meaningless. With the bill-of-rights compromise that had worked elsewhere, Virginia voted in favor. In New York, aggressive speechmaking and buttonholing by Alexander Hamilton, combined with John Jay's gentler persuasion, carried the day for ratification.

Who elected George Washington the first President?

In its wisdom and foresight, not to mention its fear of the rabble, the Framers of the Constitution had created a remarkably curious beast when it came to selecting the President. The "electoral college" was the Constitution's last-ditch defense against an overdose of democracy.

In the Framers' scheme, each state would choose electors equal to its representation in Congress (House seats plus Senate seats). How the electors were chosen was a decision left to the separate states. The electors would then meet in their states and vote for two persons for President. The winner was the man with a majority. The Framers figured nobody—besides George Washington, that is—could win a clear majority, in which case the election would be decided in the House of Representatives, where each state got one vote.

Political parties were not only absent at this time, but were considered contemptible. Ideally in a debate, men would line up on one side or the other and then fall back into nonalignment, awaiting the next issue. The men who made the Constitution did not foresee the rise of the two-party system as we know it, although its beginnings were apparent in the debate over ratification. The Federalists, led by Alexander Hamilton and John Adams, would be the first political party formed in America.

Although February 4, 1789, has come down as the traditional first presidential election date, that was actually the day on which the first electors cast their ballots. It was preceded by a crazy quilt of elections taking place in late 1788 and the first months of 1789, with each state setting its own rules as to who could vote for what. Some states allowed the electors to be chosen directly by voters; in other states, electors were chosen by the state legislature. While being a male freeholder (property owner) was generally the key to a vote, some states had very ambiguous voting rules. In New Jersey, for instance, women indeed did vote for President in the first election. In Pennsylvania, any taxpayer was eligible.

But the result was the same. On March 4 the first Congress was supposed to convene in New York, but a quorum wasn't reached until April 1. Finally, on April 6, the Senate counted the electoral ballots and declared the inevitable. Washington was elected unanimously. John Adams had been named on enough ballots to qualify as Vice-President. Officially informed of his election on April 14, Washington left Mount Vernon two days later for an eight-day triumphal journey past adoring crowds along the way, and on April 30, 1789, he took the oath of office at Federal Hall in New York, which would be the seat of government for the next year and a half.

What was the Bill of Rights?

For the new government, no order of business was more pressing than delivering on a promised set of amendments to the Constitution. These were demanded during ratification by those who feared the states would be destroyed by the new central government. Madison took the lead in preparing the amendments and on September 25, 1789, a list of twelve were submitted for ratification by the states. Ten of the twelve amendments were finally ratified and in force on December 15, 1791, and became known as the Bill of Rights.

Although England had a Bill of Rights, it was narrower and could be repealed by Parliament. The American version was broader, and repeal could only be made through the states. The intention of the amendments was to guarantee freedoms not specifically named in the original Constitution. While legal scholars argue that such guarantees may have been logically unnecessary, they have become an integral part of the American legal system and remain at the core of many of the major controversies in American history, including those confronting contemporary America.

Rights Guaranteed by the Bill of Rights

First Amendment. Guarantees separation of church and state and freedom to worship; freedom of speech and the press; the right to assemble and petition for changes.

Second Amendment. The right to bear arms. (The key to the legal-gun debate. Those who favor gun control point to the Bill's specification of "a well-regulated militia," while advocates of gun ownership cite this amendment in its literal sense.)

Third Amendment. Soldiers cannot be housed in a private home without the consent of the owner. (A reaction to the British Quartering Act, one of the "intolerable acts" leading to the Revolution.)

Fourth Amendment. The right to be free from "unreasonable search and seizure." (Another "hot" issue, criminal rights versus law enforcement, hinges on the interpretation of this amendment.)

Fifth Amendment. Provides for laws concerning prosecution, including the requirement of a grand-jury indictment and the protection from testifying against oneself. (See "Who was Miranda?" in Chapter 8.)

Sixth Amendment. Guarantees the right to a speedy, public trial in the district where the crime has been committed, as well as other protections for the accused.

Seventh Amendment. Guarantees trial by jury.

Eighth Amendment. Prohibits "cruel and unusual punishment," the amendment at the heart of the capital-punishment debate.

Ninth Amendment. Defines the rule of the construction of the Constitution.

Tenth Amendment. Guarantees that any powers not specifically delegated to the federal government or denied to the states in the Constitution rest with the states or the people.

   (Two proposed amendments dealing with the apportionment of members and congressional compensation were not ratified.)

Amended by the Bill of Rights, the Constitution was still a political document, not an act of God. Like most works of men, it was flawed and imperfect in many ways—its flagrant denial of the rights of blacks, women, and Indians chief among its flaws. Many modern commentators argue that the Constitution was the perfectly realized means of assuring the control of the wealthy over the weak, with enough table scraps for the working and middle classes to assure popular support. From the beginning, critics have said the Constitution and Bill of Rights were selectively enforced and often ignored, as in the case of the Alien and Sedition Acts of the Adams Administration (1798), which clearly trampled the guarantees of the First Amendment.

On the other hand, what was the alternative? If the northern delegates had taken the moral high ground and not compromised on the issue of slavery, the Constitutional convention would have disintegrated. Under the Articles of Confederation, the states would have remained economically weak and ripe for invasion by awaiting foreign forces.

Why didn't Jefferson like Hamilton?

Under Washington and the new Congress, the government moved rapidly toward organization. Drawing from a rich array of political talent, Washington selected appointees to the key posts in his administration, often turning to old friends and war veterans, such as Henry Knox, who became Secretary of War. A 1,000-man army was established, principally to confront the Indians on the western frontier. The Supreme Court was created, and John Jay was chosen first Chief Justice. But the two giants of this administration, and the men who would personify the great debate and division within the country in the years ahead, were Thomas Jefferson and Alexander Hamilton. Dumas Malone, Jefferson's most prominent biographer, has stated their difference simply. "No other statesman has personified national power and the rule of the favored few so well as Hamilton, and no other has glorified self-government and the freedom of the individual to such a degree as Jefferson."

America's envoy in Paris as the Bastille was stormed in 1789, beginning the French Revolution, Jefferson returned to New York to lead the State Department. Once Washington's wartime confidential secretary, Hamilton had become an attorney in New York, founder of the Bank of New York and one of that state's and the nation's most powerful men. He would fill the critical role of Washington's chief adviser in money matters. Hamilton had his work cut out for him. The nation's finances were chaotic. America owed money to foreign nations, principally France and the Netherlands, and there was massive domestic debt. Even worse, there was no money to pay them off. The government needed money, and a series of excise taxes were passed, not without a little argument from congressmen, who either wanted local products free from taxes, or overseas products protected by tariffs. Many of them were the same items that had been taxed by the English a few years earlier, prompting the first rebellious actions in the colonies.

There were two key components of Hamilton's master plan for the financial salvation of America. The first came in his *Report on Public Credit,* which provoked a firestorm of controversy by recommending that all creditors of the government be given securities at par with old, depreciated securities. Since most of these older securities were in the hands of speculators (mostly northern) who had bought them from original holders (mostly southern farmers) for a fraction of their worth, Hamilton was attacked viciously for selling out to the "eastern" speculators.

When he added the suggestion that the federal government assume the debts of the states, he was also pilloried by the southern states because most of them had already paid their debts, and Hamilton's plan would be a boon to the "eastern" states.

A real-estate deal solved this problem. Opposed to Hamilton's plan, Jefferson and James Madison, the latter a leader in the House of Representatives, swung the South to support it in exchange for an agreement establishing the site for a new federal city in the South. The nation's future capital would be located on the banks of the Potomac. (Until the new city was ready, Philadelphia would become the nation's capital.) But this compromise did not patch up the differences between Hamilton and Jefferson. Their political differences over almost every issue confronting the new government eventually grew to personal enmity.

The second major component of Hamilton's master plan was the establishment of a national bank to store federal funds safely; to collect, move, and dispense tax money; and to issue notes. The bank would be partly owned by the government, but 80 percent of the stock would be sold to private investors. Again, Jefferson balked. It was unconstitutional, he argued; the government had no such power. Hamilton responded by arguing that the bank was legal under the congressional power to tax and regulate trade. This time there was no compromise, and President Washington went along with Hamilton.

The differences between Jefferson and Hamilton extended to foreign affairs. With England and France again at war and the French Revolution under way, Hamilton openly favored the English. Jefferson admired the French and their Revolution, which America had certainly helped inspire even if he detested the rushing rivers of blood that the guillotine was creating. The lines were similarly drawn over Jay's Treaty, a settlement made with the British in the midst of another English-French war that threatened to involve the United States. Under its terms, British soldiers withdrew from their last outposts in the United States, but other portions of the treaty were viewed as excessively pro-British, and it was attacked by Jefferson's supporters. (The treaty was ratified by the Senate in 1795.)

As part of their ongoing feud, both men supported rival newspapers whose editors received plums from the federal pie. Jefferson's platform was the *National Gazette,* and Hamilton's was the *Gazette of the United States,* both of which took potshots at the opposition. These were not mild pleasantries, either, but mudslinging that escalated into character assassination. More important, the feud gave birth to a new and unexpected development, the growth of political parties.

To this point, organized parties were viewed as sinister. There was no scheme for a two-party system consisting of a government party and a loyal opposition. Instead this sytem evolved piecemeal, and the seeds were sown in the Jefferson-Hamilton rivalry. Jefferson and James Madison, a Federalist during the ratification debate but now swung to Jefferson's views, began to organize factions to support their growing opposition to Washington's Federalist Administration. Their supporters eventually adopted the name Democratic Republicans in 1796. (Now stay with this: the name was shortened to Republicans, but during Andrew Jackson's presidency, they became Democrats.) These first Republicans generally favored a democratic, agrarian society in which individual freedoms were elevated over strong, centralized government. Hamilton and his supporters coalesced in 1792 as the Federalist party, favoring a strong central government, promoting commercial and industrial interests and supported by the elite and powerful of the nation. Under Washington, who openly disdained any "factions," the Federalists held most of the power in Washington for several years to come, dominating Congress during the two Washington administrations and the Adams presidency.

To call these two groups the forerunners of the modern Democrats and Republicans is a bit of an oversimplification. The process leading to the present two-party system was a long, slow one, with several interruptions along the way. If he were alive today, would Jefferson be a Democrat or Republican? Hard to say. His notions of less federal government would sit well with conservative Republicans who want to dismantle the federal bureaucracy. His preoccupation with civil liberties would seem more at home with the Democrats. And Hamilton? Certainly his commercial and banking instincts would place him in the Republican mainstream. But his insistence on a powerful federal government pulling the economic strings would be heresy to laissez-faire Republicans.

The 1790 Census

To determine how many delegates each state would have in the House of Representatives, the Census Act was passed in 1790. The first was completed in August 1790. Some highlights:
* Total U.S. population: 3,929,625
* Black population: 697,624 slaves; 59,557 free blacks. (Massachusetts reported no slaves.)
* Philadelphia is the largest city, with 42,000; New York is second, with 33,000.
* Virginia is the most populous state, with more than 820,000 people.
* Nearly half of the population (48.5 percent) lives in the southern states, with the rest divided between New England and the Middle States.
* America is youthful: 490 of every 1,000 whites is under the age of sixteen.

What were the "Whiskey Rebellion" and the "Revolution of 1800?"

With a last hurrah, Washington led troops once more in 1794 to suppress the so-called Whiskey Rebellion in the frontier of western Pennsylvania. Like Shays's Rebellion, it was a revolt of backwoods farmers against the Establishment, this time over a stiff excise tax placed on whiskey. With 13,000 troops—more men than he had led during the war—Washington rode out in uniform, with Alexander Hamilton by his side, to put down the uprising with ease.

In September 1796, Washington made the last of his many retirement speeches in his "Farewell Address," warning against political parties and "passionate attachments" to foreign nations.

He was ignored on both counts. The first true presidential campaign then got under way. Gathering in a "caucus," the Federalist congressmen selected John Adams, the Vice-President, as their standard-bearer, with Thomas Pinckney of South Carolina as a second candidate. The other Federalist leader, Hamilton, was deemed too strong-willed and monarchist for even the staunchest of Federalists. Jefferson was the obvious choice of the Democratic Republicans, with their second on the ticket being Aaron Burr, an ambitious New Yorker who brought control of Tammany Hall, the first "political machine," to the ticket.

Shrewd and ambitious, Hamilton thought he could pull a power play by getting Pinckney elected and becoming the man pulling the strings, but this strategem backfired when New England Federalists caught on to Hamilton's plan and voted for Jefferson instead. Adams squeaked into the presidency, and Jefferson, although of the opposing party, won the second most electoral votes and became Vice-President. Obviously, it would be back to the drawing board for presidential elections.

Adams's years in office were distinguished mostly by the animosity that had been unleashed between the two competing parties. Although the Federalists had held sway through Washington's administrations and into Adams's, their power was beginning to decline. Neither the Jay Treaty nor Adams was broadly popular, and Adams endured much abuse from the Republican press. His greatest accomplishment was managing to avoid war with France when it seemed likely; his low point came with passage of a series of repressive measures called the Alien and Sedition Acts, which expressed the fear of foreigners in the young nation while attempting to suppress all criticism of the Federalist administration.

Yet the next election, in 1800, would be a close one, in more than one way. Adams once again led the Federalist ticket, with Charles C. Pinckney (the brother of Thomas Pinckney) as his party's number-two choice. Jefferson and Burr were again the Republican nominees. The campaign produced a torrent of slurs and abuses from both sides. And newspapers loyal to either party were filled with crude rumors of sexual philandering by both Adams and Jefferson. To the Federalists, Jefferson was an atheist who would allow the excesses of the French Revolution to come to America. When the ballots were counted, however, the Republicans held the day. But the problem was, which Republican? Since there was no separate election of President and Vice-President, Jefferson and Burr had collected seventy-three votes each. Under the Constitution, the tie meant the House of Representatives, still under Federalist control, would decide the question.

Faced with a choice between these two, Hamilton lobbied for Jefferson. He hated Jefferson but he detested Burr, in his opinion a "most unfit and dangerous man." Burr played his hand cautiously, not campaigning for himself, but not withdrawing either. The votes of nine states were needed to win, and Jefferson failed to gain them through thirty-five ballots. The crisis was real, and some historians believe that civil war over this election was not only possible but likely. Some Republican leaders were threatening to call out their state militias to enforce the popular will. Finally, Jefferson privately assured the Federalists that he would maintain much of the status quo, and the House elected him on February 17, 1801. He was inaugurated on March 4, 1801, in the new federal capital of Washington. (The difficulties of selecting the President in 1800 resulted in passage of the Twelfth Amendment in 1804, which provides for separate balloting for the Vice-President and President.)

This electoral crisis marked a triumph of level heads in both parties, who put the orderly succession and continuity of government first. This "Revolution of 1800," as Jefferson himself called it, was a bloodless one, but its impact was real. The Federalist party was all but guillotined; it lost both the presidency and Congress, but John Adams had made certain that their influence did not die with his defeat.

What was Marbury v. Madison?

In his last weeks before leaving the presidency, John Adams did what Franklin D. Roosevelt, Ronald Reagan, and other Presidents have only dreamed of accomplishing. Working with a "lame duck" Federalist Congress that would soon be out of power, Adams created dozens of new judgeships. He signed appointments until late into the night before Jefferson was inaugurated, and these "midnight appointments" of staunch Federalists throughout the federal courts resulted in the most successful "court-packing" operation in American judicial history. In doing so, Adams influenced the course of events long after his rather inconsequential four years in office were over.

Most prominent among these "midnight appointments" was that of John Marshall, Adams's Secretary of State, as Chief Justice of the Supreme Court in 1801. Although he had studied law only briefly and had no judicial experience, Marshall held that post until his death in 1835. He placed a stamp on the court and the young nation that is still felt today. Of his many decisions, one of the most important came in the 1803 case of *Marbury v. Madison.*

The case grew out of the ongoing political fight to the death between the Federalists and the Jeffersonian Democratic Republicans, and directly resulted from Marshall's own actions as Secretary of State. In the last-minute rush to appoint judges who would uphold the Federalist principle of a strong central government, William Marbury was named to a lower federal court. But Marshall, as Secretary of State, failed to present Marbury with his commission, and James Madison, the Secretary of State for the incoming Jefferson administration, refused to grant Marbury's commission. Marbury appealed to the Supreme Court—now with Marshall presiding—to order Madison to grant the commission.

But Marshall refused the request in a brilliant ploy that sacrificed Marbury as a pawn. Although he said Marbury was theoretically entitled to the post, Marshall denied him, ruling that a section of the Judiciary Act of 1789, which had established the federal court system, was unconstitutional and void. For the first time the Supreme Court had overturned an act of Congress. Although Marshall's decision in this case affected only the right of the court to interpret its own powers, the concept of judicial review, a key principle in the constitutional system of "checks and balances" (see pages 88–89), got its first test.

American Voices

From Chief Justice Marshall's decision in *Marbury v. Madison:*

It is emphatically the province and duty of the judicial department to say what the law is. . . . Thus the particular phraseology of the constitution of the United States confirms and strengthens the principle, supposed to be essential to all written constitutions, that a law repugnant to the constitution is void. . . .

How did America purchase Louisiana?

While America enjoyed its bloodless "Revolution of 1800," France was still in the throes of its more violent contortions. In 1799, Napoleon Bonaparte engineered the coup that overturned the Revolutionary Directory, eventually making himself ruler of France. While most of Napoleon's grandiose plans focused on Europe, America had a place in the little colonel's heart. His first step was to force a weak Spain to return the Louisiana Territory to France, which it did in 1800. The second step was to regain control of the Caribbean island of St. Domingue. In 1793, at the time of the French Revolution, the island had come under control of a self-taught genius, General Toussaint L'Ouverture, who had led a successful slave revolt. To launch any offensive in North America, Napoleon needed the island as a base, and he sent 20,000 troops to retake it.

All of this French scurrying around in America's backyard alarmed President Jefferson, who knew that French control of New Orleans and the western territories would create an over-whelming threat to America. Jefferson had an option play ready. Although he preferred neutrality between the warring European nations, Jefferson dropped hints to the British about an alliance against the French, and found them receptive. At the same time he directed Robert Livingston and James Monroe to offer to buy New Orleans and Florida from France. Such a sale seemed un-likely until the French army sent to St. Domingue was practically wiped out by yellow fever after regaining control of the island. (The French withdrew to the eastern half of St. Domingue and the western half was renamed Haiti, the original Arawak name for the island, with Toussaint's successor, Dessalines, proclaiming himself Emperor. The island, Columbus's Hispaniola, remains split today between Haiti and the Dominican Republic.)

Without the safe base on the island, a French adventure into Louisiana was out of the question. Preparing to open a new European campaign, Napoleon wrote off the New World. He needed troops and cash. Almost on a whim, he ordered his foreign minister, Talleyrand, to offer not only New Orleans and Florida but the whole of the Louisiana Territory to America. Livingston and Monroe dickered with the French over price, but in May 1803 a treaty turning over all of Louisiana was signed. Nobody knew exactly what Napoleon sold, but under the treaty's terms, the United States would double in size for about $15 million, or approximately four cents an acre. Left unclear were the rights to Texas, western Florida, and the West Coast above the Spanish settlements in California. Spain had its own ideas about these territories. Ironically, the purchase was made with U.S. bonds, the result of Hamilton's U.S. Bank initiative, which Jefferson had resisted as unconstitutional.

Who were Lewis and Clark?

Months before the purchase was made, Jefferson had the foresight to ask Congress for $2,500 to outfit an expedition into the West. Ostensibly its purpose was to "extend the external commerce" of the United States, but Jefferson had several other motives: to get America into the fur trade; to feel out the political and military uses of the West; and, reflecting his philosophy as a true Enlightenment man, to collect scientific information about this vast, uncharted land.

With the purchase complete, the little expedition now became a major adventure to find out what exactly America now owned. For this job Jefferson selected Meriwether Lewis (1774–1809), his private secretary, an army veteran and a fellow Virginian. Lewis selected another Virginian soldier, William Clark (1770–1838), a veteran of the Indian wars, as his co-commander. With some forty soldiers and civilians, they set out from St. Louis in the winter of 1803–04 aboard three boats, a fifty-five-foot keelboat with twenty-two oars and two *pirogues* or dugout canoes, each large enough to hold seven men. Working their way upstream was arduous, and strict martial discipline was maintained with regular floggings, but the company reached what is now North Dakota in the fall of 1804, built Fort Mandan (near present-day Bismarck), and wintered there.

In the spring of 1805 they set out again for the West, now joined by a French-Canadian trapper and his pregnant Indian squaw, Sacagawea, who acted as guides and interpreters. Crossing the Rockies in present Montana, they built boats to take them down the Clearwater and Columbia rivers, reaching the Pacific Coast in November, where they built Fort Clatsop (near the site of Astoria, Oregon). Hearing the Indians speak some "sailor's" English, presumably learned from traders, the expedition believed a ship might pass and they decided to winter there. When no ship appeared, they set off for an overland return, splitting the expedition in two after crossing the Rockies to explore alternate routes. The parties reunited at the site of Fort Union, and arrived together in St. Louis on September 23, 1806.

After twenty-eight months of incredible hardships met in traveling over difficult, uncharted terrain, in skirmishes with Indians, and in encounters with dangerous animals from rattlesnakes to grizzly bears, the Lewis and Clark expedition had suffered only a single casualty: one man had succumbed to an attack of appendicitis.

The journals they kept, the specimens they brought or sent back, the detailed accounts of Indians they had encountered and with whom they had traded were of inestimable value, priming an America that was eager to press westward.

While William Clark lived long and was influential in Indian affairs, Lewis suffered from melancholy and committed suicide, although many historians claim it was murder. Contrary to common myth, Sacagawea died in her twenty-eighth year.

Why did Aaron Burr shoot Alexander Hamilton?

Thomas Jefferson did not sit around idly while waiting for his two adventurers to return. The deal with France was the centerpiece of Jefferson's first administration, and while the few remaining Federalists in Congress tried to undermine it on constitutional grounds, the acquisition and the President were so popular that resistance was futile.

Jefferson had earlier made the historically popular move of cutting taxes, including repeal of the Whiskey Tax that Washington had led an army to enforce. He won more admirers when he balked at the widely accepted practice of paying tribute to pirates based in North Africa—the "Barbary pirates." A brief naval war followed, which did not end the tribute payments, but did give America some new naval heroes (Stephen Decatur chief among them), inspired the line in "The Marines' Hymn" about "the shores of Tripoli," and earned America a new measure of international respect.

By election time in 1804, Jefferson's popularity was so great that opposition Federalism was all but dead.

But a group of Federalists known as the "Essex Junto" did attempt a bizarre break from the Union. Their conspiracy would have been historically laughable had it not ended in tragedy. Part of their plan was to support Aaron Burr for governor of New York. No friend of Jefferson's, Burr had been frozen out of power in the Jefferson administration, and then unceremoniously dumped by his party as candidate for Vice-President (and replaced by George Clinton, the aging governor of New York). The long-standing hatred between Burr and Alexander Hamilton resurfaced as Hamilton used all his influence to defeat Burr in the governor's race. To Hamilton, Burr was a "dangerous man, and one who ought not to be trusted with the reins of government." That was the polite attack; others were aimed at Burr's notorious sexual exploits. (Hamilton, it should be noted, was no paragon of marital fidelity, either, and Burr pulled no punches in his counterassaults.)

Hamilton's political destruction of Burr was successful, but with awful results. A few months after the election, Burr challenged Hamilton to a duel, and they met on the morning of Wednesday, July 11, 1804, on the cliffs above the Hudson in Weehawken, New Jersey. Hamilton's son had died in a duel, and he opposed the idea of dueling, but personal honor and that of the fading Federalist party forced his hand. The accepted version of events is that Hamilton fired his pistol but deliberately missed. Others dispute that, and say Hamilton just missed. Burr did not. (As Gore Vidal's fictional Aaron Burr put it in the novel *Burr,* "at the crucial moment his hand shook and mine never does.") Hamilton was mortally wounded, and suffered for thirty hours before dying. Aaron Burr, who had nearly been President a few years before, was now a fugitive.

But Burr was hardly finished as a factor in American politics, or as a thorn in Thomas Jefferson's side. Perhaps inspired by Napoleon, an ambitious colonel who had become an emperor, Burr envisioned securing a western empire he intended to rule. With James Wilkinson, one of Washington's wartime generals who was appointed by Jefferson to govern Louisiana, but who was secretly on the Spanish payroll, Burr organized a small force in 1806 to invade Mexico and create a new nation in the West. For some reason, Wilkinson betrayed Burr and the conspiracy was foiled. Burr was captured and placed on trial for treason, with Chief Justice John Marshall presiding. Jefferson's hatred for Burr was unleashed as he did everything in his power to convict his former Vice-President. But the crafty old Federalist Marshall saw the trial as another way to undermine Jefferson, and his charge to the jury all but acquitted Burr. Following a second treason charge, Burr jumped bail and fled to Europe, where he remained for five years, attempting to persuade Napoleon to organize an Anglo-French invasion of America. He did return to New York in 1812, where he continued a colorful and lusty life until his death in 1836.

Thomas Jefferson and Sally Hemings: Did he or didn't he?

While Jefferson won the election of 1804 in a landslide, the campaign was notable for the one juicy bit of mudslinging gossip it produced. A popular Federalist claim of the day was that Jefferson had carried on an affair with a slave girl named Sally Hemings while he was envoy in Paris, and that the young slave had given birth to Jefferson's illegitimate children. Jefferson remained silent on the charges, and they certainly had no impact on the election.

The controversy gained new life with the publication of two

books, *Jefferson: The Intimate Man* (1974), Fawn Brodie's "psychobiography," and Barbara Chase Riboud's novel *Sally Hemings*
(1979), both of which became best-sellers by claiming the relationship was real. Defenders of Jefferson counter that while Jefferson
certainly had a love affair while in Paris, it was with Maria Con-
way, the wife of a painter, and whether it was consummated is a
matter of conjecture. Others, including Virginius Dabney, author
of *The Jefferson Scandals* (1981), a refutation of the Sally Hemings
rumor, point to two of Jefferson's nephews as Sally's lovers and
the sires of her children.

What was "impressment"?

Following Washington's example, Jefferson declined an
opportunity to run again. (There was no constitutional limitation
on the number of presidential terms of office a single individual
might serve until after Franklin Delano Roosevelt's unique
election to a fourth term in 1944. The Twenty-second Amendment, ratified in 1947, limits a President to two terms or to a
single elected term for a President who has served more than
two years of his predecessor's term. When Ronald Reagan left
office in 1989, he stated his opposition to this limitation on
principle, expressing the belief that the people should be entitled to vote for the candidate of their choice.) Although Jefferson had been reelected at the peak of his popularity, he left
under less happy circumstances, primarily because of his unpopular Embargo Act.

Passed in 1807, the act was the result of America's international weakness at a time when Napoleon had turned the
world into a battleground with England and its allies. Jefferson
wanted to keep America—a weak, third-rate nation with no real
army and a skeleton navy—neutral in the wars that had left
Napoleon in control of Europe and had made the British masters
of the seas. America had actually flourished economically during
the fighting, as the warring nations eagerly bought American
goods and ships. But American neutrality did not protect her
merchant ships from being stopped by British vessels, which
could take any British subject off the ship and "impress" him into
Royal Navy service. On board the ships, legal distinctions such as

"naturalized citizenship" were meaningless, and Americans were being seized along with British subjects.

The Embargo Act, which prohibited all exports into America as economic retaliation for the British impressment policy and as a means to keep America out of war, was one of the most unpopular and unsuccessful acts in American history. In his last week in office, Jefferson had it abolished, replaced by the Nonintercourse Act, which prohibited trade only with England and which provoked only more impressment attacks.

Jefferson's hand-picked successor was his Secretary of State, fellow Virginian and longtime ally, James "Jemmy" Madison, who was elected in 1808 for the first of two terms. He was the first President to occupy the new Executive Mansion that would later be christened the White House, which his charming and amply endowed wife Dolley decorated with $26,000 granted by Congress for the purpose. When Madison took office, war with England and perhaps with France seemed inevitable.

Who were Tecumseh and "the Prophet"?

The coming war got some provocation from one of the most remarkable Indian leaders of American history. A young Shawnee chief from the Ohio valley, Tecumseh envisioned a vast Indian confederacy strong enough to keep the Ohio River as a border between Indians and whites, preventing further westward expansion. He and his brother, Tenskwatawa, "the Prophet," an Indian mystic who called for a revival of Indian ways and a rejection of white culture, traveled extensively among tribes from Wisconsin to Florida. With Tecumseh's organizing brilliance and the Prophet's religious fervor, younger warriors began to fall in line, and a large army of braves gathered at the junction of the Tippecanoe and Wabash Rivers.

General William Henry Harrison, governor of the Indiana Territory (and a future President), took 1,000 men out to camp near the Indians. On one of his organizing and recruiting trips, Tecumseh was absent when the Prophet ordered a badly calculated attack on Harrison's troops in November 1811. The Indians inflicted heavy losses, but were eventually driven back and scattered. Harrison destroyed their food stores, their village, and the

Prophet's claim of invincible magic, shattering Indian confidence and ending hopes for Tecumseh's confederation.

To western Americans, the Indian confederation was a convenient excuse to fan anti-British sentiment in Congress. Calling Tecumseh's movement a British scheme, land-hungry Westerners heightened the war fever, clamoring for the expulsion of the British from North America, even if it meant invading Canada to do it.

What was the War of 1812 about?

The continuing controversy over English impressment of sailors taken from American ships, and the cry of the land-crazed "war hawks" of the West, led by the bellicose but powerful young House Speaker, Henry Clay of Kentucky, pushed Madison to what Jefferson had tried to avoid, a war with England. The War of 1812 finally got under way in June, in the midst of the presidential campaign.

It was not a war that America was ready to fight. A regular army of 12,000 was scattered and led by political appointees rather than by experienced commanders. There was a small navy, hardly equal in numbers or experience to England's.

The results showed in a meandering war effort that went on for the next two and a half years, ending early in 1815. After its humbling experience in the Revolution, and preoccupied with Napoleon's armies on the Continent, England fought a reluctant war. English commercial interests saw America as an important market and supplier, so their support for war was halfhearted. America didn't lose this war. Nor did it really win. The greatest American victory in the war, at the Battle of New Orleans, came after peace had already been signed.

Milestones in the War of 1812

1812

July Aiming to conquer Canada, American troops under General William Hull launch an assault. British-Canadian troops, augmented by 1,000 of Tecumseh's braves, send Hull's army reeling.

Hull is later court-martialed and sentenced to death for cowar
dice, but is pardoned by Madison.

August–December A series of surprising American sea victorie
by the *Constitution* ("Old Ironsides") and the *United States* com
manded by Stephen Decatur are morale boosters, but have n
influence on the war's outcome.

December Madison is reelected President, beginning an Amer
ican political tradition: no President has been turned out of offic
in wartime. Madison's new Vice-President is Elbridge Gerry,
signer of the Declaration, who wins a place in posterity for creat
ing another political tradition. Gerry carved Massachusetts int
election districts that favored his party. These districts, say hi
opponents, were shaped like wriggling salamanders, giving th
American political dictionary a new word, *gerrymander*.

December The British begin a naval blockade of Chesapeake an
Delaware Bays.

1813

March Commodore Isaac Chauncey, with the assistance of youn
Captain Oliver Perry, begins to build warships on Lake Erie t
control the Great Lakes.

April American forces capture York (Toronto) and burn govern
ment buildings there.

May American forces under Winfield Scott take Fort George
forcing British withdrawal from Lake Erie.

June The American frigate *Chesapeake* is captured by the British
Before dying, the American captain, James Lawrence, orders hi
men, "Don't give up the ship." They listened, prevailed, and th
words soon become the American navy's rallying cry.

September The American fleet on Lake Erie, led by Olive
Hazard Perry, defeats a British counterpart, giving the Unite
States control of this strategic waterway. Perry's message to
happy President Madision: "We have met the enemy and they ar
ours."

October The Battle of the Thames. Americans under Willian
Henry Harrison defeat retreating British and Indian forces. Har
rison's Indian adversary, Tecumseh, is killed in the battle, depriv

ing the Indians of the strong leader who might have united them.

November American forces under James Wilkinson are defeated at Montreal. A disgraced Wilkinson is later court-martialed for cowardice, but is acquitted.

November The British navy extends its blockade north to Long Island. Only ports in New England remain open to commerce, and merchants in New York and New England continue to supply the British.

1814

March While the war against the British goes on, General Andrew Jackson of the Tennessee militia has been fighting the Creek Indian War. Jackson achieves a decisive victory in this war at the Battle of Horseshoe Bend in Alabama ending the Creek War.

April Napoleon Bonaparte is overthrown, freeing some 14,000 British troops to concentrate on the war in America.

April The British blockade is extended to New England. The Americans retaliate by privateering, and capture 825 British vessels by the summer.

July Battle of Chippewea. Outnumbered American forces under Winfield Scott defeat British forces.

August Peace negotiations begin in Ghent.

August After routing an American army at Bladensburg in a battle watched by President Madison, British troops march un-opposed into Washington, D. C. In retaliation for the earlier American buring of York, the British set fire to the Capitol, the White House, and other government buildings. The British withdraw from the capital for an attack on Baltimore, and Madison returns to Washington at the end of August.

September An American victory on Lake Champlain forces the British to abort a planned offensive south from Canada.

September The siege of Baltimore. A successful defense of the city and Fort McHenry is witnessed by Francis Scott Key, an American civilian held on board a British ship, who is inspired to write "The Star-Spangled Banner." Two elements of the British strategy, one assault from Canada and another into the Middle

States, have now been thwarted, leaving a third British army
aimed at the Gulf Coast.

December Andrew Jackson arrives in New Orleans, unaware that
a large British invasion fleet is sailing there from Jamaica. When
he learns of the attacking force, he begins preparing a defense of
New Orleans and an elaborate system of fortifications is completed just before Christmas.

December 24 The Treaty of Ghent is signed, ending the war. The
treaty leaves unresolved most of the issues that led to the fighting,
including impressment, now a moot point because the end of the
Napoleonic wars ends the British need for more sailors. Clear
boundaries between Canada and the United States are set, and a
later agreement demilitarizes the Great Lakes. The Oregon Territory in the Pacific Northwest is placed under joint British-
American control for a period of ten years.

1815

January The Battle of New Orleans. Unaware that peace was
made two weeks earlier, the British attack. The American defenders, under General Andrew Jackson, are aided by the French
privateer Jean Lafitte, who has been courted by the British as well
Heavily outnumbered by British troops fresh from the victory
over Napoleon's armies, the Americans use artillery and
sharpshooting riflemen to repulse numerous British charges
against their defensive position, inflicting massive losses. The
British suffer more than two thousand dead; U.S. casualties are
eight dead and a small number wounded. Although the war's
outcome is unaffected by this rout, Jackson becomes an instant
national hero. The news of the Treaty of Ghent finally reaches
America in February.

What was the Monroe Doctrine?

America suffered one notable casualty in the War of 1812
The Federalist Party, which had opposed the war, was mortally
wounded. Peace had delivered a large political bonus for Madison
and his party. In 1816 the Federalists barely mounted opposition

to Madison's chosen successor, James Monroe, next in the "Virginian Dynasty" that started with Washington, was delayed by Adams, and continued through Jefferson and Madison.

Elected at age fifty-eight, Monroe had seen much in his life. A veteran of the War of Independence, he had fought at Trenton, was twice governor of Virginia and then a senator from that state. As a diplomat he helped engineer the Louisiana Purchase. Like Jefferson and Madison before him, he had served as Secretary of State, giving that post and not the vice-presidency the luster of heir apparent's office.

With the great foreign disputes settled and the nation comfortably accepting one-party rule, Monroe's years were later dubbed "The Era of Good Feelings." It was a period of rapid economic expansion, especially in the Northeast, as manufacturing began to replace shipbuilding as the leading industry. These calm years saw the beginnings of the machine age, as men like Eli Whitney, Seth Thomas of mechanical clock fame, and Francis Cabot Lowell were bringing America into the first stages of the Industrial Revolution. A series of postwar treaties with the British solidified the nation's boundaries and eliminated the threat of another war with England.

But the most notable historical milestone in this administration came in an address given to Congress in 1823. The speech was as much the work of Monroe's Secretary of State, John Quincy Adams, son of the second President, but some decades later it came to be called the Monroe Doctrine.

In this speech, Monroe essentially declared that the United States would not tolerate intervention in the Americas by European nations. Monroe also promised that the United States wouldn't interfere with already established colonies or with governments in Europe. In one sense, this declaration was an act of isolationism, with America withdrawing from the political tempests of Europe. But it was also a recognition of a changing world order. Part of this new reality was the crumbling of the old Spanish empire in the New World, and rebellions swept South America, creating republics under such leaders as Simon Bolívar, José de San Martín, and—the most unlikely name in South American history—Bernardo O'Higgins, the son of an Irish army officer and leader of the new republic of Chile. By 1822, America recognized the independent republics of Mexico, Brazil, Chile, Argentina, and La Plata (comprising present-day Colombia, Ecuador, Venezuela, and Panama).

On the positive side, the Doctrine marked what might be called the last step in America's march to independence, which had begun in the Revolution and moved through post-independence foreign treaties, the Louisiana Purchase, the War of 1812, and the postwar agreements. But from another historical perspective, the Doctrine became the basis for a good deal of highhanded interference in South American affairs as the United States embarked on a path of meddling in Central and South America that, as the Nicaragua situation of the 1980s proves, is not yet finished.

What was the Missouri Compromise?

As proof of the "Good Feelings," Monroe was almost unanimously reelected in 1820, winning 231 of the 232 electoral votes cast that year. Popular legend has it that one elector withheld his vote to preserve Washington's record as the only unanimously elected President. But the facts show that the one elector who voted for Secretary of State John Quincy Adams did not know how everyone else would vote, and simply cast his ballot for Adams because he admired him.

While it may have been "The Era of Good Feelings," not everyone felt so good. Certainly the Indians who were being decimated and pushed into shrinking territories by the rapacious westward push didn't feel so good. Nor did the slaves of the South, who now had to harvest a new crop in cotton, which had replaced tobacco as king. And it was the question of slavery that led to the other noteworthy milestone in the Monroe years—one about which Monroe had little to say—the Missouri Compromise of 1820.

From the day when Jefferson drafted the Declaration, through the debates at the Philadelphia convention, slavery was clearly an issue that America would be forced to confront. The earlier compromises of the Declaration and Constitution were beginning to show their age. Even though the slave trade had been outlawed in 1808 under a provision of the constitutional compromise, an illicit trade in slaves continued. The chief argument of the day was not about importing new slaves, however, but about the admission of new states to the union, and whether they would be free or slave states.

It is important to realize that while strong abolitionist movements were beginning to gather force in America, the slavery debate was essentially about politics and economics rather than morality. The "Three-Fifths" compromise written into the Constitution, allowing slaves to be counted as part of the total population for the purpose of allocating congressional representation, gave slave states a political advantage over free states. Every new state meant two more Senate votes and a proportional number of House votes. Slave states wanted those votes to maintain their political power. Of course, there was an economic dimension to this issue. Wage-paying northerners were forced to compete against slave labor in the South. For southerners, wealth was land. With Eli Whitney's cotton gin (the wood *gin* is short for "engine") allowing huge increases of efficiency in production, and the new factories of Lowell in New England to make cloth, the market for cotton was booming. Slave-holding southerners needed more land to grow more cotton to sell to the textile mills of the northeast and England and slaves were needed to work that land. If gaining new land to plant meant creating new states, slaveholders wanted them to be slave states.

By adding massive real estate to the equation under the Louisiana Purchase, the United States brought the free-state/slave-state issue to a head, particularly in the case of Missouri, which petitioned for statehood in 1817. With Henry Clay taking the lead, Congress agreed upon another compromise. Under Clay's bill, Missouri would be admitted as a slave state, but slavery would not be allowed anywhere else north of Missouri's southern border. But every politician in America, including an aging Thomas Jefferson, could see the strict sectional lines that were being drawn, and few believed that this Missouri Compromise would solve the problem forever. Of course, the issue would soon explode.

The Union in 1821

The following is an alphabetical list of the twenty-four states in the Union following the Missouri Compromise, divided into free and slave states. The dates given denote the date of entry into the union or ratification of the Constitution for the original thirteen states; the number following the date denotes order of entry.)

Free States	Slave States
Connecticut (1788; 5)	Alabama (1819; 22)
Illinois (1818; 21)	Delaware (1787; 1)
Indiana (1816; 19)	Georgia (1788; 4)
Maine (1820; 23)	Kentucky (1792; 15)
Massachusetts (1788; 6)	Louisiana (1812; 18)
New Hampshire (1788; 9)	Maryland (1788; 7)
New Jersey (1787; 3)	Mississippi (1817; 20)
New York (1788; 11)	Missouri (1821; 24)
Ohio (1803; 17)	North Carolina (1789; 12)
Pennsylvania (1787; 2)	South Carolina (1788; 8)
Rhode Island (1790; 13)	Tennessee (1796; 16)
Vermont (1791; 14)	Virginia (1788; 10)

The possessions of the United States at this time also included the Florida Territory, ceded by Spain in 1819; the Arkansas Territory, which extended west to the existing border with Mexico (farther north than the modern border); the Michigan and Missouri Territories, comprising the Midwest to the Rockies; and the Oregon Country, then under joint British-American rule.

According to the census of 1820, the U.S. population was 9,638,453. New York had become the most populous state with 1.3 million people, followed by Pennsylvania with a little over a million. The population in the northern free states and territories was 5,152,635; the total for the southern states was 4,485,818.

What was the "corrupt bargain"?

There is a good deal of talk today about the problem of negative advertising in presidential campaigns. We like to look back fondly to the genteel days of the past, when high-minded gentlemen debated the great issues in the politest terms. Take 1824, for example. Candidate Adams was a slovenly monarchist who had an English wife. Candidate Clay was a drunkard and a gambler. And candidate Jackson was a murderer.

If America needed any evidence that Monroe's "Era of Good Feelings" was over, it came with the election of 1824. For a second time, the choice of a President would be sent to the House of Representatives after a ruthlessly bitter campaign demonstrated how clearly sectionalism, or the division of the country into geographic areas with their own agendas, had replaced party loyalties. The leading candidates for President in 1824 were all ostensibly of the same party, the Democratic Republicans of Jefferson, Madison, and Monroe. Even John Quincy Adams, son of the last Federalist President, was now a member of this party and, as Monroe's Secretary of State, a leading contender for the presidency. The other chief candidates, all from the South or West, were General Andrew Jackson, senator from Tennessee; House Speaker Henry Clay of Kentucky; William H. Crawford, Monroe's Treasury Secretary from Georgia; and Secretary of War John C. Calhoun of South Carolina. After considerable infighting, Calhoun dropped from the race and opted for the vice-presidency, with an eye on a future presidential bid.

Crawford was the choice of the congressional power brokers who nominated him in caucus. But given the growing popular resentment against the caucus system, that designation did more harm than good. When Crawford suffered a stroke during the campaign, his candidacy was left crippled. Issues became negligible in the campaign; personalities were the only subject of debate, and slanderous charges were thrown about by all. Adams and Jackson took the lead as popular favorites, but the election was inconclusive, with neither winning a majority of electoral votes, and the choice was given to the House, as it had been in 1800. Jackson, with 43.1 percent of the popular vote and ninety-nine electoral votes, had a legitimate claim to the office. But Clay, also a powerful westerner, wanted to keep his rival Jackson from the office. It is more than likely that Clay legitimately believed Adams was the more experienced candidate but that an Adams election would clearly benefit Clay's political future at the expense of Jackson's. Clay threw his considerable influence in the House behind Adams, who won on the first ballot. Adams then named Clay to be his Secretary of State. Jackson supporters screamed that "a corrupt bargain" had been made between the two. In Jackson's words, Clay was the "Judas of the West."

Whether a deal was made in advance or not didn't matter. The damage was done. In the public eye, the people's choice had been circumvented by a congressional cabal. Brilliant in many ways and well intentioned, Adams was an inept politician. His administration was crippled from the start by the political furor over the "corrupt bargain," and Adams never recovered from the controversy. The Tennessee legislature immediately designated Jackson its choice for the next election, and the campaign of 1828 actually began in 1825.

What were "Jacksonian Democracy" and the "spoils system"?

Jackson got his revenge in 1828, after a campaign that was even more vicious than the one of four years earlier. The label of murderer was reattached to Jackson, an outgrowth of the general's numerous dueling encounters and his penchant for strict martial law, which had led to hangings of soldiers under his command. One Adamsite newspaper claimed that Jackson's mother was a prostitute brought to America by British soldiers, and that she had married a mulatto. Jackson's own marriage became an issue as well. He had married Rachel Robards in 1791, after she had presumably been divorced from her first husband. But the first husband had not legally divorced her until after her marriage to Jackson. Jackson remarried Rachel following the official divorce, but Adams supporters asked, "Ought an adultress and her paramour husband be placed in the highest offices?" One popular campaign ditty went,

Oh Andy! Oh Andy!

How many men have you hanged in your life?

How many weddings make a wife?

(The attacks on his wife particularly enraged Jackson, as Rachel was sick and died soon after the election.)

John Quincy Adams was not safe from character assault either. For purchasing a chess set and a billiard table, he was accused of installing "gaming furniture" in the White House at public expense. In another campaign charge, Adams was charged with having procured a young American girl for the pleasure of Tsar Alexander I when he had served as minister to Russia in 1809–11, under Madison.

Jackson won a substantial victory in the popular vote, and took 178 electoral votes to Adams's eighty-three. For the first time in America's brief history, the country had a President who was neither a Virginian nor an Adams. (John Quincy Adams left the White House and returned to Congress as a representative from Massachusetts, the only former President ever to serve in Congress. He served there with considerable dignity and distinction, leading the antislavery forces in Congress until his death in 1848.) That a new American era was born became apparent with Jackson's victory and inaugural. A large crowd of Old Hickory's supporters, mostly rough-hewn western frontiersmen with little regard for niceties, crowded into Washington, flush with the excitement of defeating what they saw as the aristocratic power brokers of the Northeast. When Jackson finished his inaugural address, hundreds of well-wishers stormed into the White House, where tables had been laid with cakes, ice cream, and punch. Jackson was hustled out of the mansion for his own protection, and the muddy-booted mob overturned chairs and left a chaotic mess. All of the Adamsite fears of rule by "King Mob" seemed to be coming true.

This was the beginning of so-called Jacksonian democracy. Part of this new order came with reformed voting rules in the western states, where property ownership was no longer a qualification to vote. Unlike the earlier "Jeffersonian democracy," which was a carefully articulated political agenda voiced by Jefferson himself, this new democracy was, in modern political language, a grassroots movement. Jackson was no political theorist and hardly a spokesman for the changing order, but he was its symbol. Orphan, frontiersman, horseracing man, Indian fighter, war hero, and land speculator, Andrew Jackson embodied the new American spirit and became the idol of the ambitious, jingoistic younger men who now called themselves Democrats. At its best, Jacksonian democracy meant an opening of the political process to more people (although blacks, women, and Indians still remained political nonentities). The flip side was that it represented a new level of militant, land-frenzied, slavery-condoning, Indian-killing greed.

A large number of the unruly crowd that upset the ice cream in the White House had come to Washington looking for jobs. It was expected that Jackson would sweep out holdovers from the hated Adams administration. They had won the war and were looking for the "spoils" of that war in the form of patronage jobs in the Jackson White House. There was nothing new about this "spoils system"; it had been practiced by every administration from the beginning of the republic. But the widespread and vocal calls for patronage that followed Jackson's election have linked the "spoils system" to Jackson. Ironically, only a few new patronage jobs were created during his years in office, with most posts going to previous jobholders, all established Washington insiders—proof once again that the more things change, the more they stay the same.

What was the "Trail of Tears"?

From the moment Columbus stepped onto the sands of San Salvador, the history of European relations with the natives they encountered could be written in blood. It was a story of endless betrayals, butchery, and broken promises, from Columbus and the *conquistadores* through John Smith, the Bay Colony, the French and Indian War, right up to the War of 1812. From the outset, superior weapons, force of numbers, and treachery had been the Euro-American strategy for dealing with the Indians in manufacturing a genocidal tragedy that surely ranks as one of the cruelest episodes in man's history.

Hollywood has left the impression that the great Indian wars came in the Old West during the late 1800s, a period that many think of simplistically as the "cowboy and Indian" days. But in fact that was a "mopping-up" effort. By that time the Indians were nearly finished, their subjugation complete, their numbers decimated. The killing, enslavement, and land theft had begun with the arrival of the Europeans. But it may have reached its nadir when it became federal policy under President Jackson.

During the Creek War of 1814 that first brought him notice, Jackson earned a reputation as an Indian fighter, and a particularly ruthless one. To the Indians, Jackson became "Long Knife." Confronted by a tenacious Creek Nation in the South as commander of the Tennessee militia, Jackson had used Cherokees, who had been promised governmental friendship, to attack the Creeks from the rear. As treaty commissioner, Jackson managed to take away half the Creek lands, which he and his friends then bought on attractive terms.

In 1819 he embarked on an illegal war against the Seminoles of Florida. Claiming that Florida, still in Spanish hands, was a sanctuary for escaped slaves and marauding Indians, Jackson invaded the territory, unleashing a bloody campaign that left Indian villages and Spanish forts smoldering. Jackson's incursion set off a diplomatic crisis, eventually forcing the Spanish to sell Florida to the United States in 1819 on terms highly favorable to the Americans. Again, Jackson became governor of the newly conquered territory. As a land speculator, Jackson knew that he and his friends would profit handsomely by moving the Indians off the land.

But the harsh treatment of the Indians by Jackson as a general, as well as throughout earlier American history, was later transformed. It went from popular anti-Indian sentiment and sporadic regional battles to official federal policy initiated under Jackson and continued by his successor, Martin Van Buren. The tidy word given this policy was "removal," suggesting a sanitary resolution of a messy problem, an early-nineteenth-century equivalent of Hitler's "final solution." The Indians called it the Trail of Tears.

Some historians ascribe humane motives to Jackson's call for the wholesale forced migration of Indians from the southeastern states to unsettled lands across the Mississippi. Better to move them, argued Jackson, than to slaughter them, which was already happening. In 1831, for instance, Sac tribes under Black Hawk balked at leaving their ancestral lands in Illinois. But when a group of some 1,000 Indians attempted to surrender to the militia and the regular army, they were cut off by the Mississippi River and cut down by bayonets and rifle fire, with about 150 surviving the slaughter.

The removals were concentrated on the "Five Civilized Tribes" of the Southeast. Contrary to popular sentiment of the day and history's continuing misrepresentation, the Choctaw, Chickasaw, Creek, Cherokee, and Seminole tribes had developed societies that were not only compatible with white culture, but even emulated European styles in some respects. The problem was that their tribal lands happened to be valuable cotton-growing territory. Between 1831 and 1833 the first of the "removals" forced some 15,000 Choctaws from Mississippi into the territory west of Arkansas. During the winter, pneumonia took its toll, and with the summer came cholera, killing the Choctaws by the hundreds. The Choctaws were followed by the Chickasaws and then the Creeks. In the new Indian Territory, 3,500 of 15,000 immigrants died of hardship, disease, and exposure.

The final removal began in 1835, when the Cherokees, centered in Georgia, became the target. Like the other tribes that had been forced out, the Cherokees were among the "Civilized Tribes" who clearly provided proof that the "savages" could coexist with white, Euro-American culture. The Cherokees, at the time of their removal, were not nomadic savages. In fact, they had assimilated many European-style customs, including the wearing of gowns by Cherokee women. They built roads, schools, and churches, had a system of representational government, and were becoming farmers and cattle ranchers. A written Cherokee language had also been perfected by a warrior named Sequoya. The Cherokees even attempted to fight removal legally by challenging the removal laws in the Supreme Court and by establishing an independent Cherokee Nation.

But they were fighting an irresistible tide of history. In 1838, after Long Knife Jackson left office, the United States government forced out the 15,000–17,000 Cherokees of Georgia. About 4,000 of them died along the route, which took them through Tennessee and Kentucky, across the Ohio and Missouri rivers, and into what would later become Oklahoma (the result of another broken treaty). This route and this journey were the Trail of Tears.

The strongest resistance to removal came from the Seminoles of Florida, where the Indians were able to carry out another costly war, in which 1,500 U.S. soldiers died and some $20 million was spent. The leader of the Seminoles was a young warrior named Osceola, and he was only captured when lured out of his camp by a flag of truce. He died in a prison camp three months later. With Osceola gone, the Seminole resistance withered and many Seminoles were eventually removed to the Indian Territory. But several bands remained in the Everglades, continuing their struggle against the Federals.

Who was Tocqueville, and why did he say all those things about America?

One of the most eloquent witnesses to the cruelties against the Indians was a young French magistrate studying America's penal system. Observing a Choctaw tribe—the old, the sick, the wounded, and newborns among them—forced to cross an ice-choked Mississippi River during the harsh winter, he wrote, "In the whole scene, there was an air of destruction, something which betrayed a final and irrevocable adieu; one couldn't watch without feeling one's heart wrung." The Indians, he added, "have no longer a country, and soon will not be a people."

The author of those words was a young aristocrat named Alexis Charles Henri Clerel de Tocqueville (1805–1859), who arrived in America in May 1831 with his friend Gustave de Beaumont. As young men who had grown up in the aftermath of the French Revolution and the Napoleonic empire, they came to examine American democracy with an eye to understanding how the American experience could help form the developing democratic spirit in France and the rest of Europe. The two spent nine months traveling the nation, gathering facts and opinions, interviewing Americans from President Jackson to frontiersmen and Indians. On their return to France, Tocqueville reported on the U.S. prison system, and Beaumont wrote a novel exploring the race problem in America.

But it is for an inspired work combining reportage, personal observation, and philosophical explorations, and titled *Democracy in America,* that Tocqueville's name became a permanent part of the American sociopolitical vocabulary. The book appeared in two volumes, the first of which appeared in 1835, the second in 1840. More than 150 years after its appearance, *Democracy in America* remains a basic text in American history and political theory. With his keen insight into the American character and his extraordinary prescience, Tocqueville is still regarded as a valuable commentator on American politics and democracy in general.

While he admired the republican system, Tocqueville found what he considered a great many shortcomings. Perhaps his aristocratic background left Tocqueville unprepared for the "general equality of condition among the people" he found. There were clearly class differences in America, but Tocqueville found that the lines were not as sharply or as permanently drawn as they were in Europe, with its centuries of aristocratic tradition. Admittedly, he also spent most of his time with the upper and middle classes, overlooking much of the rank poverty that existed in America among the working poor. Most of the latter were gathered in the sprawling urban centers of New York, Philadelphia, and other northern cities, where waves of poor European immigrants were drawn by the millions and consigned to the spreading inner-city slums and tenements. In this "equality of condition," Tocqueville saw a social leveling that would result, in his opinion, in a reign of mediocrity, conformity, and what he called the "tyranny of the majority."

Although many of his commentaries and observations were remarkably astute, and seem to apply as neatly to modern America as they did to the United States he found in 1831, Tocqueville did not always bat a thousand. Perhaps one of his greatest overights was his assessment of the presidency as a weak office. In fact, he wrote at a time when Andrew Jackson was shaping the office as preeminent among the three branches, establishing the mold of a strong presidency that would be repeated in such chief executives as Lincoln and the Roosevelts. Critical of slavery (as well as the treatment of the Indians), the Frenchman could see civil strife ahead. However, his prediction that the Union would fall in the face of such a regional conflict was wide of the mark.

In many more matters, however, he was right on target and remains eerily correct about the American addiction to practical rather than philosophical matters and the relentless and practically singleminded pursuit of wealth. As he observed, "I know of no country, indeed, where the love of money has taken a stronger hold on the affections of men. . . ."

Perhaps his most accurate and astute forecast was the prediction of the future competition that would arise between the United States and Russia.

What made the South fear a slave named Nat Turner?

Nothing struck deeper fear into the hearts of southerners, whether they held slaves or not, than the idea of a slave revolt. Contrary to the popular image of docile slaves working in peaceful servitude, there had been numerous small rebellions and uprisings of slaves, often in union with Indians or disaffected whites, as far back as slavery in the New World under the Spanish. These were not limited to the South, as murderous uprisings took place in colonial Connecticut, Massachusetts, and New York. One of the bloodiest of these uprisings occurred in South Carolina in 1739, when slaves killed some twenty-five whites under the leadership of a slave named Jemmy.

But the greatest horror for young America came from the Caribbean, where Toussaint L'Ouverture, a former carriage driver and a natural military genius, led the slaves of St. Domingue (Haiti and the Dominican Republic) in a successful rebellion during the 1790s. Inspired by the revolutions in America and France, L'Ouverture's rebellion resulted in some 60,000 deaths and a republic of freed slaves on the island. Yet Toussaint was a remarkable administrator as well, and successfully integrated the white minority into the island's government. In 1800, Napoleon sent troops to retake the island with little success until Toussaint was lured to the French headquarters under a truce flag, arrested, and jailed in the Alps, where he died in a jail cell.

Slaveholders tried for years to keep the news of Toussaint and his rebellion from their slaves. But as Lerone Bennet writes in *Before the Mayflower,* "Wherever slaves chafed under chains, this man's name was whispered." In 1831 a new name came to the fore as the most fearful threat to white control, that of Nat Turner (1800–1831). Nat Turner's rebellion followed two earlier unsuccessful rebellions by slaves. The first was of some thousand slaves led by Gabriel Prosser in an aborted assault on Richmond, Virginia, in 1800. The second, in Charleston in 1822, was led by another charismatic slave, Denmark Vesey, and failed because of betrayals.

Although Turner's rebellion also ultimately failed, it changed the South. Born in 1800, Turner was also marked by birth for an unusual life. A mystic and preacher, he used his visions and biblical authority to build a devoted following. In August 1831, Turner and about seventy followers started their rampage. Beginning with his own masters, Turner embarked on a death march that spared no one. The whites around Southampton, Virginia, were thrown into utter panic, many of them fleeing the state. Turner's small army, lacking discipline, halted their march, allowing a group of whites to attack. Turner counterattacked, but was soon vastly outnumbered and went into hiding. Thousands of soldiers were pressing the search for this one man who had thrown the country into hysterical terror. A massacre of any slaves even suspected of complicity followed. Turner eluded capture for some two months, during which he became a sort of bogeyman to the people of the South. To whites and slaves alike, he had acquired some mystical qualities that made him larger than life, and even after his hanging, slaveowners feared his influence. Stringent new slave laws were passed, strict censorship laws aimed at abolitionist material were passed with Andrew Jackson's blessing, and, perhaps most important, the militant defense of slavery took on a whole new meaning.

American Voices

William Lloyd Garrison (1805–1879), in the first issue of the abolitionist journal *The Liberator* (1831):

> On this subject I do not wish to think, or speak, or write, with moderation. No! no! Tell a man whose house is on fire, to give a moderate alarm; tell him to moderately rescue his wife from the hands of the ravisher; tell the mother to gradually extricate her babe from the fire into which it has fallen; but urge me not to use moderation in a cause like the present. I am in earnest—I will not equivocate—I will not excuse—I will not retreat a single inch—AND I WILL BE HEARD. . . .

Who were the Whigs?

Andrew Jackson's Democratic party was largely an outgrowth of Jackson's personality and individual opinions rather than of the strict orthodoxy associated with modern party politics. And Jackson's popularity was undeniable, resulting in his handy 1832 reelection (55 percent of the popular vote; 77 percent of the electoral vote), which also brought in New York politico Martin Van Buren (1782–1862) as the new Vice-President.

Jackson's personal platform was fairly simple: suspicion of the upper classes and big business, typified by the Bank of the United States, which Jackson vetoed in 1832; freedom of economic opportunity, including elimination of Indians to open up their lands for white expansion; increased voting rights (for white men, at least); and a general opening of the political process to the middle and lower classes, which had been closed out by the earlier, gentry-based administrations. On the growing question of the Union versus states' rights, Jackson tiptoed a cautious path, proclaiming a strong Unionist position but tending to limit the powers the federal government held over the states, the ostensible reason behind his opposition to the Bank of the United States.

Jackson's general popularity almost completely stifled opposition, but not entirely. Out of the ashes of the old Federalists came heirs of Hamilton who believed in a national approach to economic problems, coupled with the more extremist states'-rights advocates and those who simply disliked Jackson and feared his unchecked power. From this loose coalition a new party started to take life with two congressional giants, Daniel Webster (1782–1852) and Henry Clay (1777–1852), its most prominent leaders. In 1834 they took the name Whigs, recalling the pre-Revolution days when patriots adopted that name to contrast themselves with Tories loyal to the British crown. For this new generation of Whigs, the tyrant was not a foreign monarch but "King Andrew," as Jackson was called by friend and foe alike.

The Whigs mounted their first presidential campaign in 1836, but failed to coalesce behind a single nominee, sending out three "favorite sons" instead. William Henry Harrison, a former general, did best, with Hugh White and Daniel Webster finishing far out of the running. Easily outdistancing them was Martin Van Buren, Jackson's Vice-President and handpicked successor, who also carried the distinction of being the first President born an American citizen. An adept tactician, Van Buren had begun to master the new politics of group voting, or "machine politics," and was responsible for delivering New York's electoral votes to Jackson. But he utterly lacked Jackson's ability to win popular support. A severe economic depression during his term—the Panic of 1837—ruined Van Buren's chances for a second term, but he was really undone by a new Whig strategy that turned the tables on Andrew Jackson's earlier campaign against John Quincy Adams, which had cast Adams as a remote aristocrat.

In the "log cabin" campaign of 1840, the Whigs cast Van Buren, nicknamed "Martin Van Ruin," as a bloated aristocrat. They presented themselves as the people's party and General Harrison (1773–1841), their candidate, as a common man living in a log cabin. In fact, he was from a distinguished family, the son of one of the Declaration's signers. He was also presented as a war hero in Jackson's image for his battles against Tecumseh at Tippecanoe. With Virginia's John Tyler (1790–1862) as his running mate, their campaign slogan was the memorable "Tippecanoe and Tyler too!" The campaign of 1840 was a raucous affair, with huge rallies, an impressive voter turnout, and plenty of hard cider spilled. One linguistic legacy of the campaign: a distiller named E.

C. Booz bottled whiskey in log-cabin-shaped containers. Although the word "booze" was derived from the Dutch word "bowse," Booz reinforced the use of the word, and soon it became a permanent part of the language.

One month after he was inaugurated, Harrison fell ill with pneumonia and died. John Tyler, his Vice-President, a Virginian and an ardent states' righter, became the first "accidental President."

Who fought at the Alamo?

When Jackson left office, there were clearly unanswered questions about the nation's future. Southern politicians were already setting forth the argument that because states had freely joined the Union, they could just as freely leave. And while there was much talk of tariffs and banks, the real issue was slavery. The slave question pervaded the national debate on almost every question before Congress, including the momentous one regarding the fate of Texas, then a part of Mexico.

Led by Stephen F. Austin (1793–1836), Americans settled the area at the invitation of Mexican authorities. President Jackson, and Adams before him, offered to buy Texas from Mexico, but were turned down. By 1830, more than 20,000 white Americans had been drawn to the fertile, cotton-growing plains, bringing with them some 2,000 slaves. They soon outnumbered the Mexicans in the territory, and in 1834 Austin asked the authorities in Mexico City to allow Texas to separate from Mexico as a prelude to statehood. Besides the obvious reason that these Americans wanted to remain American, an overriding cause for their request was Mexico's prohibition of slavery. Austin was arrested and jailed. By 1836, President Santa Anna of Mexico announced a unified constitution for all Mexican territories, including Texas.

The Americans in Texas decided to secede. With an army of 6,000 men, Santa Anna marched against what he viewed as the treasonous Texans. With a force of 3,000, Santa Anna approached San Antonio, held by 187 men under the command of Colonel William B. Travis. The defenders took a defensive stand behind the walls of a mission called the Alamo. For ten days, in a now-legendary stand, the small group fended off Santa Anna's massed troops, inflicting tremendous casualties on the Mexicans. But the numbers were insurmountably in the Mexicans' favor. As the Mexican bands played the *Degüello*, literally "throat-cutting," artillery breached the walls of the Alamo, and Travis's band was overrun. The five American survivors of the final onslaught, including the wounded, were executed. All of the Americans' corpses were soaked in oil and then set on fire. Among the dead were the Bowie brothers, a pair of slave smugglers who are better known for Jim's famous long knife, and Davy Crockett (1786–1836), the professional backwoodsman, congressman, and veteran of Andrew Jackson's Creek War. (Unlike Jackson, Crockett had grown to respect the Indians and had become friendly with them.) Only three Americans came out of the Alamo alive: a woman named Susanna Dickinson, her fifteenth-month-old baby, and Travis's slave Joe. They were freed by Santa Anna to warn Sam Houston (1793–1863), commander of the Texas army, of the fate that awaited them if they continued to resist.

A second slaughter, in which hundreds of Texans were slain by Santa Anna's troops at the town of Goliad, stoked the flames higher. Santa Anna pressed the small Texan army that remained under Houston until the forces met at San Jacinto in April 1836. With "Remember the Alamo!" as their rallying cry, the vastly outnumbered Texans swept into the Mexican lines, who had been granted a siesta by the self-assured Santa Anna. The battle was over in eighteen minutes. With the loss of nine men, the Texans killed hundreds of Mexicans, captured hundreds more, including Santa Anna, and sent the bulk of the Mexican army into a confused retreat across the Rio Grande.

The Texans immediately ratified their constitution, and Houston, who nearly died from gangrene after the San Jacinto battle, was made President of the new Republic. They then petitioned for annexation into the United States. Jackson did nothing until his last day in office, when he recognized Texan independence. Van Buren also hesitated. Both men feared war with Mexico, but more seriously, the admission of Texas added fuel to the burning slave debate. The southern states wanted another slave territory. The North saw annexation of Texas as breaching the balance that had been reached in the Missouri Compromise (under which slave-state Arkansas and free-state Michigan had been admitted as the twenty-fifth and twenty-sixth states). For the next nine years the Texas question simmered, further dividing North and South over slavery, and pushing relations with Mexico to the brink of war.

What was "Manifest Destiny"?

The annexing of Texas was a symptom of a larger frenzy that was sweeping through America like a nineteenth-century version of "Lotto fever." In 1845 this fervor was christened. In an expansionist magazine, *The United States Magazine and Democratic Review,* journalist John L. O'Sullivan wrote of "the fulfillment of our manifest destiny to overspread the continent allotted by Providence for the free development of our yearly multiplying millions."

O'Sullivan's phrase, quickly adopted by other publications and politicians, neatly expressed a vision that sounded almost like a religious mission. Behind this vision was some ideological saber-rattling, but the greatest motivator was greed, the obsessive desire for Americans to control the entire continent from Atlantic to Pacific. As each successive generation of Americans had pressed the fringes of civilization a little farther, this idea took on the passion of a sacred quest. The rapid westward movement of large groups of settlers was spurred by the development of the famous trails to the West. The Santa Fe Trail linked Independence, Missouri, with the Old Spanish Trail to Los Angeles. The Oregon Trail, mapped by trappers and missionaries, went northwest to the Oregon Territory. The Mormon Trail, first traveled in 1847, first took the religious group and then other settlers from Illinois to Salt Lake City. And in the Southwest, the Oxbow Route, from Missouri west to California, carried mail under a federal contract.

The fact that California, with its great ports, was still part of Mexico, and that England still lay claim to Oregon, only heightened the aggressiveness of the American desire to control all of it.

Why did the Mormons move west?

While the majority of nineteenth-century Americans believed that God's plan was to send them west, others in America were finding other religious paths. The early part of the century saw an extraordinary period of spiritual reawakening that produced such groups as the Shakers, founded in New York in 1774 by an Englishwoman called Mother Ann Lee. They flourished for some years, but eventually died out when their policy of celibacy became self-induced extinction. Other "spiritual" movements of this period included the utopian communities of Oneida, where, in contrast to the Shakers, promiscuity was encouraged, and Brook Farm, the retreat of the New England Transcendentalists.

But the most historically significant and prominent new religious group to emerge in this period was the Church of Jesus Christ of Latter-Day Saints, also called the Mormons. The group was founded in western New York in 1820 by Joseph Smith, a visionary who claimed that he had been given, by an angel named Moroni, an ancient text, *The Book of Mormon,* written in hieroglyphics on golden plates. Smith and a small band of followers moved to Ohio, where their communal efficiency attracted converts but their unorthodox religious views attracted the ridicule and enmity of traditional Christians, setting off a pattern of antagonism that would send the Mormons on an odyssey in search of a home in the wilderness. With his church growing in numbers of converts, Smith was gaining political clout as well, but resentment exploded into persecution when another of Smith's visions called for polygamy. In 1844 a mob killed Smith and his brother, Hyrum.

The group was held together under the autocratic hand of Brigham Young, who saw the church's future in the far West, away from further persecution. In 1847, Young and small band of Mormons pushed to the basin of the Great Salt Lake, the new Promised Land. They began a community that became so entrenched as a Mormon power base that Young was able to dictate federal judgeships. As waves of Mormons pressed along the trail to Utah, it became a major route to the West, and the Mormons profited handsomely from the thousands heading for California and gold.

American Voices

From "The Raven" by Edgar Allan Poe (1845):

And the Raven, never flitting, still is sitting, *still* is sitting
On the pallid bust of Pallas just above my chamber door;
And his eyes have all the seeming of a demon's that is dreaming,
And that lamp-light o'er him streaming throws his shadow on the floor;
And my soul from out that shadow that lies floating on the floor
    Shall be lifted—nevermore!

Drug addict. Alcoholic. Cradle robber. Necrophiliac. These are some of the epithets associated with Poe (1809–1849). Most of them were the creations of a vindictive literary executor who spread the lies following the poet's death. Later research proved many of those charges to be unfounded slanders. But there was still plenty about Poe that was strange, and his work certainly seemed to justify those bizarre stories.

Born in Boston, Poe was raised by an uncle after the death of his parents when he was three. He first attended the University of Virginia, but dropped out, then later went to West Point, but managed to get dismissed from that institution also. He turned to newspaper editing and writing, and published a few poems and short stories. He also married his thirteen-year-old cousin—an act considered less outrageous in those days than it seems now. In 1845, *The Raven and Other Poems* appeared, winning Poe instant recognition. He continued as a successful magazine editor, at the same time writing the short stories of mystery, horror, and the supernatural—"The Murders in the Rue Morgue," "The Gold Bug" "The Fall of the House of Usher"—for which he is most famed. After the death of his wife, he suffered a nervous breakdown. Two years later, while on a train taking him to a planned second marriage, he died of unexplained causes.

Poe was a member of America's first generation of noteworthy authors, including Hawthorne, Melville, Emerson, and Thoreau, who began to flourish in this period. They represented, as Poe did, the Romantic spirit in writing that flowered in the early nineteenth century, as well as a burst of American cultural maturity that reflected a nation moving out of adolescence.

Chapter Four

Apocalypse Then: To Civil War and Reconstruction

- Why was there a war with Mexico?

- Milestones in the Mexican War

- What did America gain from the Mexican War?

- How did Frederick Douglass become the most influential black man of his time?

- Where did the Underground Railroad run?

- What was the Compromise of 1850?

- Why was *Uncle Tom's Cabin* the most important and controversial novel of its time?

- What forced the Republicans to start a new political party?

- Why was Kansas "Bloody"?

• What was the difference between a man named Dred Scott and a mule?

• What did Lincoln and Douglas debate?

• Why did John Brown attack a federal arsenal?

• Why did the South secede from the United States?

• Milestones of the Civil War

• What did the Civil War cost America?

• Was "Abe" really "honest"?

• Why did the North win the war?

• Who killed Lincoln?

• What was Reconstruction?

• Why was President Johnson impeached?

• Who were the carpetbaggers?

The space of time separating George Washington's first inauguration in April 1789 from Lincoln's first in March 1861 was only seventy-two years, a mote in the eye of history. But that slice of history contained extraordinary events. From a third-rate republic, a sliver of sparsely populated seaboard extending inland from the Atlantic for a few hundred miles, threatened by foreign powers and dangerous Indian tribes, America had become a pulsing, burgeoning world economic power whose lands stretched across the entire continent.

It was a nation in the midst of powerful growth. Canals were spreading across the country, connecting the inland regions to the bustling Atlantic ports. The first generation of steamships were beginning to make use of those canals as well as carrying prospectors around Cape Horn to California. The first railroads were being built, linking the great, growing cities across the widening landscape of America. A new generation of invention was alive with Americans turning their attention, as Tocqueville noted, to practical pursuits. In 1834, Cyrus McCormick patented his horse-drawn reaper that would begin a revolution in American agriculture. Borrowing from an earlier invention, Eli Whitney improved on a machine that made cotton king in the South—the famous cotton "gin," short for engine—and then set up a factory in the North utilizing the idea of interchangeable parts to ease mass production—an idea that helped produce the guns that would help the North defeat the South. In 1843, Congress voted funds to construct a telegraph line from Baltimore to Washington, and Samuel Morse (1791–1872) perfected the design of the telegraph and devised a code to utilize it. By 1851, America's mass-produced innovations—clocks and locks, Colt revolvers and sewing machines, reapers and railroads—were the talk of Europe.

Writing from Paris in the throes of France's bloody Revolution, Jefferson had once almost giddily expressed the notion that "a little rebellion" was good for the republic. Had Jefferson known how devastating the rebellion would be, he might have acted more forcefully to forestall it during his years of power and influence. History is an unending stream of such speculations and backward glances.

Why was there a Civil War? Could it have been avoided? Why didn't the North just let the South go? (A popular sentiment in 1860.) These questions have troubled and fascinated Americans ever since the war took place. No other period in American history has been written about more often, and with more sentiment and emotion—and even romance. Each year, dozens of new volumes appear in the vast library of books about slavery, the South, and the war and its aftermath. It is hardly surprising that America's most popular novel—and the equally adored film it inspired—is set during the Civil War era. Without arguing its historical or literary merits, there is no question that Margaret Mitchell's *Gone With the Wind* typifies—and is responsible for—the American passion and romance for this period.

But as other historians and novelists have made much clearer, very little was truly romantic about the Civil War. It was four years of vicious, devastating warfare that cost hundreds of thousands of lives, murderously divided families and friends, and left half of the country smoldering. Political and military bungling occurred on both sides, as well as military atrocities of the worst sort. Even today the issues behind the Civil War and the wounds it left continue to underscore the political and social debate in America.

To comprehend the roots of the Civil War, it is helpful to think of America in the first half of the nineteenth century not as one large country but as two separate nations. The America of the North was rushing toward modernity as it underwent its urban and industrial revolutions. While agriculture was still an important component of the North's economic structure, it was the enormous commercial enterprises—railroads, canals, and steamship lines; banks and booming factories—that were shaping the northern economy. Its population was mushrooming as massive influxes of European immigrants escaping the famines and political turmoil of Europe came to its cities, lured by the growing myth of America's unlimited wealth and opportunity. Starting in 1845, the first year of the potato blight and famine in Ireland, some 1.5 million Irish came to America over the course of the next several years. By 1860, one-eighth of America's 32 million people were foreign-born, and most of them had settled in the North, drawn to the mill towns of Rhode Island, Connecticut, New Jersey, and Pennsylvania. It was these foreign workers who would feed the ravenous appetite of the new industrial machine and be pressed into the sprawling slums and tenements of the cities, where they were held captive by companies that were far from enlightened. They dutifully joined the political machines that claimed to represent them, and ultimately provided cannon fodder under the Civil War's conscription laws.

The South, on the other hand, had remained the agrarian, slave-based economy it was in Jefferson's time, when the gentlemen planters of Virginia had helped create the nation. The basis of its wealth was now cotton—produced only to be shipped to the textile factories of Great Britain and New England—and the slaves who produced that cotton, as well as the tobacco, rice, and corn that were staples in the Southern states. Although importation of slaves had been outlawed in 1807, the slave population continued to grow at an astonishing rate. And though overseas slave trade was prohibited, trading slaves between states was an enormous business. This contradiction of logic—no foreign slave trade, but a lively domestic one—was one of the laws that many southerners felt were unfairly forced upon them by the North.

But even without African trade, the slave numbers were incredible. The nearly 700,000 slaves counted in the census of 1790 had swollen to 3.5 million in 1860. At the same time, the general population of the South grew far more slowly, absorbing few of the immigrants flocking to American shores. It was room to grow more cotton, and slaves to plant, pick and produce it, that underscored all debate about America's expansion, prompting at least one foreign war and southern talk of the conquest of Cuba and other lands to the south.

The United States was now two countries, two cultures, two ideologies destined for a collision. The simplest explanation for the war might be that southerners, in a very basic expression of human nature, did not want to be told how to live their lives—with respect to slavery, politics, or any number of other questions. This basic resistance to being ruled by someone else had been ingrained into the American character before the Revolution, became part of the national debate from the time Jefferson drafted the Declaration, and was written into the compromises that created the Constitution. But it was a powder keg with a long-burning fuse, an emotional question of ideology that simmered for those brief decades between Washington and Lincoln, factoring into every question facing the nation and every presidential election of that time, until it ultimately exploded with such horrifying results.

Why was there a war with Mexico?

If you thought Vietnam was a nasty little war, you should have seen the Mexican War. For the first time in America's short history, the nation didn't go to war with a foreign power over independence, foreign provocation, or global politics. It was a war fought unapologetically for territorial expansion. One young officer who fought in Mexico later called this war "one of the most unjust ever waged by a stronger against a weaker nation." He was Lieutenant Ulysses S. Grant.

The war with Mexico was the centerpiece of the administration of James K. Polk, the most adept of the Presidents between Jackson and Lincoln. Continuing the line of Jacksonian Democrats in the White House after Tyler's abbreviated Whig administration, Polk (1795–1849) was even dubbed "Young Hickory." A slaveholding states'-rights advocate from Virginia, Polk slipped by Van Buren in the Democratic convention and was narrowly elected President in 1844. His victory was possible only because the splinter antislavery Liberty party drew votes away from Whig candidate Henry Clay. A swing of a few thousand votes, especially in New York State, which Polk barely carried, would have given the White House to Clay, a moderate who might have been one President capable of forestalling the breakup of the Union and the war.

It was a "Manifest Destiny" election. The issues were the future of the Oregon Territory, which Polk wanted to "reoccupy," and the annexation of Texas, or, in Polk's words, "reannexation," implying that Texas was part of the original Louisiana Purchase. (It wasn't.) Even before Polk's inauguration, Congress adopted a joint resolution on his proposal to annex Texas. The move made a war with Mexico certain, which suited Polk and other expansionists. When Mexico heard of this action in March 1845, it severed diplomatic relations with the United States.

Treating Texas as U.S. property, Polk sent General Zachary Taylor into the territory with about 1,500 troops in May 1845, to guard the undefined "border" against a Mexican "invasion." After months of negotiating to buy Texas, Polk ordered Taylor to move to the bank of the Rio Grande. This so-called army of observation numbered some 3,500 men by January 1846, about half of the entire U.S. Army. Escalating the provocations, Polk next had Taylor cross the Rio Grande. When a U.S. soldier was found dead and some Mexicans attacked an American patrol on April 25, President Polk had all the pretext he needed to announce to Congress, "War exists." An agreeable Democratic majority in the House and Senate quickly voted—with little dissent from the Whig opposition—to expand the army by an additional 50,000 men. America's most naked war of territorial aggression was under way.

Milestones in the Mexican War

1846

May 3 An indication of the war's course comes in the first battle. At Palo Alto, 2,300 American soldiers scatter a Mexican force twice their size. In the ensuing Battle of Resaca de la Palma, 1,700 Americans rout 7,500 Mexicans. Accompanied by a group of Whig newspapermen, General Taylor is made an immediate national hero and is touted as the next Whig President. President Polk orders a blockade of Mexican ports on the Pacific and the Gulf of Mexico.

June 6 In the related conflict with the British over the jointly controlled Oregon Territory, Polk submits a treaty with England setting a boundary between Canada and the United States at forty-nine degrees north latitude. Eliminating the threat of war with Great Britain, Polk can concentrate on the Mexican invasion.

June 14 American settlers in California, also a Mexican possession, proclaim the independent Republic of California. On July 7, Commodore John Sloat lands at Monterey and claims California for the United States. In August, California is annexed by the United States, and Commodore David Stockton establishes himself as governor there.

August 15 Colonel Stephen Watts Kearney arrives in Las Vegas and announces the annexation of New Mexico, also a Mexican territory, by the United States. Kearney occupies Santa Fe without firing a shot, and sets up a provisional government there.

September 20–24 General Taylor captures the city of Monterey, Mexico, but he agrees to an armistice allowing the Mexican army to evacuate the city, earning President Polk's great displeasure.

November 16 General Taylor captures Saltillo, the capital of Mexico's Coahuilla province. The successful military exploits of General Taylor, a Whig, are increasing his heroic stature at home to the annoyance of both President Polk and General Winfield Scott, the commanding general in Washington and also a Whig.

The three men know well the political dividends brought by battlefield success, having cut their political teeth in the age of Andrew Jackson. Facing political pressure, Democrat Polk places General Winfield Scott in command of an expeditionary force that sails for the Mexican fortress city of Vera Cruz.

1847

January 3 General Scott orders a force of 9,000 of General Taylor's men to assault Vera Cruz by land.

February 22–23 The Battle of Buena Vista. Ignoring Scott's orders, Taylor marches west to Buena Vista and, after refusing to surrender to a superior Mexican force commanded by Santa Anna, Taylor's 4,800 men, mostly raw recruits, defeat a Mexican army of 15,000 largely untrained peasants. One of the heroes on the American side is Jefferson Davis, who leads a Mississippi infantry regiment in a counterattack using eighteen-inch Bowie knives. With loyal Whig newspapers trumpeting another triumph for Taylor, his run for the next presidency seems assured.

February 28 Marching south from El Paso, Colonel Alexander Doniphan wins a battle against massed Mexican forces at Sacramento Creek, Mexico, and occupies the city of Chihuahua the next day.

March 9–29 The Battle of Vera Cruz. Scott's forces land near Vera Cruz, the most heavily fortified city in the Western Hemisphere. Scott lays siege to the city. After a long bombardment with high civilian casualties, the city falls three weeks later. Scott's losses are minimal.

April Pressing his offensive, Scott begins a march toward Mexico City. By mid-May he takes the cities of Cerro Gordo, capturing 3,000 prisoners, and Puebla, only eighty miles from Mexico City.

June 6 Through a British intermediary, Nicholas P. Trist, chief clerk of the U.S. State Department, begins peace negotiations with Mexico.

August 20 As Scott nears Mexico City, Santa Anna asks for an armistice. Peace negotiations fail, and the armistice ends on September 7.

September 8 Scott takes Molino del Rey. In another hard-fought battle, although heavily outnumbered, Scott takes the heights of Chapultepec, overlooking Mexico City. Formal peace is still several months away, but the actual fighting concludes with the triumphal entry of Scott's army into the Mexican capital.

November 22 Nicholas Trist leaves Washington to negotiate a peace treaty with Mexico.

December 22 A somewhat obscure freshman congressman from Illinois rises to speak against the Mexican War. It is Abraham Lincoln's first speech as a member of the House of Representatives.

1848

February–March The Treaty of Guadalupe Hidalgo, ending the war with Mexico, is signed and then ratified by the Senate. Under its terms, the United States receives more than 500,000 square miles of Mexican territory, including the future states of California, Nevada, Utah, most of New Mexico and Arizona, and parts of Wyoming and Colorado, as well as Texas. The border with Mexico is set at the Rio Grande. In return, Mexico is paid $15 million and the United States takes on claims against Mexico by Americans, totaling another $3.25 million. One Whig newspaper announces, "We take nothing by conquest. . . . Thank God."

What did America gain from the Mexican War?

Won quickly and at relatively little expense, the Mexican War completed the dream of Manifest Destiny. Then came what seemed a heavenly confirmation of the popular notion that God had ordained America to go from coast to coast. On the morning of January 24, 1848, James Marshall, a New Jersey mechanic building a sawmill for Johann Sutter on the American River, east of San Francisco, spotted some flecks of yellow in the water. These proved to be gold, sparking the mad California Gold Rush of 1849, which sent a hundred thousand people or more racing west that year. During the next few years, some $200 million worth of gold would be extracted from the hills of California.

Apart from the profitable return on investment brought

about by the Gold Rush, the aftermath of the Mexican War and the Oregon Treaty brought other, less happy dividends. The addition of these enormous parcels of new territory just made the future of slavery a bigger question; there was now that much more land to fight about. From the outset of the fighting, opposition to the war was heard from abolitionists like the zealous William Lloyd Garrison (1805–1879) of the American Anti-Slavery Society, who said the war was waged "solely for the detestable and horrible purpose of extending and perpetuating American slavery." Garrison was joined in his views by antislavery pacifist Horace Greeley (1811–1872), who protested the war from its beginning in his New York *Tribune*. Another ornery gadfly went to jail in Massachusetts for his refusal to pay poll taxes that supported a war he feared would spread slavery. Henry David Thoreau (1817–1862) spent only a single night in jail—an aunt paid his fine—but his lecture "Resistance to Civil Government" (later titled "Civil Disobedience") was published in 1849 in the book *A Week on the Concord and Merrimack Rivers*.

The most ironically horrible aftermath of the war with Mexico was the practical battle experience it provided for a corps of young American officers who fought as comrades in Mexico, only to face each other in battle fifteen years later, when North met South in the Civil War. Among the many young West Pointers who fought in Mexico were two lieutenants named P. T. Beauregard and George McClellan, who served on General Scott's staff. Beauregard would lead the attack on Fort Sumter that would begin the Civil War. McClellan later commanded the armies of the North. Two other comrades at the battle of Churubusco, Lieutenants James Longstreet and Winfield Scott Hancock, would face each other at Gettysburg. A young captain named Robert E. Lee demonstrated his considerable military abilities as one of Scott's engineers. A few years later, Scott urged Lincoln to give Lee command of the Union armies, but Lee would remain loyal to his Virginia home.

American Voices

From "Civil Disobedience" by Henry David Thoreau (1849):

Unjust laws exist: shall we be content to obey them, or shall we endeavor to amend them, and obey them until we have succeeded, or shall we transgress them at once? Men generally under such a government as this, think that they ought to wait until they have persuaded the majority to alter them. They think that, if they should resist, the remedy would be worse than the evil. But it is the fault of the government itself that the remedy *is* worse than the evil. *It* makes it worse. Why is it not more apt to anticipate and provide for reform? Why does it not cherish its wise minority? Why does it cry and resist before it is hurt? . . . Why does it always crucify Christ, and excommunicate Copernicus and Luther, and pronounce Washington and Franklin rebels?

The American ideals of individual freedom and the democratic spirit found an extreme expression in the literature of the New England writers known as the Transcendentalists. Chief among them was Ralph Waldo Emerson (1803–1882), who urged Americans to stop imitating Europe and "go beyond the world of the senses." Emphasizing individuality and an intuitive spirituality, he balked at the emerging industrial society around him.

A student and friend of Emerson's, Henry David Thoreau took Emerson's ideas a step further, removing himself from society to the cabin on Walden Pond, near Concord, Massachusetts, that provided the experience for his masterpiece *Walden* (1854). Thoreau's writings deeply influenced Mahatma Gandhi, who adopted Thoreau's notion of "civil disobedience" as the means to overthrow British rule in India; and Gandhi, in turn, influenced Martin Luther King's philosophy of nonviolent resistance.

Also part of this "flowering of New England," as it was called by the critic Van Wyck Brooks, was Nathaniel Hawthorne (1804–1864). But the author of the American classics, *The Scarlet Letter* (1850) and *The House of the Seven Gables* (1851), rejected the Transcendentalists and Emerson, whom he called "a seeker for he knows not what." The Transcendentalist utopian community Brook Farm was the model for Hawthorne's *Blithedale Romance*. Depicting the New England obsession with sin and guilt, Hawthorne expressed a rejection of the grim Puritanism that dominated the era.

How did Frederick Douglass become the most influential black man of his time?

Among the most outspoken critics of the Mexican War was a man who called the war "disgraceful, cruel and iniquitous." Writing from Rochester, New York, in his newspaper, the *North Star,* Frederick Douglass criticized other opponents of the war for their weak response. "The determination of our slaveholding President to prosecute the war, and the probability of his success in wringing from the people men and money to carry it on, is made evident, rather than doubtful, by the puny opposition arrayed against him.... None seem willing to take their stand for peace at all risks."

For anyone to write so defiantly against a generally popular war was remarkable. That the author was an escaped slave writing in his own newspaper was extraordinary.

Frederick Douglass (1817–1895) was born to a slave mother and most likely sired by his first owner. He was taught to read by the wife of one of his masters—although she had been told that it was illegal and unsafe to teach a slave to read—and taught himself to write in the shipyards of Baltimore. In 1838 he escaped, disguising himself as a sailor to reach New York and then Massachusetts, finding work as a laborer in bustling New Bedford, the shipbuilding and whaling center. After making an extemporaneous speech to an antislavery convention in Nantucket, Douglass began a life devoted to the cause of freedom, for women as well as blacks. In the process he became one of the most famous men in America, black or white. A speaker of extraordinary power, Douglass was first employed by William Lloyd Garrison's Anti-Slavery Society. His lectures were grand performances that would leave his audiences in turns laughing and then tearful. He braved hecklers, taunts, eggs, and death threats, and with each lecture his fame and influence grew. In 1845 the Society printed his autobiography, *Narrative of the Life of Frederick Douglass.*

It remains one of the most chilling accounts of life as a

Maryland slave, containing the power to provoke utter revulsion at the "peculiar institution." The book's appearance and Douglass's growing celebrity as a speaker forced him to move to England out of fear that he would be seized as a fugitive. He returned to America in 1847 and began publication of the *North Star* in Rochester, putting him in the front lines of the abolitionist forces. Douglass and Garrison later fell out over tactics, but his stature continued to grow. In one of his most famous speeches, given in 1857, Douglass said, "Those who profess to favor freedom and yet deprecate agitation, are men who want crops without plowing up the ground, they want rain without thunder and lightning. They want the ocean without the roar of its many waters."

During the Civil War, he became an adviser to Lincoln, recruiting black soldiers for the Union cause and lobbying for their equal pay which was reluctantly granted. After the war he accepted a number of government appointments, and was later made ambassador to Haiti.

Where did the Underground Railroad run?

Douglass used his wits and unusual abilities to escape slavery. The *Narrative* was deliberately vague about the assistance he received along the way. Douglass did not want to endanger those who aided him, or make it easier for slave-chasers to figure out his route, thereby making escape difficult for other slaves. But he was helped by some brave individuals along the road.

For thousands of other blacks who refused submission between 1840 and 1861, the mostly anonymous people who led the way to freedom became known as the Underground Railroad. A loose network of individuals who believed that every single freed slave represented a victory against slavery, the Underground Railroad ran from the South northward through Philadelphia and New York, its two key stations, to freedom in Canada or the Northeast. While claims for the numbers of slaves it moved to freedom were vastly inflated in later years, the Railroad existed and performed a dangerous and noble service.

From "station" to "station," as each safe spot along the

treacherous route was known, the slaves slipped in the dark of night, led by the "conductors." While many of these were white abolitionists, often Quakers, the ranks of "conductors" were also joined by escaped slaves who risked far more by returning to help other slaves out. Of these, the most famous was Harriet Tubman (1820?–1913). Born a Maryland slave, like Douglass, Tubman made her way northward to freedom in 1849 and immediately returned to the South to aid other slave escapes. She made at least nineteen trips herself, and was personally responsible for bringing out at least 300 slaves, sometimes "encouraging" them to leave at gunpoint. She even succeeded in freeing her parents in 1857. Her success did not go unnoticed in the South; at one point there was a reward of $40,000 for her capture.

Although illiterate, she was a natural leader and a brilliant planner. Her life was undoubtedly saved when illness kept her from joining abolitionist John Brown's suicidal raid on the arsenal at Harper's Ferry. But during the Civil War she continued her militant defiance, serving with Union troops as a cook and as a spy behind Confederate lines. On another occasion she reportedly led 750 slaves to freedom, with the help of Union troops.

What was the Compromise of 1850?

The election of 1848 was really about the future of slavery and the Union. But you wouldn't know it from the chief candidates. The hero of the Mexican War, General Zachary Taylor, got the Whig nod without expressing or even possessing any opinions about the chief question of the day: the future of slavery in the new territories. The Democratic nominee, Lewis Cass, sidestepped the issue with a call for "popular sovereignty," or leaving the decision up to territorial governments. The only clear stand on slavery was taken by an aging Martin Van Buren, who had given up equivocating and was now running on the Free Soil ticket, a splinter group of antislavery Democrats. Taylor's image as the conquering hero won the popular imgination, and with Van Buren's third party draining Democratic votes from Cass, Taylor was elected.

As President, Taylor had no policy or plan to cope with the

new territories, including the impact of the Gold Rush on the American economy. But when California petitioned for admission as a free state in 1849, the issue was placed squarely once more before Congress, with the fate of the Union hanging in the balance. Southerners, who accepted the Oregon Territory as free, didn't want slaves kept out of another state, especially one of California's size and wealth.

Only another compromise saved the Union for the moment, this one as distasteful to abolitionists as all the others in history had been. A package of bills, mostly the work of the aging Henry Clay, were introduced and heatedly debated in the Senate, chiefly by the other two congressional giants of the age, Daniel Webster—who was willing to accept limited slavery in preservation of the Union—and John Calhoun. Because Calhoun was too ill to speak, his views were presented by Senator James Murray Mason of Virginia. Vowing secession, Calhoun died before the Compromise was signed into law. New faces on the congressional stage also joined the fray. William Seward of New York weighed in with an impassioned antislavery speech. The new senator from Illinois, Stephen Douglas, finally ramrodded the Compromise through by dividing it into five separate bills and pulling together sufficient support for each of these.

It was only Zachary Taylor's death in office in 1850 that finally allowed passage of the Compromise of 1850. Taylor's successor, Millard Fillmore (1800–1874), signed the five bills that made up the Compromise of 1850. Under these bills, California was admitted as a free state; New Mexico and Utah were organized without restrictions on slavery; Texas, also unrestricted as to slavery, had its boundaries set and received $10 million for the land that would become New Mexico; the slave trade (but not slavery itself) was abolished in the District of Columbia; a new Fugitive Slave Act provided federal jurisdiction to assist slaveowners in the recovery of escaped slaves.

It was the last of these bills that provoked the most controversy, since it gave slaveowners enormous powers to call on federal help in recovering escaped slaves. Under the law, no black person was safe. Only an affidavit was needed to prove ownership. Commissioners were granted great powers—

thoroughly unconstitutional in modern light—to make arrests. Even the expenses of capturing and returning a fugitive slave were to be borne by the federal government. Although the burden of proof was on them, accused fugitives were not entitled to a jury trial and couldn't defend themselves. And citizens who concealed, aided, or rescued fugitives were subject to harsh fines and imprisonment.

Suddenly free blacks, many of them presumably safely established for years in northern towns, were subject to seizure and transport back to the South. Angry mobs in several cities bolted at the law with violent protests. In Boston, seat of abolitionist activity, William and Ellen Craft, who gained fame when they escaped through a ruse that involved Ellen posing as the male owner of William, were defended and hidden from slave catchers. When federal marshals snatched a fugitive named Shadrach, a mob of angry blacks overwhelmed the marshals and sent Shadrach to Montreal. Outraged by this defiance of federal law, President Fillmore sent troops to Boston to remove a seventeen-year-old captured slave named Thomas Sims.

Resistance grew elsewhere. In Syracuse, New York, a large group of mixed race broke into a jail and grabbed William McHenry, known as Jerry, from his captors, spiriting him off to Canada. And in Christiana, Pennsylvania, a Quaker town that openly welcomed fugitives, troops again were called out after some escaped slaves shot and killed an owner and then escaped to Canada. President Fillmore sent marines after these slaves, but Canada refused to extradite them. In the South, these were viewed as affronts to what was considered their property and honor. New anger was spilling over into renewed threats of the Union's dissolution.

Why was Uncle Tom's Cabin *the most important and controversial American novel of its time?*

The number of blacks actually captured and sent south under the Fugitive Slave Act was relatively small, perhaps three hundred. But the law did produce one practical effect. Calling the law a "nightmare abomination," a young woman decided to write a novel that shook the conscience of America and the world.

Harriet Beecher Stowe's *Uncle Tom's Cabin* is certainly not the great American novel. It is far from the best-selling American novel. But for a long time it was surely the most significant American novel.

Harriet Beecher Stowe was the daughter, sister, and wife of Protestant clergymen. Her father, the Reverend Lyman Beecher, was a Calvinist minister who took the family to Cincinnati, where he headed a new seminary. There Harriet Beecher met and married Calvin Stowe, a professor of biblical literature. The seminary was a center of abolitionist sentiment, and a trip to nearby Kentucky provided the young woman with her only firsthand glimpse of slavery. In 1850 her husband took a teaching job at Bowdoin College in Maine, and there, after putting her children to bed at night, Stowe followed her family's urgings to write about the evils of slavery.

Uncle Tom's Cabin, or Life Among the Lowly first appeared in serial form in the *National Era,* an abolitionist journal. In 1852 a Boston publisher brought out the book in its complete form. Simplistic and overly melodramatic, the novel was also deeply affecting. The plot attempted to depict the lives of slaves and slaveholders through three primary characters: Eliza, a slave who wants to keep her child who is about to be sold off, and sets off in search of the Underground Railroad; Eva, the angelic but sickly daughter of a New Orleans plantation owner; and Uncle Tom, the noble slave sold to a series of owners, but who retains his dignity through all the degradations he suffers in hopes of being reunited with his family. That family, living together in Tom's idealized cabin on a Kentucky farm, represented the humanity of slaves, depicting them as husbands and wives, parents and children, in stark counterpoint to the common image of slaves as mere drudges.

Many of the book's characters were simply caricatures calculated to jolt tears from even the most heartless. But the book contained unforgettable images and scenes, perhaps the most famous of which was the picture of the barefoot Eliza, her child in her arms, leaping from one ice floe to another across the frozen

Ohio River to escape a ruthless slave trader. There was the cherubic child Eva, trying to bring out the good in everyone in a weepy death scene; the vicious plantation owner, Simon Legree—pointedly written as a transplanted Yankee—vainly trying to break the will and spirit of Tom; and Uncle Tom himself, resilient and saintly, the novel's Christlike central character, beaten by Legree but refusing to submit to overseeing the other slaves.

The reaction of the public—North, South, and worldwide—was astonishing. Sales reached 300,000 copies within a year. Foreign translations were published throughout Europe, and sales soon afterward exceeded 1.5 million copies worldwide, a staggering number of books for the mid-nineteenth century, when there were no paperbacks or big bookstore chains. A dramatic version played on stages around the world, making Stowe one of the most famous women in the world, although not necessarily wealthy; pirated editions were commonplace. The theatrical presentation also spawned a brand of popular minstrel entertainments called "Tom Shows," which provided the basis for the use of "Uncle Tom" as a derisive epithet for a black man viewed by other blacks as a shuffling lackey to whites.

In a time when slavery was discussed with dry legalisms and code words like "states' rights" and "popular sovereignty," this book *personalized* the question of slavery as no amount of abolitionist literature or congressional debate had. For the first time, thousands of whites got some taste of slavery's human suffering. In the South there was outraged indignation. Yet even there the book sold out. Stowe was criticized as naive or a liar. In one infamous incident, she received an anonymous parcel containing the ear of a disobedient slave. Faced with the charge that the book was deceitful, Stowe answered with *A Key to Uncle Tom's Cabin*, which provided documentation that every incident in the novel had actually happened.

In 1862, Lincoln met Harriet Beecher Stowe and reportedly said, "So you're the little woman that wrote the book that made this great war." The copies sold can be counted, but the emotional impact can't be calculated so easily. It is safe to say that no other literary work since 1776, when Tom Paine's *Common Sense* incited a wave of pro-Independence fervor, had the political impact of *Uncle Tom's Cabin*.

What forced the Republicans to start a new political party?

After Polk left the White House, America was cursed by a string of Presidents who were at best mediocre and at worst ineffectual or incompetent. Polk's successor in the White House, Zachary Taylor, had enormous battlefield experience but was ill-prepared for the political wars of his administration. Before he had a chance to grow in office, he died of cholera in 1850 and was succeeded by Vice-President Millard Fillmore (1800–1874). Overshadowed by the congressional giants of his time—Webster, Clay, and Calhoun—Fillmore made little impact in his abbreviated administration other than by winning passage of the Compromise of 1850 and dispatching Commodore Matthew C. Perry to open trade and diplomatic relations with Japan, a further extension of the "Manifest Destiny" mood that had spilled past the California coast to overseas expansionism.

The campaign of 1852 brought another ineffectual leader to the White House in Franklin Pierce (1804–1869), and his election was symptomatic of the country's problems. The two major parties, Whig and Democrat, were fracturing over slavery and other sectional conflicts. Having once been a significant third-party factor, the Free Soil Party, which had opposed the Compromise of 1850, was leaderless. Looking for the battle-hero charm to work once more, the Whigs put up General Winfield Scott, the commander during the Mexican War. But this time the charm had worn out. A northern Democrat taking a southern stand, Pierce outpolled Scott easily, but in his attempts to appease southern Democrats he lost northern support and any hope of holding the middle ground against the two ends.

The election results meant political chaos. The Whigs were in a tailspin, no longer led by Clay and Webster, the two congressional masters who once gave the party its strength. Northern Democrats, rapidly outnumbered by the growing ranks of southerners in their party, were being pushed out. Out of the chaos came a new alliance. A series of meetings, the first occurring in Ripon, Wisconsin, in 1854, resulted in the birth of a new party known as the Republicans. A group of thirty congressmen adopted this party label on May 9, 1854. Although the Republicans made antislavery claims that attracted former Free Soilers and other antislavery groups, the party's opposition to extending slavery beyond its existing boundaries came from economic and political reasoning rather than from moral outrage. Essentially, the party appealed to the free, white workingman. Its basic tenet was that the American West must be open to free, white labor. Not only were the Republicans opposed to slaves in the West; they wanted *all* blacks kept out. This was hardly the ringing message of morality that we tend to associate with the antislavery movement, but it was a message that appealed to many in the North. In 1854, the Republicans won 100 seats in Congress. Just six years after the party was born, it would put its first President into the White House.

Why was Kansas "Bloody"?

In 1854, Dorothy and Toto wouldn't have recognized Kansas. The next battlefield in the free-slave conflict, the Kansas Territory was where the debate moved from harsh rhetoric to bloodshed in what might be called the first fighting of the Civil War. At the heart of the hostilities was the long-debated question of whether slavery should be extended into new territory. Convinced that the North was trying to overwhelm them economically and politically, southerners believed the answer to the question was new slave territory. Behind that question, however, were old-fashioned greed and political ambition.

In 1854, Stephen Douglas (1813–1861), the Democratic senator from Illinois who had pushed through the Compromise of 1850, wanted to organize new territory in the West that would become Kansas and Nebraska. His motive was simple: he was a director of the Illinois Central railroad and a land speculator. The new territory would open the way for railroad development, with Chicago as its terminus. But Kansas would lie above the line marking slavery's boundary under the Missouri Compromise and would have to be free. To win approval for the new territory, Douglas bargained with southern Democrats who would not vote for a new free territory. Looking to a presidential run in 1856, for which he would need southern support, Douglas offered a solution. To win over southerners, he agreed to support repeal of the

Missouri Compromise, which had governed new territories for thirty-four years. With Douglas and his southern Democratic allies, the Kansas-Nebraska Act did just that in May 1854.

The betrayal of the Missouri Compromise just about killed the Democratic Party in the north. With opposition to the Kansas-Nebraska Act as their cornerstone, the Republican Party mushroomed. Another new party also profited from Douglas's bargain with the South. Born of fierce opposition to the waves of immigrants entering America, they were called Nativists, and an ugly racist streak lay beneath their dislike of foreigners and Catholics. Initially a secret society that preached the twin virtues of white Protestantism and defensive nationalism, they were called the "Know-Nothings" because they always answered "I don't know" when asked about their party. Their message struck home in the mid-1850s, and they became a powerful splinter party force, capturing a substantial number of Congressional seats and state legislatures.

With the Kansas-Nebraska Act calling for "popular sovereignty" in the territories, Kansas was flooded with groups from both sides of the slavery issue. Northerners opposed to slavery's expansion attempted to transport antislavery settlers to Kansas to ensure that the territory would eventually vote against slavery. Enraged by this interference from the New England "foreigners," thousands of Missourians called "Border Ruffians" poured across the line into Kansas to tip the balance in favor of slavery in the territory. In an illegal and rigged election, the pro-slave "Ruffians" won, but antislavery forces refused to concede defeat and set up a provisional free-state government in Topeka.

President Pierce denounced this government, giving the pro-slave forces justification for an offensive. And the first blow in the Civil War was struck in May 1856 when the town of Lawrence, established as an antislavery center, was sacked by pro-slave forces. Three days later in retaliation, a fanatical abolitionist named John Brown attacked a pro-slavery town on Pottawatomie Creek, slaughtering five settlers in the night. These attacks brought Kansas to a state of chaos. By October 1856, some 200 people had died in the fighting in "Bloody Kansas" and President

Pierce's mishandling of the Kansas fighting left him without support.

The political disarray produced another weak president in James Buchanan (1791–1868). Ignoring the ineffectual Pierce, the Democrats turned to Pennsylvania's James Buchanan, a Democratic Party loyalist whose chief political asset seemed to be that he was minister to England during the Kansas furor, and couldn't be blamed for it. In fact, he said little during the campaign, prompting one Republican senator to say that there was no such person as Buchanan—that "he was dead of lockjaw."

Gaining popular strength as blood was spilled in Kansas, the Republicans took a page from the old Whig playbook and chose the "Pathfinder," John C. Frémont, the celebrated western explorer and high priest of Manifest Destiny, who had led the way to California as its 1856 standard-bearer. Like the Whig generals before him, Frémont was a military man with no political experience, although his father-in-law, Senator Thomas Hart Benton, was one of the most powerful men in Congress. The Pathfinder's campaign slogan was simple: "Free Soil, Free Speech, Free Men, Frémont."

The Know-Nothings or American Nativists, also bolstered by the Kansas debacle, sent up former President Millard Fillmore. Pledging secession if the Republican Frémont was elected, southern Democrats forced preservation of the Union to the forefront of the election. Their threat carried some weight. With only 45 percent of the popular vote, Buchanan was elected as Frémont (33 percent) and Fillmore (22 percent) split the rest of the vote. The last of the Democratic heirs to Andrew Jackson, Buchanan was the weakest of all the prewar Presidents. Inaugurated in 1857, James Buchanan, the nation's only bachelor President, pledged noninterference and popular sovereignty, but it was too late for these empty slogans.

What was the difference between a man named Dred Scott and a mule?

Any desire Buchanan may have held for the settlement of the burning question of slavery in the territories and reconciliation between North and South lay with the Supreme Court. He publicly expressed his hope that the court would remove the burden of a solution from Congress and himself in his inaugural address on March 4, 1857. Whether Buchanan actually knew what the court would say is a matter of speculation. But two days later the Supreme Court altered the future of the debate and of the nation.

Instead of solving the problem, the court's ruling piled one more log on the smoldering fire. Any hopes of judicial or legislative settlement to the questions were lost in the Dred Scott decision.

The ruling came in a case brought on behalf of a Dred Scott, a legal odyssey that began 1834 when Dr. John Emerson joined the army as a surgeon. Emerson spent several years at a number of posts, including Illinois, Wisconsin Territory, and his home state of Missouri. During all of these moves, Dr. Emerson had been accompanied by his personal servant, Dred Scott, a slave. Emerson died in 1846, and with the help of a sympathetic lawyer, Scott sued for his freedom, claiming that because he had lived in territories where slavery was illegal (Illinois barred slavery under the Northwest Ordinance; Wisconsin under the Missouri Compromise), he was legally free. A St. Louis county court accepted Scott's position, but the Missouri supreme court overruled this decision and remanded Scott, his wife, and their child to slavery. On appeal, the case finally went to the U.S. Supreme Court, where the Chief Justice was Roger Taney, a former slaveowner and states'-rights advocate who had been appointed by President Andrew Jackson after serving as Jackson's Attorney General.

The Court split along regional and party lines. While each justice wrote an opinion, it was Taney's ruling that stood as the majority decision. False in some parts, in others illogical, Taney's ruling contained three principal points, all of them death blows to antislavery hopes. Free or slave, said Taney, blacks were not citizens; therefore, Scott had no standing before the court. Negroes, he wrote, "are so inferior that they had no rights which a white man was bound to respect."

Taney could have stopped there, but he went much further. Scott had never ceased to be a slave and therefore was not a citizen, but property of his owner, no different from a mule or a horse. This led to his final and most damaging conclusion. Because slaves were property, and property was protected by the Fifth Amendment in the Bill of Rights, Taney argued that Congress had no right to deprive citizens of their property—including slaves—anywhere within the United States. In his judgment, only a state could prohibit slavery within its boundaries. With one sweeping decision, Taney had obliterated the entire legislative history of compromises that restricted slavery, from the Northwest Ordinance of 1787 to the Missouri Compromise of 1820 and the Compromise of 1850.

Southerners, overjoyed by the ruling, wanted to go another step. Armed with the force of Taney's decision, southerners were poised to question the constitutionality of the 1807 law prohibiting the slave trade itself and any laws that proscribed slavery. Conciliatory northerners thought that the court had given its approval to the notion of popular sovereignty, allowing the states to set their own slavery policy.

But instead of giving slavery a new lease on life, the decision produced two unexpected results. It further split the Democrats between North and South and it strengthened the Republicans, politically and morally. Rather than accepting Taney's decision as a defeat for their position opposing slavery's spread, Republicans grew more defiant. In the North and in border states, many people who had been fence-sitters on the slavery question were driven into the Republican camp. The situation got uglier when prominent Republicans charged that President Buchanan knew in advance of the court's ruling and had conspired with Taney to extend slavery by this decision, a conspiracy theory that won popular approval in the North and advanced the Republican cause.

What did Lincoln and Douglas debate?

A year after the decision in *Dred Scott v. Sandford,* two men stood on a platform with Taney's ruling hanging over their heads like a black cloud. One of them was the dapper, short, but powerfully robust "Little Giant," Stephen Douglas. As he stood in the Illinois summer sun, Douglas must have known that he was one of the most powerful and well-known men in America, but that he was fighting for his political life and perhaps the future of the nation. Unable to win the Democratic nomination for President in 1852 and 1856, Douglas kept alive his hopes of making a run in 1860, believing that he could hold the Union together by a conciliatory approach to the South that would accept a moderate form of slavery through "popular sovereignty." But before he could run for President in 1860, Douglas had to hold on to his Senate seat.

His Republican opponent seemed unimpressive. A former one-term representative, at six feet four inches in height, Abraham Lincoln may have towered over Douglas, but he lacked the senator's stature and clout. But Douglas was not fooled. As he commented to a friend, "He is the strong man of the party—full of wit, facts, dates—and the best stump speaker, with his droll ways and dry jokes, in the West. He is as honest as he is shrewd."

Born in 1809 in Kentucky, Lincoln was the son of an illiterate pioneer farmer. At age seven, Lincoln moved with his family to Indiana, and in 1830 the Lincolns settled in southern Illinois. Upon leaving his family home, Lincoln went to New Orleans and returned to Illinois to manage a general store in New Salem. He led a detachment of Illinois militia in the Black Hawk War (see page 122), but, as he liked to say, fought nothing but mosquitoes. At twenty-five, Lincoln won a seat in the Illinois legislature while studying for the bar, and he became a lawyer in 1836. A Whig, Lincoln graduated to Congress in 1846 for a single term marked by his partisan opposition to "Polk's War" in Mexico. Although he lost his seat and returned to Springfield to build his legal practice, he joined the Republican party in 1856 and was prominent enough to win 110 votes for a vice-presidential nomination at the first Republican national convention. In 1858, after delivering his "House Divided" speech to a state Republican convention in Springfield, he was the unanimous choice of the Illinois Republicans to oppose Douglas.

Feeling that his chances would be improved by head-to-head confrontation, Lincoln challenged Douglas to a series of debates at various spots around the state. With much to lose, Douglas agreed to seven such meetings. Even though the nation had plunged into a depression in 1857 after a panic in the stock market, and there were other questions of national importance, it was clear that Lincoln and Douglas would battle over one question: their views on slavery.

Each man had a simple plan of attack. Douglas would make Lincoln look like a raving abolitionist; Lincoln would depict Douglas as pro-slavery and a defender of the Dred Scott Decision. In fact, Lincoln and Douglas were not far apart in their views, but their ambitions exaggerated their differences and their attacks on each other forced them into dangerous corners. Douglas was not afraid of race-baiting to paint Lincoln as a radical who favored racial mixing.

This attack forced Lincoln more than once into adopting conservative language that seemed to contradict some of the opinions he had stated earlier. He opposed slavery, but wouldn't force the states where it existed to surrender their rights. Lincoln stated that slavery would die gradually, but, when pressed, guessed it would take one hundred years to happen. And while he argued, in the words of the Constitution, that "all men are created equal," he balked at the notion of allowing blacks the vote, jury duty, intermarriage, or even citizenship. Lincoln said, "I am not nor ever have been in favor of bringing about in any way the social and political equality of the white and black races . . . I am not nor ever have been in favor of making voters or jurors of negroes, nor of qualifying them to hold office, not to intermarry with white people; and I will say in addition to this that there is a physical difference between the races which I believe will for ever forbid the two races living together on terms of social and political equality."

These debates paired off two men of great intellect, presence, wit, speaking ability, and political instincts. A crucial moment came when Lincoln asked Douglas if the people of a territory could exclude slavery before the territory became a state. This sprung a costly trap on Douglas. He answered that the people had the power to introduce or exclude slavery, no matter what the Supreme Court said. This was a roundabout denunciation of the Dred Scott ruling and it probably gave Douglas a temporary victory. Douglas retained his Senate seat when the Democrats maintained control of the Illinois legislature, which then selected the state's senator. But in the long run, he had shot himself in the foot. Southern Democrats would never support a man for President who equivocated about Dred Scott.

Lincoln lost the election, but it did him no harm. In fact, it increased his national visibility tremendously. With the Democrats further fracturing, along North-South lines, the Republicans were beginning to feel confident about their chances in the presidential campaign of 1860. And Abraham Lincoln had the look of a candidate who might be able to win the White House for them.

American Voices

Lincoln's "House Divided" speech at Springfield, Illinois (June 17, 1858):

"A house divided against itself cannot stand."

I believe this government cannot endure, permanently half slave and half free.

I do not expect the Union to be dissolved; I do not expect the house to fall; but I do expect it will cease to be divided. It will become all one thing, or all the other. Either the opponents of slavery will arrest the further spread of it, and place it where the public mind shall rest in the belief that it is in course of ultimate extinction; or its advocates will push it forward, till it shall become alike lawful in all the States, old as well as new—North as well as South.

Why did John Brown attack a federal arsenal?

Debates, antislavery novels, abolitionist conventions, Congress, and the Supreme Court had all failed. Some said action was needed. And the man shouting loudest for action was John Brown (1800–1859). Viewed through history as a lunatic, psychotic, fanatic, visionary, and martyr, Brown came from a New England abolitionist family, several of whom were quite insane. A failure in most of his undertakings, he had gone to Kansas with some of his twenty-two children to fight for the antislavery cause, and gained notoriety for an attack that left five pro-slavery settlers hacked to pieces.

After the massacre at Pottawatomie, Brown went into hiding, but he had cultivated wealthy New England friends who believed in his violent rhetoric. A group known as the "Secret Six" formed to fund Brown's audacious plan to march south, arm the slaves who would flock to his crusade, and establish a black republic in the Appalachians to wage war against the slaveholding South. Brown may have been crazy, but he was not without a sense of humor. When President Buchanan put a price of $250 on his head, Brown responded with a bounty of two dollars and fifty cents on Buchanan's.

Among the people Brown confided in was Frederick Douglass; Brown saw Douglass as the man slaves would flock to, a "hive for the bees." But the country's most famous abolitionist attempted to dissuade Brown, not because he disagreed with violence but because he thought Brown's chosen target was suicidal. Few volunteers answered Brown's call to arms, although Harriet Tubman signed on with Brown's little band. She fell sick, however, and was unable to join the raid.

On October 16, 1859, Brown, with three of his sons and fifteen followers, white and black, attacked the federal arsenal at Harper's Ferry, Virginia, on the Potomac River not far from Washington, D.C. Taking several hostages, including one descendant of George Washington, Brown's brigade occupied the arsenal. But no slaves came forward to join them. The local militia was able to bottle Brown up inside the building until Federal marines under Colonel Robert E. Lee and J.E.B. Stuart arrived and captured Brown and the eight men who had survived the assault.

Within six weeks Brown was indicted, tried, convicted, and hanged by the state of Virginia, with the full approval of President Buchanan. But during the period of his captivity and trial, this wild-eyed fanatic underwent a transformation of sorts, becoming a forceful and eloquent spokesman for the cause of abolition.

While disavowing violence and condemning Brown, many in the North came to the conclusion that he was a martyr in a just cause. Even peaceable abolitionists who eschewed violence, like Henry David Thoreau and Ralph Waldo Emerson, overlooked Brown's homicidal tendencies and glorified him. Thoreau likened Brown to Christ; Emerson wrote that Brown's hanging would "make the gallows as glorious as the cross."

The view in the South, of course, was far different. Fear of slave insurrection still ran deep, and the memory of Nat Turner (see Chapter 3) remained fresh. To southern minds, John Brown represented Yankee interference in their way of life taken to its extreme. Even conciliatory voices in the South turned furious in the face of the seeming beatification of Brown. When northerners began to glorify Brown while disavowing his tactics, it was one more blow forcing the wedge deeper and deeper between North and South.

American Voices

John Brown:

> I am quite certain that the crimes of this guilty land will never be purged away but with blood.

Why did the South secede from the United States?

Within days of Lincoln's election in 1860, the South Carolina legislature voted to secede from the Union. In his final message to Congress, lame-duck President Buchanan stressed that states had no right to secede, but having always favored the southern cause, Buchanan did nothing to stop such an action. In South Carolina, local militia began to seize the federal forts in Charleston's harbor. Buchanan attempted weakly to reinforce Fort Sumter, the last Charleston fort in federal hands, but the supply ship turned back.

Before Lincoln was inaugurated, five more states voted to secede, and in February 1861 these six states (Alabama, Florida, Georgia, Louisiana, Mississippi, and South Carolina) formed the Confederate States of America. Jefferson Davis (1808–1889), U.S. senator from Mississippi, was elected President. In March, the Confederacy adopted a Constitution based on the U.S. Constitution but emphasizing states' rights and the legality of slavery. By the time the war began, the first six states of the Confederacy would be joined by five more: Texas, Virginia, Arkansas, North Carolina, and Tennessee.

On March 4, 1861, after secretly slipping into Washington to foil an assassination plot that had been uncovered, Lincoln was inaugurated. In one of history's great ironies, the oath of office was administered by Chief Justice Roger Taney, author of the Dred Scott Decision, which had greatly contributed to Lincoln's election.

For years, secession had been held out as a blustering threat that both sides believed would never be used. Why did it finally happen? There were many factors: the common southern feeling that the South was being overpowered by northern political, industrial, banking, and manufacturing strength; the fear that the southern way of life was threatened by northern control of Congress; race-baiting hysteria that southern editorialists and politicians fanned with talk of black control of the South and widespread intermarriage. All of these disparate emotions and political views coalesced in the slavery issue. In the southern view, secession was the last resort to block emancipation. Faced with a legislative confrontation in which its political power was diminishing, the South resorted to the one power it possessed to control its destiny, leaving the Union.

What cannot be overlooked in any discussion of political, social, and economic reasons for the South's breaking away are human nature and historical inevitability. History has repeatedly shown that a more powerful force—in this case the north—will attempt to overwhelm a weaker one for its own interests. For those white southerners who held no slaves—and they were a majority—there was the common denominator of fear. Fear that Lincoln, the Republicans, and the abolitionist Yankees who owned the banks and the factories that set the prices for their crops would make them the slaves of free blacks. Human nature dictates that people who are pushed to the wall either break or push back. To ask why cooler heads did not prevail and settle these questions amicably overlooks the character of the south— proud, independent, individualistic, loyal to their land, and even chivalrous. For such people, a stubborn refusal to submit was the answer. As the new President of the Confederacy, Jefferson Davis, put it, "Will you be slaves or be independent? Will you consent to be robbed of your property?" To Davis, submission meant the loss of liberty, property, and honor itself.

Why didn't the North allow the South to go its own way? Some people, including such prominent abolitionist voices as Horace Greeley, argued that the North should do just that. But if the seceding states were permitted to go, it would mean the end of the United States of America as it was created in the Declaration and the Constitution. The result would be anarchy. The practical result would be economic dislocation and international weakness that could only result in the collapse of the nation's institutions.

American Voices

From Lincoln's first inaugural address (March 4, 1861):

> In your hands, my dissatisfied fellow countrymen, and not in mine, is the momentous question of civil war. The Government will not assail you. You can have no conflict without being yourselves the aggressors. You have no oath registered in heaven to destroy the Government, while I shall have the most solemn one to "preserve, protect, and defend it."
>
> I am loath to close. We are not enemies, but friends. We must not be enemies. Though passion may have strained, it must not break our bonds of affection. The mystic chords of memory, stretching from every battlefield and patriot grave to every living heart and hearthstone all over this broad land, will yet swell the chorus of the Union when again touched, as surely they will be, by the better angels of our nature.

The 1860 Census

History doesn't show whether London's touts laid odds on the war's outcome. On paper, as they say in sports, this contest looked like a mismatch. About the only thing the South seemed to

have going for it was a home-field advantage. Looking at number
alone, the South's decision and fortunes seemed doomed from
the outset. But as the history of warfare has consistently proven
Davids often defeat Goliaths—or, at the least, make them pay
dearly for their victories. The South needed no better example
than the patriots who had defeated England in the Revolution.

North

- Twenty-three states, including California, Oregon, and the
  three "border states" of Missouri, Kentucky, and Maryland, and
  seven territories.
- Population: 22 million (4 million men of combat age)
- Economy: 100,000 factories
  1.1 million workers
  20,000 miles of railroad (70 percent of U.S. total;
  96 percent of all railroad equipment)
  $189 million in bank deposits (81 percent of U.S.
  total bank deposits)
  $56 million in gold specie

South

- Eleven states
- Population: 9 million (3.5 million slaves; only 1.2 million men of
  combat age)
- Economy: 20,000 factories
  101,000 workers
  9,000 miles of railroad
  $47 million in bank deposits
  $27 million in gold specie

In addition, the North vastly outproduced the South in agricultural products and livestock holdings (except asses and mules).
The only commodity that the South produced in greater quantities than the North was cotton, raised by slave labor. The North
had the means to increase their wartime supplies and ship them
efficiently by rail. The South would have to purchase weapons,

ships, and arms from foreign sources, exposing itself to a Union naval blockade.

On the South's side of the balance sheet were several small but significant factors. The U.S. Army was largely comprised and was led by Southerners who immediately defected to the South's cause. Southerners were for the most part better riders, more at home with weaponry, and probably possessed their own rifles, and showed a greater martial spirit than their northern counterparts. The armies of the North were largely made up of conscripts from urban areas, many of them immigrants who spoke little or no English, less familiar with arms and tactics, and fighting on "foreign" turf for the dubious goals, in their minds, of "preserving the Union" and stopping the spread of slavery. All of this gave the southern armies an immediate advantage in trained soldiers and command leadership. In addition, the war would be fought primarily in the South. All the advantages of fighting at home—familiarity with terrain, popular partisan support, the motivation of defending the homeland—which had contributed to the American defeat of the British in the Revolution, were on the side of the Confederacy.

Milestones in the Civil War

1861

April 12 The war officially begins when South Carolina militia forces commanded by General Pierre G. T. Beauregard (1818–1893), second in the West Point class of 1838, bombard Fort Sumter, the Federal garrison in the harbor at Charleston, South Carolina. Lacking sufficient supplies, the fort's commander surrenders.
April 15 Declaring a state of "insurrection," Lincoln calls for 75,000 volunteers for three months' service.
April 17 Virginia secedes, the most influential state to do so. Poorly defended, Washington, D.C., lies but a hundred miles from Richmond, seat of the Confederacy. From the White House, Lincoln can see Confederate flags flying over Arlington, Virginia.
April 19 In Baltimore, crowds sympathetic to the South stone

Union troops marching to reinforce the capital; four soldiers are killed, the first casualties of the war. President Lincoln orders a naval blockade of southern ports. The blockade will prevent cotton, the South's principal cash crop, from being shipped to Europe and limit imports of munitions and other supplies crucial to the South's war effort. The Union navy is small at the time, and many of its commanders and sailors are Southerners who defect, but the American merchant marine is powerful, and merchant ships are pressed into service. Coupled with a major shipbuilding effort, the navy soon has hundreds of ships—including the first generation of ironclad warships—available to enforce the blockade, making this strategy a significant element of the Union's eventual victory.

At the suggestion of General Winfield Scott, the seventy-five-year-old, arthritic and overweight commander of the U.S. Army, Lincoln asks Robert E. Lee (1807–1870) to take field command of the Union forces. Instead, Lee resigns his U.S. Army commission on April 20 and assumes a commission in the Confederate army. Torn over the oath he took upon entering the United States Army, Lee decides he cannot take up arms against his home state of Virginia.

Lee is not alone. Many of the battle-tested commanders in the U.S. Army are Southerners who join the Confederate forces. In the war's early period, the Union armies will be led by generals who are political appointees. This disparity in leadership quality is a major factor in keeping the Confederacy's military hopes alive and prolonging the war.

July 21 The First Battle of Bull Run (or First Manassas). In Virginia, Confederate armies under Generals Joseph E. Johnston (1807–1891) and Beauregard rout Union troops. Poor Union generalship is largely to blame, a problem that bedevils the Union war effort as Lincoln searches for effective commanders. During the fighting, Confederate General Thomas J. Jackson (1824–1863), West Point class of 1846 and a professor of military tactics and natural philosophy at Virginia Military Institute, is given the nickname "Stonewall" for his leadership of the stand made by his troops that turned the tide of battle.

August 5 After the crushing defeat at Bull Run, the North realizes that this is not going to be a ninety-day war. To pay for the war, Congress passes the first income-tax law, and enlistment periods are increased from three months to two years.

August 10–30 In the West, Union forces are defeated at Wilson's Creek, Missouri, and one of the Union's most experienced commanders General Frémont, "the Pathfinder," withdraws, surrendering much of Missouri, a border state that had not joined the Confederacy. To reverse his military losses, Frémont declares martial law and announces that the slaves of secessionists are free. Lincoln requests that this order be withdrawn, but Frémont refuses and Lincoln removes him from command.

October 21 Battle of Ball's Bluff (Virginia). Another rout of Union forces with some 1,900 Union troops killed.

November 1 Lincoln forces aging General Winfield Scott to retire, and replaces him with George B. McClellan (1826–1885) as general-in-chief.

1862

January 27 Lincoln issues General War Order Number 1, calling for a Union offensive; McClellan ignores the order.

January 30 The Union ironclad ship *Monitor* is launched.

February 6 Opening a Union offensive in the West, General Ulysses S. Grant (1822–1885) initiates a campaign in the Mississippi Valley, capturing Fort Henry on the Tennessee River. Ten days later, Grant takes Fort Donelson, near Nashville.

March 9 In the first battle between two ironclad ships, the Union *Monitor* engages the Confederate *Virginia* (formerly the *USS Merrimac*) off Hampton Roads, Virginia. The battle is inconclusive, but the *Virginia* is scuttled to prevent her capture.

March 11 Annoyed at McClellan's inaction, Lincoln removes him as general-in-chief, replacing him with General Henry W. Halleck, but makes him head of the Army of the Potomac.

April 4 The Union Army of the Potomac begins the Peninsular Campaign aimed at Richmond, capital of the Confederacy. Stonewall Jackson will successfully tie up these Union troops for two months.

April 6–7 Battle of Shiloh (Pittsburg Landing, Tennessee). Confederate forces under General Albert S. Johnston (1803–1862) attack Grant's army. Union forces are nearly defeated, but reinforcements arrive and drive off the Confederate army. Losses are staggering: 13,000 Union troops and 11,000 Confederate soldiers are lost in the two days of fighting; the combined losses are more than the total American casualties in the Revolution, the War of 1812, and the Mexican War put together.

May 4–14 McClellan's army takes Yorktown, Williamsburg, and the White House, only twenty miles from Richmond. But in spite of his numerical superiority, the overcautious McClellan halts to await reinforcements instead of pressing the offensive.

June 2 Robert E. Lee takes command of the Confederate Armies of Northern Virginia.

June 26–July 2 The Seven Days' Battles. Lee attacks McClellan and eventually drives him away from Richmond. The Peninsular Campaign, which might have captured Richmond and ended the war, is over.

July 11 Lincoln appoints General Henry W. Halleck (1815–1872) general-in-chief.

August 9 Battle of Cedar Mountain (Virginia). Confederate forces under Stonewall Jackson defeat Union troops.

August 30 Second Battle of Bull Run (Second Manassas). Confederate Generals Lee, Jackson, and James Longstreet (1821–1904) defeat Union forces under General John Pope (1822–1892), forcing Union troops to evacuate all the way back to Washington. In less than a month, Lee has pushed two Union armies twice the size of his from the gates of Richmond all the way back to the Union capital. Pope is sacked and McClellan is reinstated.

September 17 Battle of Antietam (Sharpsburg, Maryland). With Pope's retreat, Lee takes the offensive, but in one of those small moments that alter history, a copy of his orders falls into Union hands, allowing McClellan to anticipate Lee's strategy. In the single bloodiest day of the war, McClellan's Union forces meet Lee's advancing army. The dead and wounded exceed 10,000 for both sides. Lee pulls back, his invasion blunted, but McClellan fails to pursue the retreating Confederate army. The battle is a critical turning point. With Lee's offensive stalled, the likelihood of European recognition of the South is reduced.

September 22 With the Union success at Antietam, Lincoln feels he can issue the Emancipation Proclamation from a position of strength. The proclamation is published in northern newspapers the following day.

Lacking the magisterial prose of some of his other famous speeches, this is a dry legalistic document. By itself, the Emancipation Proclamation doesn't free a single slave, but does change the character and course of the war. Lincoln's contemporary critics and cynical modern historians point to the fact that Lincoln freed only the slaves of the Confederacy, not those in border states or territories retaken by Union forces; as one newspaper of the day comments, "The principle is not that a human being cannot justly own another, but that he cannot own him unless he is loyal to the United States."

Lincoln's position is that under his war powers he can legally free only those slaves in rebel-held territory; it is up to Congress or the states to address the question of universal emancipation. But abolitionist voices, such as Frederick Douglass and William Lloyd Garrison, welcome Lincoln's decision.

In the South, of course, the proclamation simply seems to confirm what secessionists have always believed: that Lincoln plans to force them to surrender slavery, a right they believe to be theirs, constitutionally granted and protected. They also see the proclamation as an incitement to slave rebellion, and stiffen their resolve to defend the South against Yankee encroachment.

The proclamation produces two other results. First, because of it, France and England end a tense diplomatic dance, finally resolving not to recognize the Confederacy. To do so would endorse slavery, which is illegal and politically unpopular in both countries. Second, in the North, the proclamation has the effect of making the war considerably less popular. White workers, who were volunteering freely when the cause was the Union's preservation, are less interested in freeing slaves who they think will overrun the North, taking jobs and creating social havoc. The serious decline in enlistments forces passage of the Conscription Act in March 1863, which applies to all men between twenty and forty-five—unless they are wealthy enough to pay a substitute—and later leads to violent anti-conscription reaction.

November 5 McClellan is relieved as the head of the Army of the Potomac and is replaced by Ambrose Burnside, with disastrous results. General Burnside (1824–1881) has enjoyed early successes in devising an amphibious assault on the North Carolina coastline, but when it comes to command of the entire army, even Burnside feels he is out of his depth. He will soon be proved correct.

December 13 Battle of Fredericksburg (Virginia). Despite an overwhelming numerical advantage, General Burnside's Union troops are routed by Lee with severe casualties, losing 12,000 to the Confederates' 5,000.

1863

January 1 The Emancipation Proclamation is signed.

January 2 Battle of Murfreesboro (or Stone River, Tennessee). The Union advance toward Chattanooga, the South's rail center, is checked after a costly draw.

January 25 The hapless General Burnside is replaced as head of the Army of the Potomac by General Joseph Hooker (1814–1879). Despite his failure as a military leader, Burnside earns historical notoriety for his bushy "muttonchop" facial hair, which will come to be called, in a reversal of his name, "sideburns."

January 26 The Secretary of War authorizes the governor of Massachusetts to recruit black troops. While blacks fought in every previous American war, a 1792 law barred them from the army. The 54th Massachusetts Volunteers are the first black regiment recruited in the North. Eventually, 185,000 black soldiers in the Union army will be organized into 166 all-black regiments. Nearly 70,000 black soldiers come from the states of Louisiana, Kentucky, and Tennessee. While most are pressed into support units forced into the most unpleasant tasks, and are paid less than their white counterparts, black troops are involved in numerous major engagements, and sixteen black soldiers will receive the Medal of Honor. Their impact is even greater in the navy, where one in four sailors is black; four of these will win Medals of Honor.

May 2–4 Battle of Chancellorsville (Virginia). In another devastating battle, losses for both sides exceed 10,000 men. Lee's army defeats Hooker's Army of the Potomac. During the fighting, Stonewall Jackson leads a daring rear-end attack, forcing the Union withdrawal. But as he returned to Confederate lines, he is mistakenly shot by a Confederate soldier and dies of pneumonia on May 10, costing the Confederates one of their most effective field generals.

May 14 Battle of Jackson (Mississippi). Union Generals William Tecumseh Sherman (1820–1891), named at birth for the notorious Indian chief and adding the William later, defeats the Confederates under General J. E. Johnston.

May 22 General Grant, in concert with Sherman, begins the long siege of the Confederate citadel at Vicksburg, Mississippi, the key to control of the Mississippi River. The U.S. War Department establishes the Bureau of Colored Troops to supervise recruitment and enlistment of black soldiers.

June 20 Pro-Union West Virginia, severed from Virginia, is admitted as the thirty-fifth state, with a state constitution calling for gradual emancipation.

June 24 Planning an invasion of Pennsylvania that signals a shift in southern strategy, Lee's army crosses the Potomac and heads toward Gettysburg, Pennsylvania, with the idea that a victory there will give Lee a clear road to Washington.

June 25 General George Meade (1815–1872) is put in charge of the Army of the Potomac after General Hooker is removed by Lincoln for his failure to be more aggressive. Meade begins organizing his army for the coming confrontation with Lee.

July 1–3 The Battle of Gettysburg. Confederate troops in search of shoes meet up with a detachment of Union cavalry. Reinforcements are poured in. In three days of ferocious fighting that mark the final turning point in the war, the Union army takes a strong defensive position and turns back repeated Confederate assaults. Confederate losses reach 28,000 killed, wounded, or missing, a third of the army's effective strength, to the Union's 23,000. Now severely undermanned, Lee retreats to Virginia, unable to press his drive against the North. His army in tatters, Lee seems ripe for picking, and Lincoln wants the remnants of the Confederate army destroyed, ending the war. But Meade, licking his own wounds and cautious as ever, fails to press Lee, allowing him to cross the Potomac and escape safely into Virginia.

July 4 General U. S. Grant's long siege of Vicksburg ends in victory as he demands an unconditional surrender, giving new popular meaning to his initials. More than 29,000 Confederate troops lay down their arms, and the Union now possesses control of the Mississippi River, effectively splitting the Confederacy in two, east from west.

July 13–16 In New York, resentment against the Union Conscription Act turns into rioting in which blacks are lynched. Federal troops eventually quell the riots. Similar riots occur in several major northern cities. The crowd's anger has two sources: the idea of fighting to free the slaves, and the unfairness of the ability of the wealthy to avoid conscription by paying a substitute. In some northern counties, taxes are raised to pay for large numbers of substitutes so that residents of those counties will not have to fight.

August 21 While most of the war is fought between organized armies, in the western states of Kansas, Missouri, and Arkansas, a cruel form of partisan fighting takes place, with its roots in the "Bloody Kansas" wars. Of these partisan guerrillas, the most vicious is William C. Quantrill, whose "raiders" include the psychopathic "Bloody Bill" Anderson, who carries his victims' scalps on his saddle, and the future outlaws Jesse James and Cole Younger. With 450 men, Quantrill raids Lawrence, Kansas, and slaughters more than 180 civilians. The following October, he commits another such raid of terror in Baxter Springs, Kansas. In 1865, Quantrill will head east, intending to assassinate Lincoln, but will be killed in Kentucky by Union soldiers in May after the war's official end.

September 19–20 The Battle of Chickamauga (Georgia). The Union armies led by Generals William Rosencrans (1819–1898) and George H. Thomas (1816–1870) are defeated by Confederates under General Braxton Bragg (1817–1876). Once again, losses for both sides are extremely high: 16,000 Union casualties to 18,000 Confederate. The Union army retreats to Chattanooga.

October 16 Grant is given command of Union forces in the West;

Grant replaces Rosencrans in Chattanooga with General George Thomas, nicknamed "the Rock of Chickamauga" for his heroic stand in that battle.

November 19 Dedicating a military cemetery on the notorious Pennsylvania battlefield, Lincoln delivers the "Gettysburg Address," one of the immortal speeches in history. (Written in snatches over several days and completed the morning he delivered it, the speech was *not* written on the back of a letter, as myth has it.)

November 23–25 In a stunning assault, Grant sweeps up over mountains to drive General Bragg's Confederate forces away from Chattanooga. Tennessee is again brought under Union control. Grant's Union forces, having split the South east from west by controlling the Mississippi, can now split it horizontally with a march through Georgia to the sea that will be led by General Sherman.

December 8 Looking toward the end of the war, Lincoln offers a Proclamation of Amnesty and Reconstruction that will pardon Confederates who take an oath of loyalty.

1864

January 14 General Sherman begins his march across the South by occupying Sheridan, Mississippi. His strategy is simple—total war. Sherman either destroys or takes anything that might be used by the enemy to continue fighting. He demonstrates his planned tactics for the march ahead by burning and destroying railroads, buildings, and supplies.

March 10 His star rising after Vicksburg and Chattanooga, Grant is named commander of the Union armies, replacing General Halleck.

April 17 Grant suspends prisoner-of-war exchanges with the Confederates. His intention is to further weaken the Confederate forces. While it is effective, this strategy leads to the deaths of many Union soldiers held prisoner in overcrowded camps where food supplies are meager.

May 4 Grant begins an assault on Virginia with an army of 100,000 aimed at Lee's Virginia army.

May 5–6 Battle of the Wilderness (Virginia). During two days of inconclusive but bloody fighting, many of the wounded on both sides die when caught by brushfires ignited by gunfire in the dense woods of the battleground.

May 8–12 Battle of Spotsylvania (Virginia). Another five days of inconclusive fighting make Grant's plan clear: a war of attrition that will wear down Lee's outnumbered forces.

May 13–15 In Georgia with an army of 110,000, Sherman defeats General Johnston, but Johnston preserves his smaller army with a skillful retreat.

June 3 Battle of Cold Harbor (Virginia). Ignoring horrible losses, Grant continues to assault Lee's impregnable defense, a ghastly mistake that Grant later admits. To date, in this campaign, Grant has suffered more than 60,000 casualties, a number equal to Lee's entire army. One southern general comments, "This is not war, this is murder." But Grant's costly strategy is accomplishing its purpose of wearing out Lee's army.

June 15–18 Grant begins the long siege of Petersburg, Virginia, recalling the tactics he used earlier against Vicksburg.

June 27 Johnston's Confederate forces turn back Sherman at Kenesaw Mountain, Georgia.

July 2–13 A year after Gettysburg, Confederate forces under General Jubal Early (1816–1894) raid Maryland, heading toward Washington, D.C. With a small force, Early continues to harry Union troops in Virginia.

July 14 General Early is slowed down by Union General Lew Wallace (1827–1905). The lightly defended city of Washington is reinforced, although Early reaches the District of Columbia but then withdraws. (Later governor of New Mexico and minister to Turkey, General Wallace gains his greatest fame as the author of the novel *Ben Hur*.)

July 17 Despite his success at preserving his forces against Sherman's assault, Johnston is replaced by General John B. Hood (1831–1879), who attempts to take the offensive against Sherman.

July 22 General Hood's first attack on Sherman outside Atlanta is turned back, as is a second assault six days later.

July 30 At Petersburg, General Burnside oversees the mining of

Confederate fortifications. In a disastrously miscalculated explosion, his own force suffers nearly 4,000 casualties. Burnside is relieved of any command.

August 5 In a Union naval attack on the key southern port of Mobile, Alabama, Admiral David Farragut (1801–1870) orders his fleet to continue to attack after mines in the harbor sink one of his ships. From the rigging of his flagship, Farragut shouts, "Damn the torpedoes. Full speed ahead!" He successfully closes the port, cutting off the South from vital supplies being smuggled in by blockade runners. Farragut is given the new rank of vice-admiral, created especially for him, and ecstatic wealthy New Yorkers gave him a purse of $50,000.

September 2 Sherman takes Atlanta after Hood's withdrawal. Much of the city is set on fire. With Atlanta and Mobile in Union hands, northern morale is lifted, providing Lincoln a much-needed boost in the coming election, in which Lincoln's chances do not look good.

September 19 and October 19 Union forces under General Philip Sheridan (1831–1888) twice defeat Jubal Early's Confederates while taking heavy losses. The Confederates are driven from the Shenandoah Valley, one of their remaining supply sources.

November 8 Lincoln has been campaigning against two generals he has sacked, John C. Frémont and George McClellan. Although Frémont withdraws from the race, Lincoln wins reelection by less than a half-million popular votes, but his margin in the electoral vote is sweeping.

November 16 Sherman begins his notorious march from Atlanta to the sea at Savannah, destroying everything in his path by cutting a forty-mile-wide swath through the heart of the South, earning him the title "Attila of the West" in the southern press. A Confederate attempt to cut Sherman's supply lines is crushed, effectively destroying General Hood's army. Three days before Christmas, Sherman marches into Savannah unopposed, completing the horizontal bisection of the South. He sends Lincoln a telegram offering Savannah as a Christmas present. Of his march, Sherman comments, "We have devoured the land. . . . To realize what war is, one should follow our tracks."

1865

January 15 Fort Fisher, North Carolina, falls to Union land and sea forces, closing off another southern port of supply.

January 16 Sherman's army wheels north through the Carolinas on a march as destructive as his Georgia campaign.

February 4 Robert E. Lee is named commander-in-chief of the Confederate army, accepting the post despite the obvious hopelessness of the cause.

February 17 Columbia, South Carolina, is burned; General Sherman and retreating Confederate forces are both blamed for setting the fires. A day later, Sherman occupies Charleston.

February 22 Wilmington, North Carolina, the last open southern port, falls to Union forces.

March 4 Lincoln is inaugurated for a second term.

American Voices

From Lincoln's Second Inaugural Address:

> With malice toward none, with charity for all, with firmness in the right, as God gives us to see the right, let us strive on to finish the work we are in, to bind up the nation's wounds, to care for him who shall have borne the battle and for his widow, and his orphan—to do all which may achieve and cherish a just and lasting peace among ourselves and with all nations.

April 1 The Battle of Five Forks (Virginia). In the last major battle of the war, General Sheridan throws back a Confederate assault.

April 2 Lee withdraws from Petersburg, ending the six-month siege. He advises President Jefferson Davis to leave Richmond. A day later, Union troops enter Petersburg and Richmond. Two days after that, Lincoln tours Richmond and sits in President Davis's chair.

April 8 Surrounded and facing starvation, Lee surrenders to Grant at the village of Appomattox Courthouse in Virginia. At

Lincoln's request, the terms of surrender are generous, and Confederate officers and men are free to go home with their horses; officers may retain their sidearms, although all other equipment must be surrendered.

April 11 In his last public address, Lincoln urges a spirit of generous conciliation during the reconstruction.

April 14 While watching a comedy at Ford's Theatre, Lincoln is shot and mortally wounded by the actor John Wilkes Booth, a southern patriot. The first President to be assassinated, Lincoln dies the following day and Andrew Johnson, the Vice-President, takes the oath of office.

April 26 Booth is cornered and shot dead near Bowling Green, Virginia.

April 18 Confederate General Johnston surrenders to Sherman in North Carolina. Scattered resistance continues throughout the South for several weeks ahead, ending in May, when Confederate General Richard Taylor surrenders to Union General Edward R. S. Canby and General Kirby Smith surrenders western Confederate forces.

May 10 Captured in Georgia, Jefferson Davis, presumed (incorrectly) to be a conspirator in the Lincoln assassination plot, is jailed awaiting trial. Later released on bail, he is never tried. The only Southern officer executed for war crimes was Major Henry Wirz, commander of the infamous Confederate prison at Andersonville, Georgia, despite evidence showing he had tried to ease the suffering of his prisoners. In 1868, as one of his final acts in office, President Johnson grants amnesty to all southerners, including Davis, who declines to accept it.

What did the Civil War cost America?

The federal army began force reductions on April 13, 1865. According to Senate figures at the time, the Union had enlisted 2,324,516 soldiers, approximately 360,000 of whom were killed. The Confederate army peaked at about one million soldiers, with losses of some 260,000. The war cost the Union side more than six million dollars and the Confederate states about half that much.

Was "Abe" really "honest"?

After George Washington, no American President—or any American historical figure—has been draped in more mythic splendor than Abraham Lincoln. The Railsplitter. The Great Emancipator. Honest Abe. Assailed in office, nearly denied the nomination to a second term, vilified by the South and martyred in death, Lincoln eventually came to be considered this country's finest President. Was he?

Unlike other "log cabin" Presidents of an earlier era, Lincoln was truly from pioneer family stock. His father was illiterate, his family dirt poor. After his mother's death, his stepmother encouraged his bookishness and introduced him to the Bible. That was important. Without self-righteousness or false piety, Lincoln was a deeply spiritual man, and he needed every ounce of spiritual reserve for the trials he faced.

Lincoln was that quintessential American hero, the self-made man—reading law on his own, winning local election, gaining the Illinois bar and election to the House in 1847. He was unquestionably tall, at six feet four. And he could tell a good story around the general store, no small asset in American politics, as another, more recent President has shown. He was also honest, generally a political liability. Newsman John G. Scripps once remarked that Lincoln was "a scrupulous teller of the truth, too exact in his notions to suit the atmosphere of Washington as it now is."

By modern American standards Lincoln was a racist. By the standards of his day he was liberal, or, in the less polite phrase of the time, a "nigger lover." Like other Presidents who have achieved greatness, Lincoln grew in office. His grudging acceptance of slavery in the states where it existed was gradually replaced by the sentiment voiced in the Gettysburg Address, a recommitment to the Jeffersonian ideal that "all men are created equal."

A melancholy man who suffered greatly, for both public and private reasons, Lincoln was faced with problems graver than those faced by any other President, and in his ability to bend the presidency to the exigencies of the day, he did things that modern Presidents never could have done. While Congress was out of session, he created an army out of state militias, called up volunteers, blocked ports, and, most controversially of all, suspended the writ of habeas corpus in order to detain thousands without firm charges and due process of law. A breach of basic constitutional rights, this suspension was provided for, argued Lincoln, "in cases of rebellion or invasion."

During the war he faced opposition from one side by so-called Radical Republicans and abolitionists for his moderation toward slavery. More dangerous opposition came from the Peace Democrats, the remnants of the northern Democratic party who were given the name "Copperheads" by a newspaper because they were so poisonous. Sympathetic to the South, the Copperheads wanted to stop the war and considered Lincoln a dictator for his suspension of the writ of habeas corpus, the draft acts, and even the Emancipation Proclamation.

Lincoln surmounted these challenges, winning the reelection that cost him his life. By the time of his assassination, Lincoln had moved from resolute commander-in-chief, prosecuting the war at horrendous costs, to healing unifier. While some called him a dictator, there is little doubt that a weaker President might have failed in the most basic test of Lincoln's presidency—preserving the Union from its dissolution.

Why did the North win the war?

The simplest answer is that the Confederacy was fighting history, not just the North. In many respects, the South fielded an eighteenth-century army to fight a nineteenth-century war against a twentieth-century power. And while the South fought ferociously, the numbers were finally too great for them.

Outmanned two to one, the Confederate armies were worn away by Grant's woeful tactics of attrition. The successful blockade of southern ports reduced supplies of munitions, food, and other necessities to the point of bringing the South to starvation. The ultimate failure of the Confederacy to gain foreign recognition further weakened its prospects. The oft-cited superiority of southern military leadership overlooks two factors: the number of these commanders, like Stonewall Jackson, who died early in the conflict; and the rise of Grant and Sherman in the western war against the less brilliant Confederate commanders there. When Grant gained command of the army and Sherman began his march, their willingness to wage total war, matched with the manufacturing strength, wealth, and great population advantage of the North, simply proved too much for the South.

In retrospect, it was a war that also turned on a number of small moments, the speculative "ifs" that make history so fascinating. At a number of turning points, small things, as well as larger strategic decisions, might have changed the course of the war.

If McClellan hadn't been given Lee's battle plans at Antietam . . .

If Lee had listened to Longstreet at Gettysburg and attempted to outflank the Union troops . . .

If the 20th Maine hadn't pushed back a rebel assault at Gettysburg with a bayonet charge . . .

The speculation is interesting but ultimately useless, because it didn't happen that way, and any of those changes might simply have prolonged the inevitable.

Who killed Lincoln?

On Friday, April 14, 1865—Good Friday—Lincoln met with his Cabinet and then lifted the blockade of the South. His mood was high in those days, and he was preaching moderation and reconciliation to all around him, preparing a moderate plan of reconstruction that would bring the rebellious states back into the Union fold with a minimum of recriminations and punishment. That evening he took his wife and a young couple they knew to see a play called *Our American Cousin* at Ford's Theatre in downtown Washington. The Washington policeman guarding the President left his post, either for a drink or to get a better view of the play. There was a pistol shot. Lincoln slumped over. A man jumped from the President's box to the stage, in the process catching his spur on the bunting that draped the box and breaking his shin. He brandished his gun and shouted either "*Sic semper tyrannis!*" ("Thus be it ever to tyrants.") or "The South shall live." Then he escaped through a back exit to a waiting horse.

A second assassin had assaulted Secretary of State William Seward at home with a knife. Attacks on General Grant and Vice-President Johnson were planned but never carried out. Lincoln was taken to a lodging house across the street from the theater, where he died the next morning, throwing the shocked nation into a profound grief of a kind it had never experienced before. Hated and derided during the war years by the Copperheads, Radical Republicans who thought him too moderate, and a host of other groups who found fault with him for one reason or another, Abraham Lincoln had become, in death, a hero of the entire nation. Even leaders of the Confederacy spoke of his death with regret.

Secretary of War Stanton took charge, and martial law was announced in Washington. The assassin, it was soon discovered, was John Wilkes Booth, an actor like his more famous father, Junius Brutus Booth, and brother Edwin Booth. A fanatical supporter of the South—though he never joined the Confederate army—Booth first plotted with a small group of conspirators in a Washington boardinghouse to kidnap Lincoln. Then he planned instead to assassinate the President along with other key government figures.

After an intensive manhunt, Booth was trapped in a Bowling Green, Virginia, tobacco-drying barn on April 26, and shot and killed. A military tribunal sentenced four other captured conspirators, including boardinghouse owner Mary Surratt, to be hanged. Although conspiracy theories involving Jefferson Davis and most other prominent leaders of the Confederacy abounded in the press, they were all dismissed and disproven. Davis was captured and held for two years without trial, but eventually released to go home to write his version of events in the war.

American Voices

O Captain! My Captain! by Walt Whitman:

O Captain! my Captain! our fearful trip is done, The ship has weather'd every rack, the prize we sought is won,
The port is near, the bells I hear, the people all exulting,
While follow eyes the steady keel, the vessel grim and daring;

>   But O heart! heart! heart!
>   O the bleeding drops of red,
>   Where on the deck my Captain lies,
>   Fallen cold and dead.

What was Reconstruction?

In the aftermath of the war, the South was devastated, physically, economically, even spiritually. The postwar South, it has been said, was worse off than Europe after either of the twentieth-century world wars. Provisional military governors were established in the rebellious states, but Lincoln's plans for restoring the secession states to full membership in the Union was moderate and reconciliatory. Southerners could become citizens once more by taking a simple loyalty oath. When 10 percent of the citizens of a state had taken the oath, the state could set up a government. Radical Republicans, led by Thaddeus Stevens of Pennsylvania, Ben Wade of Ohio, and Charles Sumner of Massachusetts, wanted stricter terms, and the situation was at a standstill when Lincoln died and was succeeded by Andrew Johnson (1808–1875).

Johnson's life was a rags-to-riches story. A southerner from Raleigh, North Carolina, he never attended school, but became a tailor's apprentice, eventually attaining success in business. His wife later taught him to read, write, and do mathematics. He entered politics on a local level and found an affinity with the poor and working classes, from which he himself had come. A Jackson Democrat, he served as a U.S. representative and senator from Tennessee, and even campaigned for the Democratic presidential nomination in 1860. But he remained loyal to the Union after Lincoln's election, and was appointed military governor of Tennessee. In 1864, Lincoln saw Johnson as a loyal southerner who would help win votes in the border states.

After his swearing-in, Johnson favored Lincoln's moderate approach to what he called "restoration," which would readmit states after they had ratified the Thirteenth Amendment, abolishing slavery, which had been passed in December 1865. But Johnson would butt heads with the Radical Republicans, who not only wanted retribution but wanted to maintain the control of Congress they had enjoyed during the war years, when Democrats, mostly southerners, were missing from Congress.

As the southern states gradually returned to the fold, they antagonized northerners by returning to Congress the leadership of the Confederacy, and by passing so-called Black Codes, meant to control former slaves. Obviously designed to circumvent the Thirteenth Amendment, the codes outraged the Republicans, who formed a Committee of Reconstruction that soon heard tales of violence and cruelty toward freed slaves. Congress established a Freedmen's Bureau aimed at helping the approximately four million freed slaves, and then passed the Civil Rights Act of 1866, which declared blacks citizens and denied states the power to restrict their rights. Johnson vetoed the bill, but the Republicans had the votes to override the veto, for the first time in American history. Johnson was left weaker than ever. This override was a symbol of strength, giving Congress the upper hand in the power struggle that followed the war and leading to passage of a series of Reconstruction Acts.

The first of these acts divided the South into military regions under the control of generals. Unlike Lincoln's proposed plan, statehood could only be attained by adopting a state constitution allowing blacks to vote, and by accepting the Fourteenth Amendment, which extended citizenship to blacks and provided for punishment of any state that denied the vote to any of its adult male citizens. (This still fell shy of barring race as a voting qualification, and women and Indians were still left on the outside looking in.)

Why was President Johnson impeached?

Johnson's troubles did not end with his attempted veto of the Civil Rights Act of 1866; his next unfortunate first came when Johnson became the first President to be impeached. Under Article II, Section 4 of the Constitution, "the President, Vice-President, and all civil officers of the United States, shall be removed from office on impeachment for, and conviction of, treason, bribery, or other high crimes and misdemeanors."

What were Johnson's "high crimes and misdemeanors"? Ostensibly the issue was a law that Congress called the Tenure of Office Act, which prohibited the President from dismissing any official who had been appointed with Senate consent without first obtaining Senate approval. Challenging the law's constitutionality, Johnson tried to dismiss War Secretary Edwin M. Stanton, an ally of the Radical Republicans. The House promptly impeached him.

The equivalent of a grand-jury indictment, Johnson's impeachment meant he would be tried before the Republican-controlled Senate, with Chief Justice Salmon P. Chase presiding. Under the guise of constitutional law, this was a blatant partisan attempt by Congress to fundamentally alter the system of checks and balances. And it came remarkably close to success. Johnson was acquitted by a single vote on May 16, 1868. Four days later, Ulysses S. Grant was nominated by the Republicans to run for the presidency. To face the hero of the war, the Democrats chose Horatio Seymour of New York instead of the incumbent Johnson. For the remainder of his administration, Johnson was politically crippled, and the Republican Congress pressed forward with its more aggressive Reconstruction plan strengthened.

Who were the carpetbaggers?

The era of Reconstruction would prove to be a very mixed bag. Northern philanthropists opened or revitalized what would become the leading colleges of the South. More significantly, Reconstruction produced the first—albeit limited—black political power in the nation's history. Indeed, Ulysses Grant's margin in the popular ballot was based on the large black vote that turned out in his favor. Republican legislators who saw the full impact of the black vote rushed to provide for black suffrage with the Fifteenth Amendment, which would bar race as a condition for voting. The simple idea that blacks had any political power just a few years after they were released from slavery and declared citizens was an extraordinary achievement, if not a revolutionary one.

The underside of this achievement was the corruption of power the period produced, and the backlash it created among whites. Largely uneducated and illiterate, the newly freed blacks were ill-prepared for the intricacies of constitutional government. They were ripe for exploitation by whites, some of whom came from the North and were called "carpetbaggers" because they traveled with all their possessions carried in a carpetbag, a type of soft luggage made of carpet material. The traditional view has been that these carpetbaggers were charlatans who wanted to acquire power by using black votes to gain office. One such northerner was George Spencer, who made money with contraband cotton and later served in the Senate. Yet the historian Eric Foner dismisses the myth of the carpetbagger in his massive study of the period, *Reconstruction.* Rather than low-class manipulators, Foner demonstrates that many of those northerners who moved to the South were middle-class professionals who saw the South as a means for personal advancement and opportunity, just as others went west after the war. Of the so-called carpetbaggers, argues Foner, quite a few were idealists who had moved south before blacks got the vote.

Another maligned class was the "scalawag," the southern-born white Republican, even more hated than carpetbaggers by Southern Democrats, because they were seen as traitors to both race and region. Again, Foner says, the traditional view of the scalawags as corrupt profiteers exploiting illiterate blacks reflects more postwar antagonism than political reality.

Reconstruction, in the strict political sense of the word, had little to do with the physical rebuilding of the South. Emancipation had undone slavery, which had been the keystone of the southern economy. Now that four million slaves were free, what exactly were they free to do? Senator Thad Stevens, one of the Radical Republicans, proposed breaking up the largest plantations in the South and providing slaves with "forty acres and a mule." But even the most progressive thinkers of the day still believed property was sacred, and the plan went nowhere. Confusion reigned as many freedmen moved to the towns, looking for work that didn't exist. The Southern Homestead Act of 1867, which was supposed to open up public lands in the South to blacks and whites loyal to the Union, failed because the poor didn't have even the small amount needed to buy the land. Instead, most of the land went to big speculators, lumber companies, and large plantation owners.

A gap between intent and reality quickly arose, and the sharecropping system was developed to fill that gap. It was essentially slavery under a new face. Now free blacks worked the land as tenant farmers, splitting the crop with the owner, who also provided the seed and supplies at a price he set, payable in crops. Somehow the sharecroppers never seemed to earn enough to pay off their debts to the landowners.

Another problem was capital. With the end of the war, the West again beckoned to expansionists, and northern banks were sending money west to be spent on building railroads. Without hard cash to finance rebuilding, it was difficult for the South to sustain the growth it needed. Some manufacturing centers slowly came to life, especially around the coal-rich region of Birmingham, Alabama, where steel mills grew, but their development was insignificant compared with the outburst of industrial and railroad growth in the North and West. The fact that Republicans controlled the politics and the banks created a deep distrust and hatred of Republicanism that sent white southerners scrambling for the Democratic party. By 1877, most southern governments were back in conservative, white, Democratic hands. Those hands kept the South Democratic until Richard Nixon and Ronald Reagan were able to tap the region's underlying conservatism in the 1970s and 1980s.

An even more fearful outgrowth of the white backlash to Reconstruction came about as antagonized whites of the South, bitter over their losses, looked for new means of acquiring power. To a large class of white southerners, the idea of blacks in politics, and even controlling southern state legislatures, was simply unacceptable. The need to combat black political power gave rise to secret paramilitary societies dedicated to maintaining white supremacy. Some had names like the Knights of the White Camelia and the Pale Faces, but the most notorious, powerful, and ultimately long-lived was the Ku Klux Klan, which first met in Nashville's Maxwell House in April 1867.

Organized by former commanders, soldiers, and leaders of the Confederacy as well as southern churchmen, and using a combination of mystical talk, claims of being ghosts of dead Confederate soldiers—hence the white sheets—and outright terror tactics, the Klan gained enormous power in the postwar South. Through lynchings, beatings, burnings, and other forms of political terrorism, it successfully intimidated both blacks and "liberal" white Republicans. As Lerone Bennet eloquently puts it in *Before the Mayflower,* "The plan: reduce blacks to political impotence. How? By the boldest and most ruthless political operation in American history. By stealth and murder, by economic intimidation and political assassinations, by the political use of terror, by the braining of the baby in its mother's arms, the slaying of the husband at his wife's feet, the raping of the wife before the husband's eyes. By *fear.*"

Northern outrage over these injustices quickly faded as the nation busied itself with other concerns, like the spread westward. The reforms of the Reconstruction Acts, whether truly well-intentioned or powered purely by political ambition, faded as the nation turned its attention to building an empire in the West and coping with a depression, so often the aftermath of wartime economies, that followed another stock-market panic in 1873.

On balance, the era of Reconstruction created some opportunities, but fell far short of the lofty goals of true freedom for blacks in the South, as the near future would so oppressively prove.

When Monopoly Wasn't a Game: The Growing Empire from Wild West to World War I

- What happened at Custer's Last Stand?

- What happened at Wounded Knee?

- Who were the cowboys?

- Who were the Robber Barons?

- Of what was William Tweed "boss"?

- What happened at Haymarket Square?

- Who were the Populists?

- What was the "Cross of Gold"?

- What did "separate but equal" mean?

- Who was Jim Crow?

• Who fought in the Spanish-American War?

• Milestones in the Spanish-American War

• What did America gain from the Spanish-American War?

• Who built the Panama Canal?

• What was the "big stick"?

• Who were the "muckrakers"?

• Who were the Wobblies?

• Who was W. E. B. Du Bois?

• What did the Bull Moose Party stand for?

• Who was Pancho Villa?

• How did a dead archduke in Sarajevo get America into a World War?

• Who sank the *Lusitania,* and what difference did it make?

• Milestones in World War I

• What was the cost of World War I?

In thirty-five years, from Civil War's end to the twentieth century, America moved with astonishing speed from a war-torn nation of farmers to an industrial empire holding far-flung possessions. By the end of the First World War in 1918, the United States stood among the first rank of global powers.

Powering this dynamic growth was a lightningbolt of industrial development that spread railroads, built steel mills, and opened oil fields. This industrial surge was joined to a simultaneous explosion of practical invention, best exemplified by names that are now familiar parts of the American vocabulary: Edison, Bell, Westinghouse, Wright, and Pullman.

But progress carries a price tag. It was, as Mark Twain and Charles Dudley Warner titled their collaborative novel about this era, *The Gilded Age:* beautiful on the surface, but cheap, base, and tarnished underneath. For every mile of railroad laid, every ton of coal or iron ore mined, thousands of workers died. Many of them were immigrants or war veterans, miserably underpaid, working in unsafe and unsanitary conditions, with little or no political voice. The new fortunes being made opened up an era of astonishing corruption. The outlaws of the Wild West were small-time hoodlums compared with the politicians of New York and Washington, who brazenly bilked millions, and to the millionaire industrialists who kept these politicians in their pockets.

Since the Revolution, the American political process had opened up through agonizingly slow reforms, but power remained in the tight grip of the few. That was what the Founders had envisioned: a nation ruled by an enlightened aristocracy comprising gentlemen with the leisure and education to debate issues and rule judiciously. But in this period of a growing empire, more than ever before, the keys to government were pocketed by the powerful and wealthy, the great industrial and banking magnates who literally owned the government and turned it to their personal enrichment. It was what Alexander Hamilton may have had in mind when the Constitution was being debated, and it was light-years away from the agrarian republic that Jefferson envisioned.

The new industrialists were America's Medicis, and they dictated American policies as surely as those Italian bankers had owned Popes and principalities. Viewed beside Morgan, Gould, Rockefeller, and Carnegie, the postwar Presidents in office were either weak, inept, or corrupt. Not until the rise of Theodore Roosevelt—himself the scion of a wealthy, aristocratic family and certainly no liberal in the modern sense of the word—would a White House administration be powerful enough to challenge these merchant princes.

Pitted against them were the powerless. Immigrant laborers dying in the deserts and mountains as the railroad inched across the West. The urban poor working the factories and only slowly acquiring power through the unions that were fought with the deadly force of state militias and federal troops. Homesteaders who lost out to the railroad czars and cattle barons in incredible land grabs. Women filling the sweatshops of the swelling cities, yet still invisible on election day. And the Indians, last remnants of the millions in America when Columbus arrived. It was the subjugation of the few unconquered tribes that opened this era, but they did not go gently to their deaths.

American Voices

General William Tecumseh Sherman, 1867:
The more Indians we can kill this year, the less will have to be killed the next war, for the more I see of these Indians, the more convinced I am that they all have to be killed or be maintained as a species of paupers.

What happened at Custer's Last Stand?

The most famous Indian battle in American history was a final flourish to the Indian's hopelessly valiant war dance. The battle itself was simply the result of the actions of one vain, headstrong—probably deranged—soldier, George Armstrong Custer. The Indian victory at the Little Bighorn merely hastened the inevitable: the brutal end of Indian resistance and extinction for their singular way of life.

While the white men wearing blue and gray uniforms fought each other to the death, there were about 300,000 American Indians left in the West. They had been pushed and pressed inward from both coasts by the War of 1812, Manifest Destiny, the Mexican War, the California and Colorado gold rushes, and all the other reasons that whites had for stripping the Indians of their hunting lands. The "permanent Indian frontier" pledged by Andrew Jackson during the removals earlier in the century had long been breached by private and public enterprises, as had every treaty in the sad history of the Indians. When the Civil War ended, the politicians, prospectors, farmers, railroad builders, and cattlemen were ready to take up where they had left off when the war interrupted.

The most powerful and numerous of the surviving tribes were the Sioux, divided into several smaller groupings: the Santee Sioux of western Minnesota, who had tried to accept white ways; the Teton Sioux, those extraordinary horse warriors of the Great Plains, led by the Oglala chief Red Cloud; the Hunkpapas, who would produce Sitting Bull and Crazy Horse; and the Tetons' allies, the Cheyenne of Wyoming and Colorado. Farther south were other tribes: the Arapahos of Colorado; the Comanches of Texas; the Apaches, Navajos, and Pueblos of New Mexico.

For twenty-five years, from 1866 to 1891, the United States Army fought a continuous war against these Indian tribes at considerable cost in lives and money. The final thrust began when the Sioux balked at the opening of the Bozeman Trail, a route to the goldfields of California that passed through Indian territory in Montana. Under Red Cloud, the Sioux attacked, destroying the forts that the army was trying to build along the trail. A treaty in 1867 ended this phase of the fighting, but it would get worse. Herded onto small reservations overseen by the scandalously corrupt Bureau of Indian Affairs, the Indians attempted to live under the white man's rules.

Gold again proved the undoing of any hope for peace. Trespassers on the Indian reservations in South Dakota's Black Hills, led by Custer himself, found gold, and there was soon a rush into the territory. The Indians were ordered off the land, but decided to go on the warpath instead. Joined by the Cheyennes, the Sioux concentrated their strength in the Bighorn River region of southern Montana. In the summer of 1876, setting out against specific orders to refrain from attacking, Custer led his 250 men in a direct frontal assault, ignoring warnings that from 2,000 to 4,000 Indians awaited his attack. Led by Crazy Horse and Sitting Bull, the Indians destroyed Custer's force to the last soldier, allowing only a half-breed scout to escape from the Battle of the Little Bighorn on June 25, 1876.

Of course, it didn't read that way in the newspapers back East. In the midst of the nation's Centennial celebrations, an outraged nation read only of a massacre of brave soldiers by bloodthirsty Indians. The romanticized reports of "Custer's Last Stand" provoked a furious popular and political reaction, demanding total warfare on the Sioux. The army's response was savage. The remnants of the Sioux tribe were hunted down or forced to flee into Canada. Sitting Bull was later arrested, but died of a bayonet wound suffered in captivity.

After the Sioux wars came the great mopping-up battles in the Northwest, against Chief Joseph of the Nez Perce, and in the Southwest, against Geronimo and his Apaches. Captured in 1886, the ferocious chieftain Geronimo was displayed at the St. Louis World's Fair, where he sold his picture postcard for a quarter.

American Voices

From the last words of Crazy Horse (1877):
We had buffalo for food, and their hides for clothing and for our teepees. We preferred hunting to a life of idleness on the reservation, where we were driven against our will. At times we did not get enough to eat, and we were not allowed to leave the reservation to hunt.

We preferred our own way of living. We were no expense to the government. All we wanted was peace and to be left alone. Soldiers were sent out in the winter, who destroyed our villages.

Then "Long Hair" [Custer] came in the same way. They say we massacred him, but he would have done the same thing to us had we not defended ourselves and fought to the last. Our first impulse was to escape with our squaws and papooses, but we were so hemmed in that we had to fight.

What happened at Wounded Knee?

The Little Bighorn proved a costly victory for the Indians, only hastening the inevitable. Their subsequent battles against federal troops were all disastrous, as one Indian leader after another was captured or killed. But in spite of the odds, some Indians refused to submit, leading to the last resistance movement of the nineteenth century and a notorious massacre that truly marked the end of the era of the Indian wars.

In 1888 a Paiute Indian named Wovoka spawned a religious movement called the Ghost Dance. Ghost Dancers believed that the world would soon end and that the Indians, including the dead of the past, would inherit the earth. Wovoka preached harmony among Indians and rejection of all things white, especially alcohol. The religion took its name from a ritual in which the frenzied dancers would glimpse this future Indian paradise.

The religion quickly took hold and was widely adopted by Indians throughout the Plains, the Southwest, and the Far West. But it took on new importance when two Sioux medicine men claimed that "ghost shirts" worn by the dancers could stop white men's bullets, leading to a new militant fervor among some Indians.

Alarmed by the Ghost Dancers, the army attempted to arrest a number of Indian leaders, including the great chief Sitting Bull, who was then on a reservation. Like Crazy Horse, Sitting Bull was killed during the fight to capture him. Another chief named Big Foot, also sought by the army, was ill with pneumonia and wanted peace. But three days after Christmas Day in 1890, his band of some 350 women, children, and men was intercepted by an army patrol and taken to an encampment at Wounded Knee, South Dakota. As the Indians were surrendering their weapons to the soldiers, the gun of a deaf Indian named Black Coyote discharged. Whether it was an accident or deliberate is uncertain. But the soldiers immediately turned their guns and artillery pieces on the disarmed Indians. At least 150 Indians, and probably as many as 300, died in the barrage. Wounded Knee was the Indians' "last stand."

The following twenty years would be the nadir of American Indian history, as the total Indian population between 1890 and 1910 fell to fewer than 250,000. (It was not until 1917 that Indian births exceeded deaths for the first time in more than fifty years.) But nearly facing extinction, the American Indian proved resilient if nothing else. With agonizingly slow progress, Indians gradually gained legal rights. In 1924 all native-born United States Indians were granted American citizenship. The ruling was in large measure a reaction of gratitude to the large number of Indians who fought for America during World War I, yet paternalism, discrimination, and exploitation were still commonplace.

By the time of the Great Depression (see Chapter 6), the plight of the Indians on reservations was, in the words of one government report, "deplorable." During Franklin Roosevelt's tenure, a cultural anthropologist named John Collier was appointed Commissioner of Indians and proposed sweeping reforms that would recognize the right of Indian tribes to remain distinct and autonomous, with rights beyond other Americans. This was the so-called New Deal for Indians but it was a short-lived period of reform, replaced by the subsequent policy of "termination" under which the government sought to end the special status of Indians. As late as 1954, some states still kept Indians from voting. Yet, by the time of the 1980 census, there were some 1.5 million American Indians (including Aleuts and Eskimos), among the fastest-growing minority groups in America. As a group, however, they remain among the poorest and most unemployed Americans.

Who were the cowboys?

Without a native mythology, America had to manufacture its heroes. A nation turning one hundred years old had no *Odyssey*, no Saint George slaying the dragon, no Prometheus. The emerging American genius for making a lot of money was a poor substitute for King Arthur and his knights (although the Horatio Alger myth of rags to riches was good for a lot of mileage). So the mythmaking machinery of nineteenth-century American media created a suitably heroic archetype in the cowboys of the Wild West. The image was of the undaunted cattle drivers living a life of reckless individualism, braving the elements, staving off brutal Indian attacks. Or of heroic lawmen dueling with sixguns in the streets at high noon. This artificial Wild West became America's *Iliad*.

It was an image so powerful, appearing first in the newspapers and reinforced in dime novels and later through countless Hollywood movies, television series, and cigarette commercials, that it entered the American political mentality. This code of the cowboy shaped policy and Presidents, perhaps most notably Teddy Roosevelt, Lyndon Johnson, and Ronald Reagan.

The heyday of the cowboy lasted approximately twenty years, from 1867 to 1887. The life wasn't as glamorous or as romantically dangerous as it has been portrayed. The modern politicians' comparison of drug-ravaged urban streets to the Wild West does a disservice to the West. The famed cow and mining towns of Tombstone, Abilene, Dodge City, and Deadwood had fewer shootouts and killings in their combined history than modern Washington, D. C., has in a few months.

The soul of the cowboy myth was the cattle drive, and it began with the famous trails out of Texas, where Spanish cattle introduced by the *conquistadores* later mixed with the English cattle of American settlers to produce a genetic marvel, the Texas longhorn steer. Moving north from Texas along trails like the Chisholm, charted out in 1867 by a half-Cherokee named Jesse Chisholm, the drives ended at the newly opened railheads in Kansas City and Sedalia in Missouri, Cheyenne in Wyoming, and Dodge City and Abilene in Kansas. The rowdiest of the Wild West towns, Abilene was founded by an Illinois cattleman as a railhead to meet the cattle drovers from Texas. It soon sported a boisterous barroom and brothel business that grew to meet the demand of the drovers who had just traveled from Texas over rugged terrain for several months, accompanied only by cattle who fattened themselves on the open range. The situation demanded "peacekeepers," men whose histories were often more violent than those of the people they were supposed to police. The most famous was James Butler "Wild Bill" Hickok, who shot only two people while presiding over Abilene; one of them was another policeman. But Hickok, and other western legends like Jesse James, were being brought back to easterners in newspaper reports and dime novels that made the West seem romantic and adventurous.

By the 1890s the Wild West had already begun to fade. Cattlemen learned that the hearty steer could survive on the northern plains, killing off the need for the long drives. The advent of barbed wire in 1874 meant they were able to enclose huge areas of land (which they often didn't own, or claimed under very questionable authority). The freebooting days of the postwar period were gradually replaced by cattle-raising as big business, and the era of the cowboys and Wild West outlaws ended, their place taken by a much more sinister and ornery character, the American businessman.

Who were the Robber Barons?

Wall Street's insider trading scandals and the New York City corruption high jinks of the 1980s are polite misdemeanors when viewed against the wholesale corruption of American business and politics during the late nineteenth century. This was the era when political genius took a backseat to a genius expressed in accumulating and holding more private wealth and power than had been possessed in history. One illustration of this power was the financier John P. Morgan's refusal to make loans to the U.S. government because it lacked collateral. In 1895, Morgan bailed out a nearly bankrupt federal government by exchanging gold for U.S. bonds, which he promptly resold at an enormous profit.

The accumulation of American wealth in the hands of a few was nothing new; since colonial times a minority had held the vast majority of the nation's wealth. But the late nineteenth century brought this concentration of wealth to unprecedented heights.

After the war, the lands of the West were opened up, cleared of Indians, and ready for the great surge. To reach these rich lands—to bring the cattle and wheat to eastern markets to feed the factory workers who made the tools and machinery to mine the gold, silver, and copper—called for cheap, fast transportation. Building more railroads required four basic components: land, labor, steel, and capital. The federal government provided the land; immigrants on both coasts supplied cheap labor; Andrew Carnegie provided the steel. And J. P. Morgan, the banker's banker, provided the cash.

With unlimited vistas of western wealth, the plan to link East and West by railroad provided equally unlimited schemes to bilk the Treasury. Corruption came to the fore with the exposure of the Credit Mobilier Scandal in 1872. Massachusetts congressman Oakes Ames was a shovel maker and one of the directors of the Union Pacific Railroad, the company taking the line westward from Nebraska. Ames and the Union Pacific created a company called Credit Mobilier of America, which was awarded all construction contracts. The company was paid $94 million by Congress for work actually worth $44 million. Ames had smoothed the way for this deal in Washington by spreading around plenty

of Credit Mobilier shares, including some to President Grant's
first- and second-term Vice-Presidents, Schuyler Colfax and Henry Wilson, giving the "Vice" in the title a whole new dimension.

The Central Pacific, owned by Leland Stanford, built eastward from California and did the same things, winning land grants, contracts, and enormous overpayments to Stanford's railroad-owned construction company. Stanford got away with it and eventually built a university; Ames was censured by Congress for his role, but got no university out of the deal.

Besides the enormous costs in graft, the linking of East and West by rail, completed on May 10, 1869, at Promontory Point, Utah, cost thousands of workers' lives as the lines snaked their way over mountains, across deserts, or through Indian territory, decimating the buffalo as they went to feed the workers. Workers' lives and sound construction principles were cast aside, sublimated to greed and the rush to lay track to win bonuses. Bribes were paid by towns that wanted the railroad lines to run through them, and millions of acres of land were given away to the railroads as plums.

Grant's two terms were boom times for the corruptible. Besides the Credit Mobilier scandal, which reached into the White House, there was the Whiskey Ring scandal, which defrauded the government of millions in taxes with the assistance of the Treasury Department and Grant's personal secretary, Orville Babcock, a man with his proverbial finger in every pie. In the Bureau of Indian Affairs, corruption was equally widespread, with millions in kickbacks paid to administration officials all the way down the line, ending up with Indians on the reservation getting rotten food, when they were fed at all.

The millions made in these scandals were still small change when compared against the fortunes being made by the great thieves of the generation, the so-called Robber Barons—Jay Gould, Vanderbilt, Morgan, Carnegie, and Rockefeller. But they raised their form of thievery to sound business organization and called them "trusts."

For many of these men, such as Gould and Vanderbilt, the railroad was the ticket to enormous wealth. "Commodore" Cornelius Vanderbilt (1794–1877) started by building a Staten Island ferry business into a steamship empire, expanding into railroads after the war. Through graft and bribery, Vanderbilt built the New York Central into the largest single railroad line in America, passing down a vast amount of wealth to his family, who then gave new definition to "conspicuous consumption" with lavish parties at which guests dug in a trough for jewels.

Jay Gould (1836–1892), one of Vanderbilt's fiercest competitors, started with the Erie railroad line in New York, but was forced out after revelations of stock watering so blatant that officials in this "anything goes" era had to step in. Gould built a large empire with small lines in the Southwest, integrating them into a regional monopoly. In 1869, Gould and James Fisk, who had made millions selling shoddy blankets to the Union through Tammany Hall (see pages 343–346) attempted to manipulate the gold market, using an unwitting President Grant for their purposes. Slow to catch on to the scheme, Grant stopped gold sales for a time, forcing up gold prices until he realized what was going on and released $4 million in gold, driving gold prices down on "Black Friday" (September 24, 1869), causing a stock-market panic that set off a depression lasting several years.

With corruption and monopoly at the core of the railroad systems, and the depression unleashed by the "Black Friday" panic, the railroads were ripe for disaster. By the 1890s, many of the lines were nearly bankrupt from intense competition and poor economic conditions. In stepped J. P. Morgan (1837–1913).

The son of a banker, Morgan had not only avoided fighting in the Civil War, but had profited handsomely from it. By the turn of the century, Morgan had his hand in almost every major financial undertaking in America. His banking house was a millionaires' club that loaned money to other banks. Through Morgan, a small group of men were able to take control of the railroads of America, and by 1900 Morgan owned half of America's track mileage. His friends owned most of the rest, enabling them to set the railroad rates across the country.

In 1900 also, Morgan and steel king Andrew Carnegie (1835–1919) met at a party. Carnegie scribbled a figure—$492 million—Morgan agreed, and U.S. Steel was born, the first billion-dollar corporation. Unlike Morgan, Carnegie embodied at least a portion of the rags-to-riches myth. Born in Scotland, he immigrated to the United States with his family in 1848, and first worked in a cotton factory. His rise to power was mythic, going from telegraph clerk to secretary to the head of the Pennsylvania Railroad, and later becoming a Wall Street broker selling railroad commissions. When oil was found on a property he owned, Carnegie moved into the oil industry and later into iron and steel. Utilizing an improved steel production technique called the Bessemer method, which he had seen in England, Carnegie revolutionized steel production in the United States, and with ruthless efficiency he set out to control the American steel market.

Carnegie and one of his managers, Henry Clay Frick, were violently anti-union. In 1892, while Carnegie was in Scotland, Frick provoked a bloody strike when he demanded a pay cut and an end to the union at his Homestead plant in Pennsylvania. When the workers refused to accept Frick's demands, he fired the entire work force and surrounded the plant with barbed wire and hired Pinkerton guards to protect the strikebreakers he brought in. Two barges carrying the Pinkerton guards were met by thousands of strikers and their friends and families, who kept the guards from landing, in a battle that left twenty strikers dead. Stiffening his back, Frick called on the state governor to send in 7,000 militiamen to protect the replacement workers. During the four-month confrontation, a young anarchist named Alexander Berkman—the lover of "Red Emma" Goldman (1869–1940), the most notorious anarchist leader of the day—shot Frick in the stomach, but only wounded him, and he was back in his office that day.

After the militia arrived, strike leaders were charged with murder, but all were acquitted. The plant kept producing steel with workers shipped in by railroad, and other Carnegie plants failed to join the Homestead strike, a union defeat that kept labor unorganized in Carnegie plants for years to come.

Another of the era's "giants" was John D. Rockefeller (1839–1937), a bookkeeper by training who was once hired to investigate the investment promise of oil. Rockefeller told his employers it had "no future" and then invested in it himself, buying his first refinery in 1862. With a group of partners he formed the South

Improvement Company, a company so corrupt it was forced out
of business. Rockefeller responded by forming Standard Oil of
Cleveland in 1870. Standard bought off whole legislatures, made
secret deals with railroads to obtain favorable rates, and weakened
rivals through bribery and sabotage until Rockefeller could buy
them out with Standard Oil stock. By 1879, Standard controlled
anywhere from 90 to 98 percent of the nation's refining capacity
at precisely the moment when oil's value to an industrial society
was becoming apparent.

Twenty years later, Standard Oil had been transformed into
a "holding company" with diversified interests, including the
Chase Manhattan Bank. The key to this diversification had been
the invention of the "trust" by one of Rockefeller's attorneys,
Samuel C. T. Dodd, who was looking for ways around state laws
governing corporations. Standard Oil, for instance, was an Ohio
corporation prohibited from owning plants in other states or
holding stock in out-of-state corporations. Dodd's solution was to
set up a nine-man board of trustees. Instead of a corporation
issuing stock, Standard Oil became a "trust" issuing "trust certifi-
cates." Through this new device, Rockefeller gobbled up the
entire industry without worrying about breaking corporate anti-
monopoly laws. The idea was soon copied in other industries, and
by the early 1890s, more than 5,000 separate companies had been
organized into 300 trusts. Morgan's railroad trust, for instance,
owned all but 40,000 miles of track in America.

The trusts and the enormous monopolies kept prices artificially high, prevented competition, and set wages scandalously
low. They were obviously not popular among working Americans.
Standard Oil became the most hated company in America. These
monopolies had been built through graft and government subsid-
ies, on the backs of poorly paid workers whose attempts to
organize were met with deadly force. If any vague hope for
reform rested in the presidency, it was false hope.

For a generation, beginning with Andrew Johnson's abbreviated term and the Grant years, the President almost seemed
superfluous. In 1876, Rutherford B. Hayes (1822–1893) became
President because of a fraudulent election that stole the presidency from Democrat Samuel J. Tilden, resulting in a compro-

mise with Southern Democrats that killed congressional
Reconstruction and any hope for civil rights in the South. When
Grover Cleveland (1837–1908) was elected in 1884, he named
William Whitney his Secretary of the Navy. Whitney had married
into the Standard Oil fortune and set out to build a "steel navy" by
buying Carnegie steel at inflated prices.

Attempts at "reform" were mostly dogs without much bark or
bite, intended to mollify a public sick of corruption. The Interstate Commerce Commission, established during Cleveland's
administration to regulate railroads, was a charade for public
consumption. Cleveland's successor, Benjamin Harrison (1833–
1901) was a former railroad attorney who had broken railroad
strikes as a soldier. During his tenure, as a reaction to public
sentiment, Congress passed the Sherman Anti-Trust Act of 1890,
named for Senator John Sherman, brother of General William
Tecumseh Sherman, for the purpose of protecting trade against
"unlawful restraints."

It was a weak law made even more puny when the Supreme
Court ruled in 1895 that a company owning 98 percent of the
nation's sugar-refining capacity was a manufacturing monopoly,
not one of commerce, and was therefore immune to the law.
During an extremely conservative, pro-business period, the high
court also ruled that Anti-Trust laws could be used against railway
strikers who were "restraining trade." This Alice-in-Wonderland
court took its perverse interpretations another step when it ruled
that the fourteenth Amendment, passed to guarantee the rights
of freed slaves, was a protection for corporations, which the court
said were "persons deserving the law's due process."

American Voices

From Andrew Carnegie's article "Wealth," (published in the
North American Review, 1890):

The Socialist or Anarchist who seeks to overturn present
conditions is to be regarded as attacking the foundation upon
which civilization itself rests, for civilization took its start from
the day when the capable, industrious workman said to his
incompetent and lazy fellow, "If thou dost not sow, thou shalt

not reap," and thus ended primitive Communism by separating the drones from the bees. One who studies this subject will soon be brought face to face with the conclusion that upon the sacredness of property civilization itself depends—the right of the laborer to his hundred dollars in the savings bank, and equally the legal right of the millionaire to his millions. . . . Not evil, but good, has come to the race from the accumulation of wealth by those who have had the ability and energy to produce it.

Of what was William Tweed "boss"?

In New York, quite a bit of energy and ambition were directed toward acquiring wealth. But it was being acquired through massive corruption. The epidemic of greed didn't begin or end with Washington and the great captains of industry. It extended to the local level, most notoriously in New York, the seat of power of William Marcy Tweed (1823–1878), the infamous "Boss" of Tammany Hall. The word *Tammany* was a corruption of the name *Tamanend,* who was a Delaware Indian chief of the early colonial period said to be "endowed with wisdom, virtue, prudence, charity." These were qualities in conspicuously short supply in the club named for the chief.

Tammany began as one many fraternal societies that adopted Indian names in post-Revolution days. Unlike the Society of Cincinnatus, which was reserved for Washington's officers, groups like Tammany were for the common soldier, and their political value soon became apparent to clever power brokers like Aaron Burr and Martin Van Buren. By the time of the Civil War, the clubs not only had pull, but had become quite corrupt, serving as a conduit for government contracts to crooked suppliers who sold the Union shoddy blankets and maggot-ridden meat.

A mechanic by trade, Tweed rose to his greatest heights of power ostensibly as chief of the Department of Public Works in New York City. But that small title gave no sense of the grip he possessed on almost every facet of city life. As the leader of Tammany Hall, the New York City Democratic clubhouse, he built a simple but effective means of control. In exchange for the votes of the waves of immigrants, factory workers, disenchanted homesteaders returning to the city, and even their dead relatives, Tweed and his "Ring" arranged small "favors"—a job, an insurance settlement. With these votes, Tweed could maneuver favorable bills through the New York legislature at will. Rich in electoral votes, New York also wielded immense political clout in presidential politics, and Tweed used this power as well. Fraudulent contracts, patronage in the highest offices, kickbacks, false vouchers—all the usual tools of corruption were raised to an art form by Tweed's Tammany Club.

Tweed's most notable opponent was the cartoonist Thomas Nast, who once received an offer of $500,000 from Tweed not to run a particular cartoon. Tweed could well afford the bribe; conservative estimates of his rape of New York's treasury ran upwards of $30 million on every deal in New York from the building of the Brooklyn Bridge to the sale of the land for Central Park.

It was only when a Tweed associate felt shortchanged that Tweed got into trouble. In 1872, Samuel Tilden (1814–1880), a reform Democrat and future governor of New York who later lost the White House in an election scandal that stripped him of the electoral votes he rightfully deserved, finally won a conviction of Tweed. Sentenced to twelve years in jail, the "Boss" escaped to Cuba and then to Spain, only to be returned by Spanish authorities despite the lack of an extradition treaty between the two countries. While in jail, Tweed made a full and damning confession, expecting immunity. But he died in prison, the only member of the Ring to be convicted.

Tammany's shenanigans did not end with the breakup of the Tweed Ring. Powerful "sachems" continued their hold on New York's legislature into the twentieth century. When Theodore Roosevelt entered the New York State legislature in the 1880s, Tammany's influence was still prevalent in state politics, and the club held the key votes that controlled almost all legislation.

One of the most colorful of Tammany's "sachems" was George Washington Plunkitt, who once instructed a newspaper reporter on the distinction between "honest" and "dishonest" graft. "There's an honest graft," said Plunkitt, "and I'm an example of how it works. I might sum up the whole thing by sayin': 'I seen my opportunities and I took 'em.'. . . I'm tipped off, say, that they are going to lay out a new park at a certain place. . . . I go to that place and I buy up all the land I can and then there is a rush to get my land. Ain't it perfectly honest to charge a good price and make a profit on my investment and foresight? Of course, it is. Well, that's honest graft."

What happened at Haymarket Square?

While the wealth piled higher in the houses of Morgan and Rockefeller, the working men and women of America fell deeper and deeper into poverty, victimized by the periodic depressions of the late nineteenth century. The forces of labor were slow to organize, confronted by the combined power of the businessmen and banks working in league with state and federal governments. Unions also had to contend with the natural difficulties of organizing workers who did not all speak the same language and were suspicious of each other. The Irish hated the Italians. The Germans hated the Irish. They all hated the Chinese. And, of course, blacks were beyond the pale to most white workers. The idea of integrated unions was unspeakable to white workingmen, most of whom were preoccupied with fighting for jobs rather than with obtaining decent wages and safer conditions.

But small gains had been made. In 1860, shoe workers in Lynn, Massachusetts, organized a strike on Washington's Birthday. At their peak, the strikers numbered 10,000 workers marching through the city. While refusing to recognize the union, the factory owners conceded on wages, and it counted as the first real victory in American labor history.

It would be a long time before labor could claim another one. The post–Civil War period was littered with the bodies of strikers who were killed by strikebreakers, hired guards, or soldiers. Among those worst off were coal miners, who faced nightmarish dangers for pennies. In 1875, in Pennsylvania, a group of Irish coal miners organized as the "Molly Maguires," taking their name from an Irish revolutionary organization. Infiltrated by an informer, the Molly Maguires were accused of violence, leading to the execution of nineteen members of the group.

Two years later, in 1877, there were massive railroad strikes spreading across the country, brought on by wage cuts imposed on workers already laboring twelve hours a day for low pay. By the time this wave of strikes was over, more than a hundred people had died and a thousand strikers were jailed. But the idea of organized labor had begun to take root, and the first generation of powerful national unions was emerging. The first was the Noble Order of the Knights of Labor, begun in 1869, which quickly acquired a large measure of political and negotiating power. In 1884, Robber Baron Jay Gould suffered the indignity of bargaining at the same table with the Knights, whose membership blossomed to more than 700,000. But the history of the Knights would end in smoking disaster.

In Chicago, in 1886, the Knights of Labor were involved in a strike to force an eight-hour workday. On May 3, 1886, strikebreakers at the McCormick Reaper Company were attacked by striking workers, and police fired on the crowd, killing six and wounding dozens more. The next day, several thousand people gathered at Haymarket Square to protest the police action. As the police arrived to break up the rally, a bomb was thrown into their midst, killing seven officers.

Although there was no real evidence, blame fell on anarchist labor leaders. Anarchists were those who believed in the replacement of government with free cooperation among individuals. Fears of anarchist cells in America's cities incited a wave of panic across the country. Within months, several anarchist labor leaders were tried and quickly convicted. Some of them were hanged, and others received life sentences. (In 1893, three surviving anarchists still in prison were pardoned by German-born governor John Altgeld, who was convinced of their innocence but committed political suicide with the pardon.) Tarred with the anarchist brush after the Haymarket Square Riot, the Knights of Labor were badly discredited. By 1890, their membership had fallen to 100,000.

Their place would be filled by two more powerful leaders,

Eugene V. Debs (1855–1926) and Samuel Gompers (1850–1924). Debs's labor career began with work as a locomotive fireman—a dirty, dangerous job, as was almost all railroad work of the period. Thousands of workers were killed or maimed each year in accidents and boiler explosions. In the midst of another severe economic depression in 1893, Debs organized the militant American Railway Union, which absorbed remnants of the Knights of Labor and called for a strike in 1894 against the Pullman Car Company. Since Pullman cars were to be found on almost every train in the country, the strike soon became national in scope. The strike peaked when 60,000 railworkers went out, and the federal government, at the railways' behest, stepped in. Attorney General Richard Olney, a former railroad lawyer, declared that the strike interfered with federal mails; the Supreme Court agreed, and President Grover Cleveland called out troops to suppress the strike. After a pitched battle in Chicago, in which strikers were killed, Debs was arrested and jailed for contempt of court. He later joined the Socialist Party and ran for President five times.

Cigarmaker Samuel Gompers played it far more safely. Making the sweatshops of the Lower East Side of New York his base, Gompers wasn't interested in utopian dreams of improving society. Rather than organizing for political ends, Gompers stuck to "bread and butter" issues such as hours, wages, and safety, organizing the American Federation of Labor (AFL) as a collection of skilled craft unions. Presiding over the AFL almost continuously from 1886 to 1924, Gompers used the strike fiercely and effectively, winning eight-hour days, five- and six-day work weeks, employer liability, mine safety reforms, and, above all, maintaining the right of collective bargaining, a term that is accepted entirely today, but that reeked of Communism when it was introduced. The AFL's effectiveness in working for laborers' specific interests rather than for the broad social changes sought by anarchists or socialists showed in its growth. With about 150,000 members in 1886, the union passed the million-member mark in 1901.

They were impressive gains, but they might have been larger. The Federation had a great shortcoming, however, that hurt it morally and probably reduced its effectiveness in the long run. The AFL had hung out a sign that read "No Colored Need Apply."

American Voices

Samuel Gompers (1894):

Year by year man's liberties are trampled underfoot at the bidding of corporations and trusts, rights are invaded and law perverted. In all ages wherever a tyrant has shown himself he has always found some willing judge to clothe that tyranny in the robes of legality, and modern capitalism has proven no exception to the rule.

You may not know that the labor movement as represented by the trades unions, stands for right, stands for justice, for liberty. You may not imagine that the issuance of an injunction depriving men of a legal as well as a natural right to protect themselves, their wives, their little ones, must fail of its purpose. Repression or oppression never yet succeeded in crushing the truth or redressing a wrong.

Who were the Populists?

While organized labor inched painfully toward acceptance, the other people who suffered most from the economic upheavals of the period were the farmers. The millions of small farmers, principally in America's West and South, were at the mercy of many forces besides the weather that they were unable to control: eastern banks controlled credit; manufacturing monopolies controlled the price of machinery; eastern railroad trusts set freight prices; depression wiped out land values and sent crop prices spiraling downward. With the population booming and mechanization increasing farm efficiency, it should have been a time of plenty. Instead, farmers were being squeezed tighter and tighter, forced to sell their lands at panic prices and move to factory jobs in the cities.

But a backlash set in, producing a wave of Farm Belt radicalism that swept the country. Locally it produced farmers' organizations called Granges that gained sufficient political clout to press for reforms, although many of these, like the Interstate Commerce Commission, proved to be unloaded guns in the war against monopolies. In the South, for the first time since the end of the Civil War, poor blacks and working-class white farmers began to see that they shared common problems and interests, and the beginnings of an alliance of black and white farmers emerged. The farmers also reached out to join with city workers to form a powerful new alliance that might transform American politics.

Meeting in St. Louis in 1892, the Grangers and remnants of the Knights of Labor organized the People's, or Populist, Party. In a national convention later that year, the Populists put together a platform calling for national ownership of railroads and telegraph and telephone systems; a system of keeping nonperishable crops off the market; and a graduated income tax. Their platform was an eloquent indictment of the times: "We meet in the midst of a nation brought to the verge of moral, political, and material ruin. Corruption dominates the ballot-box, the Legislatures, the Congress, and touches even the ermine of the bench. The people are demoralized. . . . The newspapers are largely subsidized or muzzled, public opinion silenced. . . . The fruits of the toil of millions are boldly stolen to build up colossal fortunes for a few. . . . From the same prolific womb of governmental injustice we breed the two great classes—tramps and millionaires."

These weren't the rantings of wild-eyed college kids who had just read Karl Marx. They were working-class, backbone-of-America types who had been pushed too far by the excesses of business in league with government. The men in power did not watch idly. In the South, Democrats undermined the Populist organizing effort by heightening racial fears. The mass of urban workers were never drawn to Populism, preferring to deal with the Democratic machines that they thought were defending their interests. In the election of 1892, in which Democrat Grover Cleveland recaptured the White House he'd lost four years earlier to Benjamin Harrison, the Populists finished a distant third. But the Populists still made strides as a third party, especially in the Farm Belt states, where they captured state legislatures, a governorship, and a substantial number of congressional seats in 1894. The two major parties realized that these farmers were a force to be reckoned with.

American Voices

Populist organizer Mary Elizabeth Lease (1890):
What you farmers need to do is raise less corn and more Hell!

What was the "Cross of Gold"?

During the next few years the real issues raised by the Populist Party were drowned in an obscure argument over currency. By 1895, the conflict over gold versus silver coins had absorbed all political debate in the country. "Free silver" became the new Populist rallying cry, a demand to return America to a standard using both silver and gold coins. To many Populists, this simplistic response to the depression brought about by a panic in 1893 seemed to be a cure-all. But it was a diversion that camouflaged the serious economic problems confronting the country, and it sapped much of the Populist Party's energy.

President Cleveland was a staunch supporter of the gold standard. But when federal gold reserves fell to near-bankruptcy levels in 1896 and Cleveland had to turn to J. P. Morgan for a bail-out, his political life was finished. Morgan and his associates turned around and sold off at an enormous profit the government bonds they had received, and Cleveland was seen as a Morgan puppet, which, in the public eye, was no different from being in league with the devil.

With Cleveland politically dead, some Democrats saw the Populist manifesto as a way to hold on to the White House. A young delegate-at-large from Nebraska, William Jennings Bryan (1860–1925) spotted the political gold to be found in the "Free Silver" cry, and he seized the moment.

Addressing the Democrats' 1896 nominating convention, the silver-tongued Bryan captured the audience of 20,000 with a speech regarded as the most thrilling and effective in party convention history. Raising the banner of silver against gold, western farmers against eastern business, Bryan said, "Burn down your cities and leave our farms and your cities will spring up again as if by magic; but destroy our farms and the grass will grow in the streets of every city in the country."

With a great theatrical flourish, he concluded, "You shall not press down upon the brow of labor this crown of thorns," and extending his arms like Christ crucified, Bryan said, "You shall not crucify mankind on a Cross of Gold."

The speech was met with wild acclaim, and the following day, Bryan—who was being subsidized by western silver and copper interests—was named the Democrats' choice—at age thirty-six the youngest presidential nominee ever. With the Democrats chanting "Cross of Gold," the Populist platform had been co-opted and the Populists were forced to throw their support behind Bryan. Populism was Jonah in the belly of the mainstream Democratic whale.

In the meantime, the guiding hand and pocketbook of the wealthy Ohio industrialist "Kingmaker" Mark Hanna literally bought the Republican nomination for Ohio's Governor William McKinley (1843–1901). In a campaign thoroughly modern in its "packaging" of a candidate, the Hanna-led Republicans outspent the Democrats by $7 million to $300,000. McKinley's election marked the triumph of eastern industrial interests over western farm interests. One of McKinley's first acts in office was to kick Senator John Sherman up to the State Department, allowing Hanna to take Sherman's Senate seat. Populism as an effective political third party was just about finished, joining the long list of American third parties that had burst into prominence only to flicker and fade after a brief flash of brilliance.

What did "separate but equal" mean?

Homer Plessy was seven-eighths Caucasian and one-eighth black. But when he tried to sit in a railroad coach reserved for whites, that one-eighth was all that counted. Plessy was arrested, in accordance with an 1890 Louisiana law separating railroad coaches by race. Plessy fought his arrest all the way to the Supreme Court in 1896. Unfortunately, this was the same Supreme

Court that had protected corporations as "persons" under the fourteenth Amendment, ruled that companies controlling 98 percent of the sugar business weren't monopolies, and jailed striking workers who were "restraining trade."

In Plessy's case, the arch-conservative, business-minded court showed it was also racist in a decision that was every bit as indecent and unfair as the Dred Scott decision before the Civil War. The majority decision in the case of *Plessy v. Ferguson* established a new judicial idea in America—the concept of "separate but equal," meaning states could legally segregate races in public accommodations, such as railroad cars and public schools. In his majority opinion, Justice Henry Brown wrote, "We consider the underlying fallacy of the plaintiff's argument to consist in the assumption that the enforced separation of the two races stamps the colored race with a badge of inferiority. If this be so, it is not by reason of anything found in the act, *but solely because the colored race chooses to put that construction upon it.*" (Emphasis added.)

The problem with this fine notion, of course, was that every facet of life in the South was increasingly separate—schools, dining areas, trains and later buses, drinking fountains, and lunch counters—but they were never equal.

The lone dissenter in this case, as in so many others during this period, was John Marshall Harlan (1833–1911) of Kentucky. In his eloquent dissent, Harlan wrote, "The arbitrary separation of citizens, on the basis of race, while they are on a public highway, is a badge of servitude wholly inconsistent with the civil freedom and the equality before the law established by the Constitution. It cannot be justified upon any legal grounds.

". . . We boast of the freedom enjoyed by our people above all other peoples. But it is difficult to reconcile that boast with a state of the law which, practically, puts the brand of servitude and degradation upon a large class of our fellow-citizens, our equals before the law. . . ."

In practical terms, the Supreme Court of this period had turned congressional Reconstruction upside down. Its perversion of the fourteenth Amendment had been used to protect corporations instead of blacks. *Plessy v. Ferguson* had given the court's institutional stamp of approval to segregation. It would be another sixty years before another Supreme Court decision over-turned the "separate but equal" doctrine.

Who was Jim Crow?

With the blessing of the Supreme Court, the floodgates opened. In the years following the *Plessy* decision, almost every former Confederate state enacted "separate but equal" laws that merely gave the force of law to what had become a fact of life—slavery under a new name. And to blacks and whites alike, the name was "Jim Crow."

Like "Uncle Tom" of the minstrel shows that followed in the wake of Stowe's momentous novel, the name "Jim Crow" came from a white man in blackface. According to historian Lerone Bennet, Jr., a white entertainer named Thomas Dartmouth Rice wrote a song-and-dance tune that became an international hit in the 1830s.

> Weel a-bout and turn a-bout
> And do just so
> Every time I weel about
> I jump Jim Crow.

"By 1838," writes Bennett, "Jim Crow was wedged into the language as a synonym for Negro." And the image it conveyed was of a comic, jumping, stupid rag doll of a man.

Jim Crow railroad cars came first, creating the situation addressed in *Plessy*. Afterwards came separate waiting rooms, factory entrances, and even factory windows. Eventually Jim Crow said that white nurses couldn't tend black patients and vice versa. Black barbers couldn't cut the hair of white women and children. Perhaps most damaging was the separation of education into white and black schools, a system in which white schools regularly received ten times the funding of black schools, and teaching was as segregated as the classrooms. Some states failed to provide blacks with high schools, a fact that carried over well into the twentieth century. In fact, there was no facet of life that was untouched by Jim Crow, even criminal life; in New Orleans, prostitution was segregated.

At the roots of Jim Crow were two fears. One was sexual—the fear, either primal or institutionalized, of black men having sexual contact with white women. In the words of one notable southern politician of the time, "Whenever the Constitution comes between me and the virtue of the white women of the South, I say to hell with the Constitution."

The other fear combined politics and economics. When the Populist movement threatened to unite poor blacks and whites, the old elite white regimes in the South drove poor whites back into line with fear of black economic power. Voting fell back along strict racial lines. Ultimately, Jim Crow meant the end of black voting power in the South, as restrictive registration laws kept blacks away from the ballot boxes through poll taxes, literacy requirements, and a dozen other technical tricks.

Where laws failed to keep blacks in their place, another technique proved even more effective: the terror of lynching. Blacks were strung up throughout the South with impunity through much of the late nineteenth and early twentieth century, often but not always on the pretext of the rape of a white woman. Lynchings of blacks became so commonplace that they were advertised in newpapers, providing a sort of spectator sport.

Out of this period stretching from the late nineteenth century to the recent past, the major black voice in America was one of accommodation. Booker T. Washington (1859–1915) was born a slave but was able to receive an education under congressional Reconstruction. Working as a janitor to pay his way through Hampton Normal and Agricultural School, he became a school-teacher. He was clearly an impressive figure who could mesmerize a crowd, as Frederick Douglass had done a generation earlier. Almost singlehandedly he built Alabama's Tuskegee Institute from a shack beside a church into the major vocational training school for blacks in the country. In a sense, Washington was trying to adopt the rags-to-riches American dream for southern blacks, preaching the virtues of hard work and economic survival through education and advancement into the professions. Critics of Washington, both in his day and later, complained that his accommodation to and acceptance of the status quo was weak, even cowardly. Others have defended Washington as one man who was doing his best in a time of very limited options. After all, he lived in a time when a lynch mob needed no more excuse to hang a man than that he was "uppity."

American Voices

Booker T. Washington, "The Atlantic Compromise" (1895):
To those of my race who depend on bettering their condition in a foreign land or who underestimate the importance of cultivating friendly relations with the Southern white man, who is their next-door neighbor, I would say: "Cast down your bucket where you are. . . .

The wisest among my race understand that the agitation of questions of social equality is the extremest of folly. . . .

Who fought in the Spanish-American War?

The racism expressed in Jim Crow didn't end at southern, or even American, borders. The vigorous rise of a belief in white, Anglo-Saxon superiority extended overseas. One popular writer of 1885 was the clergyman Josiah Strong, who argued that the United States was the true center of Anglo-Saxon virtue and was destined to spread it over the world. "This powerful race," wrote Strong in the best-selling book *Our Country*, "will move down upon Mexico, down upon Central and South America, out upon the islands of the sea, over upon Africa and beyond." Then, borrowing from Charles Darwin, whose ideas were then being floated around, Strong concluded, "Can any one doubt that the result of this competition of races will be the 'survival of the fittest'?" Strong left no doubt as to who he thought the "fittest" was.

Strong's message found a receptive audience in the corridors of American power, and a few years later the message went out in a war with Spain. This was America's muscle-flexing war, a war that a young and cocky nation fought to shake off the cobwebs, pull itself out of the economic doldrums, and prove itself to a haughty Europe.

Watching England, Germany, France, and Belgium spread their global empires in Asia and Africa, America fought this war to expand and protect its trade markets overseas, capture valuable mineral deposits, and acquire land that was good for growing fruit, tobacco, and sugar. It was a war wanted by banks and brokers, steelmakers and oilmen, manufacturers and missionaries. It was a war that President McKinley didn't seem to want, and a war that Spain certainly didn't want. But there were a lot of powerful people who did want it. And, perhaps above all, it was a war the newspapers wanted. War, after all, was good for circulation.

The ostensible reason for going to war with Spain was to "liberate" Cuba, a Spanish colony. A fading world power, Spain was trying to maintain control over a native population that demanded its freedom, as America had demanded and won its independence a century earlier. When Spain sent a military governor to throw rebels into concentration camps, America acted the part of the outraged sympathizer. It was a convenient excuse. But an element of fear also played into the game. There was already one black republic in the western hemisphere, in Haiti. The United States didn't want another one in Cuba.

Forces outside the government were matched by powerful men inside it who wanted war. Chief among them were Henry Cabot Lodge (1850–1924), the influential Senator from Massachusetts, Theodore Roosevelt, then Assistant Secretary of the Navy, and Captain Alfred Mahan, author of a book called *The Influence of Sea Power Upon History, 1660–1783,* an influential work calling for expansion of American naval power to bases around the world, especially in the Pacific. Roosevelt, the great admirer of the cowboy spirit, once told a friend, "I should welcome almost any war, for I think this country needs one."

Lodge was an even more outspoken booster of American imperialism. When President Cleveland failed to annex Hawaii in 1893, Lodge lashed out angrily and spoke about his aims for America: "In the interests of our commerce and our fullest development, we should build the Nicaraguan canal, and for the protection of that canal and for the sake of our commercial supremacy in the Pacific we should control the Hawaiian Islands and maintain our influence in Samoa. . . . Commerce follows the flag, and we should build up a navy strong enough to give protection to Americans in every quarter of the globe. . . ."

Pressing the war cries from the outside were the two most powerful newspaper czars in American history, William Randolph Hearst (1863–1951) and Joseph Pulitzer (1847–1911). Both men had learned in the Civil War that war headlines sold newspapers. Tabloid headlines depicting Spanish atrocities against Cubans became commonplace, and the influential papers of both men were outdoing each other in the sensationalized screaming for war. The expansionist doctrine that had grown out of Manifest Destiny also sold newspapers, so the papers of both men were soon hawking war. When the artist Frederick Remington (1861–1909) went to Cuba to send back pictures for Hearst's papers, he told his boss he couldn't find a war. "You furnish the pictures," Hearst responded in a fury. "I'll furnish the war."

Against the urgings of party and press, and of businessmen and missionaries calling for bringing Anglo-Saxon Christianity to the world, McKinley tried to avert war. But finally he found it easier to go with the flow. Through a series of diplomatic ultimatums, McKinley pushed Spain into a corner of a room and then closed the only window that would have provided escape. What Secretary of State John Hay would call a "splendid little war" lasted a few months. But like all wars it carried a price in lives and perhaps in virtue.

Milestones in the Spanish-American War

1898

January 25 The U.S. battleship *Maine* arrives in Havana harbor. Its stated purpose is to protect the interests of Americans who are being brutalized by the Spanish governor, according to reports in the tabloids.

February 9 A private letter by Spain's ambassador to the United States is published in Hearst's *New York Journal* in which President McKinley is characterized as feebleminded, provoking a wave of indignation, fanned by the Hearst and Pulitzer newspapers.

February 15 The battleship *Maine* mysteriously explodes while anchored in Havana harbor, resulting in the deaths of 260 crew members. The newspapers and warhawks soon trumpet, "Remember the *Maine!* To hell with Spain!" as a battle cry. The source of the blast is said to be an external explosion. While the Americans claim the blast was caused by a mine in the harbor, Spanish authorities assert it was an internal explosion, perhaps in the heavily loaded ship's magazine.

March 9 By unanimous vote, Congress appropriates $50 million "for national defense," and the country moves toward a war footing.

March 27 President McKinley offers Spain several conditions to avert a war that is widely desired by the banking and military interests of the country. The conditions include negotiations with Cuban rebels; revocation of concentration camps; U.S. arbitration to settle the rebel question in Cuba. While Spain seems to express willingness to negotiate and accept McKinley's conditions, war hawks continue to apply pressure.

April 11 McKinley delivers a "War Message." Fearing peace will split his party, he ignores Spanish peace overtures as the call for war is pressed by the Hearst and Pulitzer papers, Henry Cabot Lodge in Congress, and Assistant Secretary of the Navy Theodore Roosevelt.

April 19 Congress adopts a war resolution calling for Cuban independence from Spain and evacuation of Spanish forces from the island. The measure asserts that the United States is un-interested in exerting control over the island, and the coming war is depicted as a war of "liberation" of a western colony from a European power, which will allegedly permit the Cubans to "determine their fate."

April 20 To prevent the use of diplomatic channels to avoid a war, the Spanish Ambassador's passport is returned before he can deliver the U.S. ultimatum. A day later, Spain breaks off diplomatic relations with the United States.

April 22 Congress passes the Volunteer Army Act, which calls for organization of a First Volunteer Cavalry—a "cowboy cavalry" that the press will christen "Rough Riders." Resigning his post as Assistant Secretary of the Navy and chief instigator of war within the McKinley administration, Theodore Roosevelt takes a commission as lieutenant colonel of the brigade, which is commanded by Leonard Wood. Hundreds of applications for the Rough Riders come from all over the country, and Roosevelt will draw on Ivy Leaguers as well as cowboys. The U.S. Navy also begins a blockade of Cuban ports, and a Spanish ship is captured in the first actual encounter of the war.

April 23 McKinley issues a call for 125,000 recruits.

April 24 Spain declares war on the United States.

April 25 The United States declares that a state of war exists as of April 21, the day Spain broke off diplomatic relations.

May 1 While Cuba is the focus of hostilities, the United States launches a surprise naval attack on the Philippines. Commodore (later Rear Admiral) Dewey's Asiatic Squadron has been preparing for this attack for some time, at the secret orders of Theodore Roosevelt. In a seven-hour battle outside Manila Bay, where the outdated and outgunned Spanish ships have maneuvered to avoid civilian casualties, the United States sinks all the Spanish ships, killing more than 300 Spanish at a loss of no American ships and incurring only a few wounded. With a quick and easy victory under its belt, America's hawkishness quickly explodes into outright war fever.

May 12 The United States bombards San Juan, Puerto Rico.

May 19 With American assistance, the Philippine guerrilla leader Aguinaldo arrives in Manila. At the same time, back in Cuba, the Spanish fleet moves into Santiago Harbor.

May 25 The first American troop ships leave for Manila. McKinley calls for another 75,000 volunteers.

May 29 The American fleet blockades the Spanish fleet in Santiago Harbor.

June 10 A force of 647 marines lands at Guantanamo Bay, beginning the invasion of Cuba.

June 22 Nearly 20,000 American troops arrive at the fishing village of Daiquiri, eighteen miles east of Santiago.

June 24 Led by Joseph Wheeler, formerly of the Confederate cavalry, who occasionally lapses in battle and calls the Spanish "Yankees," and Leonard Wood, 1,000 regular army and Rough Riders, accompanied by several war correspondents, win the first land battle of the war at Las Guasimas, Cuba. In his first action, Roosevelt is accompanied by two major war correspondents and is already being marked as a war hero.

July 1 The battles of El Caney and San Juan Hill. Against much smaller Spanish forces, Americans take heavy casualties in the major pitched battle of the war. An American balloon sent aloft to observe Spanish troop placements simply gives the Spanish gunners a perfect indication of American positions. More than 6,000 U.S. soldiers suffer 400 casualties at El Caney against a Spanish force of only 600. At San Juan Heights, confusion and delayed orders result in severe U.S. casualties as Spanish guns rake the waiting troops. Colonel Theodore Roosevelt finally takes the initiative, leading an assault first on Kettle Hill and a second charge on San Juan Heights. After successfully taking San Juan Heights, the American forces have command of Santiago below. But the American position is very weak. They are short of supplies and casualties are heavy. Yellow fever and malaria have already begun to take their toll, as the Spanish defenders had expected. Roosevelt himself writes to Henry Cabot Lodge, "We are within measurable distance of a terrible military disaster." After the battle of San Juan Heights, 1,572 Americans are dead or wounded, but Roosevelt achieves instant war-hero status.

July 3 Against his own belief that he is risking certain defeat, Spanish Admiral Cervera is ordered to break through the American blockade of Santiago Harbor. After the battle, the Spanish fleet is utterly destroyed. There is one American dead, another wounded.

July 4 In the Pacific, American troops take the deserted Wake Island.

July 8 Admiral Dewey takes Isla Grande near Manila.

July 10 With the destruction of the Spanish fleet guarding Santiago, U.S. troops launch a final attack on the city. By agreement with the Spanish command, there will be no resistance.

July 17 Santiago surrenders to American forces, and the U.S. flag is raised over the government building.

July 25 The town of Guánica in Puerto Rico is taken by U.S. troops.

July 26 Through the French ambassador, Spain requests peace terms. The "splendid little war" ends after three months of fighting. McKinley announces the following terms: independence for Cuba; the United States takes control of Puerto Rico; the United States will occupy Manila until further negotiations.

August 9 McKinley's terms are accepted by Spain, and a protocol of peace is signed.

What did America gain from the Spanish-American War?

There were 5,462 American deaths in the war, only 379 of which were battle casualties. Yellow fever, malaria, and other diseases were primarily responsible for most of them. Tainted meat sold to the army by the Armour Company may have led to some others. When Roosevelt and his men had opened tinned meat on the way to Cuba, they promptly tossed the putrid contents overboard.

In the aftermath of the war, several unexpected developments arose. America found itself not only in possession of Cuba and Puerto Rico as the island bases Henry Cabot Lodge hoped for, but in control of Wake Island, Guam, and the Philippines as well. President McKinley was somewhat uncertain as to what should be done with them. His choices were to give them back to Spain, or to give them to France or Germany, which seemed foolish; to leave them alone seemed equally foolish. The best remedy was to keep them for America. With the annexation of Hawaii in 1898, America had in place its "steppingstones" to a new Pacific empire.

The people in the Philippines had other ideas about who they needed protection from. Emiliano Aguinaldo, the rebel leader brought back to the Philippines by Admiral Dewey, was no more interested in American rule than he had been in Spanish rule. What followed was a war more bloody than the one with Spain: the Philippine incursion. It carried with it all the earmarks of a modern imperial war: massive strikes against civilians, war atrocities, and a brutality that had been missing from American wars with Europeans. Fighting against the "brown" Filipinos removed all excuses for civility. The Philippines would be an unhappy "protectorate" in the American Pacific for years to come. Five thousand Americans died fighting the Filipinos.

The other development that came home from Cuba was a real, live war hero in Teddy Roosevelt. Unashamedly, he rode his Rough Rider fame into the statehouse of New York in 1898, where his reform-minded ideas unsettled fellow Republicans and the industries they represented. A number of Republicans felt it would be an eminently prudent idea to stash Teddy away in the Vice-President's office, where he couldn't do any harm. Senator Mark Hanna did not join in this thinking. The Chairman of the Republican Party, Hanna commented, "Don't any of you realize there's only one life between this madman and the presidency?"

Roosevelt initially balked at the post, believing that the office was a political dead end. The bullet fired by anarchist Leon Czolgosz, which struck President McKinley in Buffalo in September 1901, changed all of that. At age forty-two, Theodore Roosevelt became the youngest President in American history. In one of his first acts in office, he invited Booker T. Washington to the White House. It was an act that the South would never forgive or forget.

Who built the Panama Canal?

While America prepared for war in Cuba, the American battleship *Oregon,* stationed off the coast of California, was ordered to Cuba. Steaming around South America, the *Oregon* was followed in the press like the Kentucky Derby. The voyage took two months, and while the *Oregon* arrived in time to take part in the battle of Santiago Harbor, it was clear that America needed a faster way to move its warships from ocean to ocean.

This wasn't a new idea. The dream of connecting the Atlantic and the Pacific had been held almost since Balboa stood on the cliffs of Darien in modern Panama. President Grant sent a survey team to look for the best route to dig a canal across Central America, and an American company later built a small railroad line to take steamship passengers across the isthmus, drastically cutting travel time from coast to coast.

Plenty of other people saw the commercial as well as strategic advantages of this undertaking. In 1880 a French group led by Ferdinand de Lesseps, chief architect of the Suez Canal, put together a company with the capital of thousands of investors to build a canal across the Isthmus of Panama, then still a part of Colombia. In the growing macho mood of America's leaders, President Hayes announced that no European country would control such a canal, saying, "The policy of the country is a canal under American control."

Corruption on a grand scale, miserable engineering plans, the harsh realities of the Central American jungle with its rainy-season floods, earthquakes, yellow fever, and malaria doomed the de Lesseps effort. After some preliminary excavations and thousands of deaths by accident and disease, the French company abandoned its canal cut amid a national scandal and left everything behind, the rusted machinery looking like some mechanical dinosaurs fossilized in the dense jungle.

After the war in Cuba and the *Oregon* incident, the American appetite for a canal was reawakened. President McKinley authorized a commission to investigate the best route for the canal. When Roosevelt, the great apostle of American sea power, took the White House, the enthusiasm became that of a raging bull. Initially, Roosevelt tilted toward a Nicaraguan canal, a longer route but thought to be an easier dig. A Nicaraguan canal also offered the advantage of being closer to American ports on the Gulf of Mexico. An angry Senate debate followed, with Senator Mark Hanna leading the way for Panama. When the French company dropped the asking price for its assets from $109 million to $40 million, the Panama route became more attractive. Only one problem remained. The "dagos" in Colombia, in Roosevelt's phrase, who still owned the territory, were asking too much.

The solution presented to Roosevelt was simple. If Colombia stood in the way, just make a new country that would be more agreeable. Led by a former director of the French canal company with U.S. Army assistance, Panamanians revolted against Colombia in November 1903. The American battleship *Nashville* steamed south and pointed its guns in Colombia's direction, and Panama was born with the U.S. Navy for a midwife.

Recognized faster than any new government had ever been,

Panama's regime received $10 million, a yearly fee of $250,000 and guarantees of "independence." In return the United States got rights to a ten-mile swath across the country—the Canal Zone—"in perpetuity." Since the zone comprised most of Panama and would be guarded by American troops, the United States effectively controlled the country. Years afterward, Roosevelt would proudly say, "I took the Canal and let Congress debate."

A few months later, Americans took over the remnants of the French project, and in 1904 the first Americans were in Panama. From day one, the work was plagued by the same problems the French met: tropical heat, the jungle, and the mosquitoes. One of the few positive results of America's Cuban experience was the discovery that mosquitoes spread yellow fever, and the disease had been eliminated from Havana during the American occupation. But there were still plenty of people who thought the idea that mosquitoes carried disease was nonsense and they keot U.S. Army doctor William Gorgas, the health officer in Panama, from carrying out a plan of effective mosquito control.

When railroad builder John Stevens came to Panama in 1905 as head of the project, to give the dig the organization it needed, he also gave Dr. Gorgas a free hand to eliminate malaria and yellow fever, a task accomplished with remarkable efficiency, given the circumstances of the environment and lack of scientific appreciation. Unfortunately, Jim Crow also came to Panama. Most of the laborers were blacks from the Caribbean. They were housed and fed separately, and paid in silver, while whites were paid in gold. According to David McCullough's epic account of the creation of the canal, *The Path Between the Seas,* the death rate by accident and disease for blacks was about five times that of whites in Panama.

Without explanation, Stevens left the dig, replaced by army engineer George W. Goethals. Roosevelt put an army man in charge so he couldn't quit as previous administrators had done in the face of the project's overwhelming difficulties. Taking over in 1907 and building on the plan and reorganization left behind by Stevens, Goethals completed the canal ahead of schedule and under budget, despite the challenges the canal posed and the enormous changes the original plan had undergone as work proceeded. More remarkably, according to McCullough, it was completed without suspicion of corruption, graft, kickbacks, or bribery.

First planned under McKinley, aggressively begun by Roosevelt, and carried out by his successor Taft, the Panama Canal was completed in 1914, under Woodrow Wilson. Ironically, the grand plans for a gala opening were canceled. War in Europe was looming, and news of the canal's completion was lost in preparations for the coming hostilities.

What was the "big stick"?

That he would start a revolution to suit his needs came as no surprise to anyone who knew Theodore Roosevelt. His record to that point—as cattle rancher, New York State legislator, Civil Service Commissioner, New York City Police Commissioner, Navy Secretary, soldier, Governor of New York, and then President—had been to act forcefully and leave questions of law, propriety, and good sense for others. His favorite saying, used often in public and private, was an old African proverb: "Speak softly, and carry a big stick; you will go far."

Although he rarely spoke softly himself, he was always ready to use a big stick, abroad and at home. His first chance to use the big stick came when 140,000 mine workers went on strike in May 1902. Underpaid, forced to buy overpriced supplies in company stores and to live in company-owned houses, the miners were kept in perpetual debt and had organized as the United Mine Workers (UMW) under John Mitchell. The mine companies, owned almost exclusively by the railroads (meaning, for the most part, J. P. Morgan), refused to recognize the union or to negotiate. As the work stoppage threatened to cripple an economy largely run on coal power, Roosevelt stepped in and threatened to use troops. But unlike the past, when they had been used as deadly strikebreakers to force workers back into the mines, these troops would operate the mines in the "public interest." With this "big stick" over their heads, the mine owners agreed to accept the ruling of an Arbitration Commission, which ruled favorably for the miners. The victory was more Roosevelt's than the union's, but it allowed the cowboy President to carve another notch on his six-shooter.

Using the strengthened Sherman law, Roosevelt went after other selected targets, subjectively labeled "bad trusts," such as the "beef trust" (*Swift & Co. v. United States*, 1905) and the American Tobacco Company. Roosevelt was hardly a radical; he believed that monopoly was fine as long as it could be regulated, and that there were benevolent trusts, such as International Harvester. But his tenure produced reforms that were significant and long-lasting, such as the strengthening of the Interstate Commerce Commission, the creation of a Cabinet-level Department of Labor and Commerce (later separated into two departments) and the passage of the Pure Food and Drug Act, a law inspired by a bunch of "muckrakers" (see below).

In foreign affairs, Roosevelt was even more willing to wield his big stick, especially in the Caribbean and the Philippines. In 1904 he sent troops into the Dominican Republic, which had reneged on debts to Great Britain. Roosevelt put Americans in charge of Dominican revenues until the debt problem was solved. This was an example of what was called the Roosevelt Corollary, which said the United States had "international police power" to correct wrongs within its "sphere of influence." Though effective, Roosevelt's overbearing treatment of nations he viewed as racially inferior won America no friends in Latin America, which had been reduced to a collection of vassal states.

Ironically, in the wake of policing the Caribbean and overseeing the subjugation of the Philippines, Roosevelt won the Nobel Peace Prize by mediating an end to the Russo-Japanese War in 1905 at Portsmouth, New Hampshire. Divvying up substantial chunks of Asia, the treaty may have created more trouble than it solved. Japan got Korea and guaranteed that it would leave its hands off the Philippines, now in the American "sphere of influence." But the high-handedness of Roosevelt's dealings left a bitter taste in Japanese mouths.

To prove to the Japanese that he meant business, Roosevelt sent forth the big stick in the form of the Great White Fleet. The result of a modernization and overhaul of the navy, this armada of sixteen ships cruised around the world in 1907, an impressive display of American naval power that also pointed up to the navy its shortcomings in being too dependent on foreign supplies at sea.

Who were the "muckrakers"?

"Big stick" was but one of Roosevelt's frequent expressions that became enshrined in the language. Among Presidents, he had a singular ear for a turn of phrase. A voracious reader with an astonishing sense of recall, he could quote at will from a wide range of sources, from African proverbs to obscure military dissertations or, in another famous case, John Bunyan's allegory *Pilgrim's Progress*. In 1907, exasperated by the work of a growing number of journalists who concentrated on exposing graft and corruption, Roosevelt compared them to Bunyan's "man with the Muck-Rake," a character so preoccupied with the filth at his feet that he fails to grasp for the "celestial crown."

The appellation "muckraker" stuck and was happily accepted by a new breed of American journalist best represented by Ida M. Tarbell, Lincoln Steffens, and Upton Sinclair. In newspapers, magazines such as *McClure's* and *The Atlantic Monthly*, and books—both nonfiction and fiction—a generation of writers had begun to attack the widespread abuses that abounded in American business and politics. In a sense, the trend began with Twain and Warner in *The Gilded Age*. But muckraking reached its heights in the early twentieth century. In 1903, *McClure's* began to serialize the articles written by Ida M. Tarbell (1857–1944) about Standard Oil. The result was her landmark investigation of the company, *History of Standard Oil Company*. At the same time, *McClure's* was running a series by Lincoln Steffens (1866–1936) about urban corruption, collected in the book *The Shame of the Cities* (1904). *McClure's* also ran early portions of social reformer Jane Addams's book *Twenty Years at Hull-House*. Addams founded Hull-House as a settlement house to assist immigrants in adjusting to American life, and more than four hundred of these sprung up in cities around America, inspired by Addams's example. At first culturally high-minded, the settlement houses eventually provided basic educational and health care that could not be found elsewhere for hundreds of thousands of immigrants in the sprawling tenements of the inner cities. But Addams and her colleagues were fighting an impossible battle in an era when government assistance to the poor was considered blasphemous and communistic.

In New York, the plight of immigrants also emerged through the reports and photographs of Jacob Riis, himself an immigrant. In his 1890 book, *How the Other Half Lives,* Riis exposed the crime, disease, and squalor of the urban slums.

A new generation of novelists was adapting these journalistic techniques to fiction as well: Stephen Crane in *Maggie, a Girl of the Streets;* William Dean Howells in *The Rise of Silas Lapham;* Frank Norris in *The Octopus.* Perhaps most famous of all was Upton Sinclair's *The Jungle,* a novel that blisteringly exposed the disgusting conditions in the meatpacking industry in Chicago. (Read the book even today, and you will swear off sausage!) Publication of *The Jungle* in 1906 cut American meat sales overnight and immediately forced the industry to accept federal meat inspection as well as passage of the Pure Food and Drug Act. These were the first toddling steps in modern consumerism, and the muckrakers were the ancestors of Ralph Nader, unsparing critics of fraud, abuse, and industrial and political corruption.

American Voices

From *Twenty Years at Hull-House,* by Jane Addams:

> Our very first Christmas at Hull-House, when we as yet knew nothing of child labor, a number of little girls refused the candy which was offered them as part of the Christmas good cheer, saying simply that they "worked in a candy factory and could not bear the sight of it." We discovered that for six weeks they had worked from seven in the morning until nine at night, and they were exhausted as well as satiated. . . .
>
> During the same winter three boys from a Hull-House club were injured at one machine in a neighboring factory for lack of a guard which would have cost but a few dollars. When the injury of one of these boys resulted in his death, we felt quite sure that the owners of the factory would share our

horror and remorse....To our surprise, they did nothing whatever, and I made my first acquaintance then with those pathetic documents signed by the parents of working children, that they will make no claim for damages resulting from "carelessness."

Who were the Wobblies?

The Jungle was more than a muckraking novel. It was the most prominent example of a Socialist novel. Besides being a scathing exposé of meatpacking practices, the book was a call to workers to unite, ending with a utopian vision of a workers' society. In fact, it had first been published in a Socialist newspaper, *Appeal to Reason.* Years of being associated with Soviet and Chinese Communism have permanently tarred Socialism in the American mind as dangerous. But for a period in the early twentieth century it was a growing political force, especially among the working class, who saw it as a way to distribute wealth through government control rather than through private enterprise. Since few workers in America were getting any wealth distributed by the Morgans and Rockefellers, they decided to give Socialism a try.

While the conservative, mainstream AFL stayed away from Socialist ideas, not wanting to be associated with the Bolshevism that was taking over Russia (where 10,000 American troops were involved in a secret war to prevent the Bolshevik revolution during World War I), another union sprang up and proudly unfurled the Socialist banner. It was the Industrial Workers of the World (IWW), and its members became better known, for reasons historically unclear, as the "Wobblies." Unlike the AFL, which was open only to white, skilled craftsmen, the Wobblies were organized to accept all workers into "one big union." At their first meeting, in 1905, were "Big Bill" Haywood (1869–1928), a miner; Eugene V. Debs, leader of the Socialist Party, and Mary Harris "Mother" Jones (1830–1930), a seventy-five-year-old organizer for the United Mine Workers.

The Wobblies' cause flared for about ten years, met with the full force of anti-union violence as its leaders were jailed, beaten, and, in the case of the legendary Joe Hill (1872?–1915), framed and executed, but granted a sort of immortality in the song "I Dreamed I Saw Joe Hill Last Night."

Under Debs, the Socialist Party attracted notable personalities, including Helen Keller, and managed to win as much as 6 percent of the presidential vote until the war intervened and in its wake the first powerful wave of anti-Communism swept the country, all but eradicating Socialism as a force in American politics and life.

Who was W.E.B. Du Bois?

One man who briefly joined the Socialists emerged from this period as the most eloquent and forceful voice for blacks since Frederick Douglass. In stark counterpoint to the accommodating spirit of Booker T. Washington (see pages 216–217), W.E.B Du Bois (1868–1963) became the trumpeter of a new spirit of "manly agitation." The great civil rights upheaval in America was still half a century away, but Du Bois was its John the Baptist, the voice in the wilderness. Born in Massachusetts, he was the first black to receive a Ph.D. from Harvard, in 1895. He taught, lectured, and wrote, his most notable work being the classic *The Souls of Black Folk* (1903). Rejecting Washington's conservative restraint, Du Bois joined in founding the National Association for the Advancement of Colored People (NAACP) in 1909, at that time a white-dominated organization, and became editor of its journal, *The Crisis,* where he served for a quarter-century.

Du Bois left the NAACP in 1934, when he promoted a more radical strategy and returned to teaching. Ten years later he rejoined the NAACP, and in 1945 was one of the Americans in attendance at the founding of the United Nations. Du Bois later joined the Communist party, left America, and renounced his citizenship, moving to Ghana, where he died.

American Voices

W.E.B. Du Bois, from *The Souls of Black Folk* (1903):

> So far as Mr. [Booker T.] Washington preaches thrift, patience, and industrial training for the masses, we must hold

up his hands and strive with him, rejoicing in his honors and glorying in the strength of this Joshua called of God and of man to lead the headless host. But so far as Mr. Washington apologizes for injustices, North or South, does not rightly value the privileges and duty of voting, belittles the emasculating effects of caste distinctions, and opposes the higher training and ambition of our brighter minds—so far as he, the South, or the nation, does this—we must unceasingly and firmly oppose them.

What was the Bull Moose Party?

Though he could have run for another term and probably would have won handily, given his popularity, Teddy Roosevelt accepted the unwritten rule observed since Washington (and unbroken until Teddy's cousin Franklin D. came along). Having served out most of McKinley's unfinished term and his own full term, Roosevelt left a handpicked successor in the White House in William Howard Taft (1857–1930). In 1908, with Roosevelt's blessing and running on the Roosevelt record, Taft easily defeated the unsinkable William Jennings Bryan, who made his third unsuccessful bid for the White House. At the time, a common joke said the name Taft stood for "Take Advice From Teddy."

Roosevelt decided that he would head off for an African safari to stay out of Taft's way. But a year of bagging big game didn't quench Teddy's political hunting instincts. When he came back, he set about to recapture the Republican nomination from Taft, whose star could never shine as brilliantly as Roosevelt's had. Pegged a conservative, Taft had actually brought more antitrust suits than Roosevelt had, including the one that broke up Standard Oil in 1911, and Teddy's backers included a former Morgan banker. But this was to be an election fought to see who appeared most progressive. And it was Roosevelt who projected himself as the champion reformer. After a bloody battle in which Taft recaptured the Republican nomination, Roosevelt led a group of dissatisfied liberal Republicans out of the fold and into the Progressive Party. Claiming at one point that he was "as strong as a bull moose," Roosevelt gave the party its popular name.

The Democrats struggled through forty-six ballots before turning to Woodrow Wilson (1856–1924), then governor of New Jersey, a surprise choice, and, for his times at least, rather liberal. The Democratic Party solidified behind Wilson, especially in the South, where Roosevelt was never forgiven for welcoming Booker T. Washington to the White House. Taft essentially threw in the towel and stayed out of the campaign—later to head the Supreme Court, the job he really always wanted. In spite of an unsuccessful assassination attempt that seemed to confirm his invincibility, Roosevelt campaigned hard, and Wilson's popular vote was less than the combined Taft-Roosevelt vote. (Socialist candidate Eugene V. Debs polled 6 percent of the vote—nearly a million votes, and an indication that the political winds had clearly shifted to the left.) But Wilson's electoral victory was sweeping. Taft won only two states and Roosevelt six. The rest of the country was solidly Democratic behind Wilson. And once again, a third-party candidacy had changed the course of American politics.

Like his opponents, Wilson ran on a progressive reform platform he called the "New Freedom." During his first administration, his legislative success was quite remarkable. Duties on foreign goods, the almost sacred weapon held by big business to keep out foreign competition, were reduced for the first time since the Civil War. The Sixteenth Amendment, imposing an income tax, was ratified. The Seventeenth Amendment, providing for election of U.S. senators by popular direct vote, was ratified. (Previously, U.S. senators had been chosen by state legislatures.) And a Federal Reserve Act gave the country its first central bank since Andrew Jackson's time. In other key reforms, the Federal Trade Commission was created and the Clayton Antitrust Act was passed; both were intended to control unfair and restrictive trade practices, exempting unions and farm groups.

The shame of Wilson's "progressive" administration was his abysmal record on civil rights. Under Wilson, Jim Crow became the policy of the U.S. government, with segregated federal offices, and blacks losing some of the few government jobs they held. Virginian-born, Wilson was a product of the post–Civil War South, and he reflected that mentality to a remarkable extent for a man who seemed so forward-thinking in other respects. But his treatment of blacks was of little concern to a nation that was warily watching the approach of a European war.

Who was Pancho Villa?

Under Woodrow Wilson, America went from "big stick" to "Big Brother" when it came to Latin America. With the nearly completed Panama Canal to defend, Wilson was going to ensure that American power in the hemisphere would not be threatened. Local unrest in the Caribbean left American troops controlling Nicaragua, Haiti, and the Dominican Republic. All were pushovers for American military might. Less simple to deal with was the instability in Mexico that produced Pancho Villa.

Mexico had undergone a series of coups and dictatorships in the early twentieth century, leaving General Victoriano Huerta installed as president in 1911 with the help of the American ambassador and the blessings of foreign investors who only wanted the stability that allowed them to exploit Mexico. But President Wilson refused to recognize Huerta's government, throwing Mexico into more turbulence. Using as a pretext the arrest of some American sailors, Wilson sent the U.S. Navy to invade Vera Cruz in 1914, and Huerta soon abdicated. The door was opened for another general, Venustiano Carranza, and two of his "generals," Emiliano Zapata and Pancho Villa. An illiterate Indian, Zapata made some claims for social reform by giving land to the poor. Villa was simply a bandit who eventually rose against Carranza and seized Mexico City.

In an attempt to undermine Carranza, Villa began to attack the United States. He killed a dozen American passengers aboard a train in northern Mexico, and then began to make raids across the border into New Mexico, murdering a group of American mining engineers. An outraged Wilson sent General John J. Pershing (1860–1948) into Mexico in pursuit of Villa. But chasing the wily outlaw general was like trying to catch the wind. Villa led the American troops deeper into Mexican territory on a nine-month fox hunt that only served to alarm Carranza, raising tensions between America and Mexico.

With involvement in Europe's war growing more likely, Wilson relented and recalled Pershing from Mexico in 1917. Within a few years, Villa, Zapata, and Carranza were all dead by assassination in the turbulent world of Mexican politics, a world that was being drawn in by the powerful pull of European war.

How did a dead archduke in Sarajevo get America into a World War?

On June 28, 1914, Archduke Francis Ferdinand, heir to the Austrian throne, was in the city of Sarajevo (in modern Yugoslavia), then part of the Austro-Hungarian empire. A group of young student nationalists who wanted to join independent Serbia to Austria's south plotted to kill the Archduke. One of them, Gavrilo Princip, shot the Archduke in his automobile. Within days the Austrian Empire declared war on Serbia, Austria's tiny neighbor to the south, claiming it was responsible for the assassination. Allied to Serbia, Russia mobilized its troops. Austria's ally Germany responded by declaring war on Russia and its ally, France. Also bound by defense treaties, Great Britain declared war on Germany as German troops began an invasion of Belgium on their way to France.

Ferdinand's death was merely the spark that ignited a short fuse that exploded into what was then called "the Great War," and only later, at the time of the Second World War, became known as World War I. Another way to put it is that the assassination was a final piece in a Rube Goldberg contraption, a crazy scheme of interlocking parts that finally sent Europe reeling into a war that covered most of the globe.

On the eve of war, Europe was more in the nineteenth century than the twentieth. The German Empire had been consolidated into the continent's leading power during the late nineteenth century by the "Iron Chancellor" Bismarck, and was linked to the Austrian Empire through aristocratic bloodlines and military alliance. Together they constituted the "Central Powers" in Europe and were also allied to the Ottoman Empire, which controlled much of the modern Middle East. The German Empire had been partly built at French expense after Germany won a war in 1870 that humiliated France and gave Germany the rich territories of Alsace and Lorraine. Resentment over this loss and surrender of French territory had never subsided between the two nations, and France, in the wake of its disastrous defeat at Germany's hands, had rearmed heavily, reorganized its armies, and become an intensely militarized nation with plans to eventually retake the steel-producing region it considered its property.

Thrown into this simmering stew of alliances was the coming revolution in Russia. Tsarist Russia was tied to England and France through mutual defense treaties and bloodlines (the King of England and the Tsar were relatives). The threat of a Socialist revolution pledged to destroy the monarchy on its eastern borders pressed on Kaiser Wilhelm, Germany's autocratic young leader who had dismissed Bismarck as Chancellor.

As tensions heightened, all these nations had armed to heavily producing a state of military readiness that did wonders for the armament industry, and the huge munitions makers of Europe happily kept the cauldron bubbling. International tension was good for profits. But whenever countries feel so well armed, they believe themselves invincible—and that was the case in the major European capitals. The urge to use such might acquires a life of its own. Fierce nationalism, visions of invincibility, complicated alliances, and antagonism from an earlier century were combining to suck Europe into a violent maelstrom. Again, as throughout history, personalities determined the course of events as much as did economics or border disputes. Cooler heads and gentlemanly diplomacy were lost to nineteenth-century ideals of honor and country in a new century in which people didn't know how powerful their destructive powers had become. Perhaps the men raised in the nineteenth century on chivalrous, aristocratic ideals and wars still fought on horseback had no idea what havoc their twentieth-century arsenals could wreak. The world of sabers and cavalry charges was giving way to such inventions as mustard gas, U-boats, and the flamethrower (perfected by Germany), the tank (developed by the British), and a new generation of hand grenades and water-cooled machine guns. When these modern tools failed, the ancient bayonet would be the weapon of last resort. The carnage was unbelievable in battles that have become legend.

Marne. Ypres. Gallipoli. Verdun. Argonne Forest. Soon these fields and plains sprouted forests of crosses.

The scenes of battle were played out for the most part in Europe, especially on the flat plains in Belgium and France, where the inhuman trench warfare would eat bodies as a flame consumes dry wood. But the real prize was elsewhere. The bottom line was that the nations of Europe were fighting over the course of empire. The spoils of victory in this Great War were Africa, Asia, and the Middle East. Whatever the professed reasons for going to war, it was the material wealth—the gold and diamonds of South Africa, the metals and rubber of Africa, the rubber of Malaysia, the oil of the Mideast—that was at the heart of the conflict.

By the time the Archduke lay dead in Sarajevo, the competition had long since commenced. Germany was a well established power in Africa, as was Belgium. France's empire extended into Indochina. England's empire covered much of Asia, Africa, and the Far East. British armies had already been bloodied in the Boer War for control of South Africa and in the Crimean War for control of the Middle East, where England had also taken over the Suez Canal. Supreme on the oceans, England was now threatened by a German Navy that was being built with only one conceivable purpose—to challenge that British supremacy for eventual control of the wealth of the Empire. The leaders of Europe knew their own national resources were exhaustible. Power, even survival, in the new age of industry and mechanization would come from contol of these resources in the colonial worlds. The dead might pile up at Verdun, Ypres, the Marne, and a dozen other storied battlefields, but to the victor would go the riches of other continents.

Who sank the *Lusitania* and what difference did it make?

For generations of American schoolchildren, the reason America finally decided to enter the war in Europe was to protect the open seas from German raiders in their U-boats who were killing innocent Americans aboard passenger ships. The most notorious example of this practice was supposedly the sinking of the passenger ship *Lusitania*. The problem with this explanation is that it has little to do with the facts.

Secure in its control of two continents and holding on to sufficient bits of an empire in Asia and the Pacific, America was wary of involving itself in Europe's war. Avoiding "entangling alliances" had been the underpinning of American foreign policy since the days of Washington and Jefferson. Neutralism and isolationism were powerful forces in America, where a good deal of the population was descended from the countries now at each other's throats in the mud of France. Eight million German-Americans had no desire to see America at war with Germany. Another 4.5 million Irish-Americans held no love for Great Britain, then in the midst of tightening its grip on Ireland as the Irish Republican movement was reaching its peak.

Early in May 1915, the German Embassy in Washington published advertisements in American papers warning Americans to avoid sailing on British ships in the Atlantic. On May 7, 1915, the Cunard liner *Lusitania* was torpedoed by a German U-boat off the coast of Ireland. In only eighteen minutes the huge ship went down, taking with it almost 1,200 of its 1,959 passengers and crew. Among the dead were 128 Americans.

President Wilson resisted the indignant clamor for war that followed the sinking, and dealt with the Germans through a series of diplomatic notes demanding reparations and German disavowal of passenger-ship attacks. William Jennings Bryan, the American Secretary of State, thought even these notes were too severe a response, and resigned. Although the German government agreed to make reparations, it held to its claim that the *Lusitania* was carrying armaments and thus was a war vessel. The British denied this, but it was later revealed that the *Lusitania* carried 4,200 cases of ammunition and 1,250 shrapnel cases, which exploded when the torpedo struck, speeding the *Lusitania*'s demise.

While the sinking definitely increased tension between America and Germany, the incident had little to do with drawing America into the war. President Wilson continued to press his policies of neutrality while seeking to negotiate a settlement. He campaigned for reelection in 1916 under the Democratic slogan

"He Kept Us out of War." It would be April 1917, almost two years after the sinking, before America entered the war, already in its closing stages.

The stated reasons for America's involvement were freedom of the seas and the preservation of democracy. But neither side in this war had a monopoly on illegal naval warfare. Nor was the democratic ideology so powerful among America's allies that Wilson thought he should fight to maintain it as far back as 1914.

In his favor, Wilson tried admirably to restrain both sides and mediate a peace. But as in almost every other war America has fought, powerful forces in industry, banking, and commerce cynically thought that war was healthy. And if the world was going to be divvied up after the fighting was over, America might as well gets its fair share of the spoils.

Milestones in World War I

1914

June 28 The Crown Prince of Austria, Archduke Francis Ferdinand, is murdered in the city of Sarajevo by Gavril Princips. Using the assassination as a pretext, the Austro-Hungarian government declares war on Serbia, its tiny southern neighbor, five days later. Russia begins to mobilize its troops in defense of Serbia.

August 1 Allied to Austria, Germany declares war on Russia. Two days later, Germany declares war on France.

August 4 Bound by mutual defense treaties, Great Britain declares war on Germany as German troops invade Belgium on the way to France.

August 5 The United States formally declares its neutrality and offers to mediate the growing conflict. In America, opinions are divided three ways: neutralists want to stay out of the war; pro-Allies (France, England, Belgium, Russia) press for aid for England, France, and Belgium, who are depicted as victims of barbarous German aggression and atrocities; and pro-Germans—mostly German-Americans—who want the United States to avoid taking sides. Pro-Allies form the Lafayette Escadrille to join the French Air Force, while other Americans join the British Army and the French Foreign Legion or, like Ernest Hemingway, become ambulance drivers. Irish-Americans denounce any assistance to Great Britain.

August 6 Germany's Central Powers ally, Austria-Hungary, declares war on Russia.

August 23 Japan declares war on Germany.

September 5 The Battle of the Marne. In the first horrific battle of the war, with each side taking casualties of 500,000, a French-English repulse of the German invasion stalls Germany's plan to quickly subdue continental Europe before Allied forces can fully mobilize. Instead, German forces fall back, beginning three years of devastating, stalemated trench warfare. The defeat also forces Germany to step up its U-boat *(Unterseeboot)* warfare to counter British naval superiority, which threatens to cut Germany off from essential war supplies. Although the German U-boats initially concentrate their attacks on warships, the submarines eventually turn to commercial and passenger shipping, a strategy that will ultimately give the United States its justification to join the Allied side.

1915

January 28 The *William P. Frye*, an American merchant ship carrying wheat to England, is torpedoed by a U-boat, the first such attack against American commercial shipping.

January 30 Colonel Edward M. House (1858–1938), a Texan who was responsible for Wilson's nomination and is now the President's most powerful adviser, sails to Europe to attempt to mediate a peace agreement. Each side feels that a quick victory is possible, and all parties decline to negotiate.

February 4 Germany declares the waters around the British Isles a war zone, threatening all shipping that approaches England.

May 1 The American tanker *Gulflight* is sunk by a German U-boat. Germany apologizes, but the ocean war is escalating as the British call for a blockade of all German ports, despite President Wilson's protest.

May 7 The British ocean liner *Lusitania* is sunk by a U-boat. Germany claims—reliably, it turns out—that the liner carried munitions; the British deny this. Nearly 1,200 of the 1,900 passengers aboard die; 128 of them are Americans who had disregarded the warnings published by Germany in American newspapers to avoid passage on vessels carrying wartime cargoes. A diplomatic crisis follows, as Germany refuses to pay reparations or disavow the attack. Secretary of State William Jennings Bryan, a pacifist, resigns in protest over what he deems a tilt toward England in Wilson's reaction to the *Lusitania*'s sinking. In a series of notes to Germany, Wilson warns against infringement of American rights. Although the sinking of the *Lusitania* has come down in history as one of the reasons the U.S. joined the war, the actual impact of the sinking was slight, and it would be almost two full years before America committed itself to war.

July 2 A German professor at Cornell University explodes a bomb in the U.S. Senate and shoots J. P. Morgan the next day. The captured professor commits suicide. A few days later, the head of German propaganda in the United States leaves on a New York subway a suitcase filled with information about the existence of a German spy ring. It is found by the Secret Service and released to the press, further arousing anti-German sentiment.

July 25 The American merchant ship *Leelanaw*, carrying flax, is sunk off the coast of Scotland by a U-boat.

August 10 General Leonard Wood of Rough Rider fame establishes the first of several private military camps that will train 16,000 "unofficial" soldiers by 1916.

November 7 Twenty-seven Americans die in an Austrian submarine attack on the Italian liner *Ancona*.

December 7 President Wilson requests a standing army of 142,000 and reserves of 400,000.

1916

January 7 Responding to American pressure, Germany pledges to abide by international rules of naval warfare.

February 2 A congressional resolution warns Americans to avoid travel on ships owned by the warring nations. In response, President Wilson declares that American rights must be protected.

March 15 The Army Reorganization Act is passed by Congress. Under this measure, the army will be brought to a strength of 175,000 and the National Guard to 450,000 by the end of June.

March 24 Three more Americans die when a French ship is torpedoed in the English Channel, and public sympathies turn increasingly in favor of the Allied cause and against Germany.

April 20 The Easter Uprising begins. Organized with German assistance, the Irish Rebellion is supposed to create a diversionary revolution in Ireland to distract Great Britain from the war in Europe. On Good Friday, April 21, a German ship delivering arms to Ireland and a German U-boat carrying Sir Roger Casement to lead the uprising are both captured by the British, who have discovered the plan through their intelligence reports. On Easter Monday, April 24, the Citizen's Army strikes in Dublin without Casement's leadership or the expected weapons, and takes over several buildings. A few days later, British troops recapture Dublin and put down the rebellion. Casement is quickly tried and hanged, as are fifteen of the rebels from Dublin. Seen as harsh "tyranny," the executions are a severe blow to British prestige in America, while the German complicity is overlooked. American sentiment for England falls to its wartime low.

June 16 Wilson is renominated by the Democrats under the slogan "He Kept Us out of War," all the while preparing the nation for entrance into the war on the Allied side. Running on a platform of "Peace and Preparedness," he is nearly defeated by Charles Evans Hughes, a Supreme Court justice and former governor of New York who has the bellicose Teddy Roosevelt's still-influential support. It takes a week after election day to confirm that Wilson has carried California, where Hughes inadvertently snubbed the popular Republican governor, who then failed to campaign for him; this gaffe may have cost Hughes the state and the White House. By a thin popular and electoral margin, Wilson wins a second term. The East is solidly Republican, but the Democrat Wilson keeps the South and West. As a referendum on war policy, the election makes it clear that Americans want to stay out of the conflict. A few weeks after the election, Wilson asks the warring powers for their conditions for peace.

1917

January 22 In a speech to Congress, Wilson calls for a league of peace, an organization to promote the resolution of conflicts. But neither side is willing to agree to negotiations while holding on to the prospect of victory.

January 31 Having rapidly built its submarine fleet to over one hundred boats, Germany resumes unrestricted submarine warfare, believing it can starve the Allies into submission in six months.

February 3 Citing the German decision, Wilson breaks diplomatic relations with Germany.

February 24 In what will become known as the "Zimmerman telegram" incident, the British Secret Service has intercepted a telegram from German Foreign Minister Arthur Zimmermann to the German Ambassador in Mexico, attempting to incite Mexico to join Germany's side in the event of war with the United States. In return, Germany promises to help Mexico recover Texas, New Mexico, and Arizona. The British have held the note until an appropriate moment when its revelations will presumably push Wilson over the brink of his wavering neutrality and into war. After the telegram is released, there is an angry public outcry over what is considered German treachery.

February 26 After asking Congress for permission to arm merchant ships, Wilson is told by his Attorney General that he has that power. He issues the directive on March 9.

March 15 The Tsar of Russia is forced to abdicate after the Russian Revolution. The U.S. government recognizes the new government formed by Aleksandr Kerensky.

March 12–21 Five more American ships are sunk, all without warning.

April 2 Wilson asks Congress to declare war on Germany.

American Voices

Wilson's War Request to Congress:

It is a fearful thing to lead this great peaceful people into war, into the most terrible and disastrous of all wars, civilization itself seeming to be in the balance. But the right is more precious than peace, and we shall fight for the things which we have carried nearest our hearts—for democracy, for the right of those who submit to authority to have a voice in their own Governments, for the rights and liberties of small nations, for a universal dominion of right by such a concert of free people as shall bring peace and safety to all nations and make the world itself at least free.

Wilson's speech was met with wild applause and Congress overwhelmingly approved war a few days later. After delivering the speech, Wilson told an aide, "My message today was a message of death for our young men. How strange it seems to applaud that."

One of the only dissenting voices in Congress is that of Nebraska Senator George W. Norris, who speaks against the declaration of war, voicing the view of the war's opponents that it is a fight for profits rather than for principles. Quoting from a letter written by a member of the New York Stock Exchange favoring the war and the bull market it would produce, Norris denounces the Wall Street view:

Here we have the man representing the class of people who will be made prosperous should we become entangled in the present war, who have already made millions of dollars, and who will make many hundreds of millions more if we get into the war. Here we have the cold-blooded proposition that war brings prosperity. . . . Wall Street . . . see[s] only dollars coming to them through the handling of stocks and bonds that will be necessary in case of war.

    Their object in having war and in preparing for war is to make money. Human suffering and sacrifice of human life are necessary, but Wall Street considers only the dollars and the cents. . . . The stock brokers would not, of course, go to war. . . . They will be concealed in their palatial offices on Wall Street, sitting behind mahogany desks. . . .

May 18 The Selective Service Act is passed, authorizing the registration and drafting of males between 21 and 30. (The Supreme Court upholds the government's right of conscription in January 1918 under the constitutional power to declare war and raise and support armies.) General John J. Pershing will lead the first contingent of Americans, the American Expeditionary Force, to France on June 24. The Rainbow Division, under Colonel Douglas MacArthur, will reach Europe on November 30.

June The Espionage Act is passed by Congress, ostensibly to prevent spying. However, it is used chiefly to silence American critics of the war. A year after its passage, Eugene Debs, the Socialist leader and presidential candidate, is arrested and sentenced to ten years in prison for making a speech that "obstructed recruiting." Debs actually ran for President again in 1920 from prison, and was eventually pardoned by President Harding after serving thirty-two months.

July 4 The first military training field for airmen opens. At the outset of war the army has fifty-five planes; by war's end there were nearly 17,000 planes in service.

November 6 The Kerensky government is overthrown by the Bolsheviks, who make peace with Germany in March 1918. The United States denies recognition of the new government.

December 7 The United States declares war on Austria-Hungary.

1918

January 8 Wilson's "Fourteen Points" for peace speech. The speech outlines a generous and liberal attempt to settle the war. The last of the points states, "A general association of nations must be formed under specific covenants for the purpose of affording mutual guarantees of political independence and territorial integrity to great and small states alike." (This point will form the nucleus of the League of Nations.) Allied reaction is tepid. French Prime Minister Clemenceau says the Fourteen Points "bore him," and adds, "Even Almighty God has only ten."

March 21 Attempting a final concentrated assault before U.S. forces are fully involved, German troops mass for an offensive on the Western Front. Their Eastern Front is safe after the November treaty with the Bolsheviks and the collapse of the Italian forces. After an initial thrust, the Germans force the Allied lines back forty miles.

April 14 Named commander of Allied forces, French General Ferdinand Foch pleads for more troops, and 313,000 soldiers arrive by July.

June 25 After two weeks of fighting, a U.S. Marine brigade captures Belleau Wood. Casualties are nearly 9,500, more than half the brigade's entire strength.

July 17 The Allies halt the German drive in the second Battle of the Marne. A German offensive is repulsed, and an Allied counteroffensive at Soissons turns the tide.

August Ten thousand American troops join in a Japanese invasion of Russian territory, occupying Vladivostok and some of Siberia. American troops become involved in the internal fighting as they join "White Russians" in the fighting against the Bolsheviks, and more than five hundred Americans die fighting in Russia.

August 10 General Pershing establishes an independent American Army with Allied permission. Colonel George C. Marshall is made operations officer.

September 14 American forces under Pershing take the salient at Saint-Mihiel.

September 26 More than one million Allied troops, including 896,000 Americans, join for an offensive in the last major battle of the war. Casualties reach 120,000. At the same time, British forces farther north crack the German line of defense, the Hindenburg Line.

October 3 Germany forms a parliamentary government as the army collapses and the navy revolts. The Kaiser abdicates, and Germany begins peace overtures based on Wilson's Fourteen Points.

October 30 Austria asks Italy for an armistice and surrenders on November 4.

November 11 Germany signs an armistice treaty at 5:00 A.M., and six hours later, at the "eleventh hour of the eleventh day of the eleventh month," fighting ends.

1919

June 28 The Treaty of Versailles is signed, under which Germany is required to admit guilt, return the rich Alsace-Lorraine region to France, surrender her overseas colonies, and pay reparations that total $32 billion—reparations that won't be collected. (Germany spent more than $100 billion to finance the war.) Under the treaty, German rearmament is strictly limited, and the Allies take temporary control of the German economy. The League of Nations is accepted by all signatories, but a Republican-controlled U.S. Senate, left out of the treaty negotiations by Wilson, refuses to ratify the treaty. Without American participation, the League of Nations is doomed to pointlessness.

September 25 On a cross-country tour to promote popular support for the Treaty of Versailles and the League of Nations, President Wilson suffers a stroke in Colorado. Only a few insiders are allowed to see him, including Wilson's wife, Edith (who literally makes presidential decisions during his recovery), his doctor, his secretary, and Bernard Baruch. Wilson should have turned over the reins of government to his Vice-President, but doesn't. By November 1, he is sufficiently recovered to appear in control once more. During his absence, the Senate has hardened against the treaty and refuses to ratify it.

What was the cost of World War I?

The cost of the "war to end all wars" was nightmarish. Some ten million died on the battlefields of Europe. Almost an entire generation of young men was decimated in Russia and France. The Russian combat death toll was 1,700,000; 1,357,000 French soldiers died, and 908,000 British. On the Central Powers side, German dead numbered 1,800,000; Austrians 1,200,000; and 325,000 Turks died in combat. Those were the dead fighters—another 20 million people died of disease, hunger, and other war-related causes. Six million more were left crippled. American losses for its short-term involvement in the war were 130,174 dead and missing and more than 200,000 wounded. The American wartime bill totaled around $32 billion.

Given these losses, the Allies were not in a forgiving mood, and the Versailles Treaty showed that they expected Germany to pay for the war that everyone had helped to start. But far more dangerous than the impossible economic terms demanded of Germany, Austria, and Turkey under the postwar settlements was the reshaping of the world map. Hungary, once part of a huge empire, lost two-thirds of its lands and was reduced to fewer than eight million people. The independent states of Yugoslavia, Czechoslovakia, and Poland, with a corridor to the Baltic, were arbitrarily carved out of former Austro-Hungarian and German territory. Almost three million Austro-Germans were incorporated into Czechoslovakia. They were known as Sudeten Germans, and that name would loom large a few years later when a rebuilt Germany decided to annex the Sudetenland. The other half of the former empire became tiny Austria. And in 1939, it too would become part of the rationale for Germany's aggression.

The lands of the Middle East that had been the Ottoman Empire (Turkey) were split among the winners, leaving Turkey a small, impoverished state. The British took Palestine, Jordan, and oil-rich Mesopotamia (modern Iraq). France won Lebanon and Syria. The German possessions in Africa were similarly divided among the victors under a League of Nations "mandate" that simply transferred control of these African lands to new colonial powers.

In all of these postwar dealings, the seeds were being sown for the next war.

Chapter Six

Boom to Bust to Big Boom: From the Jazz Age and the Great Depression to Hiroshima

- Why were Sacco and Vanzetti executed and made martyrs for a generation of leftists?

- Why was Prohibition one of the greatest social and political disasters in American history?

- Who were the suffragists?

- What was the scandal over Teapot Dome?

- Did Henry Ford invent the automobile?

- What was so "lucky" about "Lucky Lindy"?

- Why did investors panic in 1929, leading to the Great Crash?

- What was so "great" about the Great Depression?

- What was the Bonus Army?

• What were the New Deal and the Hundred Days?

• What was the WPA?

• Why did Franklin D. Roosevelt try to "pack" the Supreme Court?

• What happened to Amelia Earhart?

• What was Lend-Lease?

• Who were the Fascists?

• What did FDR know about a Japanese attack, and when did he know it?

• Milestones in World War II

• What was the cost of World War II?

• What was the Yalta Conference?

• How did FDR die?

• Did the United States have to drop atomic bombs on Hiroshima and Nagasaki?

The Great War was over. Disillusioned and shocked by its frightful toll, Americans retreated to the safe shell of prewar isolationism. The country wanted to get back to business. That meant putting Republicans back in the White House. Starting in 1921, a Republican held the presidency for the next twelve years. First was Warren G. Harding (1865–1923), who campaigned on the promise of a "return to normalcy." Elected in 1920, the highlights of his weak administration were the loud whispers of presidential philandering and the infamous "Teapot Dome" scandal of 1922.

In the midst of that scandal, Harding died and was replaced by Calvin Coolidge (1872–1933), best remembered for his pronouncement that "the business of America is business." Known as "Silent Cal," he also said, "The man who builds a factory builds a temple. And the man who works there worships there."

Under Coolidge, America seemed to prosper during the "Roaring Twenties," a period in which the booming stock market was the centerpiece of a roaring economy. This was the exuberant era in which convention and old-fashioned morality were tossed aside—in spite of Prohibition—in favor of the freewheeling spirit of the "Jazz Age," the days of wild new dances like the Charleston, of hip flasks and of women shucking Victorian undergarments and donning short skirts. It was the period that provided the inspiration for the fiction of F. Scott Fitzgerald, including the great representative character of the era, Jay Gatsby. The disillusionment with war and society also brought forth angry new literary voices like those of John Dos Passos (1896–1970), author of the World War I novel *Three Soldiers* (1921), and Ernest Hemingway (1899–1961), whose first novel was *The Sun Also Rises* (1926). Also bucking the conventions of the day were the acerbic journalist H. L. Mencken (1880–1956), whose writings skewered what he called the "booboisie," the complacent middle-class puritanical Americans who were also the target of Sinclair Lewis (1885–1951) in such books as *Main Street* (1920), *Babbitt* (1922), *Arrowsmith* (1925), and his great novel of religious hypocrisy, *Elmer Gantry* (1927), a body of work that brought Lewis the 1930 Nobel Prize, a first for an American author.

But the self-satisfied America targeted by these writers was very happy with the ways things were, thank you. A new industry in a far-off patch of California called Hollywood was producing a diversion that took America's mind off its troubles, which seemed to be few in the twenties. By 1927, a Jewish singer in blackface named Al Jolson told the country, "You ain't seen nothing yet," in the first "talkie," *The Jazz Singer,* and Hollywood was soon mounting multimillion-dollar productions to meet an insatiable demand for movies.

Seemingly contented with its wealth and diversions, America stayed the course in 1928 by electing Calvin Coolidge's Commerce Secretary, Herbert Hoover (1874–1964). An international hero as the World War I Food Administrator praised for keeping Europe from starving, Hoover's reputation as a brilliant manager faded fast. He was cursed with overseeing the greatest economic collapse in history.

In the midst of the worldwide economic collapse, Hoover was dropped in 1932 in favor of the governor of New York, Franklin D. Roosevelt (1882–1945), already crippled by polio but elected overwhelmingly by a nation that desperately wanted a new direction. The economic crisis was met in America by Roosevelt's progressivism and the "New Deal." Overseas, there were different responses. As the answer to their woes, Germany turned to Hitler and Italy to Mussolini. By the middle of the depressed thirties, the war that was not supposed to be was on the horizon.

American Voices

"Returning Soldiers" by W. E. B. Du Bois (May, 1919):

We return.
We return from fighting.
We return fighting.

Why were Sacco and Vanzetti executed and made martyrs for a generation of leftists?

Nicola Sacco and Bartolomeo Vanzetti had three strikes against them. They were Italian. They were immigrants. And they were anarchists. In 1920, those traits won no popularity contests in America.

When a payroll holdup at a shoe factory in Braintree, Massachusetts, left two men dead, an eyewitness said that two of the robbers "looked Italian." On the strength of that, Sacco and Vanzetti, known anarchists, were arrested. They were carrying guns at the time of their arrest. A few weeks earlier, another Italian anarchist had died when he "jumped" from the fourteenth floor of a building where he was in police custody. Sacco and Vanzetti were quickly tried by a judge whose mind was already made up about what he called "those anarchist bastards." The two men became darlings of the intellectual and leftist world. They eventually became martyrs. (Years later, FBI files and ballistics reports showed that Sacco was probably guilty and Vanzetti probably innocent.)

Guilty or not, the pair died because the country was in a frenzied, lynch-mob mood created by President Wilson's Attorney General, A. Mitchell Palmer (1872–1936). After a bomb exploded outside his home in 1919, Palmer unleashed a hysterical "Red Scare" that was the equal of the more infamous McCarthy era some thirty years later. Palmer was riding the nation's case of postwar jitters, a ride that he thought might take him all the way to the White House. To most Americans in 1919, the world had been turned upside down. The country went through a bout of economic dislocation of the sort that typically follows a high-powered wartime economy. Inflation was high and unemployment rose, bringing a new era of labor unrest. But it wasn't a good time for unions. During the war, the Wobblies (see pages 231–232) had been broken by the government. Wobbly leader Bill Haywood skipped bail and fled to revolutionary Russia, where he later died.

Progressivism and reform were one thing. Communism was another. The Communists had taken over in Russia. Anything faintly tainted by socialism was presumed dangerous. To many Americans, anything faintly *foreign* was dangerous. Anarchism had nothing to do with Communism, but both were lumped together in the press and in the popular mind. Most immigrants were neither Communists nor anarchists, but they were so *different*. Under Palmer, mass arrests and deportations followed. In August 1919, Palmer created the General Intelligence Division and appointed a supercharged anti-Communist named J. Edgar Hoover (1895–1972) to lead it. Most of the mass arrests led to nothing. But 556 people were deported, including the anarchists Emma Goldman and Alexander Berkman, who were sent to the Soviet Union.

With official America on the warpath against "foreign influences," private America joined the hunt. The Ku Klux Klan revived once more, with a vengeance. The economic dislocation following the war gave the Klan its opening. New leadership gave it a respectability it had lacked before. But its violence was as deadly as ever. While blacks remained the chief targets of Klan enom, the new message of hate spread to include Jews, Catholics, and foreigners. By 1924 the "new" Klan claimed between four and five million members, not limited to the South. In 1923, Oklahoma's governor, J. C. Walton, declared martial law because he feared that the Klan was creating a state of insurrection. The largest Klan rally in American history was held in Chicago. The pace of lynchings, which had slackened during the war years, was revived with vicious frenzy. In a harbinger of the race riots of the sixties, violence broke out in a number of cities such as East St. Louis, Houston, Philadelphia, Washington, and Chicago, resulting in hundreds of deaths and injuries between 1917 and 1919.

Reflecting the great fear of people and things foreign, and the retreat from Europe's affairs, Congress put the brakes on immigration. In 1921 a tight quota system began to limit immigration sharply. In 1924 the quotas were further reduced, and by 1929 the total number of immigrants allowed to enter the United States was lowered to 150,000. Most of these were white Anglo-Saxons from Great Britain.

The "huddled masses yearning to breathe free" would have to hold their breath and huddle a little longer.

Why was Prohibition one of the greatest social and political disasters in American history?

Nowadays, the night belongs to Michelob. Football stadiums ring with the chant "LESS FILLING! TASTES GREAT!" Budweiser comes wrapped in images of the workingman and the American flag. And attempts to limit beer sales at ballgames are shot down as un-American. From the late-twentieth-century perspective, it is hard to imagine that this is the same country that once outlawed alcohol.

America has always had a love affair with simple solutions to complex problems. Indians on good land? Move 'em out. You want Texas? Start a war with Mexico. Crime problem? Bring back the death penalty. Prayer in schools will solve the moral lapse of the nation. Busing schoolchildren will end racial segregation. It always seems so simple when politicians proclaim them, masses take up the cry and laws are passed with an outpouring of irresist-

ible popular support. The problem is that these broad solution
rarely work the way they are supposed to.

America's grandest attempt at a simple solution was also it
biggest failure. The constitutional amendment halting drinking in
America was supposed to be an answer to social instability and
moral decline at the beginning of the twentieth century. It should
stand forever as a massive memorial to the fact that complex
problems demand complex responses, and that Americans ball
whenever somebody tries to legislate their private morality and
personal habits.

Proposed by Congress during World War I, the Eighteenth
Amendment to the Constitution prohibited "the manufacture
sale, or transportation of intoxicating liquors" within the United
States. It also cut off the import and export of beer, wine, and
hard liquor. In January 1919 the amendment became part of the
Constitution when Nebraska voted in favor of ratification—only
Rhode Island and Connecticut failed to ratify the amendment—
and a year later it became the law of the land, when Congress
passed the Volstead Act to enforce the law.

To President Herbert Hoover, it was "a great social and
economic experiment, noble in motive and far-reaching in purpose." To Mark Twain, Prohibition drove "drunkenness behind
doors and into dark places, and [did] not cure it or even diminish
it."

Prohibition didn't just spring up as some wartime cure-all for
the nation's social ills. The Prohibition spirit had been alive in
America since colonial times, but was greatly revived in the
nineteenth century, especially in the West, where drunkenness
and immorality became inseparably linked. It was there that primarily women waged war on "demon rum" and, though they
lacked the vote, first demonstrated the political clout they carried.
The temperance movement was strongest in Midwestern and
western states in the years after the Civil War. As the primary
victims of social and economic ills spawned by alcoholism, women
held prayer vigils in the streets outside the many saloons that had
sprung up in the cattle era, then moved to grassroots organizing.
In 1874 the Women's Christian Temperance Union (WCTU)

came together to fight alcohol, becoming the first broad-based national women's organization in America.

By the turn of the century, the temperance gang lost its temper, led by the militancy of Carrie Nation (1846–1911). Striding into the saloons of Kansas with an ax and shouting, "Smash, women, smash!" Nation and her followers reduced bars, bottles, glasses, mirrors, tables, and everything else in their path to splinters and shards of glass.

The sense of dislocation left after the war, the desire for "normalcy," the fear that emerged in Red Scares and Ku Klux Klan revivals all helped pave the way for the Eighteenth Amendment. Prohibition was a notable example of the American predilection for living by one set of standards and publicly proclaiming another. In public, politicians wanted to be seen as upholding the Calvinist-Protestant ethic. Privately, most Americans consumed some alcohol before Prohibition and continued to do so afterward.

Once in place, Prohibition proved virtually unenforceable. "Bootlegger," "rum runner," and "moonshine" became part of the language. For the rich, there were "speakeasies," the ostensibly private clubs, requiring a codeword entry, that often operated under the watchful eye of the corner cop. For the poor, there was bathtub gin. Pharmacists wrote prescriptions for "medicinal" doses of alcohol, and more Catholics must have gone to mass, because production of legal sacramental wine increased by hundreds of thousands of gallons.

Some historians claim that Prohibition had some beneficial effects: alcoholism decreased and, with it, alcohol-related deaths; wages weren't being spent on alcohol; and organized crime existed before Prohibition. That is a terminal case of Pollyana thinking. It overlooks the increased fatalities from the deadly use of rubbing alcohol in "bathtub gin." It also ignores the death toll and cost of the rise of organized crime, which may have existed before Prohibition but gained its stranglehold by controlling most of the smuggling and distribution of illicit liquor—this was the heyday of Al Capone (1898–1947) in Chicago.

Few who wanted to drink were prevented. As an attempt to

restore morality, Prohibition probably produced the opposite effect. The willingness to break the law contributed to a wider decline in moral standards. Official corruption, its prevalence reduced since the earlier days of reformers and muckrakers, skyrocketed as organized crime spent millions in payoffs to government officials, from cops on the beat paid to keep a benevolent eye on the local speakeasy, to senators, judges, mayors, and governors on the criminal payroll.

While the "dry" West may have stayed sober and decent, the cities entered F. Scott Fitzgerald's "Jazz Age" under Prohibition. These were the "Roaring Twenties," the era of the hip flask filled with smuggled gin, of the "rumble seat" and the "flapper." This was the "new woman" of the twenties. With her bobbed hair, short dresses, and exotic dances, the modern woman had two other things her mother lacked. The first was birth control, in the form of diaphragms introduced through the efforts of Margaret Sanger (1883–1966), who was arrested for "distributing obscene materials" from her New York clinic. Far from being widely available, the new method of contraception nonetheless brought the subject into the open for the first time in America.

The second was the vote.

American Voices

From *The Great Gatsby* (1925), by F. Scott Fitzgerald (1896–1940):

> "Who are you, anyhow?" broke out Tom. "You're one of that bunch that hangs around with Meyer Wolfsheim—that much I happen to know. I've made a little investigation into your affairs—and I'll carry it further to-morrow."
>
> "I found out what your 'drug-stores' were." He turned to us and spoke rapidly. "He and this Wolfsheim bought up a lot of side-street drug-stores here and in Chicago and sold grain alcohol over the counter. That's one of his little stunts. I picked him for a bootlegger the first time I saw him, and I wasn't far wrong."

Who were the suffragists?

Women in America always endured plenty of suffering. What they lacked was "suffrage" (from the Latin *suffragium* for "vote").

American women as far back as Abigail Adams—who admonished her husband John to "Remember the Ladies" when he went off to declare Independence—had consistently pressed for voting rights, but just as consistently had been shut out. It was not for lack of trying. But women were fighting against the enormous odds of church, Constitution, an all-male power structure that held fast to its reins, and many of their own who believed in a woman's divinely ordained, second-place role.

But in the nineteenth century, more women were pressed to work and they showed the first signs of strength. In the 1860 Lynn, Massachusetts, shoeworker strike, many of the 10,000 workers who marched in protest were women. (At the time in Lynn, women made one dollar per week against the three dollars per week paid to men.) Women were also a strong force in the abolitionist movement, with Harriet Beecher Stowe attracting the most prominence. But even in a so-called freedom movement, women were accorded second-rate status.

To many male abolitionists, the "moral" imperative to free black men and give them the vote carried much greater weight than the somewhat blasphemous notion of equality of the sexes. In fact, it was exclusion of women from an abolitionist gathering that sparked the first formal organization for women's rights. The birth of the women's movement in America dates to July 19, 1848, when Elizabeth Cady Stanton (1815–1902) and Lucretia Mott (1793–1880) called for a women's convention in Seneca Falls, New York, after they had been told to sit in the balcony at a London antislavery meeting. Of the major abolitionist figures, only William Lloyd Garrison supported equality for women. Even Frederick Douglass, while sympathetic to women's rights, clearly thought it secondary in importance to the end of slavery. The Abolitionist movement did produce two of the most remarkable women of the era in Harriet Tubman (see pages 147–148), the escaped slave who became an Underground Railroad "conductor" and later a Union spy during the Civil War, and Sojourner Truth, a charismatic black spiritual leader and prominent spokeswoman for the rights of women.

With the Civil War's end, abolition lost its steam as a moral issue and women pressed to be included under the protection of the Fourteenth Amendment, which extended the vote to black males. But again women had to wait as politicians told them that the freed slaves took priority, a stand with which some women of the day agreed, creating a split in the feminist movement over goals and tactics. Hardliners followed Elizabeth Cady Stanton into the National Woman Suffrage Association (NWSA); Moderates willing to wait for black male suffrage started the American Woman Suffrage Association (AWSA), leaving a rift that lasted twenty years. (The two wings of the women's movement reunited in 1890 in the National American Woman Suffrage Association, or NAWSA, with Stanton as its first president.)

Much of the political energy absorbed by abolition was shifted to the temperance movement after the war. Groups like the WCTU, whose greatest strength lay in the West, proved to women that they had organizational strength. Amelia Bloomer (1818–1894) didn't invent the pantaloons that bore her name, but she popularized them in her newspaper, *The Lily*, a journal preaching temperance as well as equality.

Susan B. Anthony (1820–1906), called "the Napoleon of women's rights," came from the same Quaker-abolitionist-temperance background as Stanton, and the two women became friends and powerful allies, founding the NWSA together. A forceful and tireless organizer and lobbyist, she pushed for local reforms in her home state of New York while continuing to urge the vote for women at the national level. But by the turn of the century, Anthony's position fell from favor. Women shifted tactics, concentrating on winning the vote state by state, a strategy that succeeded in Idaho and Colorado, where grassroots organizations won the vote for women. After 1910, a few more western states relented, and the movement gained new momentum.

At about the same time, the suffragists took a new direction, borrowed from their British counterparts. The British "suffragettes" (as opposed to the commonly used American term "suffragist") had been using far more radical means to win the vote. Led by Emmeline Pankhurst, British suffragettes chained themselves to buildings, invaded Parliament, blew up mailboxes, and burned buildings. Imprisoned for these actions, the women called themselves "political prisoners" and went on hunger strikes that were met with force-feedings. The cruelty of this official response was significant in attracting public sympathy for the suffragette cause.

These militant tactics were brought back to America by women who had marched with the British. Alice Paul (1885–1977) was another Quaker-raised woman who studied in England and had joined the Pankhurst-led demonstrations in London. At the 1913 inauguration of Woodrow Wilson, who opposed the vote for women, Paul organized a demonstration of 10,000. Her strategy was to hold the party in power—the Democrats in this case—responsible for denying women the vote. By this time, several million women could vote in various states, and Republicans saw, as they had in winning the black vote in Grant's time, that there might be a political advantage in accepting universal suffrage.

President Wilson's views were also dictated by politics. He needed to hold on to the support of the Democratic South. That meant opposing women's voting. Southern Democrats were successfully keeping black men from voting; they certainly didn't want to worry about black women as well. Ironically, Wilson's wife, Edith Galt, proved how capable women could be at running things. During the period when Wilson was immobilized by a stroke in 1919, she literally took over the powers of the presidency, making presidential-level decisions for her invalid husband.

After Wilson's 1916 reelection, in which women in some states had voted against him two to one, the protest was taken to Wilson's doorstep as women began to picket around the clock outside the White House. Eventually imprisoned, Paul and others imitated the British tactic of hunger strikes. Again, sympathies turned in favor of the women. After their convictions were overturned, the militant suffragists returned to their White House protests.

In 1918, Paul's political tactics paid off as a Republican Congress was elected. Among them was Montana's Jeannette Rankin (1880–1973), the first woman elected to Congress. Rankin's first act was to introduce a constitutional suffrage amendment onto the House floor. The amendment was approved by a one-vote margin. It took the Senate another eighteen months to pass it, and in June 1919, the Nineteenth Amendment was submitted to the states for ratification. Now fearful of the women's vote in the approaching presidential election, Wilson shifted to support of the measure. One year later, on August 26, 1920, Tennessee delivered the last needed vote, and the Nineteenth Amendment was added to the Constitution. It stated simply that "the right of citizens of the United States to vote shall not be denied by the United States or by any State on account of sex."

It took more than 130 years, but "We, the People" finally included the half of the country that had been kept out the longest.

What was the scandal over Teapot Dome?

Does this sound familiar? A genial, well-intentioned, "hands-off" Republican President, called lazy by some critics, delegates responsibility to subordinates and doesn't pay too much attention to what they are up to; he believes in cutting taxes for the wealthy as a means to stimulate the economy; but his administration is bedeviled by scandal when some of his Cabinet members are caught in influence-peddling and other corrupt schemes.

Tired of the war and eight years of Democrat Woodrow Wilson, a weary nation welcomed the noncontroversial Warren G. Harding, a small-town, self-made businessman. Opposed by James M. Cox—who ran with Wilson's young Assistant Secretary of the Navy Franklin D. Roosevelt—Harding and his running mate Calvin Coolidge, the governor of Massachusetts, won easily in a small-turnout election. (Socialist Eugene V. Debs garnered 3.5 percent of the vote.)

Harding's was a classic Republican administration. Tax cuts. Help for big business. An America-first foreign policy that rejected Wilson's League of Nations and set up stiff tariffs to protect American industry.

But his administration would also soon be dogged by what came to be called the Harding Scandals. The first of these involved the siphoning of millions of dollars allocated for Vererans Administration hospitals. In another seamy episode, Harding's Attorney General Harry Daugherty was implicated in fraud related to the return of German assets seized during the war, and only avoided conviction by invoking the Fifth Amendment.

But the most famous of the Harding Scandals involved a place called Teapot Dome. Two federal oil reserves—one in Elk Hills, California, and the other in Teapot Dome, Wyoming—were marked for the future use of the U.S. Navy. But the Interior Secretary, Albert B. Fall, contrived to have these lands turned over to his department. He then sold off drilling leases to private developers in return for hundreds of thousands of dollars in bribes and kickbacks in the form of cash, stock, and cattle. In August 1923, as this scandal was being uncovered by a Senate investigation, Harding suffered a fatal heart attack—misdiagnosed by an incompetent Surgeon General as food poisoning—while in San Francisco on his way home from a trip to Alaska. Interior Secretary Fall was later convicted for accepting a bribe, thereby achieving the distinction of becoming the first Cabinet officer in American history to go to jail.

Calvin Coolidge, untainted by the scandals, took Harding's place and handily won reelection in 1924.

Did Henry Ford invent the automobile?

Autos and airplanes. The prosperity of the twenties was due in large part to a shift from the nineteenth century's Industrial Revolution, symbolized by the railroads, to a twentieth-century revolution in technology. The invention and development of both the automobile and the airplane defined that shift. And during this period, both industries were defined by two American icons, Henry Ford and Charles A. Lindbergh. In their day, both men were revered. History has not been so kind.

Henry Ford (1864–1947) did not invent the automobile or

the assembly line. But his perfected versions of them made him one of the richest and most powerful men in America. The son of an Irish immigrant farmer, Ford had a mechanical inclination. In 1890 he went to work for the Edison company in Detroit and built his first gasoline-driven car there. Europeans had taken the lead in the development of the automobile, and the Duryea brothers of Massachusetts were the American pioneers. Ford borrowed from their ideas, envisioning the auto as a cheap box on wheels with a simple engine, and brought out his first Model T in 1909. In a year he sold almost 11,000 of them.

But Ford envisioned a car for the masses. When Ford and his engineers introduced the moving assembly line, an idea proposed in a 1911 book by Frederick W. Taylor, the mass-produced Model T revolutionized the auto industry. The efficiency of the assembly line cut the price tag on the Model T from $950 in 1908 to under $300. By 1914, Ford Motors turned out 248,000 Model T's, almost half of all autos produced, at the rate of one every 24 seconds. Realizing enormous profits, Ford made headlines by paying his workers five dollars per day, almost double the going rate. He wouldn't have done it if he couldn't afford it; at the same time, Ford himself was clearing up to $25,000 per day. Paying his workers more money was Ford's only way to keep them from quitting the monotonous, dehumanizing assembly line. He also realized that it was one way to enable his workers to buy Fords.

For Americans, it was love at first sight with the automobile. It is fair to say the Model T revolutionized American life. When Congress enacted highway fund legislation in 1916 and the country embarked on a massive road-building era, the American dream of freedom on the open road became a new reality. In a short time the auto industry became the keystone of the American economy, in good times and bad. New industries in roadside services sprung to life all over the country. Service stations, diners, and motels all came into being. The country cottage was no longer the exclusive preserve of the Vanderbilts and Morgans. The auto gave the working and middle classes a sense of accomplishment. The new, auto-induced sense of freedom, and the economic prosperity created by the automobile and related industries, helped to open up American society in the 1920s.

Henry Ford cared little for social improvements or the broad sweep of history. "History is more or less bunk," he said. Autocratic and conservative, he tyrannized his workers. He fired anyone caught driving a competitor's model. Gangster tactics were used to maintain discipline in plants, and unionizing efforts were met with strikebreaking goon squads. Unions were kept out of Ford plants until 1941. Ford's attitude was that workers were unreliable and shiftless. In the midst of the Depression, he blamed the workingman's laziness for the nation's economic problems. "The average worker," said Ford, "won't do a day's work unless he is caught and can't get out of it."

His conservatism spilled over into his political beliefs. An isolationist in foreign policy—although his plants won big defense jobs during both World Wars—Ford was also an outspoken anti-Semite. Ford bought a newspaper, the *Independent,* that became an anti-Jewish mouthpiece. The paper was involved in the American publication of *The Protocols of the Elders of Zion,* an anti-Semitic propaganda tract that had first appeared in Russia in 1905 to castigate Jews. But Ford's conservative, stubborn streak cost him in the long run. Unwilling to adapt to changing styles, Ford Motors later slipped behind more aggressive competitors like General Motors. Yet at his death in 1947, Henry Ford remained an American folk hero for personifying the rags-to-riches American myth.

What was so "lucky" about "Lucky Lindy"?

"Lucky Lindy" was the other great hero of the era. Like Ford, Charles Lindbergh (1902–1975) invented nothing. The Wright brothers had begun their famous experiments at Kitty Hawk, North Carolina, in 1903, and the Lockheed brothers built their early commercial planes in 1913. Strictly speaking, Lindbergh wasn't even the first to fly across the Atlantic. A pair of Englishmen had flown from Newfoundland to Ireland in 1919 (a route considerably shorter than Lindbergh's).

But the war in Europe had given a real boost to the commercial potential of the airplane. While the air industry was not as economically crucial to the twenties as Ford's automobile, it was symbolic of the venturesome spirit of the times. Lindbergh's design of his aircraft, which he called *The Spirit of St. Louis,* allowed him to become the first man to fly solo across the Atlantic. It was an act of enormous daring, skill, and flying ability. The 3,600-mile flight began on Long Island on May 20, 1927. Lindbergh, attempting to win a $25,000 purse promised to the first pilot to go from New York to Paris, carried only a few sandwiches, a quart of water, and letters of introduction. He wouldn't need those. When he landed in Paris thirty-three hours later, Lindbergh was smothered in the adulation of France and the rest of Europe. His hero's welcome would be repeated around the world as he became, like Ford, the symbol of do-anything American inventiveness and daring. A reclusive personality, Lindbergh became best known by his newspaper nickname, "Lucky Lindy," and he was the world's most familiar celebrity.

That celebrity led to the tragedy in his life. After his marriage to Anne Spencer Morrow, daughter of a U.S. senator and later a renowned writer, he lived in the glare of international publicity. In May 1932, their son, nineteen-month-old Charles Junior, was kidnapped and a $50,000 ransom demand was met. But the child was found murdered. Like the Sacco and Vanzetti affair, the case of Bruno Hauptmann, the man electrocuted for the crime in 1936, has never quite gone away. Fifty years after his execution, there are many who claim Hauptmann was innocent, the victim of a frame-up. There is little question that the country's anti-foreign frenzy at the time helped convict him, but the evidence in the case was always strong against him. The infamous kidnapping, which dominated newspapers in the midst of the Depression's worst year, prompted congressional passage of a measure making kidnapping across state lines a capital crime.

Ford and Lindbergh shared something besides their fame and success. By the late 1930s, both men were notorious for their conservative, isolationist, and anti-Semitic political views. Lindbergh made several trips to Germany to inspect the German air force (Luftwaffe) and, in 1938, was presented with a medal by Hermann Goering, first leader of Hitler's storm troopers, founder of the Gestapo, and Hitler's air minister. Ford also received a medal from Hitler himself in 1938. After pronouncing Germany's military superiority, Lindbergh returned to America to become an outspoken leader of the isolationist "America First" movement, funded with Ford money, that tried to keep the United States out of World War II. In one speech, Lindbergh nearly killed the movement when he warned Jews in America to "shut up" and borrowed the well-worn Nazi tactic of accusing "Jewish-owned media" of pushing America into the war. Although he was in the Air Corps Reserve, Lindbergh's criticism of Roosevelt forced him to resign his commission. During the war he served as a consultant to Ford and later flew combat missions in the Pacific. After the war, he was a consultant to the Defense Department. His heroics kept his reputation intact.

American Voices

From Herbert Hoover's "Rugged Individualism" campaign speech (October 22, 1928):

> When the war closed, the most vital of all issues both in our own country and throughout the world was whether Governments should continue their wartime ownership and operation of many instrumentalities of production and distribution. We are challenged with a peace-time choice between the American system of rugged individualism and a European philosophy of diametrically opposed doctrines—doctrines of paternalism and state socialism.
>   . . . Our American experiment in human welfare has yielded a degree of well-being unparalleled in all the world. It has come nearer to the abolition of poverty, to the abolition of fear of want than humanity has ever reached before.

Why did investors panic in 1929, leading to the "Great Crash"?

When Herbert Hoover made that speech, America did seem to be a place of unlimited opportunity. Apart from a huge underclass of the unemployed and poor farmers that Hoover overlooked and prosperity bypassed, the bulk of the country probably agreed with Hoover's sentiment. The year 1927 was one more in the prosperous years of the Roaring Twenties. Lindbergh's 1927 flight to Paris came in the midst of the country's "Coolidge Boom." An avatar of unlimited potential, Lindbergh added another boost to American feelings of confidence, invincibility, and Hoover's "rugged individualism."

With such good feelings in the air, Hoover was elected by a huge margin in 1928. But another factor in his election was the religion of his Democratic opponent, New York Governor Al Smith, a Roman Catholic. "A vote for Smith is a vote for the Pope," proclaimed campaign banners in 1928. Smith also favored repeal of Prohibition, and another slogan said Smith would bring "Rum, Romanism, and Ruin" to America. But more than anything else, the Hoover victory was made possible by "general prosperity."

And nowhere was the prosperity more conspicuous than on Wall Street, home of the New York Stock Exchange. During the 1920s, new companies like General Motors had issued stock that was making many an investor, large and small, seemingly wealthy. An ambitious young man like Joseph P. Kennedy (1888–1969), unfettered by the restraints of any regulatory authority (the Securities and Exchange Commission was a later creation), could make a large fortune for himself with not-always scrupulous means. In fact, a great number of the most successful men in those days were operating in shady territory. Working in "pools," crooked manipulators bought cheap shares of stock, drove up the prices among themselves, then lured outside investors into the pool. The "pool" operators then dumped their stocks at artificially inflated prices, leaving the "sucker" holding a bag of overpriced stock.

The most notorious of the wealthy crooks of the day was the "Swedish match king," Ivar Kreuger. Claiming to be an intimate of the crowned heads of Europe, Krueger built a huge financial empire on credit granted by some of the era's leading financial institutions. Featured on the cover of *Time* as a giant of business, Krueger was a con man of the first water, whose empire was based on deception. He issued worthless securities and later counterfeited Italian government bonds. Equally notorious was Samuel Insull, a "self-made" millionaire who used millions put up by working-class investors—many of them public employees caught in the spell of Insull's magnificent wealth—to build a public-utilities empire, all the while manipulating stock prices to his benefit. Before the Crash, Insull controlled an empire of holding companies, and he personally held eighty-five directorships, sixty-five board chairmanships, and eleven company presidencies.

The paper wealth being acquired masked a rot in the American economy. American farmers continued to struggle following the postwar collapse of agricultural prices. Before the Great Depression, unemployment was already high as factories became mechanized and the worker at the bottom was let go. Housing starts fell in 1927, always an ominous sign in the American economy. The problems were not only America's. International production intensified, but demand slackened and warehouses filled up. The wealth of the world was concentrated in the hands of a small class at the top. The wealth trickling down from the top was not enough. The great bulk of the population simply couldn't create the demand needed to keep up with the increasing supply. The American consumer could not consume all of the goods that American manufacturers were producing.

Yet thousands of Americans were drawn to the lure of fortunes made in the market. Like moths to the flame, people pulled their life savings from banks and put them into stocks and securities, like Insull Utilities Investments. The easygoing rules of the day meant that investors only had to put down ten to twenty percent in cash to buy stock; the rest was available on cheap credit. The Federal Reserve fed the frenzy with artificially low interest rates set by old-line Republicans beholden only to their corporate pals. Banks loaned millions to feed speculative schemes. The American public was in enormous debt and their "wealth" was all on paper.

By late 1929, barely a year after Hoover had spoken about the abolition of poverty, the cracks in the foundation began to show. Steel and automobile production, two centerpieces of the American economy, were in decline. Yet still the stock market rose, reaching its peak in late September of 1929. But the house of cards was about to tumble. Skittish European investors began to withdraw their investments in the United States. When brokers called customers to pay off the amounts owed on stocks bought with borrowed money, these investors had to sell off their stocks to raise cash. This created a wave of fear—the fear of losing everything—that quickly gained momentum. As stock prices fell, more brokers called on customers to put up more cash, and a vicious cycle was unleashed, sending prices on the stock exchange plunging. On "Black Thursday," October 24, 13 million shares of stock were sold off. A combine of bankers led by John P. Morgan, Jr., set up a pool of cash to prop up prices, as Morgan's father had done in 1907 during a similar panic in the market. This attempt to inspire confidence failed. By the following week, on October 29—"Black Tuesday"—more than 16 million shares were sold off as panic swept the stock exchange. (In today's world, well over a hundred million shares change hands daily. But in 1929 the market was much smaller and there were no computers recording deals.) Within days, the "wealth" of a large part of the country, which had been concentrated in vastly inflated stock prices, simply vanished.

American Voices

Frederick Lewis Allen, in his social history of the period, *Since Yesterday:*

> The official statistics of the day gave the volume of trading as 16,410,030 shares, but no one knows how many sales went unrecorded in the yelling scramble to sell. There are those who believe that the true volume may have been twenty or even twenty-five million. Big and small, insiders and outsiders, the high-riders of the Big Bull Market were being cleaned out: the erstwhile millionaire and his chauffeur, the all-powerful pool operator and his suckers, the chairman of the board with his two-thousand-share holding and the assistant bookkeeper with his ten-share holding, the bank president and his stenographer. . . . The disaster which had taken place may be summed up in a single statistic. In a few short weeks it had blown into thin air *thirty billion dollars*—a sum almost as great as the entire cost of the United States participation in the (first)

World War, and nearly twice as great as the entire national
debt.

What was so "great" about the Great Depression?

Wall Street's Great Crash of 1929 did not "cause" the decade
of Great Depression that followed, any more than the assassination of Archduke Ferdinand had "caused" World War I. The
Crash was a symptom of the economy's serious disease. It was the
fatal heart attack for a patient also suffering from terminal can-
cer. By the time the market rallied a few years later in the Little
Bull Market, it was too late. The damage had been done. The
Crash had been the last tick of a time bomb that, when it exploded, brought down the world economy.

America had suffered depressions before. But none of them
had been capitalized like the Depression of the 1930s. None had
ever lasted so long, and none had ever touched so many Americans so devastatingly. After the Crash, the economy was para-
lyzed. In one year, 1,300 banks failed. There was no such thing as
Federal Deposit Insurance guaranteeing the savings of working
people. Hard-earned savings disappeared as 5,000 banks closed
during the next three years, their assets tied up in the speculating
that created wealth but disappeared in the Crash, or in mortgages
that the jobless could no longer pay. Without banks to extend
credit and capital, businesses and factories closed, forcing more
workers onto unemployment lines. In 1931, Henry Ford blamed
the laziness of workers for the calamity. A short time later, he
closed a plant and, with it, 75,000 jobs were lost.

The jolted American system got two more shocks when the
empires of Ivar Kreuger and Samuel Insull came tumbling down.
Insull had built a pyramid of holding companies and used them to
push up the value of his stock. By 1932 the artificial values had
fallen to their true worth, declining in value by some 96 percent.
Indicted by a Chicago grand jury, Insull fled to Greece, where he
hoped to escape extradition. When Greece later signed an extradition treaty with the United States, the man who had once
surrounded himself with three dozen bodyguards, disguised himself as a woman and sailed for Turkey. Eventually he was brought

back to the United States and tried. But Insull escaped punishment. The holding companies he had used were outside regulation; all of his manipulations were technically legal.

Ivar Kreuger was less lucky. Living in a luxurious Paris apartment, he was also revealed as a swindler. Once an adviser to President Hoover, he had stolen more than $3 million from investors. Kreuger didn't wait for an indictment. He shot himself in the spring of 1932, before the worst of his schemes was even brought into the open.

Before the Great Depression, America had absorbed periodic depressions because most people lived on farms and were able to produce what they needed to survive. But the American and world economy had been thoroughly revolutionized in the early twentieth century. This was an urbanized, mechanized America in which millions were suddenly unemployed, with no farms to go home to. Statistics are virtually meaningless when it comes to the magnitude of joblessness. Official numbers said 25 percent of the work force was unemployed. Other historians have said the number was more like 40 to 50 percent.

Through his last three desperate years in office, Herbert Hoover continued to voice optimism. Like most economists of his day, Hoover believed that depressions were part of the business cycle. America had suffered them before and had shaken them off after a period of dislocation. But this time was different. Hoover made a long, steady stream of pronouncements about how the corner had been turned. Instead, things turned bleaker. As millions were losing their homes, unable to pay rent or mortgages, Hoover and other members of the wealthy class made some incredible statements. When the International Apple Shippers' Association, overstocked with apples, decided to sell its vast surplus to unemployed men on credit so that they could resell them on streetcorners for a nickel apiece, Hoover remarked, "Many people have left their jobs for the more profitable one of selling apples." Henry Ford, who put 75,000 men out of work and on the road as "hoboes" in search of work, said of the hundreds of thousands of wandering men, women, and children, "Why, it's the best education in the world for those boys, that traveling around! They get more experience in a few months than they would in years at school." J. P. Morgan believed that there were 25 or 30 million families in the "leisure class"—that is, able to employ a servant. He was startled to learn that there were fewer than two million servants in the entire country.

Hoover clung to his optimistic line. "Business and industry have turned the corner," he said in January 1930. "We have now passed the worst," was the cheery word in May. Prosperity was always right around the corner. But the country never seemed to reach that corner. Hoover has come down in history as a do-nothing Nero who fiddled while Rome burned. That portrait is not quite accurate. The problem was that just about everything he tried either backfired or was too little, too late. In 1930 he went along with a protectionist bill—the Hawley-Smoot Tariff Bill—which threw up trade barriers around the United States. This simply prompted the European countries to do the same thing, worsening the crisis both in the United States and in Europe. By 1931 the Depression had spread throughout Europe, where the scars of the war were still not healed and the crush of wartime debt contributed to the crisis. Austria, England, France, and, most ominously, Germany were all sucked into a violent whirlpool of massive unemployment and staggering inflation.

Hoover was steadfast in his refusal to allow the government to help the jobless, homeless, and starving through government relief programs he viewed as Socialist and Communist. He did, at least, ignore the advice of one of the nation's wealthiest men, Treasury Secretary Andrew Mellon (1855–1937), whose tax policies in the 1920s had contributed to underlying flaws in the American economy. Mellon advised a complete laissez-faire response, proposing to "liquidate labor, liquidate stocks, liquidate the farmer, liquidate real estate." He thought that through this scorched-earth policy, "people will work harder, live a more moral life. Values will be adjusted and enterprising people will pick up the wrecks from less competent people." Hoover eased the aging Mellon out of the Treasury and made him ambassador to England.

Hoover set up a belated public-works program that, by the time it started, was woefully inadequate, unable to replace all the local building projects that had been killed by the banking collapse. In 1932, bowing to the pressure of the time and going against his deep conservative grain, Hoover created the Reconstruction Finance Corporation, which loaned money to railroads and banks.

But even in this, Hoover was snakebit. To the millions of unemployed and starving, the RFC was a bitter symbol of Hoover's willingness to aid corporations while showing complete indifference to the poor. In spite of the growing misery, the lengthening bread lines, the "Hoovervilles" of cardboard shacks being thrown up in America's large cities, the utter despair of hundreds of thousands without homes or hope, Hoover staunchly refused to allow government to issue direct aid. By his lights, it was socialism to do so, and was completely contrary to his notion of "rugged individualism."

What was the Bonus Army?

In the midst of the Depression, buglers called President Hoover and the First Lady to seven-course dinners served by a small army of white-gloved servants. President Hoover thought that keeping up regal trappings and spiffy appearances was good for national morale. Outside, Americans were fighting for scraps from garbage cans. But some "rugged individuals" were going to give Hoover an unpleasantly close look at life on the other side of the Depression fence.

In the summer of 1932, the Depression's worst year, 25,000 former "doughboys"—World War I infantrymen, many of whom were combat veterans—walked, hitchhiked, or "rode the rails" to Washington, D.C. Organizing themselves into a penniless, vagrant army, they squatted, with their families, in abandoned buildings along Pennsylvania Avenue and pitched an encampment of crude shacks and tents on the banks of the Anacostia River. They had come to ask Congress to pay them a "bonus" promised to veterans in 1924 and scheduled to be paid in 1945. Starving and desperate men, they had families going hungry, no jobs, and no prospects of finding one. They needed that bonus to survive. Calling themselves the Bonus Expeditionary Force (BEF), they were better known as the "Bonus Army."

Their pleas for relief fell on deaf ears. To Hoover, Congress, lawmen, and the newspapers, these weren't veterans but "Red agitators." (Hoover's own Veterans Administration surveyed the Bonus Army and found that 95 percent of them were indeed veterans.) Instead of meeting the BEF's leaders, Hoover called out the troops, commanded by General Douglas MacArthur (1880–1964) with his young aide Dwight Eisenhower (1890–1969). The assault was led by the Third Cavalry, sabers ready, under the command of Major George Patton (1885–1945). Behind the horses, the U.S. Army rolled out to meet the ragged bunch of men, women, and children with tear gas, tanks, and bayonets.

Patton's cavalry first charged the Bonus Marchers, now mixed with curious civilians who were getting off from work on this hot July afternoon. Following the cavalry charge came the tear-gas attack, routing the Bonus Army from Pennsylvania Avenue and across the Eleventh Street Bridge. Disregarding orders—a common thread running through his career—MacArthur decided to finish the job by destroying the Bonus Army entirely. After nightfall, the tanks and cavalry leveled the jumbled camp of tents and packing-crate shacks. It was all put to the torch. There were more than one hundred casualties in the aftermath of the battle, including two babies suffocated by the gas attack.

Pushed out of the nation's capital, the Bonus Army dissipated, joining the other two million Americans "on the road." Some states, like California, posted guards to turn back the poor. The violence in Washington, D.C., was the largest but not the only demonstration of a growing anger and unrest in America. During 1931 and 1932 there had been a number of riots and protests, mostly by the unemployed and hungry, sometimes by children, that were put down with harsh police action.

The assault on the Bonus Marchers came as the 1932 presidential campaign was getting under way. A grim Herbert Hoover had been renominated in June by the Republicans on a platform that promised to balance the budget, keep tariffs high on foreign goods, and—in a reversal of its position four years before—repeal Prohibition, allowing the states to control alcohol.

Believing that only a major disaster could prevent them from recapturing the White House, held by Republicans for twelve years, the Democrats met in Chicago. Three leading candidates emerged for the nomination: Al Smith, the 1928 standard-bearer who had been swamped by Hoover; the powerful Speaker of the House, John Nance Garner of Texas, who had the support of newspaper czar William Randolph Hearst, who in turn controlled the California delegation; and Al Smith's handpicked successor as governor of New York, Franklin D. Roosevelt (1882–1945). Roosevelt led after the first ballot, but lacked the votes to win the nomination. In a classic "smoke-filled room" deal, Garner was promised the vice-presidency in return for his support of Roosevelt. On the fourth ballot, with Hearst throwing California's delegates to Roosevelt, the popular governor won the nomination. Roosevelt immediately wanted to demonstrate that he was not going to be bound by any traditions. He flew to Chicago to accept the nomination, launching the tradition of the nominee's speech to the convention. Roosevelt also wanted to demonstrate to the country that although crippled by polio, he would not be stopped from going where he wanted.

Not everyone agreed that it was a great choice. Two of the leading newspapermen of the day were H. L. Mencken and Walter Lippmann (1899–1974). Mencken said the convention had nominated "the weakest candidate." Lippmann, perhaps the most influential columnist in the country at the time, was even more disparaging. He called FDR an "amiable boy scout" who lacked "any important qualifications for the office."

It didn't matter. The Democrats could have run a real Boy Scout that year and won. The country may not have been sure about wanting FDR, who ran a conservative campaign but promised a "new deal" for the country and the repeal of Prohibition, establishment of public works, and aid to farmers. But they were sure they didn't want Herbert Hoover. "General prosperity" led the way for Hoover in 1928. But "general despair" knocked him out in 1932. Roosevelt won the election with 57 percent of the popular vote, carrying forty-two of forty-eight states. The Democrats also swept into majorities of both houses of Congress.

After Roosevelt's inauguration, the Bonus Army returned to Washington. Roosevelt asked his wife Eleanor (1884–1962) to go and speak to the men, and let them have plenty of free coffee. The First Lady mingled with the marchers and led them in songs. One of them later said, "Hoover sent the army. Roosevelt sent his wife."

American Voices

From Franklin D. Roosevelt's first inaugural address, March 4, 1933:

This is pre-eminently the time to speak the truth, the whole truth, frankly and boldly. Nor need we shrink from honestly facing conditions in our country today. This great nation will endure as it has endured, will revive and will prosper.

So first of all let me assert my firm belief that the only thing we have to fear is fear itself—nameless, unreasoning, unjustified terror which paralyzes needed efforts to convert retreat into advance.

Most of Roosevelt's campaign speeches had been written for him, but a handwritten first draft of the inaugural address shows this to be Roosevelt's own work. Yet the speech's most famous line was old wine in a new bottle. Similar sentiments about fear had been voiced before. The historian Richard Hofstadter notes that Roosevelt read Thoreau in the days before the Inauguration and was probably inspired by the line "Nothing is so much to be feared as fear."

What were the New Deal and the Hundred Days?

When he took the Democratic nomination with a ringing acceptance speech, Roosevelt promised the people a "new deal." In his inaugural, he promised a special session of Congress to deal with the national economic emergency. He came through on both promises.

The legislative centerpiece of Roosevelt's response to the Great Depression, the "New Deal" was a revolution in the American way of life. A revolution was required because Roosevelt's election did not signal a turnaround for the depressed American economy. Between election day and the inauguration, the country scraped bottom. Bank closings continued as long lines of panicky depositors lined up to get at their savings. Governors around the country began to declare "bank holidays" in their states. On March 5, his first day in the White House, Roosevelt did the same thing, calling for a nationwide four-day bank holiday. That night he talked to Americans about how banking worked in the first of his "fireside chats"—radio addresses aimed at educating the public, soothing fears, and restoring the confidence and optimism of a nation that had little left.

Then he called Congress to a special emergency session. From March through June, the "One Hundred Days," the U.S. Congress passed an extraordinary series of measures, sometimes without even reading them. Roosevelt's approach was, "Take a method and try it. If it fails, try another."

The result was the "alphabet soup" of new federal agencies, some of them successful, some not.

Like the other President Roosevelt of an earlier era, FDR looked to the nation's human resources and created the Civilian Conservation Corps (CCC), which provided jobs for young men from eighteen to twenty-five years old in works of reforestation and other conservation.

The Agricultural Adjustment Administration (AAA) was created to raise farm prices by paying farmers to take land out of production. This plan had two major drawbacks. The nation was outraged to see pigs slaughtered and corn plowed under by government decree to push up farm prices while there were so many people starving. And thousands of mostly black sharecroppers and tenant farmers, lowest on the economic pecking order, were thrown off the land when farmers took their land out of production.

The object of even greater controversy, the Tennessee Valley Authority (TVA), a federally run hydroelectric power program, was one of the most radical departures. Under the TVA Act, the federal government created a huge experiment in social planning. The TVA not only produced hydroelectric power, but built dams, produced and sold fertilizer, reforested the area, and developed recreational lands. (The TVA also created the Oak Ridge facility, which later provided much of the research and development of the atomic bomb.) It was an unprecedented involvement of government in what had once been the exclusive—even sacred—domain of private enterprise, and was wildly condemned as communistic.

The Hundred Days also saw creation of the Federal Deposit Insurance Corporation (FDIC), designed to protect savings; the Home Owners Loan Corporation, which refinanced mortgages and prevented foreclosures; and a Federal Securities Act to begin policing the activities of Wall Street. In 1934 the Securities and Exchange Commission (SEC) was created, and Roosevelt appointed Joseph Kennedy, a notorious speculator in his day, to be its first chief. The thinking was that Kennedy would know all the tricks that any crooked brokers might try to pull. In May 1933 the Federal Emergency Relief Administration (FERA) was created and given $500 million in federal relief funds for the most seriously destitute, the beginning of a federal welfare program.

One of the final acts of the Hundred Days was passage of the most controversial New Deal bill, the National Industrial Recovery Act, aimed at stimulating industrial production. This act was a huge attempt at government control of production, labor, and costs. To gain the acceptance of business and labor, it contained goodies for both. It allowed manufacturers to create "business codes," a legal form of price-fixing that would have been forbidden under antitrust laws while giving workers minimum wages, maximum hours and collective bargaining rights.

To its organizers, the NRA took on the trappings of a holy crusade. To oversee the law, the National Recovery Administration (NRA) was created, with its Blue Eagle symbol. Companies and merchants pledged to the NRA displayed the eagle and the motto "We Do Our Part," and consumers were advised to buy only from those places that displayed the NRA symbol. Massive marches and parades in support of the program took place across the country. A million people marched in an NRA parade in New York City.

But abuses by industry were widespread. Prices were fixed

high, and production was limited in most cases, creating the opposite of the intended effect of increasing jobs and keeping prices low. The NRA did spur labor-union recruitment, and the United Mine Workers under John L. Lewis (1880–1969) grew to half a million members. A barrel-chested dynamo, Lewis then joined with other unions to form the Committee for Industrial Organization (CIO), which splintered off from the conservative AFL in 1938 but soon was its rival in numbers and influence.

The first "Hundred Days" came to an end with passage of the NIRA bill but the Great Depression was still far from over. Yet in this short time, Roosevelt had not just created a series of programs designed to prop up the economy. His New Deal marked a turning point in America as decisive as 1776 or 1860. It was nothing less than a revolutionary transformation of the federal government from a smallish body that had limited impact on the average American into a huge machinery that left few Americans untouched. For better or worse, Roosevelt had begun to inject the federal government into American life on an unprecedented scale, a previously unthinkable reliance on government to accomplish tasks that individuals and the private economy were unwilling or unable to do. From the vantage point of the late 1980s, there is so little in modern America that is unaffected by the decisions made in Washington that it is difficult to imagine a time when a President, creating the federal machinery designed to carry the country out of crisis, was viewed as a Communist leading America down the road to Moscow.

What was the WPA?

The New Dealers worked overtime but the Depression went on. While production and consumption rose, they remained well below pre-Crash levels. The unemployment figures never fell much below 10 percent, and they were much higher in some cities. The mid-thirties brought the droughts and winds that created the Dust Bowl of the Plains states, sending thousands of farmers off the foreclosed farms and on the road. This was the woeful exodus immortalized by John Steinbeck in *The Grapes of Wrath*.

With the "try anything" approach, Roosevelt set up new programs. For each program that died or failed to do its job, he was ready to create a new one. When the Supreme Court unanimously killed the NRA as unconstitutional, Roosevelt tried the WPA. The Works Progress Administration, created in 1935 with Harry Hopkins (1890–1946) as its head, was set up for federal construction projects. (In 1939 its name was changed to the Work Projects Administration.) Critics immediately called the WPA a "makework boondoggle," and it provoked the common image of the workman leaning on a shovel. But under Hopkins, the WPA was responsible for 10 percent of new roads in the United States, as well as new hospitals, city halls, courthouses, and schools. It built a port in Brownsville, Texas, roads and bridges connecting the Florida Keys with the mainland, and a string of local water-supply systems. Its large-scale construction projects included the Lincoln Tunnel under the Hudson River connecting New York and New Jersey, the Triborough Bridge system linking Manhattan to Long Island, the Federal Trade Commission building in Washington, the East River Drive (later renamed the FDR Drive) in Manhattan, the Fort Knox gold depository, and the Bonneville and Boulder dams. (Boulder Dam was renamed Hoover Dam by a Republican-controlled Congress in 1946). Apart from building projects, the WPA set up artistic projects that employed thousands of musicians, writers, and artists.

But Roosevelt's greatest contribution may have been psychological rather than simply legislative. He possessed a singular, natural gift for restoring confidence, rebuilding optimism, and creating hope where all hope seemed to have been lost. Herbert Hoover had embarked on some of the same paths that FDR took toward recovery. But the stern, patrician Hoover, totally removed from the people, lacked any of the sense of the common person that FDR possessed naturally, despite being a child of wealth and privilege. His "fireside chats" over the radio gave listeners the distinct impression that Roosevelt was sitting in their parlors or living rooms speaking to them personally. While Roosevelt's name was unmentionable in conservative Republican households, where he was referred to as "that man," he was practically deified by the larger American public, including blacks who began to desert the Republican party, their home since Reconstruction days, for Roosevelt's Democrats.

American Voices

From *The Grapes of Wrath* (1939), by John Steinbeck (1902–1968):

> The moving, questing people were migrants now. Those families which had lived on a little piece of land, who had lived and died on forty acres, had now the whole West to rove in. And they scampered about, looking for work; and the highways were streams of people, and the ditch banks were lines of people. Behind them more were coming. The great highways streamed with moving people. There in the Middle- and Southwest had lived a simple agrarian folk who had not changed with industry, who had not formed with machines or known the power and danger of machines in private hands. They had not grown up in the paradoxes of industry. Their senses were still sharp to the ridiculousness of the industrial life.
>
> And then suddenly the machines pushed them out and they swarmed on the highways. The movement changed them; the highways, the camps along the road, the fear of hunger itself, changed them. The children without dinner changed them. They were migrants. And the hostility changed them, welded them, united them—hostility that made the little towns group and arm as though to repel an invader, squads with pick handles, clerks and storekeepers with shotguns, guarding the world against their own people.

Why did Franklin D. Roosevelt try to "pack" the Supreme Court?

The New Deal and the NRA in particular were bitter medicine to conservative Wall Streeters and corporate leaders, most of them Republicans. To them, they reeked of socialism and Communism. Even though things were getting better, obscene whispers and cruel jokes were common about the crippled Roosevelt and his wife, Eleanor: Eleanor had given FDR gonorrhea, which she had contracted from a Negro; she was going to Moscow to learn unspeakable sexual practices. Some of the rumors were tinged with anti-Semitism, like the one that Roosevelt was descended from Dutch Jews who had changed their names. Roosevelt was undaunted by the critics. He was only interested in results. And the larger public seemed to agree.

The first proof came in the 1934 midterm elections. Traditionally the party in power loses strength between presidential contests. Instead, the Democrats tightened their control of both the House and Senate. In the presidential race of 1936, Roosevelt's popularity climbed to new heights. He told Raymond Moley, the Columbia professor who led Roosevelt's "brain trust" of academic advisers, that there was only one issue in the campaign of 1936: "It's myself," said Roosevelt, "the people must either be for me or against me." Opposed by Kansas Governor Alf Landon, a Progressive Republican, FDR racked up an overwhelming reelection victory with more than 60 percent of the popular vote, carrying every state but Maine and Vermont. After the election, someone suggested FDR balance the budget by selling the two states to Canada.

Following his reelection, FDR seemed at the peak of his power and prestige. But he was about to be dealt the most crushing defeat of his political life. A year after it was created, the National Recovery Administration was killed. In *Schechter v. United States* (May 1935), the Supreme Court, dominated by aging, conservative Republicans, ruled that the NRA was unconstitutional. This was followed by Court decisions that killed off the Agricultural Administration, the Securities and Exchange Act, a coal act, and a bankruptcy act. In all, the conservative judges shot down eleven New Deal measures. Emboldened by his recent victory, Roosevelt went on the offensive against the Court. Reviving an old proposal that would allow the President to appoint an additional justice for each member reaching the age of seventy, Roosevelt wanted to "pack" the Supreme Court with judges who would be sympathetic to New Deal legislation.

It was the greatest misjudgment of his career. Even when one of the older judges retired and Roosevelt was able to appoint Hugo Black, a New Dealer, FDR remained committed to the bill. But he was almost alone. Alarmed by the measure's threat to the system and constitutional checks and balances, the Senate beat it back. It was Roosevelt's first loss in Congress in five years, and it opened a small floodgate of other defeats. In 1938, Roosevelt, looking to avenge his Court measure defeat, targeted a number of southern senators who had opposed his Supreme Court plan for defeat in the midterm elections. The strategy backfired, resulting in a costly election-day defeat for Roosevelt's handpicked candidates. Roosevelt's once-invincible armor seemed to be cracking.

But even after the "court-packing" debacle and his 1938 political defeats, Roosevelt remained the most powerful man in the country and perhaps the world. Only one man might have rivaled FDR's power at the time. Ironically, he had come to office in March 1933, a few days before Roosevelt's first inauguration. Like Roosevelt, he had come to power largely because he offered a desperate nation a means of dealing with its economic crisis. He too would have the young men of his country go into the countryside in a uniformed group like Roosevelt's CCC. But these young men would be called "Brownshirts." When the Reichstag (the German parliament building) burned to the ground in February 1933, Adolf Hitler (1889–1945) was only the Chancellor of Germany, appointed to the post by an aging and weak German President Hindenburg. Blaming the Communists for the fire that destroyed the seat of Germany's Parliament, Adolf Hitler's National Socialist Party had the scapegoat it needed to unite the country behind its cause and its Fuehrer.

Roosevelt may have lost the fight with the "nine old men" of the Supreme Court in 1937, but he was looking to Europe and what surely would be much bigger battles.

What happened to Amelia Earhart?

After Charles Lindbergh, the most famous flier of the day was Amelia Earhart (1897–1937). Born in Kansas, she graduated high school in Chicago in 1915 and became something of a wanderer, taking up flying along the way. In 1928 she flew across the Atlantic with two men, becoming overnight an outspoken American heroine and a model of "rugged feminism." When she married the publisher George Putnam in 1931, Earhart made it clear that she would continue her career. By 1932 she had set the record for a transatlantic flight and was going on to pile up an impressive list of achievements.

Her boldest plan came in 1937, when she planned to fly around the world with navigator Fred Noonan. Departing from Miami, Florida, in June, Earhart reached New Guinea and took off for Howland Island in the Pacific on July 1. Then her radio messages stopped and she disappeared. A naval search found no sign of the plane, and speculation about the flier's fate fed newspapers for months. The remains of her plane were never found. Many people believed that she was a great pilot—others, a lousy one—who had attempted the impossible. Lost over the Pacific, Earhart simply ran out of fuel and crashed in the vast expanses, ending in a watery grave.

But another of those theories, strongly held by the historian William Manchester, indicates the temper of the times. The late 1930s was an era of increasing military buildup in answer to the economic crisis of the Depression, especially by Italy, Germany, and Japan, the three nations that would later join in the Axis. Looking to become predominant in its Asian sphere, Japan was arming heavily and building strong defenses on a string of Pacific islands it had been granted in 1919 under the Treaty of Versailles. Saipan, Guam, and Tinian were part of the Mariana Islands chain, unknown to most Americans at the time but soon to become a painful part of America's wartime vocabulary. Passing over the Marianas, Earhart caught a glimpse of the fortifications that the Japanese were building on the islands, Manchester contends in his book *The Glory and the Dream*. Under existing treaties, these fortifications were illegal and an indication of Japan's intentions. Manchester says, "She was almost certainly forced down and murdered."

The irony may be that given the country's isolationist temper at the time, even if Earhart had seen this buildup and lived to tell what the Japanese were doing, her warnings would have been ignored. In 1937, America was in no mood for joining anybody else's wars.

What was Lend-Lease?

"Suppose my neighbor's house catches fire," said FDR to a press conference on December 17, 1940. "If he can take my garden hose and connect it up with his hydrant, I may help him put out the fire. Now what do I do? I don't say to him, 'Neighbor, my garden hose cost me fifteen dollars; you have to pay me fifteen dollars for it.' What is the transaction that goes on? I don't want fifteen dollars—I want my garden hose back after the fire is over."

This was part of FDR's brilliance. What was complex, he made simple; the dangerous seemed innocuous. With this homey analogy, President Roosevelt was preparing to bring the country one step closer to a reality it had been avoiding for most of a decade. The neighbor's house was not only on fire—it was about to burn to the ground.

Even as Roosevelt spoke, the German Luftwaffe was throwing everything it had at England during the devastating Battle of Britain. In this sixteen-week air war, which cost Britain more than nine hundred planes and thousands of civilian lives, while Germany lost 1,700 aircraft, London and the industrial heart of England were being bombed into ruin. Down to only $2 billion in gold reserves, England was about to run out of the cash it needed to keep its defenses alive. Publicly pledged to neutrality, FDR was doing everything in his power—and even beyond his legal powers—to assist the British cause. But his hands were tied by the strong isolationist mood in the country and in Congress, and the President could only watch and wonder how to stop Hitler.

The answer came a few weeks after the "garden hose" press conference, as Roosevelt introduced the Lend-Lease bill. Under it, he was granted unprecedented powers to aid any country whose defense was deemed vital to the defense of the United States. America would "lend" tanks, warplanes, and ships that could be returned "in kind" after the war. Congress almost unanimously sided with Roosevelt, except for the hard-line isolationists like Senator Robert A. Taft, who compared the loan of war equipment not to a garden hose but to chewing gum—you wouldn't want it back.

The path to Lend-Lease had been a long and torturous one for Roosevelt. Preoccupied with the Depression crisis, Roosevelt was little concerned with events in Europe. Too many Americans had fresh memories of the horrors of 1918, and isolationist sentiment in the country was overwhelming. When a congressional investigation showed that munitions makers had garnered enormous profits during World War I, the desire to avoid Europe's problems gained greater strength.

Of even less concern than events in Europe was the changing scene in Asia. In 1931, while Herbert Hoover was still in office, the Japanese invaded China and established a puppet state called Manchukuo in Manchuria. Little was said or done by the United States or anyone else. A few months later, Japan bombarded Shanghai and extended its control over northern China. The League of Nations condemned Japan, which laughed and withdrew from the League. Adolf Hitler, who became Chancellor of Germany in 1933, a few days before Roosevelt was inaugurated, watched with interest as Japan's aggressive empire-building went unpunished.

Who were the Fascists?

The word *fascist* gets thrown about quite a bit these days. In the 1960s, the police were called "fascist pigs." Anybody who doesn't like another government simply calls it "fascist." Generally, *fascism* has come to mean a military dictatorship built on racist and powerfully nationalistic foundations, generally with the broad support of the business class (distinguishing it from the collectivism of Communism.) But when Benito Mussolini adopted the term, he used it quite proudly.

The first of the modern dictators, Benito Mussolini (1883–1945), called *Il Duce* (which simply means "the leader"), was the son of a blacksmith who came to power as prime minister in 1922. A preening bully of a man, he organized Italian World War I veterans into the anti-Communist and rabidly nationalistic "black-shirts," a paramilitary group that used gang tactics to suppress strikes and attack leftist trade unions. Riding the anti-Communist fervor in Italy, he was accepted by a people who wanted "order." His rise to power was accompanied by the beatings of opponents and the murder of a key Socialist party leader.

In 1925, Mussolini installed himself as head of a single-party state he called *fascismo*. The word came from *fasces,* a Latin word referring to a bundle of rods bound around an ax, which had been a Roman symbol of authority. While most of Europe disarmed, Mussolini rearmed Italy during the twenties. A failure at actual governing, Mussolini saw military adventurism as the means to keep the Italian people loyal, and Italy embarked on wars in Africa and in support of General Francisco Franco's Spanish rebels.

The rise to power of the three militaristic, totalitarian states that would form the wartime Axis—Germany, Japan, and Italy—as well as Fascist Spain under General Franco, can be laid to the aftershocks, both political and economic, of the first World War. It was rather easy, especially in the case of Germany and Italy, for demagogues to point to the smoldering ruins of their countries and the economic disaster of the worldwide depression and blame their woes on foreigners. Under the crushing weight of the war's costs, the people might be said to have lacked the will *not to believe*.

Mussolini blamed Italy's problems on foreigners, and promised to make the trains run on time. (Contrary to popular belief, he did not.) The next step was simply to crush opposition through the most ruthless form of police state. In Germany, Adolf Hitler (1889–1945) made scapegoats not only of the Communists and foreign powers who he claimed had stripped Germany of its land and military abilities at Versailles, but also of Jews, who he claimed were in control of the world's finances. The long history of anti-Semitism in Europe, going back for centuries, simply fed the easy acceptance of Hitler's argument.

Like Mussolini and his blackshirts, Hitler organized his followers into a strongarm gang of Brownshirts, and later into an elite uniformed guard called the SS. In 1930, his National Socialist (Nazi) party, with its platform of placing blame for Germany's Depression problems on Jews, Marxists, and foreign powers, attracted the masses of unemployed and began to win increasing numbers of seats in Germany's parliament, the Reichstag, and Hitler was named Chancellor by an aging President Hindenburg. When the Reichstag burned and Communists were blamed, Hitler had the incident he needed to grab dictatorial powers and concentrate them under a police state that simply crushed all opposition. Bathed in nationalistic theatrics, bankrolled by militant industrialists, supported by an increasingly powerful army and secret police, and led by a man with an uncanny ability to captivate and enthrall his country with pomp and jingoism, Hitler was the essence of the Fascist leader.

Hitler made no secret of his plans. From the start, he announced that he wanted to reunite the German-speaking people separated when the map of Europe was redrawn following the Treaty of Versailles. He also pledged to rearm Germany so that it would never be forced to accept terms as it had at Versailles in 1918. By 1935, Germany was committed to a massive program of militarization, modernizing its armaments and requiring universal military service. That same year, Mussolini invaded Ethiopia, which bordered Italian Somaliland in Africa. American attempts to avoid entanglement in these "European" problems led to passage of the Neutrality Act in 1935, which barred the sale of munitions to all belligerents. Facing strong isolationist sentiment, led by Henry Ford, Charles Lindbergh, and the vitriolic, anti-Semitic Catholic "radio priest," Father Charles Coughlin (1891–1979), Roosevelt had to swallow the unpleasant bill. Curiously unrestricted by the embargo were petroleum products. Oil and gasoline sales to Italy tripled as the modernized Italian army crushed the nearly primitive Ethiopian resistance.

In 1936 the Spanish Civil War broke out. The Fascist (Falangist) rebels under General Francisco Franco (1892–1975), with the military support of Germany and 50,000 Italian troops, sought to overthrow the left-leaning Spanish Republic, which in turn was receiving support from the Soviet Union. The Spanish Civil War was a proxy war in which German arms, weapons, and tactics were being battle-tested. Again, America's official position remained neutral and isolationist, even as many Americans went to Spain to fight in the losing Loyalist or Republican cause.

The pace of events became more rapid. In July 1937, Japan attacked China once more, this time conquering Peking. The following October, Roosevelt made a subtle shift from isolationism. Like Wilson before the First World War, Roosevelt's sympathies were always with England, and like Wilson, Roosevelt professed a desire to avoid American involvement in the war. Saying that "America actively engages in the search for peace," he recommended "quarantining" the aggressors, acknowleding without identifying them.

In March 1938, Germany absorbed Austria in the *Anschluss* (annexation), and in September, Hitler demanded the return of the German Sudetenland, which had been incorporated into Czechoslovakia after 1918. At a conference in Munich, the prime ministers of Great Britain and France accepted this demand and pressed the Czechs to turn over the land. That was simply Hitler's prelude to a more ambitious land-grab.

Recognizing the paucity of resistance, Hitler simply took the rest of Czechoslovakia in early 1939. He next set his sights on Poland, demanding the city of Danzig (modern-day Gdansk). Hitler now had Roosevelt's full attention, but Roosevelt lacked the votes at the time even to overturn the Neutrality Act that prevented him from arming France and Great Britain for the war that everyone now knew was surely coming.

In August 1939, Germany and the Soviet Union signed a nonaggression pact, a prelude to a joint attack on Poland by Germany from the west and Russia from the East. France and England could stand by and appease Hitler no longer. Both countries declared war on Germany on September 3.

As the German military had planned in 1914, Germany went for a quick, decisive victory that would crush France and give it control of Europe. But unlike 1914, when the British and French held off the German assault, the Nazi plan was far more successful. The Nazi onslaught, the *Blitzkreig* ("lightning war") leveled resistance in Denmark, Norway, the Netherlands, Belgium, and France. By the summer of 1940, Hitler controlled most of western

Europe, and the British and French armies had been sent reeling from Dunkerque, on the Strait of Dover.

Roosevelt was able to force through a stopgap "cash and carry" bill that allowed the Allies to buy arms. After Italy joined Germany in the attack on France, Roosevelt froze the assets of the conquered nations still held in the United States, to prevent the Germans from using them. Without legal authority, FDR began to sell the English "surplus" American arms. After the fall of France, FDR came up with the idea of "trading" aging American destroyers to the British in exchange for bases, the deal that was the prelude to Lend-Lease.

What did FDR know about a Japanese attack, and when did he know it?

No question has tantalized historians of the wartime period more than this one. Did Roosevelt know the Japanese were going to attack Pearl Harbor, and did he deliberately allow the attack that took more than 2,000 American lives?

There are two basic views about America's entry into the war. The first says that FDR was preoccupied with the war in Europe and didn't want war with Japan. American strategic thinking, perhaps reflecting Anglo-Saxon racism about Japanese abilities, dismissed the Japanese military threat.

The other says that FDR viewed Japan, allied to the German-Italian Axis, as his entrée into the European war. This stand holds that FDR made a series of calculated provocations that pushed Japan into war with America. The ultimate conclusion to this view is that FDR knew of the imminent Japanese attack on Pearl Harbor and not only failed to prevent it, but welcomed it as the turning point that would end isolationist obstruction of his war plans.

Neither view is seamless, and the reality may lie in a combination of the two, with such factors as human frailty, overconfidence on both sides, and the tensions of a world already at war thrown in. You might also cast a vote for historical inevitability. A clash between Japan and the United States and other Western nations over control of the economy and resources of the Far East and

Pacific was bound to happen. A small island nation with limited resources but great ambitions, Japan had to reach out to control its destiny. That put it on a collision course with the Western nations that had established a colonial presence in the Pacific and Asia, and had their own plans for exploiting that part of the world.

With that in mind, there are certain facts that remain. Japanese-American relations were bad in the 1930s, and worsened when the Japanese sank an American warship, the *Panay*, on the Yangtze River late in 1937, a clear violation of all treaties and an outright act of war. But America was not ready to go to war over a single ship. Attempting to influence the outcome of China's struggle against Japan, Roosevelt loaned money to the Nationalists in China and began to ban exports to Japan of certain goods that eventually included gasoline, scrap iron, and oil.

Were these provocations to force Japan into war, or sensible reactions to Japanese aggression in China and elsewhere in Asia? Historical opinion divides on this point. It is clear that moderation on either side might have prevailed. But in the United States, the Secretary of State was demanding complete Japanese withdrawal from their territorial conquests. At the same time in Japan, hawkish militants led by General Hideki Tojo (1884–1948) had gained power. Moderation was tossed aside and the two speeding engines continued on a runaway collision course.

By late in 1941, it was more than apparent that war was coming with Japan. American and foreign diplomats in Japan dispatched frequent warnings about the Japanese mood. And more significantly, the Japanese diplomatic code had been broken by American intelligence. Almost all messages between Tokyo and its embassy in Washington were being intercepted and understood by Washington.

There is no longer any doubt that some Americans knew that "Zero Hour," as the Japanese ambassador to Washington called the planned attack, was scheduled for December 7. They even knew it would come at Pearl Harbor. According to John Toland's account of Pearl Harbor, *Infamy*, Americans had not only broken the Japanese code, but the Dutch had done so as well, and their warnings had been passed on to Washington. A British double agent code-named Tricycle had also sent explicit warnings to the United States.

Here is where human frailty and overconfidence, and even American racism, take over. Most American military minds expected a Japanese attack to come in the Philippines, America's major base in the Pacific; the American naval fortifications at Pearl Harbor on Oahu were believed to be too strong to attack, as well as too far away for the Japanese. The commanders there prepared for an attack by saboteurs, which explains why the battleships were packed together in the harbor, surrounded defensively by smaller vessels, and why planes were parked in neat rows in the middle of the airstrip at Hickam Field, ready to be blasted by Japanese bombing runs.

Many Americans, including Roosevelt, dismissed the Japanese as combat pilots because they were all presumed to be "nearsighted." The excellence of their eyes and flying abilities came as an expensive surprise to the American military. There was also a sense that any attack on Pearl Harbor would be easily repulsed. The Japanese would get a bad spanking, and America would still get the war it wanted in Europe.

Whether or not the attack was invited and specific warnings were ignored, the complete devastation of the American forces at Pearl Harbor was totally unexpected. Even today, the tally of that attack is astonishing. Eighteen ships were sunk or seriously damaged, including eight battleships. Of these eight, six were later salvaged. Nearly two hundred airplanes were destroyed on the ground, and 2,403 people died that morning, nearly half of them aboard the battleship *Arizona*, which took a bomb down its smokestack and went to the bottom in minutes.

A day after the attack, Roosevelt delivered his war message to Congress. The long-running battle between isolationists and interventionists was over.

American Voices

From Franklin D. Roosevelt's war message to Congress (December 8, 1941):

Yesterday, December 7, 1941—a date which will live in infamy—the United States of America was suddenly and deliberately attacked by naval and air forces of the Empire of Japan.

The United States was at peace with that nation and, at the solicitation of Japan, was still in conversation with its government and its emperor, looking toward the maintenance of peace in the Pacific.

. . . The attack yesterday on the Hawaiian Islands has caused severe damage to American naval and military forces. I regret to tell you that very many American lives have been lost. . . .

Yesterday, the Japanese Government also launched an attack against Malaya.

Last night, Japanese forces attacked Hong Kong.

Last night, Japanese forces attacked Guam.

Last night, Japanese forces attacked the Philippine Islands.

Last night, the Japanese attacked Wake Island.

And this morning, the Japanese attacked Midway Island.

. . . No matter how long it may take us to overcome this premeditated invasion, the American people, in their righteous might, will win through to absolute victory.

Milestones in World War II

1938

March 13 The *Anschluss* (annexation of Austria). German troops march into Austria to "preserve order." Hitler declares Austria "reunited" with Germany.

September 30 The Munich Pact. The British and French allow Hitler to annex the Sudetenland, an area of Czechoslovakia with a largely German-speaking population. Through this policy of "appeasement," Prime Minister Neville Chamberlain (1869–1940) believes that Germany will be satisfied and that there will be "peace in our time." Winston Churchill, later First Lord of the Admiralty, thinks otherwise. "Britain and France had to choose

between war and dishonor," say the future Prime Minister. "They chose dishonor. They will have war."
October 3 Hitler triumphantly enters the Sudetenland.

1939

March 14 After taking the Sudetenland, Germany invades the rest of Czechoslovakia.
April 1 The three-year-old Spanish Civil War ends with German- and Italian-supported Fascist victory. The United States recognizes the new government of General Francisco Franco (1892–1975).
April 7 Italy invades Albania, its small neighbor across the Adriatic Sea.
July 14 Reacting to growing international tension over Germany's provocations in Europe, President Roosevelt asks Congress to repeal an arms embargo so that the United States can sell arms to England and other non-Fascist countries.
September 1 Germany invades Poland. Claiming a Polish attack on German soldiers, Germany's modernized forces overrun the small, unprepared, and outdated Polish army.
September 3 After Hitler ignores their demand for German withdrawal from Poland, Great Britain and France formally declare war on Germany.
   Twenty-eight Americans die aboard a British ship torpedoed by a German submarine, but Roosevelt proclaims American neutrality in the war. Five days later he declares a limited national emergency, giving him broad powers to act. A few weeks later he announces that all U.S. offshore waters and ports are closed to the submarines of the warring nations.
September 28 Germany and Russia partition Poland, which Russia invaded from the east on September 17, two weeks after Germany entered Poland from the west. The United States refuses to recognize the partition, and maintains diplomatic relations with a Polish government-in-exile in Paris.
October 11 A letter written by Albert Einstein is delivered to Roosevelt by Alexander Sachs, a financier and adviser to the President. In it, Einstein discusses the implications of a nuclear

chain reaction and the powerful bombs that may be constructed. He says, "A single bomb of this type, carried by boat and exploded in a port, might very well destroy the whole port, together with some of the surrounding territory." Roosevelt immediately begins a secret military undertaking that will result in the atomic bomb.

November 4 The Neutrality Act is signed. This measure will allow the United States to send arms and other aid to Britain and France.

1940

January "The Battle of the Atlantic." German submarines begin torpedo attacks on Allied shipping, sinking nearly 4.5 million tons of ships in the first two months of the year.

March 18 Mussolini and Hitler announce Italy's formal alliance with Germany against England and France. Mussolini calls this the "Axis" on which Europe will revolve.

April 9 Norway and Denmark are overrun by Germany.

May 10 Luxembourg, Belgium, and the Netherlands are invaded by Germany. On the same day, Winston Churchill replaces the disgraced Neville Chamberlain as Prime Minister.

May 26–June 4 Dunkerque. Pressed to the coast of France, British and French troops converge on this small coastal town on the Dover Strait. The Royal Navy, assisted by hundreds of small fishing and merchant ships, evacuates more than 300,000 troops as the advancing Germans bomb and shell the fleeing troops. Churchill makes one of his memorable speeches: "We shall fight on the beaches, we shall fight on the landing grounds, we shall fight in the fields and the streets. . . . We shall never surrender."

June 5 Germany invades France. Ten days later, Paris falls. By **June 22,** France surrenders and a pro-German government is installed in the city of Vichy. In London, a Free French government headed by General Charles de Gaulle (1890–1970) vows to resist.

June 10 President Roosevelt announces a shift from neutrality to "non-belligerency," meaning more active support for the Allies against the Axis.

June 28 The Alien Registration Act (the Smith Act) is passed. it requires aliens to register and makes it illegal to advocate the violent overthrow of the U.S. government.

July 10 The Battle of Britain. The first aerial attack on England by the German air force begins the devastating air war over England. For four months, German bombers pound London and other strategic points. Taking heavy civilian and military losses, the staunch British air defense destroys 1,700 German planes. Failure to control the airspace over England is a key factor in the Nazi decision not to launch an invasion across the Channel.

July 20 Congress authorizes $4 billion for the construction of a two-ocean navy.

September 3 Roosevelt gives fifty American destroyers to England in exchange for the right to construct bases in British possessions in the Western Hemisphere. This trade inspires the Lend-Lease program.

September 16 The Selective Training and Service Act requires men from twenty-one to thirty-five years of age to register for military training.

September 26 President Roosevelt announces an embargo on shipments of scrap metal outside the Western Hemisphere, aimed at cutting off supplies to Japan.

November 5 Roosevelt wins reelection to an unprecedented third term, defeating Republican Wendell Willkie by 449 electoral votes to 82.

December 29 In a year-end "fireside chat," Roosevelt says that the United States will become the "arsenal of democracy." Many peacetime factories are converted to war production, and this shift to a wartime economy shakes off the last effects of the Great Depression. During the war, America will produce 297,000 planes, 86,000 tanks, 12,000 ships, and enormous quantities of other vehicles, arms, and munitions. As in the case of the North in the Civil War and the United States in World War I, the American industrial capacity to mass-produce war materials provides the margin of victory. America and its allies do not so much outfight Germany and Japan as outproduce them.

1941

March 11 The Lend-Lease Act is signed into law. It narrowly passes Congress as isolationist sentiment remains strong.

May 27 A limited state of emergency is declared by President Roosevelt after Greece and Yugoslavia fall to the Axis powers. An American merchant ship, *Robin Moor*, is sunk by a U-boat near Brazil.

June 14 German and Italian assets in the United States are frozen under President Roosevelt's emergency powers. Two days later, all German consulates in the United States are ordered closed, and on June 20, all Italian consulates are also shut down.

June 22 Germany invades Russia, breaking the "nonaggression" pact signed in 1939. Two days later, President Roosevelt promises U.S. aid to Russia under Lend-Lease.

July 25 After the Japanese invade French Indochina, President Roosevelt freezes Japan's assets in the United States, halting trade between the countries and cutting off Japanese oil supplies. This move is later cited by the Japanese as a cause for attacking the United States.

August 14 After meeting secretly on warships stationed near Newfoundland, Roosevelt and Churchill announce the Atlantic Charter, a document that lays out eight goals for the world, including open trade, international economic cooperation, safe boundaries, freedom of the seas, and abandonment of the use of force. Its call for "self-determination" is aimed at freeing nations under Axis domination rather than the many Allied colonial interests in such places as India, Indochina, and the Philippines.

October 17 The U.S. destroyer *Kearney* is torpedoed by a U-boat, leaving eleven Americans dead. Two weeks later, the destroyer *Reuben James* is sunk by a U-boat, with one hundred Americans lost. Hitler knows that war with the United States is now inevitable.

November 3 The U.S. Ambassador to Japan, Joseph Grew, warns of a possible Japanese surprise attack. Roosevelt and the Cabinet receive his message on November 7.

November 17 Japanese envoys in Washington propose removing restrictions on trade. American Secretary of State Cordell Hull rejects the proposal, calling for Japanese withdrawal from China and Indochina.

December 7 One day after President Roosevelt appeals to Emperor Hirohito to use his influence to avert war, the Japanese attack

Pearl Harbor, the major U.S. base in Hawaii, killing 2,403 American soldiers, sailors, and civilians. Nineteen ships and 150 planes are destroyed. Defying all American expectations of their military capabilities, the Japanese make simultaneous strikes on Guam, Midway, and British bases in Hong Kong and Singapore. Japan declares war on the United States.

December 8 Addressing a joint session of Congress, Roosevelt asks for a declaration of war on Japan. The Senate vote is unanimously in favor; the House approves 388–1, with pacifist Jeanette Rankin, the first woman elected to the House, the lone dissenter.

December 11 (Europe) Responding to the state of war between the United States and Japan, Germany and Italy declare war on the United States, giving President Roosevelt the fight with Hitler that he wanted.

December 17 (Pacific) Admiral Chester Nimitz (1885–1966) is given command of the Pacific fleet, replacing Admiral Kimmel, who was in charge of Pearl Harbor and is the scapegoat for the disaster. Nimitz will organize and direct the American counterattack in the Pacific.

December 23 (Pacific) The Japanese take Wake Island, an American possession in the middle of the North Pacific.

December 25 (Pacific) Hong Kong falls to Japan.

1942

January 2 (Pacific) Japan takes control of the Philippines as General MacArthur withdraws to Corregidor, an island fortress in Manila Bay.

January 14 (Home front) A presidential order requires all aliens to register with the government. This is the beginning of a plan to move Japanese-Americans into internment camps in the belief that these people might aid the enemy.

January 26 (Europe) For the first time since the end of World War I, American troops arrive in Europe, landing in Northern Ireland.

February 20 (Home front) Roosevelt approves the plan to remove Japanese-Americans from their homes and send them to internment camps in Colorado, Utah, Arkansas, and other interior states. Eventually 100,000 Japanese-Americans will be moved, losing their homes and possessions. Many of the young men who are relocated join special U.S. army units that perform with high honor.

February 23 (Home front) In one of the only assaults on the continental United States, an oil refinery in California is shelled by a Japanese submarine.

February 27–March 1 (Pacific) A Japanese fleet virtually destroys the American and British fleet in the Java Sea.

March 11 (Pacific) General MacArthur leaves the Philippines for Australia, vowing, "I shall return." General Jonathan Wainwright (1883–1953) is left in command of American forces, who move to the Bataan Peninsula.

April 9 (Pacific) Seventy-five thousand American and Philippine troops surrender to the Japanese after a stoic resistance to overwhelming Japanese numbers. The captives are marched over one hundred miles in the infamous "Bataan Death March," during which thousands of prisoners are executed or die of starvation and thirst before they reach Japanese prison camps. A few weeks later, General Wainwright is captured by the Japanese, surrendering all American forces in the Philippines. (A classic photograph later shows an emaciated Wainwright embracing MacArthur after the Japanese surrender.)

April 18 (Pacific) Led by Major General James Doolittle, U.S. bombers raid Tokyo and other Japanese cities. Although the raids have little military effect, carrying the war to Japan provides an important psychological boost to American morale and alters Japanese strategic thinking.

April 28 (Home front) Coastal "blackouts" go into effect along a fifteen-mile strip on the Eastern Seaboard. Following Pearl Harbor, there are real fears of bombing attacks by Germany as well as the more realistic threat of German U-boats operating in the Atlantic.

May 4–8 (Pacific) The Battle of the Coral Sea. In an early turning point off New Guinea, U.S. Navy planes severely damage a Japanese fleet, forestalling a Japanese invasion of Australia. For the first time in naval history, ships in battle do not engage each other directly; all the fighting is carried out by carrier-launched planes.

May 15 (Home front) Gasoline rationing goes into effect. A few days later, price ceilings on many retail products take effect.

June 3–6 (Pacific) The Battle of Midway. In a major naval confrontation off the small North Pacific island, the U.S. Navy wins another crucial battle in the Pacific war. Although the carrier *Yorktown* is damaged, the Japanese lose four carriers and many of their best-trained pilots, and the Japanese naval advantage is eliminated, ending the threat to Australia. By this time the Japanese control an enormous area extending westward to Burma, north to Manchuria, south to New Guinea, and including the small islands of the Pacific. The territory represents about 10 percent of the Earth's surface.

June 13 (Home front) Eight German saboteurs land in various spots on the East Coast from submarines. They are quickly captured and tried as spies, and six are executed.

In Washington, two important new agencies are established. The Office of War Information (OWI) will become the government's wartime propaganda arm and home to numerous writers and filmmakers. The Office of Strategic Services (OSS), led by William Donovan (1883–1959), is the country's espionage agency and forerunner to the postwar CIA.

August 7 (Pacific) In the first U.S. offensive of the war, marines land on Guadalcanal in the Solomon Islands, northeast of Australia. It is the beginning of a two-pronged offensive aimed at dislodging the Japanese from islands that will provide stepping-stones for an eventual invasion of Japan. The war in the Pacific has been given a strategic backseat to the war in Europe, and American Pacific forces will often be poorly supported, lacking ammunition and other supplies. This is the case on Guadalcanal, the first in a series of bloody, savagely fought battles in the Pacific.

August 22 (Europe) The Battle of Stalingrad. The Germans begin an offensive against the city that they expect will complete their conquest of the Soviet Union. This is the beginning of an epic Russian stand that costs hundreds of thousands of lives on both sides, but is a turning point as Hitler's eastern offensive ends in a harsh failure.

October 25–26 (Pacific) Attempting to stop the American landing on Guadalcanal, the Japanese fleet is met by the U.S. Navy in the Battle of Santa Cruz. The Japanese again suffer heavy aircraft losses.

November 12–15 (Pacific) In the naval battle of Guadalcanal, the U.S. fleet under Admiral William Halsey (1882–1959) destroys a Japanese fleet, sinking twenty-eight warships and transports, rendering the Japanese unable to reinforce their troops on Guadalcanal.

November 18 (Home front) The draft age is lowered to eighteen years.

November 25 (Europe) The three-month siege of Stalingrad has turned against the German army, which is eventually surrounded. By the time the German army surrenders, in February 1943, its casualties will surpass 300,000. The Russian victory marks the end of the German offensive in Russia, and Germany begins its long retreat from the Eastern Front.

December 1 (Home front) Coffee and gasoline join the list of rationed items.

1943

January 14–24 (Europe) Meeting at the Casablanca Conference, Roosevelt and Churchill map out strategy for the eventual invasion of Europe.

February 7 (Home front) Shoe rationing is announced, limiting civilians to three pairs of leather shoes per year.

February 9 (Pacific) U.S. Marines take control of Guadalcanal after four months of savage combat in which they have been cut off from supplies and were reduced to eating roots.

February 14–25 (Europe) At the Kasserine Pass in Tunisia, the Afrika Korps of Field Marshal Erwin Rommel (1891–1944) defeats U.S. forces. But American troops regroup under the new command of George S. Patton (1885–1945) and stop Rommel's drive. They eventually link up with British forces under Field Marshal Bernard Montgomery (1887–1976), who was chasing Rommel from Egypt. Probably Germany's best wartime field commander, Rommel is recalled to Germany and is later involved in a botched attempt to assassinate Hitler, which will lead to Rommel's suicide.

March 2–4 (Pacific) The U.S. Navy scores another major victory over a Japanese convoy in the Battle of the Bismarck Sea off New Guinea.

April 1 (Home front) Meats, fats, and cheese are now rationed. Attempting to stem inflation, President Roosevelt freezes wages, salaries, and prices.

May 7 (Europe) In a pincer action, Montgomery and Patton link their armies in Tunis, forcing the surrender of all German and Italian troops in North Africa. Ignoring the warnings of Rommel to withdraw these troops, Hitler and Mussolini have pressed more troops into North Africa in a drive aimed at gaining control of the Suez, through which England's oil supply moves. In a few weeks, more than 250,000 Axis soldiers lay down their weapons. Combined with combat casualties, more than 350,000 Axis troops are killed or captured in North Africa, against 18,500 American casualties.

May 16 (Europe) In Warsaw, Poland, the last fighters in the Jewish ghetto are overwhelmed after their stoic but doomed resistance against the Nazis. The survivors are shipped to death camps, and the ghetto is razed.

May 27 (Home front) President Roosevelt issues an executive order forbidding racial discrimination by government contractors. At about this time, anti-black riots in Detroit leave thirty-four people dead.

May 29 (Home front) An issue of *The Saturday Evening Post* is published with a cover illustration by Norman Rockwell that introduces an American icon known as "Rosie the Riveter." The character is a sandwich-munching, brawny, yet innocent-looking woman in coveralls, cradling her rivet gun in her lap, goggles pushed up onto her forehead. Rockwell borrowed the idea for "Rosie" from a figure in Michelangelo's Sistine Chapel frescoes. Rockwell's "Rosie" is an admiring tribute to the more than 6 million women who have entered the job force during the war, many of them taking up positions in what was considered "man's work," including the defense industries. However, the image is destined to last only as long as the war.

July 10 (Europe) The Invasion of Sicily. Allied forces under General Dwight D. Eisenhower's command begin an assault that will capture the strategic island by August 17, giving the Allies control of Mediterranean shipping and a base from which to launch an invasion of mainland Italy. Allied casualties in the five weeks of fighting top 25,000, while more than 167,000 Germans and Italians are killed or wounded.

July 19 (Europe) Preceded by an air drop of millions of leaflets calling upon Italians to surrender, the Allies begin to bomb targets in and around Rome. Within a week, Mussolini is forced to resign by King Victor Emmanuel, and the new prime minister, Pietro Badoglio, considers an Italian surrender. By September 3, when the Allies launch an invasion of the mainland from Sicily, Prime Minister Badoglio has signed a secret armistice ending Italian military resistance.

September 9 (Europe) The invasion of Salerno. More than seven hundred ships deliver an Allied invasion force that meets fierce resistance, as the Germans have prepared for this invasion by reinforcing Italy with their best troops. Every inch of the Allied advance is hard-fought, as the Germans are dug into well-defended mountain positions and the Italian winter is one of the harshest on record. By October 1, the port of Naples is in Allied hands, but the departing Germans put the torch to books and museums as retribution for Italy's "betrayal." Italy declares war on Germany.

November 20 (Pacific) The Battle of Tarawa. One of the equatorial Gilbert Islands, the Tarawa atoll possesses an airstrip, an important prize in the Pacific fighting. Using British guns captured at Singapore, the Japanese are well defended on the small island of Betio, about half the size of Central Park. Ignoring islanders' warnings of tricky tides, the landing's commanders send in waves of marines who are trapped before reaching the beaches. The marines' casualties total 3,381, although the airstrip is eventually taken.

November 28–December 1 (Europe) The Teheran Conference brings together Roosevelt, Churchill, and Josef Stalin, the first time all three have met in person. They confer about the coming invasion of Europe.

1944

January 22 (Europe) The invasion of Anzio. Allied forces hit this coastal town near Rome in an attempt to encircle German forces in central Italy. But Germans pin down the Americans on Anzio's beach. At the inland monastery town of Monte Cassino there is fierce fighting that takes a heavy toll on both sides.

January 31 (Pacific) After taking control of the airstrip at Tarawa, the U.S. amphibious invasion force under Admiral Nimitz continues its step-by-step sweep into the North Pacific with an invasion of the Marshall Islands.

February 20–27 (Europe) The U.S. Army Air Corps begins a massive bombing campaign against German aircraft production centers. A week later, on March 6, more than six hundred U.S. bombers make their first raid on Berlin. While it is presumed that the strategic bombing has been costly to the German economy and morale, a survey initiated by President Roosevelt will later show that the bombing was devastating but did not work "conclusively." Just as the British economy has survived the German Blitz, the Germans are able to shift production around with no discernible fall-off.

May 3 (Home front) Meat rationing ends, except for certain select cuts.

May 18 (Europe) The German stronghold at Monte Cassino in central Italy finally falls. It has been under Allied siege for three months, a costly campaign of dubious strategic value. A few weeks later, at Anzio, Americans trapped on the beaches for months break through as British troops mount an offensive from Italy's west. The Allies are driving toward Rome, and arrive in the city on June 4.

June 6 (Europe) D-Day. The Allied invasion of Europe, code-named Operation Overlord, commences just after midnight. The largest invasion force in history, it comprises 4,000 invasion ships, 600 warships, 10,000 planes, and more than 175,000 Allied troops. Although an invasion has been expected by the Germans, the secret of Overlord is well kept. The plan, at the mercy of the weather, includes a feint farther north near Calais, but the true objective is the Normandy coast between Cherbourg and Le

Havre—beaches that have been given names like Juno and Sword,
Omaha and Utah. It takes four days of fierce fighting and heavy
casualties on both sides before the two main beachhead armies are
joined. Despite heavy casualties, the Allies send the Germans
backwards toward Germany and a million Allied troops are soon
on the Continent. But this is only the beginning of the end. It will
take almost a full year of fierce combat before the German surrender.

June 13 (Europe) Germany launches the world's first guided
missiles, the ramjet-powered V-1 "buzz bombs," across the English Channel at London; only one reaches its target but by the
end of summer, they kill some 6,000 people. These "vengeance
weapons" are the creation of a team of rocket scientists led by Dr
Wernher von Braun, who will become an American citizen in
1955 and boost the American space program.

June 15 (Pacific) B-29 Superfortress bombers, based in China
begin to raid Japan. At the same time, U.S. troops begin an
offensive on the Marianas—Saipan, Guam, and Tinian. The first
target, Saipan, is supposed to be captured in three days. But these
islands have been held by the Japanese for twenty-five years and
their defenses are strong. The battle for Saipan is a month-long
fight that claims 3,400 American lives and more than 27,000
Japanese. A grisly aftermath of the fighting is the mass suicide of
civilians who jump from a cliff because Japanese propaganda has
warned them of American sadism.

June 22 (Home front) President Roosevelt signs the Servicemen's
Readjustment Act that will provide funds for housing and education after the war. It is better known as the GI Bill.

June 27 (Europe) The French port of Cherbourg is captured by
the Allies, although it has been badly sabotaged and booby
trapped by the departing Germans.

July 9–25 (Europe) After the British take Caen, and St.-Lo falls
Patton's tank troops of the Third Army break through a German
line, isolating German troops in Brittany.

July 20 (Europe) With defeat becoming more certain, a group of
German officers plot to kill Hitler and take control of the government. The coup fails when Hitler escapes injury from a bomb
planted in a suitcase at his headquarters. The leaders of the plot

are discovered and executed, and thousands of possible con-spirators are killed.

August 10 (Pacific) Guam falls to U.S. forces after three weeks of intense fighting. The Japanese losses are put at 17,000; 1,200 Americans die and another 6,000 are wounded. The completed conquest of the Marianas will give the United States an airbase from which to begin a large-scale bombardment of Japan. Napalm is used for the first time in these bombings, and the island of Tinian is the base from which the *Enola Gay* will make its fateful flight a year later.

August 14 (Home front) With war production requirements eas-ing, production of vacuum cleaners and other domestic products is allowed to resume.

August 15 (Europe) A second invasion front is opened in south-ern France as Allied troops sweep up the Rhone River valley, meeting little resistance.

August 25 (Europe) French troops led by General LeClerc retake Paris. On the following day, General de Gaulle, leader of the Free French, enters Paris in a ceremonial parade. On August 27, Eisenhower and other Allied leaders enter Paris. Relatively un-touched by the war, Paris has flourished under German occupa-tion, and the great fashion houses have prospered. Frenchwomen who are suspected of having slept with Germans are led into the streets to have their heads shaved.

September 12 (Europe) The second wave of von Braun's missiles, the V-2s, which are the first modern rockets, are launched across the Channel. Five hundred hit London. These are more accurate, but they are too few, too late to make any impact on the war's outcome.

October 20 (Pacific) General Douglas MacArthur, in the now-famous photograph, wades ashore at Leyte Island, the Philip-pines, fulfilling his promise to return. Three days later, the Battle of Leyte Gulf results in a major Japanese naval defeat. The Japanese now begin to resort to the infamous *kamikaze* suicide attacks, in which Japanese pilots attempt to crash their explosive-laden planes into American ships. Kamikaze attacks will result in the loss of some four hundred ships and nearly 10,000 American seamen.

November 7 (Home front) President Roosevelt wins his unprecedented and unequaled fourth term by defeating New York governor Thomas Dewey.
December 16 (Europe) The Battle of the Bulge. In the last major
German counteroffensive, Allied troops are pushed back in Belgium's Ardennes Forest. (As Allied lines fall back, a "bulge" is
created in the center of the line, giving the battle its familiar
name.) Two weeks of intense fighting in brutal winter weather
follow before the German offensive is stopped. One of the most
famous moments in the long battle comes when the American
101st Airborne Division is encircled by Germans in Bastogne.
When the German general demands surrender, General Anthony
McAuliffe reportedly replies, "Nuts." The 101st is relieved a few
days later as Patton sends in his tanks. This last-gasp German
gamble is followed by rapid defeat for Germany.

1945

February 1 (Europe) One thousand American bombers raid Berlin. At about this time, Dresden, a city of little strategic value, is
firebombed by U.S. planes, killing more than 100,000 Germans.
February 4–11 (Europe) The Yalta Conference. Meeting in he
Crimea, Churchill, Stalin, and an ailing Roosevelt discuss plans
for the final assault on Germany, and agree to create a peace
organization that will meet in San Francisco on April 25 and will
become the United Nations. More significantly, the meeting also
produces the groundwork for the postwar division of Europe
among the Allies.
February (Pacific) A month-long siege in the Philippines ends
with U.S. troops retaking Manila.
March 7 (Europe) American forces cross the Rhine River at Re-
magen, and by the end of the month, all German forces have been
pushed back into Germany.
March 9 As U.S. planes begin to bombard Japan more heavily, a
massive firebombing of Tokyo kills some 100,000 Japanese.
March 16 (Pacific) Iwo Jima. A month-long struggle for this
rocky, eight-square-mile piece of volcanic island comes to an end.
Possessing Japan's last line of radar defense to warn against

American air attacks, Iwo Jima is a strategically significant prelude to the invasion of Okinawa. The combined naval and ground attack begins one of the most terrible and hard-fought battles of the war. The famous image of the six marines—three of whom will die on Iwo Jima—raising the flag atop Mount Suribachi becomes an American icon of the day. Losses on both sides are horrifying, with the U.S. Marines suffering some 25,000 casualties.

April 1 (Pacific) In the next steppingstone, U.S. troops invade Okinawa on Easter Sunday, or, as the soldiers note ironically, April Fool's Day. The Japanese allow the troops to land, and then systematically attempt to destroy their naval support, beginning a fight that will last almost three months, the bloodiest battle of the Pacific, which will eventually cost 80,000 American casualties.

April 11 U.S. troops reach the Elbe River (in what is now East Germany). They halt there and meet advancing Russian troops on April 25.

April 12 (Home front) After suffering a massive cerebral hemorrhage, President Roosevelt dies at his retreat in Warm Springs, Georgia. Vice-President Harry S. Truman (1884–1972) is sworn in as President.

April 24 President Truman is told of the program called the Manhattan Project, which has developed the atom bomb. Truman is initially reluctant to use the weapon, and orders a search for alternatives.

April 30 With Russian shells falling on Berlin, Hitler marries his mistress, Eva Braun, in his bombproof Berlin bunker. He then poisons her and kills himself. His remains are never recovered.

May 7 (Europe) The Germans formally surrender to General Eisenhower at Rheims, France, and to the Soviets in Berlin. President Truman pronounces the following day V-E Day.

June 5 (Europe) The United States, Russia, England, and France agree to split occupied Germany into eastern and western halves, and to divide Berlin, which is within the eastern, Russian-occupied half of Germany.

June 21 (Pacific) Okinawa falls. The Japanese have lost 160,000 men in fighting on the island; more than 12,500 Americans die on Okinawa.

July 5 (Pacific) General MacArthur completes the recapture of the Philippines; 12,000 Americans have died in the ten-month fight for the islands. With the reconquest of the Philippines and the securing of Okinawa as a base, the United States begins to plan for an invasion of Japan.

July 16 (Home front) The first atomic bomb is successfully detonated in a secret test at Alamogordo, New Mexico, the fruits of the top-secret Manhattan Project begun in 1943 by President Roosevelt and continued under Truman.

August 6 (Pacific) Hiroshima. The U.S. B-29 Superfortress *Enola Gay* drops the atomic bomb on this industrial city. The destructive capacity of this now-primitive weapon levels the city, killing some 80,000 immediately, seriously injuring another 100,000 (out of a total population of 344,000), and leveling 98 percent of the city's buildings. The bomb's force astounds even its makers, who have not truly understood its destructive potential or the effects of radiation. Three days later, on August 9, a second bomb is dropped on Japan, this one on the city of Nagasaki, and Stalin declares war on Japan, launching an invasion of Manchuria.

August 14 (Pacific) Fighting ends in the Far East. Three days later the Allies divide Korea along the 38th parallel, with Soviet troops occupying the northern half and U.S. troops holding the south.

September 2 (Pacific) General MacArthur, named Supreme Commander of Allied Powers in Japan, accepts the formal, unconditional surrender of Japan aboard the USS *Missouri* in Tokyo Bay. In December, MacArthur is appointed by Truman to attempt to negotiate a settlement between the Nationalist Chinese under Chiang Kai-shek and the Communists under Mao Zedong.

What was the cost of World War II?

While there is no "official" casualty count for the Second World War, it was clearly the greatest and deadliest war in history, costing more than 38 million lives. The estimates of battle losses are numbing: 7.5 million Russians; 3.5 million Germans; 1.2 million Japanese; 2.2 million Chinese. Great Britain and France each lost hundreds of thousands of men. The civilian toll was even higher. Probably 22 million Russians died during the war years.

The German "final solution," or extermination of the Jews, took the lives of at least 6 million Jews, most of these dying in the concentration camps. Millions more Slavs, Eastern Europeans, gypsies, and homosexuals were similarly engulfed by the Holocaust. For the United States, combat casualties were close to 300,000 dead and nearly 700,000 wounded.

The wartime cooperation between the Soviets and the West, the creation of the United Nations, and the frightful power of the atomic bomb raised hopes that this truly would be the war to end all wars. But just three months into the new year, former Prime Minister Winston Churchill, turned out of office in the 1945 elections, addressed a college audience at Fulton, Missouri. He told the gathering and the world, "An Iron Curtain has descended across the continent, allowing 'police governments' to rule Eastern Europe,"

One war was over. The next—the Cold War—was under way.

What was the Yalta Conference?

In February 1945, the war in Europe was moving toward its final days. Soviet armies were already in Hungary and Poland and approaching Berlin. On the Western Front, Allied forces pushed back Hitler's personally planned counteroffensive in the Ardennes forest in the brutal Battle of the Bulge. American and Soviet troops were moving toward their meeting on the Elbe River. But the Pacific war was still going strong. Japan was far from defeated, although plainly in retreat.

Against this background the Allied Big Three—Winston Churchill, Franklin D. Roosevelt, and Josef Stalin (1879–1953), the men who conducted the war against Germany—met together in Yalta, in a former Tsarist palace on the Black Sea. This was to be a "mopping-up" meeting. The major wartime decisions had been made earlier at meetings between Roosevelt and Churchill at Casablanca, and at a summit of the Big Three in Teheran.

Recently inaugurated for a fourth term, but greatly aged by twelve years of governing a fractious nation through the Depression and the war, Roosevelt was in poor health. He came to Yalta with three goals: to establish a meaningful United Nations;

to persuade the Russians to declare war on Japan and thereby to hasten the end of that part of the war; and to decide the fate of Poland, that sizable chunk of territory which had been at the heart of the war since Germany and Russia both invaded it.

Of these three issues, Russian commitment to the war against Japan was uppermost in Roosevelt's mind. Work on a secret weapon to be used against Japan was still going on, but even the few who knew of the existence of the Manhattan Project held no great hopes for the atomic bomb's usefulness. Roosevelt had to consider the advice of his generals, like MacArthur, who conservatively estimated that a million American casualties would result from the eventual invasion of Japan. To Roosevelt and Churchill, obtaining Stalin's commitment to join the fight against Japan was crucial. To Roosevelt's generals, it was worth any price.

Stalin knew that.

Roosevelt and Churchill, who had held most of the cards during the war, found themselves in the dangerous position of dealing with the master of the Soviet Union from a position of weakness. Stalin finally agreed to enter an anti-Japanese alliance, but the price was substantial: the Soviets would control Manchuria and Mongolia, and would be ceded half of Sakhalin Island and the Kurile Islands, off northern Japan; a Soviet occupation zone would be created in Korea; and in the United Nations, a veto power would be given to the major nations, of which the Soviet Union was one, along with the United States, Great Britain, France, and China (still under the wavering control of Chiang Kai-shek's American-supported Nationalists).

Later it would be said that Roosevelt, the "sick man" of the Yalta Conference, had given away Poland (and the rest of Eastern Europe). In fact, he couldn't give away what wasn't his to give. The Red Army and Communist partisan forces in Eastern Europe held control of almost all of this territory. In private, Churchill urged Eisenhower to continue pushing his armies as far east of the Elbe River as possible, a position with which U.S. General George Patton was in complete agreement. But Ike disagreed. Patton had to pull back, and the Russians "liberated" Czechoslovakia, eastern Germany, and Berlin.

At Yalta, the Polish issue was "solved" by redrawing its borders and, in a replay of Versailles, adding lands that had been Germany's. In the spirit of Allied unity, Stalin agreed to guarantee all Eastern European countries the right to choose their governments and leaders in free elections. Roosevelt believed that a United Nations, with American commitment (which the League of Nations lacked), could solve problems related to these issues as they arose. Perhaps more tragically, Roosevelt saw his personal role as the conciliator as a key to lasting peace.

As the historian James McGregor Burns wrote in *The Crosswinds of Freedom*, "Holding only weak hands in the great poker game of Yalta, Roosevelt believed he had won the foundations of future peace. It was with hope and even exultation that he and his party left Yalta for the long journey home. Above all he left with confidence that, whatever the problems ahead, he could solve them through his personal intervention."

How did FDR die?

Any hopes Roosevelt had of maintaining peace through his personality went to his grave with him. On April 12, 1945, Roosevelt suffered a cerebral hemorrhage while resting at his retreat in Warm Springs, Georgia, where he was staying with his longtime mistress, Lucy Rutherford. His death left the nation and much of the world dizzy and disoriented. Even the Japanese issued a sympathetic message. He was still vilified by many, but to most Americans FDR had been an immutable force, a Gibraltar-like presence on the American scene. He had guided America as it licked the Great Depression and the Nazis. To younger Americans, including many of those in uniform, he was the only President they had known.

Practically beatified by a generation of Americans, Franklin D. Roosevelt appears, forty-five years after his death—like Washington, Lincoln, and other "great men" of American history—less a saint than a man flawed by his humanity. He was foremost a politician, perhaps the greatest ever in America, and like all politicians, he made bargains. There are large questions left by his legacy. For instance, although he was greatly admired and overwhelmingly voted for by blacks, FDR's approach to the question of blacks in America was confused. His wife, Eleanor, consistently pushed for greater social equality for blacks and all minority groups. But American life and the army remained segregated, although blacks slowly reached higher ranks, and war contractors were forbidden to practice segregation.

Another lingering question has concerned his response to the Holocaust. Prior to the American entry into the war, the Nazi treatment of Jews evoked little more than weak diplomatic condemnation. It is clear that Roosevelt knew about the treatment of Jews in Germany and elsewhere in Europe, and about the methodical, systematic destruction of the Jews during the Holocaust. Clearly, saving the Jews and other groups that Hitler was destroying en masse was not a critical issue for American war planners.

The Pearl Harbor issue also refuses to go away. Few historians are willing to go so far as to condemn Roosevelt for sentencing two thousand Americans to die when they might have been saved. Instead, the consensus is that his military advisers underestimated the abilities of the Japanese to reach Hawaii, and exaggerated the U.S. military's ability to defend itself against such an attack. The internment of Japanese-Americans during the war is an everlasting stain on Roosevelt and the entire nation.

In a private light, FDR was later shown to have carried on a long-term relationship with Lucy Rutherford. If revealed, this secret might have brought him down. But in contrast to what has befallen politicians in more recent times, no stories about FDR and Rutherford ever appeared, much less film or photographs. He was protected by the press and the Secret Service, just as John F. Kennedy would be for sexual behavior far more indiscreet and dangerous than Roosevelt's love affair had been.

Yet FDR's legacy remains. Just as Washington was "the indispensable man" of his time, so was FDR in the era of depression and war. If history does come down to the question of personality, was there another man in America who could have accomplished what Roosevelt did? Despite flaws and contradictions, he knew that a failure to improve the nation's economic and psychological health might produce a victory for the forces of racism and militarism that produced different leaders in other countries. Few Presidents—none since Lincoln during the Civil War—held the

ear-dictatorial powers Roosevelt commanded during the De-
ression and the war. Yet, if he was a quasi-dictator at the height
f his political power, FDR's overall record is certainly benign.
he same economic shock waves that brought Roosevelt to power
roduced Mussolini and Hitler, demagogic madmen with visions
f world conquest, who ruled brutal, racist, police states. Like
aany another canonized American hero, Roosevelt was far from
ainthood. Yet consider the alternative.

)id the United States have to drop atomic bombs on Hiroshima
nd Nagasaki?

Okay, Mr. President. Here's the situation. You're about to
ivade Japan's main islands. Your best generals say hitting these
eaches will mean half a million American casualties. Other es-
mates go as high as a million. General MacArthur tells you that
he Japanese will continue guerrilla-style resistance for ten years.
ased on horrific battle experience—from Guadalcanal to Okina-
a—you believe the Japanese will fight to the death. They have
ix million battle-hardened troops who have shown complete
illingness to fight to the death for their homeland—a samurai
radition of complete devotion to the divine Emperor that is
icomprehensible to Americans. Japanese civilians have jumped
ff cliffs to prevent capture by Americans, and there are reports
hat mainland Japanese civilians are being armed with sharpened
amboo spears. But you also remember Pearl Harbor and the
ataan Death March and other wartime atrocities committed by
apanese. Vengeance, in the midst of a cruel war, is not in-
omprehensible.

Now you have a bomb with the destructive power of 20,000
ons of TNT. It worked in a test, but it may not work when you
rop it out of a plane. Why not give a demonstration to show its
ower? Your advisers tell you that if the show-detonation is a dud,
he Japanese resistance will harden.

Modern history has presented this pair of options—the Big
ivasion versus the Bomb—as "Truman's Choice." It was a choice
ruman inherited with the Oval Office. President Roosevelt had
esponded to Albert Einstein's 1939 warning—a warning Einstein

later regretted—of the potential of an atomic bomb by establish
ing the Manhattan Project in 1943. Known to a handful of men
Truman not among them, the project was a $2-billion (in pre
inflation 1940s dollars) effort to construct an atomic weapon
Working at Los Alamos, New Mexico, under the direction of J
Robert Oppenheimer (1904–1967), atomic scientists, many o
them refugees from Hitler's Europe, thought they were racing
against Germans developing a "Nazi bomb." That effort was late
proved to be far short of success. The first atomic bomb wa
exploded at Alamogordo, New Mexico, on July 16, 1945. Truma
was alerted to the success of the test at a meeting with Churchil
and Stalin at Potsdam, a city in defeated Germany.

Before the test detonation, there were already deep misgi
ings among both the scientific and military communities abou
the morality of the bomb's destructive power. Many of its creator
did not want it to be used, and lobbied to share its secrets with th
rest of the world to prevent its use. Truman ignored that advice
With Churchill and China's Chiang Kai-shek, he issued the "Pots
dam Declaration," warning Japan to accept a complete and un
conditional surrender or risk "prompt and utter destruction.
Although specific mention of the bomb's nature was considered
this vague warning was the only one issued.

When the Japanese first failed to respond to, and then re
jected, his ultimatum, Truman ordered the fateful go-ahead. I
was a self-perpetuating order that took on a life of its own. Afte
Hiroshima, nobody said, "Don't drop another one," so the mer
proceeded under the orders they had been given.

Almost since the day the first bomb was dropped on Hiroshi
ma, critics have second-guessed Truman's decision and motives
A generation of historians have defended or repudiated the nee
for unleashing the atomic weapon. The historical justification wa
that a full-scale invasion of Japan would have cost frightful numb
ers of American and Japanese lives.

Many critics have dismissed those estimates as implausibl
high, and say that the Japanese were already nearing their deci
sion to submit when the bombs were dropped. A study made afte
the war by a U.S. government survey team reached that ver

conclusion. But coming as it did a year after the war was over, that judgment didn't help Truman make his decision.

Other historians who support the Hiroshima drop dispute that criticism. Instead, they point to the fact that some of the strongest militarists in Japan were planning a coup to topple a pro-surrender government. Even after the Japanese surrender, Japanese officers were planning kamikaze strikes at the battleship on which the surrender documents would be signed. The view that accepts "atomic necessity" offers as evidence the actual Pacific fighting as it moved closer to Japan. And it is a convincing exhibit. Each successive island that the Americans invaded was defended fanatically, at immense cost on both sides. The Japanese military code, centuries old and steeped in the samurai tradition, showed no tolerance for surrender. Indeed, even in Hiroshima itself, there was anger that the Emperor had capitulated.

But was the Bomb versus an invasion the only option? Or was there another reality? A top-secret study made during the period and revealed in the late 1980s says there was, and destroys much of the accepted justification for the Hiroshima bombing. According to these army studies, the crucial factor in the Japanese decision to surrender was not the dropping of the bombs but the entry of the Soviet Union into the war against Japan. These documents and other recently revealed evidence suggest that Truman knew at Potsdam that Stalin would declare war against Japan early in August. Nearly two months before Hiroshima, Army Chief of Staff George C. Marshall had advised the President that the Soviet declaration of war would force Japan to surrender, making the need for an American invasion unnecessary. It was a fact with which Truman seemed to agree.

So if the estimates of an invasion's costs and ending the war quickly were not the only considerations, why did the United States use these terrible weapons?

What history has confirmed is that the men who made the bomb really didn't understand how horrifying its capabilities were. Of course they understood the destructive power of the bomb, but radiation's dangers were far less understood. As author Peter Wyden tells it in *Day One*, his compelling account of the making and dropping of the bomb, scientists involved in creating what they called "the gadget" believed that anyone who might be killed by radiation would die from falling bricks first.

But apart from this scientific shortfall, was there another strategic element to the decision? Many modern historians unhesitatingly answer "Yes." By late 1945 it was clear to Truman and other American leaders that victory over Germany and Japan would not mean peace. Stalin's intention to create a buffer of socialist states surrounding the Soviet Union and under the control of the Red Army was already apparent. Atomic muscle-flexing may have been the overriding consideration in Truman's decision.

The age of nuclear saber-rattling did not begin with the dropping of the bomb on Hiroshima, but with the Potsdam meeting, where Stalin and Truman began the deadly dance around the issue of atomic weaponry. Truman was unaware that Stalin, through the efforts of scientist-spy Klaus Fuchs, who was working at Los Alamos and passing secrets to the Soviets, knew as much about the atomic bomb as the President himself—if not more.

Some historians have pointed to the second attack on Nagasaki as further proof of this atomic "big stick" theory. Having demonstrated the uranium bomb at Hiroshima, Truman still wanted to show off the plutonium bomb used against Nagasaki to send a clear message to the Soviets: We have it and we're not afraid to use it.

If Truman viewed these bombs as a message to the Soviets, that message, and the frightful nuclear buildup on both sides in the postwar years, dictated American and Soviet policies in the coming decades of Cold War confrontation.

Chapter

———————

Seven

———————

Commies, Containment, and Cold War: America in the Fifties

- What was the Truman Doctrine?

- What were the Pumpkin Papers?

- Why were the Rosenbergs executed for espionage?

- What was McCarthyism?

- Who fought in the Korean War?

- Milestones in the Korean War

- What were the results of the Korean War?

- What was *Brown v. Board of Education?*

- Why did the arrest of a woman named Rosa Parks change American life?

- Why did President Eisenhower send the army into Little Rock, Arkansas?

• What was Sputnik?

Wﾠhat we think of as the fifties really began in 1945. The war was over. The boys came home. America was triumphant, now first among nations. "The American Century" proclaimed earlier by *Time* magazine's publisher Henry Luce seemed to be fully under way.

It was time to enjoy Uncle Miltie, Lucy, and daring novels like *Forever Amber* and *Peyton Place*. Most people fondly recall the postwar era as a respite of prosperity and social normality, a comfortable time. For eight of those years, Dwight D. Eisenhower (1890–1969), the gentle-faced golfer whom America called "Ike," held office, a comforting President. His campaign buttons simply read "I Like Ike," and that said it all. With his wife, Mamie, as First Lady, it was like having everyone's favorite aunt and uncle sitting in the White House.

America started to watch television—more than 4 million sets were sold in 1950—and listen to the comfortable sound of Perry Como. There was no hip-swiveling jailhouse rocker on the scene. Yet.

America moved to the comfortable suburbs; 13 million new homes went up between 1948 and 1958, many of them in the cookie-cutter fashion pioneered by developer William J. Levitt's phenomenally successful Levittown, Long Island. Coming back from the Big War and later the Korean conflict, former GIs wasted no time, and America's maternity wards were overflowing—76.4 million "baby boomers" were born between 1946 and 1964. The country was reading Dr. Spock's *Baby and Child Care* and Norman Vincent Peale's *The Power of Positive Thinking*.

But not everything was rosy—even though America saw Red wherever it looked. There were commies everywhere. In Eastern Europe and Asia. In the State Department and the army. They seemed to be under every rock. Even in Hollywood!

There was also a generation of young writers looking at the underside of this dream, straining against the new American dream and its conformist constraints. In his first novel, *The Naked and the Dead* (1948), Norman Mailer (b. 1923) presented a different and uncomfortable picture of the American GI in combat. A short-story writer named J. D. Salinger (b. 1919) would capture the alienation of youth forever in his novel *The Catcher in the Rye* (1951). In several novels of the period, including *The Adventures of Augie March* (1953), Saul Bellow (b. 1915) would also express the angst of a generation. By 1955 with *On the Road,* Jack Kerouac (1922–1969) would help lead a generation of "beats" who broke the era's social restraints, becoming self-proclaimed outcasts from a nation that prized stability and "normality" above all. Books like David Riesman's *The Lonely Crowd* (1950) and William Whyte's *The Organization Man* (1956) also examined this peculiar American need to conform, an American characteristic that Tocqueville had perceptively brought to light more than a hundred years earlier.

What was the Truman Doctrine?

Any dreams for an era of postwar cooperation between the two new giants of the world, the United States and the Soviet Union, quickly evaporated. The map of Europe had been redrawn and, in Churchill's ominous phrase, an "Iron Curtain" had descended across Eastern Europe as the Soviets under Stalin established a ring of socialist states around its flanks. The future, it appeared, would produce a string of flare-ups as the two nations contended for power and influence.

In 1947, when it appeared that Greece and Turkey were the next targets for Communist takeovers, and the British informed President Truman that they would be unable to prevent such takeovers, Truman asked Congress for aid to both governments. In what became known as the Truman Doctrine, the President told Congress, "I believe that it must be the policy of the United States to support free peoples who are resisting subjugation by armed minorities or by outside pressures."

With $400 million worth of American advisers and military aid, the Greek and Turkish governments prevailed. But instead of installing representative government in the so-called cradle of democracy, Athens came under the rule of an oppressive, right-wing military regime, as did Turkey. But that was less important to political leaders of the United States at the time than that both countries remain aligned with the United States.

The theoretical underpinnings of the Truman Doctrine came from a State Department official named George F. Kennan. Writing under the pseudonym "X" in the influential journal *Foreign Affairs,* Kennan introduced the pivotal concept of "containment," which essentially meant using American might to counter Soviet pressure wherever it developed. "Containment" of the Communist threat would color every foreign-policy decision in America for decades to come, as well as help bring about the great domestic fear of Communism that swept the country during the 1950s. Besides the Truman Doctrine, "containment" also led to the establishment of the North Atlantic Treaty Organization (NATO) in 1949 to defend Western Europe against Soviet Bloc attack, and the Marshall Plan to address the serious economic crisis in postwar Europe.

American Voices

From Secretary of State George C. Marshall's Harvard commencement address justifying the European Recovery Program, known as the Marshall Plan (June 5, 1947):

> The truth of the matter is that Europe's requirements for the next three or four years of foreign food and other essential products—principally from America—are so much greater than her present ability to pay that she must have substantial additional help, or face economic, social and political deterioration of a very grave character.
>
> . . . Aside from the demoralizing effect on the world at large and the possibilities of disturbances arising as a result of the desperation of the people concerned, the consequences to the economy of the United States should be apparent to all. It is logical that the United States should do whatever it is able to do to assist in the return of normal economic health in the world, without which there can be no political stability and no assured peace. Our policy is directed not against any country

or doctrine but against hunger, poverty, desperation, and chaos.

Conceived by Undersecretary of State Will Clayton and first proposed by Secretary of State Dean Acheson (1893–1971), the Marshall Plan pumped more than $12 billion into Europe in the next four years. It provided the economic side of Truman's policy of containment by removing the economic dislocation that might have fostered Communism in Western Europe. It also set up a Displaced Persons Plan under which some 300,000 Europeans, many of them Jewish survivors of the Holocaust, were granted American citizenship.

By most accounts, the Marshall Plan was an enormously successful undertaking to return a devastated Europe to a state approaching health. But was it simply pure American altruism, as we learned in school—the goodhearted generosity of America's best intentions? Not so, say critics on the left. To them, the Marshall Plan was simply an extension of a capitalist plan for American economic domination, a calculated Cold War ploy to rebuild European capitalism. Or, to put it simply, if there was no Europe to sell to, who would buy all those products the American industrial machine was turning out?

What were the Pumpkin Papers?

To America, Communism was on the march around the world. Roosevelt and his liberal coterie had "given away" Eastern Europe at Yalta. In a test of U.S. resolve, the Soviets had tried to close off Berlin, forcing the United States to conduct a massive airlift in 1948 that finally cracked the Russian hold on the city. In China, the Nationalists were crushed by Mao's Communist forces in 1949. At about the same time, it was revealed that the Soviets had the Bomb. The world seemed to be in the grasp of a Communist conspiracy of international domination, and the President had responded with the "Truman Doctrine," with the complete support of a bipartisan Congress.

The obsessive fear of Communism in America was nothing new. Americans had been battling the Red Menace for years, and the first wave of Red hysteria had followed World War I. (See Chapter 6.) But it seemed as if the fears were much more real now, heightened by the terror of the mushroom cloud. Communism was the cutting issue on which people voted. To be "soft" on communism was political suicide, and ambitious young men, like Representative Richard M. Nixon (1913–1994) of California, could see that Communist-bashing was the ticket to the future.

Responding to this anti-Red pressure, Truman had set up loyalty boards in 1947 to check on reports of Communist sympathizers in the federal government. Thousands were investigated, but there was no meaningful trace of subversion, even though careers were destroyed as suspicion replaced evidence. These were the first of the anti-Communist "witch hunts" in which the burden of proof was on the accused, who couldn't face or know his unnamed accusers. Hearsay testimony from unreliable witnesses became Holy Writ.

The fear got front-page headlines in 1949, when Whittaker Chambers (1901–1961), a "reformed" Communist Party member and later an editor at *Time* magazine, charged that Alger Hiss was a Communist spy. To those who knew Hiss, this was nonsense that took the paranoia too far. A Roosevelt New Dealer, Hiss (b. 1904) was born and bred to the Eastern Establishment, with impeccable credentials as a progressive. But to conservatives, Hiss was blemished because he had been with Roosevelt at Yalta and was Secretary General of the United Nations organizing conference in 1945–46. Both Yalta and the UN were increasingly viewed as parts of the Communist scheme for weakening America and achieving world domination. In 1947, Hiss became president of the Carnegie Endowment for International Peace. But his integrity and loyalty were unquestioned.

Disheveled, overweight, and a somewhat ill-bred character, Chambers claimed that in the 1930s, Hiss had been a Communist who had given Chambers classified documents to be passed on to Moscow. Pressed by Congressman Richard Nixon in a hearing before the House Un-American Activities Committee investigating alleged Communist subversion in government, Hiss denied the allegations. Everything in his demeanor and bearing seemed to demolish the allegations made by the unseemly Chambers. But there were also some damaging revelations that left nagging suspicions. The most sensational of these came to light when Chambers produced copies of old purloined microfilm that had allegedly been concealed inside a hollowed-out pumpkin in Chambers's garden. Overnight, these became the "Pumpkin Papers."

The case might have blown over, except that Hiss sued Chambers for libel, and the evidence against this paragon of American progressive-liberalism turned out to be strong. In the courtroom, Chambers showed that he knew intimate details of Hiss's life, and even produced papers showing that Hiss had once given him an old car. While the statute of limitations protected Hiss from espionage charges, he was indicted for perjury for lying to a congressional committee. Tried and convicted in January 1950, he was sentenced to five years in prison. And people still argue this case with passion.

Why were the Rosenbergs executed for espionage?

At about the same time Hiss's story held the headlines, Americans learned that Klaus Fuchs, a respected European scientist who had total access to Los Alamos during the war, had been passing secrets to the Russians. Harry Gold, an American associate of Fuchs, was caught at the same time as an American couple, David and Ruth Greenglass. Greenglass, who also worked at Los Alamos, testified that he had passed on crude drawings of atomic weapons to his brother-in-law and sister, Julius and Ethel Rosenberg.

Claiming innocence at their trial, the Rosenbergs relied on the Fifth Amendment when asked if they were Communists. Their day in court came in the midst of the Korean War, presided over by a judge who, in a throwback to the Sacco and Vanzetti case, was totally in league with the prosecution. The Rosenbergs' defenders—then and now—have claimed that the Rosenbergs were framed, convicted, and executed in an atmosphere of anti-Semitic, anti-Communist frenzy.

The other conspirators were given prison sentences, including Fuchs himself, because they all agreed to help the prosecution, which the Rosenbergs refused to do. And that was ultimately the reason they were sent to the electric chair. While the evidence against them was strong, what has emerged is a consensus that Julius Rosenberg may have indeed been a spy, but that the secrets he passed along were far less damaging than those Fuchs turned over. The government wanted to make the Rosenbergs symbols of its fervent anti-Communism. But the years have turned the couple into the martyrs of America's rabid, irrational fears.

What was McCarthyism?

It was from this toxic cloud of hysteria that Senator Joseph McCarthy (1909–1957) emerged, and was taken up by the right-wing press as a new Paul Revere. He was the freshman senator from Wisconsin, elected to the Senate in 1946 by lying about his wartime service record and smearing his primary- and general-election opponents. In a short time this scruffy, mean-spirited alcoholic was lining his pockets with lobbyist money and was generally thought of as the "worst senator" in Washington. By 1950 he was looking for the issue that would keep his leaky political boat from sinking.

McCarthy found that issue when he was fed some obsolete documents relating to old investigations of Communists in government jobs. In February 1950, McCarthy told a women's club in Wheeling, West Virginia, that he held, "here in my hand," a list of 205 men in the State Department named as members of the Communist Party who were part of a spy ring. The numbers changed from day to day, and even McCarthy wasn't sure where he had gotten them. His bulging briefcase of "evidence" generally held only a bottle of bourbon. But this was the beginning of his "Big Lie," consisting of evidence and charges fabricated by a desperate man. In the following days, the emptiness of McCarthy's "evidence" should have ended his Senate career. But it didn't work out that way. In 1950, America was more than ready to believe what Senator McCarthy had to say.

Although a Senate committee investigated and then refuted everything McCarthy claimed, their findings were ignored. True or not, McCarthy's irresponsible accusations caught the public ear, made headlines, and sold newspapers. The Senate investigations dismissing his charges got buried on the back pages with the ship sailing notices.

Time has altered the meaning of "McCarthyism." In 1950 it meant a brave, patriotic stand against Communism, with the broad support of the media and people. Now it has come to mean a smear campaign of groundless accusations from which the accused cannot escape, because professions of innocence become admissions of guilt and only confessions are accepted. Many of those who came before McCarthy, as well as many who testified before the powerful House Un-American Activities Committee (HUAC), were willing to point fingers at others to save their own careers and reputations. To fight back was to be tarred with McCarthy's "Communist sympathizer" brush. For many, particularly in the entertainment industries of radio, motion pictures, and television, that meant "blacklisting" that ruined careers. In this cynical atmosphere, laws of evidence and constitutional guarantees didn't apply to "devious Communists." For four years, McCarthy was as powerful as any man in Washington. He could force the President to clear appointments through him, and McCarthy's rampage forced President Eisenhower to institute a new round of "loyalty" programs to prove that he too was "tough" on Communism.

But in 1954, McCarthy took up a battle that turned against him when he challenged the U.S. Army to purge supposed Communists from the Pentagon. With the resourceful assistance of Roy Cohn, a young attorney whom McCarthy had earlier dispatched overseas to eradicate "communistic books" from U.S. International Information Administration libraries, McCarthy had begun to attack certain army officers as Communists. Once again he captivated the public imagination with his charges. But this time he overreached himself. The Army was Ike's turf. Eisenhower and the army started to hit back, first by investigating David Schine, Roy Cohn's wealthy companion on his book-purge trip, who, having subsequently been drafted into the army, had used McCarthy's influence to win soft military assignments.

The media also turned on him. CBS's legendary reporter Edward R. Murrow (1908–1965), the man who had brought the Blitz of London live to America on radio during the war, took aim at McCarthy on his TV program "See It Now," a predecessor to "60 Minutes." By simply showing clips of McCarthy without editorializing, Murrow allowed the senator's bluster to undermine him, exposing McCarthy for the charlatan he was.

During the thirty-six days of the Army-McCarthy hearings, McCarthy finally came undone, his cudgel-like attacks, remorseless crudeness, and unfounded accusations being revealed in an unpleasant light. The daily televised hearings dissolved as Joseph Welch, the respected lawyer representing the army, turned the tables on McCarthy and routed him in public. The hearings ended inconclusively, but the rest of the Senate smelled blood. By the end of 1954, McCarthy was condemned by his peers, and his public support eroded. His hold on the Senate and the public gone, McCarthy spiraled downward in a pathetic drunken tailspin. He died in May 1957 of health problems brought on by his alcoholism.

American Voices

Joseph N. Welch (1890–1960), special counsel for the army at the 1954 Army-McCarthy hearings, in response to an attack by McCarthy on a young associate in Welch's law firm:

> Until this moment, Senator, I think I never really gauged your cruelty or your recklessness. . . . Have you no decency, sir, at long last? Have you left no sense of decency?

Who fought in the Korean War?

As if Hiss and the Rosenbergs, Mao's millions and McCarthyism, and the Soviet bomb weren't enough to strike fear into 1950s America, 90,000 North Koreans did the trick. In June 1950, after a large-scale artillery barrage, the sound of bugles signaled the massed charge of North Koreans who came down out of the mountains to roll over an American-sponsored government in South Korea. Armed and trained by the Soviets, this was the most efficient fighting force in Asia after the Soviet Red Army.

This was the onset of the Korean War, a "hot war" in the

midst of the Cold War maneuvering, and one that cost more than two million Korean lives as well as 100,000 American casualties. As political strife in South Korea continues even today to move through successive phases of protests and militaristic repression, it is still not really over.

Most contemporary American perceptions of the Korean War come from the TV series "M*A*S*H." The Korean conflict remains something of an ambiguity, unlike the "people's war" that preceded it or the unpopular war that followed it. For Americans at home in the 1950s, Korea wasn't the "good war." Korea was a far-off mystery, and fighting for "containment" lacked the moral urgency behind the crusade against the Nazi scourge and the "murderers" of Pearl Harbor and Bataan. But American boys were being soundly whipped by the Korean invaders. President Truman and General MacArthur said we should fight, and in 1950 that was good enough for most Americans.

Americans still relied on radio and newsreels for their news, rather than the television that would bring Vietnam into the living room with such astonishing immediacy. But there are some clear parallels between Korea and America's tragedy in Vietnam. (Moreover, the first American involvement in Vietnam actually came during the Korean War, in the form of aid to the French anti-Communist effort in Indochina.) In both wars, an American-supported right-wing government was under attack by Communist insurgents supported by the Soviet Union and China. Both wars were fought to "contain" Asian Communism in nations split by postwar agreements with the Soviets. The Asian Communists were assumed in 1950 to be part of a worldwide Communist conspiracy that reached right into the heart of America's government—as Senator McCarthy was "proving."

While the rebels in both places were fighting a civil war for reunification under their control, the stakes were higher in Washington and Moscow, which poured in the military support to keep the wars going. While the United States provided the bulk of the troops and funds in Korea and Vietnam, both wars were ostensibly fought by an alliance of nations. But although the United States actually fought in Korea under a United Nations flag, it held no such pretensions in Vietnam. There is one other significant difference. In Vietnam, the United States fought against a mainly Vietnamese force of both guerrillas and North Vietnamese regulars. In Korea, the fighting started out against the North Koreans, but it quickly escalated into a much deadlier and more dangerous war against the massive armies of Red China.

At home, both wars produced "hawks" who supported total commitment to the effort. In the Korean period, they were led by General MacArthur and the powerful "China lobby" of senators and media moguls like Henry Luce who wanted all-out war against Communism—including an assault on Mao's China. Although Korea never produced the broad social divisions that came later with Vietnam, the American people had little heart for the fighting in Korea.

As with Vietnam, the war in Korea helped end the presidency of a Democratic President—Harry S. Truman, in this case, and opened the way for a Republican—Dwight D. Eisenhower. (The Twenty-second Amendment, ratified in 1947, limits a President to two terms or to a single elected term for a President who has served more than two years of his predecessor's term, as Truman had. Truman was exempt from these provisions, however, and could have run again in 1952, but chose not to.)

American Voices

From the "Checkers Speech" by Richard Nixon (September 1952):

> I should say this—that Pat [Nixon's wife] doesn't have a mink coat. But she does have a respectable Republican cloth coat. And I always tell her that she would look good in anything.
>
> One other thing I should probably tell you, because if I don't they'll be saying this about me, too. We did get something, a gift, after the nomination. A man down in Texas heard Pat on the radio mention the fact that our two youngsters would like to have a dog and, believe it or not, the day before we left on this campaign trip we got a message from Union Station in Baltimore, saying they had a package for us. . . . You know what it was?

It was a little cocker spaniel dog in a crate that he had sent all the way from Texas—black and white, spotted, and our little girl Tricia, the six-year-old, named it Checkers. And you know the kids, like all kids, love that dog and I just want to say this, right now, that regardless of what they say about it, we're going to keep it."

Nixon's speech came in the midst of Eisenhower's campaign against Adlai Stevenson. While the Republicans ran on a platform of scourging Democratic corruption in Washington, Nixon was accused of keeping a "secret slush fund" provided by "fat cat" contributors. It certainly existed, but was legal. The appearance of the "war chest" was terrible for the Republicans, however, and Nixon was on the verge of resigning from the ticket. Instead, he took to the airwaves in a televised speech that would be called maudlin and mawkish by the media. But the speech won heartland votes and it saved Nixon's career and the Republican ticket's chances.

Milestones in the Korean War (1950–1953)

1950

June 25 Trained and equipped by the Soviet Union, 90,000 North Korean troops pour over the 38th-parallel border and invade the Republic of Korea. The following day, President Truman authorizes the U.S. Navy and Air Force to assist South Korean armies in defending against the invasion. Within three days North Korean troops, encountering token resistance from what is essentially a South Korean military police force, capture the capital, Seoul, located only forty miles south of the border.

June 27 The United Nations Security Council first adopts a ceasefire resolution. The Soviet Union's envoy to the UN is not present, as he is boycotting the Security Council because it recognizes Nationalist China instead of Communist China. The resolution passes the Security Council 9–0. In a few weeks, a second resolution will commit a UN force to support the South Korean government.

June 30 General Douglas MacArthur visits the collapsing South Korean front lines and calls for U.S. troops. President Truman commits U.S. ground troops to South Korea, announces a naval blockade of the Korean coast, and extends the draft for another year. He also increases aid to the French fight against Communist rebels in Indochina.

July 8 A third UN resolution acknowledges American leadership of UN forces and Gen. Douglas MacArthur is placed in command of UN troops in South Korea. Although U.S. and South Korean troops will form the bulk of the UN forces, soldiers from sixteen nations, including Australia, Great Britain, and the Philippines, also see action. Initially, U.S. troops prove woefully unprepared for combat. Pulled from soft occupation duty in Japan, they lack training and are out of shape and ill-armed. American military strength is at its lowest state of readiness since Pearl Harbor. In the first weeks of fighting, U.S. forces are pushed back to a defensive perimeter at Pusan. American air power, which controls the skies over Korea and harasses North Korean supply routes, is the only reason North Korea fails to overwhelm the South.

August 6 The North Korean offensive is finally stopped by the line around Pusan.

September 15 In what is usually considered the single most brilliant stroke in his long military career, General MacArthur leads an amphibious assault on the port city of Inchon, deep behind North Korean lines. The invasion force encounters light resistance and moves quickly toward Seoul. With dangerously overextended supply lines, the North Koreans are trapped between MacArthur's landing force and the defenders at Pusan. They begin an immediate retreat back across the border. Two weeks after the landing at Inchon, Seoul is recaptured by UN troops, who meet unexpectedly stiff resistance from remaining North Korean troops in the capital.

September 29 The UN forces reach the 38th parallel, marking the boundary separating North and South. Presumably, the aims of the war have been accomplished with the North driven back across its border. But Korean President Syngman Rhee announces his intention to continue the war by uniting Korea under his rule and punishing the North for its aggression. This plan is fully supported by MacArthur, a staunch anti-Communist, and the American military command in Washington, but any action against China is expressly ruled out.

October 7 Shifting from the containment policy to a goal of overthrowing a Communist government, MacArthur's UN forces invade North Korea. The move is denounced by the Communist government of China, which says it will not stand idly by. The Chinese threat is ignored as a bluff. The United States has no relations with China, and only recognizes the Nationalist government of Chiang Kai-shek on Taiwan (Formosa). Nearly one million Chinese troops had been massed in Manchuria.

October 15 President Truman and General MacArthur meet on Wake Island. Truman wants to rein in the headstrong soldier who has spent his career countering presidential orders. Truman leaves Wake thinking that MacArthur is resolved to abide by his general orders.

October 20 UN troops capture the North Korean capital of Pyongyang and continue to advance north toward the Yalu River, the border with Manchuria.

November 1 Massing under the cover of smoke from huge forest fires, Chinese troops attack South Korean troops in the North, destroying one army.

November 2 General MacArthur announces that the Chinese constitute a serious threat. Under attack by the Chinese, the U.S. Eighth Army retreats south.

November 4 A massive Chinese counteroffensive begins. MacArthur reports that the Chinese are in Korea in such numbers that they threaten his command, and demands reinforcements.

November 6 Abandoning their concealment tactics, a million Chinese move into Korea. U.S. pilots watch a steady stream of Chinese troops cross the Yalu River separating Korea from Manchuria. MacArthur announces a plan to bomb the Yalu bridges, but it is overruled by Washington. MacArthur begins a political offensive in favor of all-out war against the Chinese that will not only reunite Korea but topple the Communist government in China, allowing Chiang Kai-shek to retake the mainland. In his worst strategic maneuver, MacArthur has split his armies, and the Chinese easily drive through the center of the UN forces.

December 5 In the face of enormous Chinese manpower willing to accept huge casualties, UN troops abandon Pyongyang and are eventually pushed out of the North. The Chinese continue their offensive, promising to drive the Americans into the sea. MacArthur reports to Truman, "We face an entirely new war."

December 8 President Truman announces an embargo on U.S. goods shipped to China.

December 16 President Truman declares a national emergency and calls for an army buildup to 3.5 million men. Three days later, Dwight Eisenhower, who is serving as president of Columbia University, is named supreme commander of Western European defense forces.

December 29 General MacArthur announces that the United States should attack China, and advocates atomic attacks on China and the use of half a million Nationalist Chinese troops to overthrow the Communist government in China.

1951

January 4 Chinese troops capture Seoul. MacArthur complains about being hampered by Truman's decision not to bomb Chinese supply dumps in China. UN troops eventually regroup and halt the Chinese offensive.

March 14 UN forces recapture Seoul and eventually push Chinese troops back across the border.

April 5 In the United States, Julius and Ethel Rosenberg are sentenced to death on their conviction of passing atomic secrets to the Soviet Union. The execution will be carried out in June 1953.

April 11 President Truman removes General MacArthur as commander in Korea after MacArthur openly defies Truman's plan to negotiate a Korean peace. In March, General Matthew B. Ridgway takes command of forces in Korea. Returning to the States as a national hero and greeted by huge crowds (some reports put New York crowds welcoming MacArthur in a ticker-tape parade at 7 million), MacArthur later addresses a joint session of Congress with a speech urging an expanded war against China. There is a huge popular outcry against Truman, and thousands of letters calling for his impeachment descend on the White House and Congress.

American Voices

President Harry S. Truman on the firing of General MacArthur, from Merle Miller's biography of Truman, *Plain Speaking* (1973):

> I fired him because he wouldn't respect the authority of the President. That's the answer to that. I didn't fire him because he was a dumb son of a bitch, although he was, but that's not against the law for generals. If it was, half to three-quarters of them would be in jail.

July 10 While fighting continues, the United States joins peace talks between the UN and China. The U.S. goal is a negotiated truce confirming the staus quo before the war—a return to the containment policy.

1952

January 24 Peace talks with the Chinese are declared stalled. The war continues, fought primarily in a seesaw battle in North Korea's cold, rugged mountain terrain. These battles, for Heartbreak Ridge, Bloody Ridge, the Punchbowl, and other hills essentially end in a bloody stalemate, bringing to mind the trench warfare of World War I.
November 4 Dwight D. Eisenhower is elected President. Richard M. Nixon is his Vice-President. His opponent, Democrat Adlai Stevenson, has won only nine states.
December 5 President-elect Eisenhower visits troops in Korea and attempts to break the stalemate in truce talks.

1953

July 27 An armistice is signed at Panmunjon, halting the Korean fighting. The war ends where it started, at the 38th parallel.

What were the results of the Korean War?

The war cost America more than 54,000 dead and another 100,000 casualties. More than 2 million Koreans were killed in the fighting. After three years, the situation in Korea was almost exactly what it had been when the North first attacked the South. All of the fighting and deaths had changed almost nothing, and it has remained that way to this day. At home, the war produced a massive call for militarization and a buildup of American conventional and nuclear forces—strengthening what President Eisenhower himself would later label "the military-industrial complex."

American Voices

From *Invisible Man,* by Ralph Ellison (1952):

> I am an invisible man. No, I am not a spook like those who haunted Edgar Allan Poe; nor am I one of your Hollywood-movie ectoplasms. I am a man of substance, of flesh and bone, fiber and liquids—and I might even be said to possess a mind. I am invisible, understand, simply because people refuse to see me. Like the bodiless heads you sometimes see in circus sideshows, it is as though I have been surrounded by mirrors of hard, distorting glass. When they approach me they see only my surroundings, themselves, or figments of their imagination—indeed, everything and anything except me.

What was Brown v. Board of Education?

Every day, eight-year-old Linda Brown wondered why she had to ride five miles to school when her bus passed the perfectly lovely Sumner Elementary School, just four blocks from her home. When her father tried to enroll her in Sumner for fourth grade, the Topeka, Kansas, school authorities just said no. In 1951, Linda Brown was the wrong color for Sumner.

In July 1950, a year before Linda was turned away, segregated black troops from the 24th Infantry Regiment scored the first American victory of the Korean War when they recaptured Yechon. A few months after that, Pfc. William Thompson was awarded the Medal of Honor for heroism in Korea—the first black so honored since the Spanish-American War. (It's hard to win combat awards when the army will only let you peel potatoes and dig slit trenches.) In September 1950, Gwendolyn Brooks (b. 1917) won the Pulitzer Prize for poetry for her book *Annie Allen,* the first black ever cited by the Pulitzer Committee. And that month, American diplomat Ralph J. Bunche (1904–1971) was awarded the Nobel Peace Prize for his mediation of the Palestinian conflict, the first black to win that honor.

For most of the 15 million American blacks—in 1950 they were Negroes—these accomplishments held little meaning. In the first place, a good many of those 15 million people couldn't read about these achievements. Illiteracy among America's largest racial minority (approximately 10 percent of the total population in 1950) was commonplace. Schools for blacks, where they existed, didn't offer much in the way of formal education. The law of the land remained "separate but equal," the policy dictated by the Supreme Court's 1896 *Plessy v. Ferguson* ruling. (See pages 213–215.) "Separate but equal" kept Linda Brown out of the nearby Topeka schoolhouse and dictated that everything from maternity wards to morgues, from water fountains to swimming pools, from prisons to polling places, were either segregated or for whites only. Exactly how these "separate" facilities were "equal" remained a mystery to blacks: If everything was so equal, why didn't white people want to use them?

Nowhere was the disparity more complete and disgraceful than in the public schools, primarily but not exclusively in the heartland of the former Confederacy. Schools for whites were spanking new, well maintained, properly staffed, and amply supplied. Black schools were usually single-room shacks with no toilets, a single teacher, and a broken chalkboard. If black parents wanted their children to be warm in the winter, they had to buy their own coal. But a handful of courageous southern blacks—mostly common people like teachers and ministers and their families—began the struggle that turned back these laws.

Urged on by Thurgood Marshall (b. 1908), the burly, barb-tongued attorney from Baltimore who led the NAACP's Legal Defense and Educational Fund, smalltown folks in Kansas, South Carolina, Virginia, and Delaware balked at the injustice of "separate but equal" educational systems. The people who carried these fights were soon confronted by threats ranging from loss of their jobs to dried-up bank credit and ultimately threats of violence and death. In 1951, one of these men was the Reverend Oliver Brown, the father of Linda Brown, who tried to enroll his daughter in the all-white Topeka school. Since Brown came first in the alphabet among the suits brought against four different states, it was his name that was attached to the case that Thurgood Marshall argued before the Supreme Court in 1953.

Marshall seemed to have momentum on his side. In 1950 the Supreme Court had already made three important decisions that chipped away at *Plessy:* the *Sweatt* decision said equality involved more than physical facilities; the *McLaurin* decision said black students in state universities could not be segregated after admission; and in the *Henderson* case, railroad dining-car segregation was banned. But these were limited, circumscribed cases without broader interpretations.

There had also been a change in the makeup of the Court itself. After the arguments in *Brown v. Board of Education* were first heard, Chief Justice Fred M. Vinson, the Truman appointee who had ordered the other justices flown back to Washington to ensure that the Rosenberg execution would proceed on schedule, died of a heart attack. In 1953, with reargument of the case on the horizon, President Eisenhower appointed Earl Warren (1891–1974) Chief Justice of the Supreme Court. No legal giant, Warren was a good Republican soldier, a fairly moderate California governor, and the vice-presidential candidate on the 1948 Dewey ticket. His past held only one black mark—at least in retrospect. As California's attorney general, he had pressed the cause of internment of Japanese-Americans during World War II, a policy he had then helped carry out in his first term as California's governor. But in 1953, that seemed like evidence of good sense rather than the grievous smudge it would be today.

Certainly nobody at the time suspected that Warren would go on to lead the Court for sixteen of its most turbulent years, during which the justices took the lead in transforming America's approach to racial equality, criminal justice, and freedom of expresssion. President Eisenhower, the good general and hero of democracy who marched firmly in place when it came to civil rights, later said the appointment of Warren was "the biggest damfool mistake I ever made."

From the moment the justices began to confer on the case, Warren—as yet unconfirmed by the Senate—made it clear that he would vote to overturn *Plessy* because he believed that the law could no longer tolerate separating any race as inferior, which was the obvious result of "separate but equal" laws. But Warren was an adroit politician as well as a jurist. He knew that the case was so important and politically charged that it demanded unanimity. Achieving that unanimity was less simple than forming his own decision. But through gentle persuasion, Warren was able to shape the consensus he wanted—and what the case needed. All nine of the brethren not only voted to overturn *Plessy*, but allowed Warren's single opinion to speak for them. When Warren read the simple, brief ruling, it was the judicial equivalent of the shot heard 'round the world.

In *Simple Justice,* a monumental study of the case and the history of racism, cruelty, and discrimination that preceded it, Richard Kluger eloquently assessed the decision's impact:

> The opinion of the Court said that the United States stood for something more than material abundance, still moved to an inner spirit, however deeply it had been submerged by fear and envy and mindless hate. . . . The Court had restored to the American people a measure of the humanity that had been drained away in their climb to worldwide supremacy. The Court said, without using the words, that when you stepped on a black man, he hurt. The time had come to stop.

Of course, *Brown* did not cause the scales to fall from the eyes of white supremacists. The fury of the South was quick and sure. School systems around the country, South and North, had to be dragged kicking and screaming through the courts toward de-segregation. The states fought the decision with endless appeals and other delaying tactics, the calling out of troops, and ultimately violence and a venomous outflow of racial hatred, targeted at schoolchildren who simply wanted to learn.

American Voices

Chief Justice Earl Warren, from the unanimous opinion in *Brown v. Board of Education of Topeka* (May 17, 1954):

> We come then to the question presented: Does segregation of children in public schools solely on the basis of race, even though the physical facilities and other "tangible" factors may be equal, deprive the children of the minority group of equal educational opportunities? We believe that it does. . . .
>
> To separate them from others of similar age and qualifications solely because of their race generates a feeling of inferiority as to their status in the community that may affect their hearts and minds in a way unlikely ever to be undone. . . .
>
> . . . We conclude that in the field of public education the doctrine of "separate but equal" has no place. Separate educational facilities are inherently unequal.

Why did the arrest of a woman named Rosa Parks change American life?

In its historic judgment, the Supreme Court gave the civil rights movement its Ten Commandments. What the movement lacked was its Moses. Rosa Parks may not have been Moses, but she certainly was a voice crying out from Egyptian bondage. In 1955, Egypt was Montgomery, Alabama.

A forty-three-year-old seamstress who worked in a downtown Montgomery department store, Rosa Parks was on her way home from work on a December day. Loaded down by bags filled with her Christmas shopping, Rosa Parks boarded a city bus and moved to the back—legally, traditionally—and, it seemed, eternally—the Negro section. Finding no seats there, she took one toward the middle of the bus. When the driver picked up more white passengers, he called out, "Niggers move back," an order to vacate the white seats even if it meant standing. Mrs. Parks refused. Active in the local chapter of the NAACP, Rosa Parks had already decided that she would make a stand if asked to give up her seat.

Unwilling to leave that seat, Rosa Parks was arrested for violating Montgomery's transportation laws. Mrs. Parks was ordered to court on the following Monday. But over the weekend, the blacks of Montgomery found their Moses. Meeting to protest Mrs. Parks's arrest and the reason for it, the black community of Montgomery selected the twenty-seven-year-old pastor of Mrs. Parks's church, the Dexter Avenue Baptist Church, as its leader. Calling for a peaceful form of resistance, the young minister urged his people to boycott the buses of Montgomery. His name was Martin Luther King, Jr. (1929–1968). In a short time the bus boycott and the movement it inspired in Montgomery would raise him to world fame and make him one of the nation's most admired and reviled men.

King was born in Atlanta, the son of one of that city's prominent black ministers and grandson of the man who had organized a protest that created Atlanta's first black high school, named for Booker T. Washington, which King himself attended. He went on to Atlanta's Morehead College, studied theology and philosophy at Crozier Theological Seminary and the University of Pennsylvania, and had completed his Ph.D. in systematic theology from Boston University in 1955 when he took the call at Dexter Avenue. Buttressed by the twin principles of nonviolence and civil disobedience inspired by Henry David Thoreau and India's Mahatma Gandhi, King planned to shape a civil rights movement using the fundamental moral teachings of Christianity—love, forgiveness, humility, faith, hope, community—as its bedrock. The Montgomery boycott, begun on December 5, 1955, presented him with the first opportunity to try this approach.

For more than a year the boycott was hugely effective. Angry because they couldn't make these Negroes ride the buses, the whites of Montgomery looked for other ways to retaliate. Mrs. Parks was rearrested for failing to pay her fine. King was arrested, first on a drunk-driving charge and later for conspiring to organize an illegal boycott. Insurance companies cancelled the auto insurance on cars being used to circumvent the buses. When peaceful means failed, black homes were firebombed. A shotgun blast broke the windows of King's home. And of course the KKK appeared on the scene, to march through the streets of Montgomery.

The case wound its way back to Washington, where the Supreme Court, now armed with the *Brown* precedent, was beginning to roll back "separate but equal" statutes in all areas of life. The Court ordered an end to Montgomery's bus segregation in November 1956, and on the morning of December 21, 1956, the blacks of Montgomery went back to the buses. They had won a battle, but the war was just beginning. The peaceful boycott movement gathered momentum and was duplicated throughout the South. For the next ten years these peaceful protests led the civil rights movement until the painfully slow process finally boiled over in the urban racial violence of the mid-1960s.

Despite the success of the protest, the international notoriety Martin Luther King had gained created some dissension within the ranks, according to David J. Garrow's book *Bearing the Cross.* Mrs. Parks, who lost her job as a seamstress, later took a job at the Hampton Institute in Virginia, and remained a living symbol of the civil rights movement.

In 1957, King moved to Atlanta and organized the Southern Christian Leadership Conference (SCLC). Later that year he led the first civil rights march to Washington in a Prayer Pilgrimage. This time 50,000 blacks joined him. In the future he would return with hundreds of thousands.

In the meantime, the Supreme Court had issued a second ruling in May 1955, known as *Brown II,* which attempted to address some of the practical concerns of its desegregation order. Walking a dangerous tightrope without a safety net, the Court reasserted that the states in the suits must begin to make a prompt, reasonable start toward full compliance with the 1954 ruling. But Warren concluded with the now-famous phrase that this process should move with "all deliberate speed." The Court had told the country to go fast slowly. Of course, to the advocates of integration, the emphasis was on speed. To segregationists, "deliberate" meant sometime in the days of Buck Rogers.

Why did Eisenhower send the army into Little Rock, Arkansas?

Through all of these Supreme Court decisions and during the Montgomery boycott and other peaceful protests that followed, the Eisenhower White House stood as a vacuum of moral leadership on the civil rights issue. While the Cold War general was making the world "safe for democracy," his own vision of a free society seemed to have no room for blacks.

Apparently fearful of alienating the powerful bloc of "Dixiecrats," the southern Democratic congressmen whose votes he needed, Eisenhower was ambiguous in his public comments. He promised to uphold the laws of the land, but refrained from endorsing the Court's rulings. At the time, a word of leadership or outrage at Jim Crow conditions from this popular President might have given the civil rights movement additional vigor and force. Instead, Eisenhower was ultimately forced to act, with great reluctance, in a showdown that was more about presidential power than about the rights of black children.

In September 1957, the governor of Arkansas, Orville Faubus, posted 270 men from the Arkansas National Guard outside Little Rock Central High School. Fully armed, their duty was to prevent nine black children from entering the previously all-white school. On American television and all over the world, people watched with revulsion as the children tried to enter school and were turned away by the guard as an angry, jeering mob spat and cursed at them, all under the watchful eyes of the guardsmen. A federal district court order forced Faubus to allow the children into the school, but the governor withdrew the Arkansas state guard, leaving the protection of the black children to a small contingent of resentful local policemen, some of whom refused to carry out the order.

Finally Eisenhower, in order to defend the sovereignty of the federal court, had to order 1,100 paratroopers from the 101st Airborne to Little Rock and place the state national guard under his direct orders. For the first time since Reconstruction, U.S. troops were in the South to protect the rights of blacks. Eisenhower had not acted out of concern for the students' rights or safety, but because he believed that he couldn't allow the force of federal law to be ignored.

The troops remained in Little Rock Central High for the rest of the school year, and eight of the black students stayed through the year despite curses, harassment, and abuse. Whatever else it proved, Little Rock showed that the civil rights movement was going to need the full force of the federal government to enforce the laws that the Supreme Court had created.

American Voices

From "The Southern Manifesto" signed by ninety-six congressmen from the South in response to the *Brown* decision (March 12, 1956):

> . . . This unwarranted exercise of power by the court, contrary to the Constitution, is creating chaos and confusion in the states principally affected. It is destroying the *amicable relations between the white and Negro races that have been created through ninety years of patient effort by the good people of both races.* (Emphasis added.) It has planted hatred and suspicion where there has been heretofore friendship and understanding.

What was Sputnik?

On the educational Richter scale, *Brown* had been the equivalent of the Great San Francisco Earthquake. It leveled everything. While *Brown*'s tremors sent shock waves across the country, America got another tremendous jolt that shook the country to its foundations. On October 4, 1957, the Soviet Union launched Sputnik (whose name in Russian meant "little traveler"), man's first artificial satellite.

Weighing in at about 185 pounds, Sputnik was a little bigger than a basketball and traveled 18,000 miles per hour some 560 miles about the earth, emitting a steady *beep-beep-beep* radio signal. The launch was not only an unexpected technological achievement but a work of propaganda genius. The Soviets had given Sputnik an orbit and trajectory that sent the satellite over the earth's most populous areas and low enough that it could be seen at times with the assistance of powerful binoculars. Ham radio operators could pick up the distinctive message it beamed back to Earth.

The Sputnik shock was redoubled in November when the Russians lofted a second satellite, dubbed Sputnik II. Not only was this a substantially larger satellite, weighing more than 1,100 pounds, but it carried a passenger. A small dog was strapped into the satellite, hooked up to monitoring equipment that relayed information about the physical effects of space travel.

The paranoia that the twin Sputnik launchings induced was extraordinary, and it worked on two levels. The first was the gut reaction of fear: If the Russians can put something like this up in the sky, maybe they can send up something that will drop bombs on us. More realistically, it meant that the Soviets had taken the lead in development of the intercontinental ballistic missile, thereby fundamentally altering the balance of power between the two competing powers. Sputnik obliterated the American assumption of its nuclear superiority. It was all the more reason for wives to yell at their husbands to forget the baseball game and get back to work on digging that fallout shelter in the backyard.

The fear of the bomb merged with the reality of man moving into space and the constant drumbeat of anti-Communist hysteria to produce a paranoid pop culture that blossomed in the science fiction books and films of the fifties. Before World War II, science fiction had been a respectable sort of fantasy, most popularly practiced by H. G. Wells or the pleasant utopian visions of Edward Bellamy's novel *Looking Backward*. Radio's Buck Rogers gave new life to notions of space travel and futuristic death rays, but that was mostly child's play. The specter of totalitarian police states in Germany and the Soviet Union, heightened by the threat of the bomb, had turned science fiction darker. The trend began with such classics as George Orwell's *1984* and Aldous Huxley's *Brave New World*, and was later reflected in such books as Ray Bradbury's *Fahrenheit 451*, the classic about a futuristic society in which all books are burned, which was written in the midst of Senator McCarthy's witch hunts and a movement to purge American libraries of "subversive" works. In the movies, the paranoia was reflected in films like *Invasion of the Body Snatchers*.

A more serious but equally hysterical fear rocked the American education system, reeling under the pressures of desegregation. Already struggling against the Soviets in an arms race, America now found itself left at the starting line in the new "space race." Worse than that, America didn't even have its sneakers on.

To all the wise men in the land, the reason for America's sad technological performance while the Soviets had leapt into space was obvious: the American education system was falling down, while the Soviet system, which rigorously drilled its children in math and the sciences, was producing a super-race of mathematicians and scientists who would rapidly outdistance the American child in their achievements.

The decline in American standards was blamed on that favorite of whipping boys, "progressive education." In the late 1950s, "back to basics" was the call to arms. It is a story that was replayed in the mid-1980s, when it was determined that America's schools were falling prey to a "rising tide of mediocrity." The eighties also produced a new archvillain who was out-educating America's children. Instead of the Soviets, the new bogeyman was the Japanese, and the media were filled with reports of the superiority of the Japanese educational system, an uncanny reprise of the debate in the late fifties. Once again, "back to basics" was the simplistic answer to the problems of the miserable American school systems.

The practical response to Sputnik was a total overhaul of American education, with a new commitment on the part of the federal government to aid public schools, along with an overhaul of research and development in the rocketry field, spearheaded by a compelling urgency to overtake the Soviets in the area of missile delivery systems. Sputnik had been the space equivalent of the Russian atomic bomb. In the years ahead, the United States would devote enormous resources to victory in the new space race.

Success would be built on failures. And the first of these was nearly devastating. On December 6, 1957—uncomfortably close to the anniversary of Pearl Harbor in many minds—a Vanguard rocket that was to carry America's first satellite into space blew up on the launching pad. It was an inauspicious beginning to America's race for the moon.

American Voices

From Dwight D. Eisenhower's farewell address (January 17, 1961):

[The] conjunction of an immense military establishment and large arms industry is new in the American experience. The total influence—economic, political, even spiritual—is felt in every city, every state house, every office of the federal government. We recognize the imperative need for the development. Yet we must not fail to comprehend its grave implications. Our toil, resources, and livelihood are all involved; so is the very structure of our society.

In the councils of government, we must guard against the acquisition of unwarranted influence, whether sought or unsought, by the military-industrial complex. The potential for the disastrous rise of misplaced power exists and will persist.

This speech was a little bit like Dr. Frankenstein yelling "Look out!" after the monster has escaped the laboratory. As the leading proponent of Cold War containment, Eisenhower had presided over the rise of this "military-industrial complex," created to give the United States the military might it needed to carry out the containment policy, a policy that continued to dictate American decision-making in the White House and Congress in the decades ahead.

Chapter Eight

The Torch Is Passed:
From Camelot to
Hollywood
on the Potomac

- How did Richard Nixon's five-o'clock shadow spoil his 1960 campaign for President?

- What happened at the Bay of Pigs?

- What was the Cuban Missile Crisis?

- What was *The Feminine Mystique*?

- Who killed JFK?

- Did *Mississippi Burning* really happen?

- What was the Tonkin Resolution?

- Milestones in the Vietnam War

- What happened in Watts?

- Who was *Miranda*?

- What happened at My Lai?

- Why did Richard Nixon and Henry Kissinger try to stop *The New York Times* from publishing the "Pentagon Papers"?

- Why did "Jane Roe" sue Wade?

- How did a botched burglary become a crisis called Watergate and bring down a powerful President?

- A Watergate Chronology

- How did the Arabs of OPEC cripple America during the 1970s?

- What was "voodoo economics"?

- Why was Ronald Reagan called the "Teflon President"?

- Can a man called "Bubba" become President?

*C*amelot. The Age of Aquarius. "All You Need Is Love." Hippies and Haight-Ashbury. "Be Sure to Wear Some Flowers in Your Hair." "Tune In. Turn On. Drop Out." Free love. Men on the moon. Woodstock.

It has come down as "the sixties," a romantic fantasy set to a three-chord rock beat. But the era viewed so nostalgically as the days of peace, love, and rock and roll didn't start out with much peace and love. Unless you focus on the fact that Enovid, the first birth-control pill, was approved by the FDA in 1960.

The flip side of the sixties was a much darker tune. Riots and long, hot summers. Assassinations. Rock-star obituaries etched in acid. A war that only a "military-industrial complex" could love. *Sympathy for the Devil.* Altamont Speedway.

The "bright shining moment" of the JFK years—the media-created myth of *Camelot* manufactured in the wake of Kennedy's death—began with the same Cold War paranoia that set the tone of the previous decade. The "liberal" Kennedy campaigned in 1960 as a hard-line anti-Communist, and used a fabricated "missile gap" between the United States and the Soviet Union as a campaign issue against Republican candidate Richard Nixon.

What we call the sixties ended with the death throes of an unpopular, costly war in a quagmire called Vietnam.

But it was an extraordinary era in which all the accepted orthodoxies of government, church, and society were called into question. And, unlike the glum, alienated mood of the fifties, the new voices questioning authority had a lighter side. Joseph Heller (b. 1923) was one of the first to capture the new mood of mordant humor in his first novel, *Catch-22* (1961), which was a forecast of the antimilitary mood that would form to oppose the war in Vietnam. But the new generation of poets was more likely to use an amplified guitar than a typewriter to voice its discontent. In the folk music of Peter, Paul, and Mary and Bob Dylan, and later in the rock-and-roll revolution, "counterculture" was blasting out of millions of radios and TVs. Of course, the record business found it a very profitable counterculture. And it spilled into the mainstream as entertainers like the Smothers Brothers brought irreverence to prime time—which promptly showed them the door.

The seventies got under way with the downfall of a corrupt White House in a sinkhole called Watergate. Vietnam and Watergate seemed to signal a change in the American political landscape. The years that followed were characterized by a feeling of aimlessness. Under Gerald Ford (b. 1913), who replaced the disgraced Nixon, and Jimmy Carter (b. 1924), America suffered the indignity of seeing its massive power in a seeming decline. But this slide was not the result of a superpower confrontation with the archvillain Soviets. Instead, a series of smaller shocks undid the foundation: the forming of OPEC by major oil-producing countries to place a stranglehold on the world's oil supplies; the acts of international terrorists, who struck with seeming impunity at the United States and other western powers, culminating in the overthrow of the once-mighty Shah of Iran; and the imprisonment of American hostages in the American embassy in Teheran.

More than anything else, it was that apparent decline, reflected in America's economic doldrums, that brought forth a President who represented, to the majority of Americans, the cowboy in the white hat who they always believed would ride into town. After the doubt and turmoil produced by the Seventies,

Ronald Reagan (b. 1911) seemed to embody that old-fashioned American can-do spirit. For many critics, the question was who was going to do what, and to whom? A throwback to Teddy Roosevelt and his big stick, Reagan also saw the White House as a "bully pulpit." His sermon called back the "good old days"— which, of course, only appeared so good in hindsight.

Though it is still too soon to assess properly the long-term impact of his presidency, Ronald Reagan has already begun to be judged by history. To those who admire him, he was the man who restored American prestige and economic stability, and forced the Soviet Union into structural changes through a massive buildup of American defenses. To critics, he was the President who slept through eight years in office while subordinates ran the show. In some cases, those underlings proved to be corrupt or simply cynical. In perhaps the most dangerous instance, a lieutenant colonel working in the White House was allowed to make his own foreign policy.

How did Richard Nixon's five-o'clock shadow spoil his 1960 campaign for President?

"If you give me a week, I might think of one." That's what President Eisenhower told a reporter who asked what major decisions Vice-President Richard Nixon (1913–1994) had participated in during their eight years together. Although Ike later said he was being facetious, he never really answered the question, and the remark left Nixon with egg on his face and the Democrats giddy.

That was in August 1960, as Nixon and John F. Kennedy (1917–1963) ran neck-and-neck in the polls. How many wavering Nixon votes did Ike's little joke torpedo? It would have taken only a shift of about a hundred thousand votes out of the record 68,832,818 cast to change the result and the course of contemporary events.

Most campaign historians cite Ike's cutting comment as a jab that drew blood, but that was not the knockout punch in this contest. Posterity points instead to the face-off between the contenders—the first televised debates in presidential campaign history—as the flurry of verbal and visual punches from which Nixon never recovered. In particular, the first of these four meetings is singled out as the blow that sent the Vice-President to the canvas. More than 70 million people watched the first of these face-to-face meetings. Or maybe "face-to-five-o'clock shadow" is more accurate.

Recovering from an infection that had hospitalized him for two weeks, Nixon was underweight and haggard-looking for the debate. Makeup artists attempted to conceal his perpetual five-o'clock shadow with something called "Lazy Shave" that only made him look more pasty-faced and sinister. Jack Kennedy, on the other hand, was the picture of youth and athletic vigor. While radio listeners thought there was no clear winner in the debates, television viewers were magnetized by Kennedy. If FDR was the master of radio, Kennedy was the first "telegenic" candidate, custom-tailored for the instant image-making of the television age.

Broadcast on September 26 from Chicago, the first debate focused on domestic affairs, an advantage for Kennedy because Nixon was acknowledged to be more experienced in international matters. It was Nixon, after all, who had stood face-to-face with Nikita Khrushchev in Moscow, angrily wagging a finger at the Soviet leader during their "kitchen debate" in 1959. But in the first TV debate, Kennedy had Nixon on the defensive by listing the shortcomings of the Eisenhower administration. With deft command of facts and figures, Kennedy impressed an audience that was skeptical because of his youth and inexperience. He stressed his campaign theme that the Republicans had America in "retreat," and he promised to get the country moving again.

The audience for the three subsequent debates fell off to around 50 million viewers. The impressions made by the first debate seemed to be most lasting. Kennedy got a boost in the polls and seemed to be pulling out in front, but the decision was still too close to call. Invisible through most of the contest, Eisenhower did some last-minute campaigning for Nixon, but it may have been too small an effort, too late.

Two events in October also had some impact. First, Republican Henry Cabot Lodge promised that there would be a Negro in the Nixon cabinet. Nixon had to disavow that pledge, and whatever white votes he won cost him black support. A second Kennedy boost among black voters came when Martin Luther King, Jr., was arrested prior to the final debate. Kennedy called King's wife, Coretta, to express his concern, and Robert Kennedy helped secure King's release on bail. Nixon decided to stay out of the case. King's father, who had previously stated he wouldn't vote for a Catholic, announced a shift to Kennedy. "I've got a suitcase of votes," said Martin Luther King, Sr., "and I'm going to take them to Mr. Kennedy and dump them in his lap." He did just that. When Kennedy heard of the senior King's earlier anti-Catholic remarks, he won points by humorously defusing the situation, commenting, "Imagine Martin Luther King having a bigot for a father. Well, we all have fathers, don't we?"

Kennedy certainly had a father. Joseph Kennedy, Sr., FDR's first chairman of the Securities and Exchange Commission and later his ambassador to Great Britain, where his anti-Semitic and isolationist views won him no points, stayed in the background in the campaign. Bankrolling and string-pulling, Joseph Kennedy had orchestrated his son's career from the outset with his extensive network of friends in the media, the mob, and the Catholic church. A few examples: Writer John Hersey's "Survival," the now-deflated account of Kennedy's wartime heroics aboard PT-109, overlooked the fact that Kennedy and his crew were sleeping in a combat zone when a Japanese destroyer rammed them. Joe Kennedy made sure his son was decorated by a high-ranking navy official. When JFK ran for the House, Joe arranged for the Hersey article to appear in *Reader's Digest* and then made sure every voter in Kennedy's district got a copy. Publication of JFK's first book, *Why England Slept,* was arranged by Kennedy pal journalist Arthur Krock, who then reviewed the book in the *New York Times.* Kennedy's second book, the best-selling and Pulitzer Prize–winning *Profiles in Courage,* was the output of a committee of scholars and Kennedy speechwriter Theodore Sorensen.

Other friends of Joe Kennedy, like Henry Luce and William Randolph Hearst, had added to building the Kennedy image. Through Frank Sinatra, another Joe Kennedy crony, funds of dubious origin were funneled into the Kennedy war chest.

Through Sinatra, JFK also met a young woman named Judith Campbell, who would soon become a regular sexual partner. What Kennedy didn't know at the time was that Judith Campbell was also bedding Mafia chieftain Sam Giancanna and a mob hit man named John Roselli. In a few months, they would all converge as Giancanna and Roselli were given a "contract" to pull off the CIA-planned assassination of Fidel Castro.

The debate; his father's war chest; his appeal to women (the public appeal, not the private one, which remained a well-protected secret); the newly important black vote;. vice-presidential candidate Lyndon B. Johnson's role in delivering Texas and the rest of the South all played a part in what was the closest presidential election in modern history. Nixon actually won more states than Kennedy, but it was a Pyrrhic victory. Kennedy had sewn up the biggest electoral-vote states. The margin of difference in the popular vote was less than two-thirds of a percentage point.

But close only counts in horseshoes. Despite some Republican protests of voting fraud in Illinois, Nixon went back to California after telling reporters, "You won't have Nixon to kick around anymore." America got its youngest President, his beautiful young wife, its youngest Attorney General in Jack's brother Robert F. Kennedy (1925–1968), and a new royal family whose regal intrigues were masked by sun-flooded pictures of family games of touch football.

American Voices

From John F. Kennedy's inaugural address (January 20, 1961):

> Let the word go forth from this time and place, to friend and foe alike, that the torch has been passed to a new generation of Americans—born in this century, tempered by war, disciplined by a hard and bitter peace, proud of our ancient heritage—and unwilling to witness the slow undoing of those human rights to which this nation has always been committed, and to which we are committed today at home and around the world. . . .

Now the trumpet summons us again—not as a call to bear arms, though arms we need—but a call to bear the burden of a long twilight struggle, year in and year out, "rejoicing in hope, patient in tribulation"—a struggle against the common enemies of man: tyranny, poverty, disease and war itself.

. . . And so, my fellow Americans: ask not what your country can do for you—ask what you can do for your country.

What happened at the Bay of Pigs?

In March 1961, during his first hundred days in office, Kennedy announced a program that perfectly symbolized his inaugural appeal to "ask what you can do for your country." The Peace Corps would dispatch the energy of American youth and know-how to assist developing nations. Directed by another family courtier, Sargent Shriver, husband of John's sister Eunice, the Peace Corps was the new generation's answer to Communism, promoting democracy with education, technology, and idealism instead of the fifties rhetoric of "containment." Linked with the Alliance for Progress, a sort of Marshall Plan aimed at Latin America, the Peace Corps was the visible symbol of the vigor that Kennedy wanted to breathe into a stale American system.

What the Peace Corps idealism masked was a continuing policy of obsessive anti-Communism that would lead to one of the great disasters in American foreign policy. This failure would bring America to its most dangerous moment since the war in Korea and, in the view of many historians, helped create the mind-set that sucked America into the Vietnamese quicksand. It took its unlikely but historically fitting name from an obscure spot on the Cuban coast, Bahía de Cochinos. The Bay of Pigs.

If the operation had not been so costly and its failed results so dangerously important to future American policy, the Bay of Pigs fiasco might seem comical, a fictional creation of some satirist trying to create an implausible CIA invasion scenario.

The plan behind the Bay of Pigs sounded simple when put to the new President by Allen Dulles (1893–1961), the legendary CIA director and a holdover from the Eisenhower era, when his brother, John Foster Dulles (1888–1959), had been the influential Secretary of State. It was Allen Dulles's underlings who dreamed up the Cuban operation involving a force of highly trained and well-equipped anti-Castro Cuban exiles called La Brigada. Supported by CIA-planted insurgents in Cuba who would blow up bridges and knock out radio stations, the Brigade would land on the beaches of Cuba and set off a popular revolt against Fidel Castro, eliminating the man who had become the greatest thorn in the paw of the American lion. The most secret aspect of the plan, as a Senate investigation revealed much later, was the CIA plot to assassinate Castro using Mafia hit men Sam Giancanna and John Roselli, who were also sleeping with Judith Campbell, the President's steady partner. The Mafia had its own reasons for wanting to rid Cuba of Castro. (Giancanna and Roselli were both murdered mob-style in 1976. Giancanna was assassinated before he could testify before the Senate Intelligence Committee; Roselli testified, but his decomposing body was later found floating in an oil drum off Florida. Both men were believed to possess information connecting the Mafia to the assassination of President Kennedy.)

For most of the century, since Teddy Roosevelt and company had turned Cuba into an American fiefdom in the Caribbean, the island's economy was in nearly total American control. Almost all of the sugar, mining, cattle, and oil wealth of Cuba was in American hands. The Spanish-American war had also given the United States a huge naval base at Guantanamo. But American gangsters had a rich share, too. While American businessmen controlled the Cuban economy, the casinos and hotels of Havana, a hot spot in the Caribbean, were controlled by the Mafia from New Orleans and Las Vegas.

All that had come to an end in 1958, when Fidel Castro and Che Guevara marched out of the hills with a tiny army and sent dictator Fulgencio Batista into exile. At first, Castro got good press notices in the United States and made a goodwill visit to Washington, professing that he was no Communist. But that didn't last long.

By 1959, Castro had formed a ruthless, Moscow-supported military regime that jailed and murdered dissidents, ended any vestige of legal process, and put Cuba on a totally socialist footing. America was now Cuba's archenemy. Betrayed by Castro, many of the rebels who had helped Castro to power found their way to exile in Miami where they were taken into the welcoming embrace of the CIA.

Cuban Communism became a campaign issue in 1960 as Nixon and Kennedy tried to outdo each other on the Castro issue. As they campaigned, the plans for La Brigada's invasion were being hatched by the CIA, a plan that had the enthusiastic encouragement of Vice-President Richard Nixon and the nominal approval of Eisenhower. When Kennedy arrived in office, the plans only awaited the presidential okay. Briefed by Dulles himself before his inauguration, Kennedy agreed that preparations should continue. After his inauguration, momentum took over.

Franklin D. Roosevelt had his "brain trust" of academics who offered advice and counsel—which Roosevelt didn't always follow. Likewise, Kennedy surrounded himself with a group of elite academics—professors and Rhodes scholars among them. Unlike FDR's brain trust, Kennedy's "best and brightest," as they were dubbed in David Halberstam's book tracing the path of American involvement in Vietnam, were going to have enormous and disastrous influence on the course of American policy. For the most part, the best and the brightest went along with what the CIA had guaranteed was a successful plan for eliminating Castro.

The CIA planners cockily pointed to their successful 1954 Guatemala coup that had installed a pro-American regime there as proof of their abilities. But Cuba, as they were sadly going to learn, was not Guatemala. From the Cuban plan's outset, the Agency men in charge of the invasion (including a fanatical CIA operative named E. Howard Hunt, who also wrote third-rate spy novels and would later be involved in the Watergate debacle) bungled and blustered. Almost every step of the plan was misguided. The CIA overestimated themselves, underestimated Castro and the popular support he enjoyed, relied on sketchy or nonexistent information, made erroneous assumptions, and misrepresented the plot to the White House.

The secret invasion proved to be one of the worst-kept secrets in America. A number of journalists had uncovered most of the plan, and several editors, including those at the *New York Times,* were persuaded by the White House to withhold the information. When the curtain finally came down, it was on a tragedy.

On April 17, 1961, some 1,400 Cubans, poorly trained, underequipped, and uninformed of their destination, were set down on the beach at the Bay of Pigs. Aerial photos of the beaches were misinterpreted by CIA experts, and Cuban claims that there were dangerous coral reefs that would prevent boats from landing were ignored by invasion planners, who put American technology above the Cubans' firsthand knowledge. CIA information showing the target beaches to be unpopulated was years out of date. The bay happened to be Fidel's favorite fishing spot, and Castro had begun building a resort there, including a seaside cabin for himself.

The invasion actually began two days earlier with an air strike against Cuban airfields, meant to destroy Castro's airpower. It failed to do that, and instead put Castro on the alert. It also prompted a crackdown on many suspected anti-Castro Cubans who might have been part of the anticipated popular uprising on which the Agency was counting. Assuming the success of the air strike without bothering to confirm it, the Agency didn't know Castro had a number of planes still operable, including two jet trainers capable of destroying the lumbering old bombers the CIA had provided to the invaders. But these planes wouldn't have counted for much if the air "umbrella" that the CIA had promised to La Brigada had materialized. President Kennedy's decision to keep all American personnel out of the invasion squashed that, and Castro's fliers had a field day strafing and bombing the invasion "fleet." The CIA-leased "navy" that was to deliver the invasion force and its supplies turned out to be five leaky, listing ships, two of which were quickly sunk by Castro's small air force, with most of the invasion's supplies aboard.

Cuban air superiority was responsible for only part of the devastation. Castro was able to pour thousands of troops into the area. Even though many of them were untried cadets or untrained militia, they were highly motivated, well-equipped troops supported by tanks and heavy artillery. While the invasion force fought bravely, exacting heavy casualties in Castro's troops, they lacked ammunition and, most important, the air support promised by the CIA. Eventually they were pinned down on the beaches, while American navy fliers, the numbers on their planes obscured, could only sit and wonder why they had to watch their Cuban allies being cut to pieces. U.S. ships, their identifying numbers also pointlessly obscured, lay near the invasion beach, also handcuffed. Frustrated naval commanders bitterly resented their orders not to fire. In Washington, Kennedy feared that any direct U.S. combat involvement might send the Russians into West Berlin, precipitating World War III.

The sad toll was 114 Cuban invaders and many more defenders killed in the fighting; 1,189 others from La Brigada were captured and held prisoner until they were ransomed from Cuba by Robert Kennedy for food and medical supplies. Four American fliers, members of the Alabama Air National Guard in CIA employ, also died in the invasion, but the American government never acknowledged their existence or their connection to the operation.

What was the Cuban Missile Crisis?

Those were the immediate losses. The long-term damage was more costly. American prestige and the goodwill Kennedy had fostered around the world dissipated overnight. Adlai Stevenson, the former presidential contender serving as the U.S. representative to the United Nations, was shamed by having to lie to the General Assembly about the operation because he was misled by the White House. In Moscow, Kennedy was perceived as a weakling. Soviet leader Nikita Kruschchev (1894–1971) immediately saw the Bay of Pigs defeat as the opening to start arming Cuba more heavily, precipitating the Missile Crisis of October 1962.

When American spy flights produced evidence of Soviet missile sites in Cuba, America and the Soviet Union were brought to the brink of war. For thirteen tense days, the United States and the USSR stood toe-to-toe as Kennedy, forced to prove himself after the Bay of Pigs, demanded that the missile sites be dismantled and removed from Cuba. To back up his ultimatum, Kennedy ordered a naval blockade to "quarantine" Cuba, and readied a full-scale American invasion of the island. On Sunday October 28, Radio Moscow announced that the arms would be crated and returned to Moscow. Disaster was averted, temporarily.

The damage done to U.S. credibility by the Bay of Pigs fiasco had seemingly been undone. But the lesson of the foolishness of committing American military support to anti-Communism hadn't really sunk in. Kennedy was still willing to make an anti-Communist stand in the world. The next scene would be as distant from America as Cuba was close, a small corner of Asia called Vietnam.

What was The Feminine Mystique?

Every so often a book comes along that really rattles America's cage. *Uncle Tom's Cabin* in 1850. Upton Sinclair's *The Jungle* in 1906. In the 1940s and 1950s, John Hersey's *Hiroshima* and the Kinsey studies, *Sexual Behavior in the Human Male* and *Sexual Behavior in the Human Female*. All of these books delivered karate chops to the American perception of reality.

In 1963 it was a book that introduced America to what the author called "the problem without a name." Betty Friedan (b 1921), a summa cum laude Smith graduate and free-lance writer who was living out the fifties suburban dream of house, husband, and family, dubbed this malady *The Feminine Mystique*.

"The problem lay buried," wrote Friedan, "unspoken for many years in the minds of American women. It was a strange stirring, a sense of dissatisfaction, a yearning. . . . Each suburban wife struggled with it alone. As she made the beds, shopped for groceries, matched slip-cover material, ate peanut butter sandwiches with her children, chauffeured Cub Scouts and Brownies, lay beside her husband at night—she was afraid to ask even herself the silent question—'Is this all?' "

The book reached millions of readers. Suddenly, in garden clubs, coffee klatches, and college sorority houses, talk turned away from man-catching, mascara, and muffin recipes. Women were instead discussing the fact that society's institutions—government, mass media and advertising, medicine and psychiatry, education and organized religion—were systematically barring them from becoming anything more than housewives and mothers.

Friedan's book helped jump-start a stalled women's-rights movement. Lacking a motivating central cause and aggressive leadership since passage of the Nineteenth Amendment after World War I (see pages 259–262), organized feminism in the United States was practically nonexistent. In spite of forces that brought millions of women into the work force—like the wartime factory jobs that made "Rosie the Riveter" an American heroine—women were expected to return to the kitchens after the menfolk came home from defending democracy. Although individuals like Eleanor Roosevelt, Amelia Earhart, Margaret Sanger, and Frances Perkins—the first woman Cabinet officer and a key player in FDR's New Deal—were proven achievers, most women were expected to docilely accept the task of managing house and family, or to hold a proper "woman's job" like teaching, secretarial work, or, for the poorer classes, factory labor. In all of these jobs, women were invisible. Once married, of course, the "ideal woman" stopped working. The idea of career as fulfillment was dismissed as nonsense, and that minority of pioneer "career women" was viewed practically as a class of social deviants. Overnight, Friedan made women question those assumptions.

The Feminine Mystique had its shortcomings. It was essentially about a white, middle-class phenomenon. It failed to explore the problems of working-class, poor, and minority women, whose worries ran far deeper than personal discontent. It also ignored the fact that a substantial portion of American women were satisfied in the role that Friedan had indicted.

But the book was like shock treatment. It galvanized American women into action at the same moment that an increasingly aggressive civil rights movement was moving to the forefront of American consciousness. And it came just as the government was taking its first awkward steps toward addressing the issue of inequality of the sexes. In one of his first acts, President Kennedy had formed a Commission on the Status of Women, chaired by the extraordinary Eleanor Roosevelt, then in her seventies. In 1964 a more substantial boost came when women actually received federal protection from discrimination because the legislative tactics of one crusty conservative congressman backfired.

Howard W. Smith of Virginia, an eighty-one-year-old vestige of the Old South, was looking for ways to shoot down the 1964 Civil Rights Act with "killer amendments." To the laughter of his House colleagues, Smith added "sex" to the list of "race, color, religion or national origin," the groups that the bill had been designed to protect. Assuming that nobody would vote to protect equality of the sexes, Smith was twice struck by lightning. The bill not only passed, but now protected women as well as blacks. Women were soon bringing appeals to the Equal Employment Opportunities Commission, even though its director complained that the bill was "conceived out of wedlock" and wasn't meant to prevent sex discrimination. That complaint came too late. Women filed more discrimination complaints with the EEOC than did any other single group. It was the foot in the door, and a new generation of activist women was ready to push the door harder.

In 1966, three hundred charter members formed the National Organization of Women (NOW) with Friedan as its first president. In the years ahead, NOW spearheaded a movement that would splinter and change as younger women grew more angry and defiant, radicalized by the same forces that were altering the civil rights and antiwar movements. But it is safe to say that no movement so fundamentally altered America's social makeup as the feminist movement of the past three decades. The workplace. Marriage and family life. The way we have babies—or choose not to have them. Few corners of American life were left untouched by the basic shifts in attitude that feminism created.

Of course, the process is far from complete. The federal government, from the White House to Congress and the judiciary, is still largely male, middle-aged, white, and wealthy. The upper crust of American corporate management remains male dominated. A considerable gap in salaries still exists between men and women. And it is still presumed impossible or at least unlikely for a woman to be elected President in this country, even though forceful leaders like Indira Gandhi, Golda Meir, Margaret Thatcher, and Corazón Aquino have shown they are capable of acting as effectively, and even as ruthlessly, as any man.

Thirty years after Friedan gave a name to the problem, the greatest irony may be the new yearning created for a generation of younger women brought up to put careers first and families second. In a strange twist on the question plaguing Friedan's generation, many successful women in their thirties—unmarried, childless women, or career-bound mothers—are looking at their designer business suits, corporate perks, and power offices with a new stirring of dissatisfaction. It is now their turn to wonder about that silent question, "Is this all?"

American Voices

From Martin Luther King's "I Have a Dream" speech in Washington, D.C. (August 1963):

> I say to you today, my friends, that in spite of the difficulties and frustrations of the moment I still have a dream. It is a dream deeply rooted in the American dream.
>
> I have a dream that one day this nation will rise up and live out the true meaning of its creed: "We hold these truths to be self-evident; that all men are created equal."
>
> I have a dream that one day on the red hills of Georgia the sons of former slaves and the sons of former slaveowners will be able to sit down together at the table of brotherhood.
>
> I have a dream that one day even the state of Mississippi, a desert state sweltering with the heat of injustice and oppression, will be transformed into an oasis of freedom and justice.
>
> I have a dream that my four children will one day live in a nation where they will not be judged by the color of their skin but by the content of their character.
>
> I have a dream today.
>
> I have a dream that one day the state of Alabama, whose governor's lips are presently dripping with the words of interposition and nullification, will be transformed into a situation where little black boys and black girls will be able to join hands with little white boys and white girls and walk together as sisters and brothers.
>
> I have a dream today. . . .

King's most memorable speech was the culmination of the massive march on Washington, D.C., that drew a quarter of a million blacks and whites to the capital. In his biography of King, *Bearing the Cross,* author David J. Garrow calls the speech the "clarion call that conveyed the moral power of the movement's cause to the millions who had watched the live national network coverage. Now, more than ever before . . . white America was confronted with the undeniable justice of blacks' demands." The march was followed by passage of the Civil Rights Act, signed into law by Lyndon Johnson in June 1964, and the awarding of the Nobel Peace Prize to Dr. King in October 1964.

Who killed JFK?

Americans probe this question like searching for a missing tooth. We keep running our tongue over the empty space.

This question has inspired a cottage industry of conspiracy theorists. In the view of an American majority, none of them has yet to answer the question to full and verifiable satisfaction. Some innate paranoia in the American makeup finds it far more appealing to believe that Kennedy's death was the result of some intricately constructed Byzantine conspiracy. The list of possible suspects reads like an old-fashioned Chinese restaurant menu. Just choose one from Column A and one from Column B. The choices include a smorgasbord of unsavory characters with the motive and ability to kill Kennedy: teamsters and gangsters; Cubans, both pro- and anti-Castro; white supremacists; CIA renegades; KGB moles; and, of course, lone assassins.

The conspiracy theories linger because the basic facts of the assassination remain shrouded in controversy. What is true is that JFK went to Texas in the fall of 1963 to shore up southern political support for a 1964 reelection bid. The Texas trip began well in San Antonio and Houston, where the President and the First Lady were met by enthusiastic crowds. Everyone agreed that Dallas would be the tough town politically, and several advisers told Kennedy not to go. A few months before, the good folks of Dallas had spat on Adlai Stevenson, JFK's UN ambassador. But even in Dallas on November 22, things were better than expected, and crowds cheered the passing motorcade. In the fateful limousine, Texas Governor John Connally's wife leaned over and told the President, "Well, you can't say Dallas doesn't love you."

Then the car made its turn in front of the Texas Book Depository and at least three shots rang out. Kennedy and Governor Connally were hit. The limousine carrying them sped off to the hospital. The President died and Lyndon B. Johnson (1908–1973) took the oath of office aboard Air Force One as a shocked and bloodied Jackie Kennedy looked on. Within hours, following the murder of a Dallas policeman, Lee Harvey Oswald was in custody and under interrogation. But two days later, as Oswald was being moved to a safer jail, Jack Ruby, owner of a Dallas strip joint, jumped from the crowd of policemen and shot Oswald dead in full view of a disbelieving national television audience.

This is where controversy takes over. A grieving, stunned nation couldn't cope with these events. Rumors and speculation began to fly as the country learned of the strange life of Lee Harvey Oswald—that he was an ex-Marine who had defected to Russia and come back with a Russian wife; that he was a Marxist and a Castro admirer; that he had recently been to the Cuban embassy in Mexico City.

Responding to these rumors, which were growing to include the suggestion that Lyndon Johnson himself was part of the conspiracy, LBJ decided to appoint a commission to investigate the assassination and to determine whether any conspiracy existed. After his first week in office, Johnson asked Chief Justice Earl Warren to head the investigation. Warren reluctantly accepted the job when Johnson said that he feared nuclear war might result if the Cubans or Soviets proved to be behind the assassination.

The Warren Commission spent ten months examining the deaths of Kennedy and Oswald. Its report, released in September 1964, concluded that Oswald had acted alone and there was no evidence of any conspiracy, domestic or foreign.

But twenty-five years after the Warren Commission tried to calm a very skittish nation, those findings are still viewed skeptically by a majority of the American public. The commission's detective work left much to be desired, and in later years, major new revelations followed. In particular, shocking facts were produced by the investigations into the activities of the CIA and the FBI during the 1970s. Among other startling discoveries, these investigations by a presidential commission and Congress uncovered the CIA's plans for assassinating Fidel Castro and other foreign leaders; that Kennedy's mistress Judith Campbell was also involved with the two gangsters hired by the CIA to kill Castro; and that FBI Director J. Edgar Hoover had ordered a cover-up of Bureau failures in the Oswald investigation in an effort to protect the Bureau's integrity and public image.

Were there only three shots fired by someone in the Texas Book Depository? Was Oswald the gunman who fired them? Or were other shots fired from the grassy knoll overlooking the route of the motorcade? Was Jack Ruby, who was both connected to the Dallas underworld and a friend of Dallas policemen, simply acting, as he said, to spare Mrs. Kennedy the pain of returning to Dallas to testify at a murder trial? Who were the two "Latins" that a New Orleans prostitute said she encountered on their way to Dallas a few days before the murder?

Dozens of books written during the past twenty-five years, from attorney Mark Lane's *Rush to Judgment* and Edward Jay Epstein's *Inquest* to David Lifton's *Best Evidence* and David Scheim's *Contract on America: The Mafia Murder of President John F. Kennedy,* have probed these and other "mysteries." All have relied on flaws in the Warren investigation and on new material the Warren Commission never saw to support a variety of possible conspiracies. All have been greeted by a public feeding frenzy.

Far less sensational is *Final Disclosure,* a 1989 book that refutes all of these theories, written by David W. Belin, the counsel to the Warren Commission and executive director of the Rockefeller Commission investigating abuses by the CIA. Obviously Belin, as a key staff member of the Warren Commission, has a personal interest to protect. But his book is well-reasoned and amply supported by evidence. Examining the Warren Commission's total evidence, the subsequent CIA and FBI revelations, and the analysis of a controversial audio tape that supposedly proved the existence of a fourth shot and a second gunman, Belin deflates the most serious charges brought by the conspiracists, often by showing they have made highly selective use of evidence and testimony.

Even so, that missing-tooth feeling remains. Can anyone say for sure that Oswald and then Ruby acted alone? It seems that few people are willing to accept that conclusion.

American Voices

From Lyndon Johnson's "Great Society" speech (May 1964):

> The Great Society rests on abundance and liberty for all. It demands an end to poverty and racial injustice, to which we are totally committed in our time. But that is just the beginning.
>
> The Great Society is a place where every child can find knowledge to enrich his mind and to enlarge his talents. It is a place where leisure is a welcome chance to build and reflect, not a feared cause of boredom and restlessness. It is a place where the city of man serves not only the needs of the body and the demands of commerce, but the desire for beauty and the hunger for community.
>
> It is a place where man can renew contact with nature. It is a place which honors creation for its own sake and for what it adds to the understanding of the race. It is a place where men are more concerned with the quality of their goals than the quantity of their goods.

In this speech, delivered during hs election campaign against Republican Barry Goldwater, Johnson laid out the foundation for the ambitious domestic social program he carried out after his landslide victory over the conservative senator from Arizona. Johnson proposed attacking racial injustice through economic and educational reforms and government programs aimed at ending the cycle of poverty. The legislative record he then compiled was impressive, although social historians argue over its ultimate effectiveness. The Office of Economic Opportunity was created. Kennedy's proposed Civil Rights Bill was passed, followed by a Voting Rights Act and the establishments of Project

Head Start, the Job Corps, and Medicaid and Medicare. But while Johnson was carrying out the most ambitious social revolution since FDR's New Deal, he was also leading the country deeper and deeper into Vietnam. And that futile and disastrous path, more than any of his domestic initiatives, would mark Johnson's place in history.

Did Mississippi Burning *really happen?*

If Hollywood gets its way, the civil-rights movement was saved when Gene Hackman and Willem Dafoe rolled into town like two gunslinging western marshals. In this revisionist cinematic version of history, two FBI men bring truth and vigilante justice to the nasty Ku Klux Klan while a bunch of bewildered Negroes meekly stand by, shuffling and avoiding trouble.

The 1989 film *Mississippi Burning* was an emotional roller coaster. It was difficult to watch without being moved, breaking into a sweat, and finally cheering when the forces of good terrorized the redneck klansmen into telling where the bodies of three murdered civil-rights workers were buried. The movie gave audiences the feeling of seeing history unfold. But in the grand tradition of American filmmaking, this version of events had as much to do with reality as did D. W. Griffith's racist "classic," *Birth of a Nation.*

The movie opens with the backroads murder of three young civil-rights activists in the summer of 1964. That much is true. Working to register black voters, Andrew Goodman and Michael Schwerner, two whites from the North, and James Chaney, a black southerner, disappeared after leaving police custody in Philadelphia, Mississippi. In the film, two FBI agents arrive to investigate, but get nowhere as local rednecks stonewall the FBI and blacks are too fearful to act. The murderers are not exposed until Agent Anderson (Gene Hackman), a former southern sheriff who has joined the FBI, begins a campaign of illegal tactics to terrorize the locals into revealing where the bodies are buried and who is responsible.

It is a brilliantly made, plainly manipulative film that hits all the right emotional notes: white liberal guilt over the treatment of blacks; disgust at the white-trash racism of the locals; excitement at Hackman's Rambo-style tactics; and, finally, vindication in the murderers' convictions.

The problem is that besides the murders, few of the events depicted happened that way. Pressed by Attorney General Robert Kennedy, FBI Director J. Edgar Hoover sent a large contingent of agents to Mississippi, but they learned nothing. The case was only broken when Klan informers were offered a $30,000 bribe and the bodies of the three men were found in a nearby dam site. Twenty-one men were named in the indictment, including the local police chief and his deputy. But local courts later dismissed the confessions of the two klansmen as hearsay. The Justice Department persisted by bringing conspiracy charges against eighteen of the men. Tried before a judge who had once compared blacks to chimpanzees, seven of the accused were nonetheless convicted and sentenced to jail terms ranging from three to ten years.

Although J. Edgar Hoover put on a good public show of anti-Klan FBI work, it masked his real obsession at the time. To the Director, protecting civil-rights workers was a waste of his Bureau's time. Although the film depicts a black agent, the only blacks employed by the Bureau during Hoover's tenure as head, were his chauffeurs. The FBI was far more interested in trying to prove that Martin Luther King was a Communist and that the civil-rights movement was an organized Communist front. Part of this effort was the high-level attempt to eavesdrop on King's private life, an effort that did prove that the civil-rights leader had his share of white female admirers willing to contribute more than just money to the cause. Hoover's hatred of King boiled over at one point when he called King "the most notorious liar" in the country. Another part of this effort involved sending King a threatening note suggesting he commit suicide.

What was the Tonkin Resolution?

When is a war not a war? When the President decides it isn't, and Congress goes along.

America was already twenty years into its Vietnam commitment when Lyndon Johnson and Kennedy's best and brightest holdovers decided to find a new version of Pearl Harbor. An incident was needed to pull American firepower into the war with at least a glimmer of legitimacy. It came in August 1964 with a brief encounter in the Gulf of Tonkin, the waters off the coast of North Vietnam.

In the civil war that was raging between North and South since the French withdrawal from Indochina and the partition of Vietnam in 1954, the United States had committed money, material, advice, and, by the end of 1963, some 15,000 military advisers in support of the anti-Communist Saigon government. The American CIA was also in the thick of things, having helped foster the coup that toppled prime minister Ngo Dinh Diem in 1963 and then acting surprised when Diem was executed by the army officers who overthrew him.

Among the other "advice" the United States provided to its South Vietnamese allies was to teach them commando tactics. In 1964, CIA-trained guerrillas from the South began to attack the North for months in covert acts of sabotage. Code-named Plan 34-A, these commando raids failed to undermine North Vietnam's military strength, so the mode of attack was shifted to hit-and-run operations by small torpedo boats. To support these assaults, the U.S. Navy posted warships in the Gulf of Tonkin, loaded with electronic eavesdropping equipment enabling them to monitor North Vietnamese military operations and provide intelligence to the South Vietnamese commandos.

One of the American ships in the Gulf of Tonkin was the destroyer USS *Maddox*. Operating approximately ten miles off the coast of North Vietnam, the *Maddox* was within North Vietnamese territorial waters rather than in international waters, as the United States would later claim. From behind an island, three North Vietnamese patrol boats suddenly appeared and sped toward the *Maddox*, which responded by firing on the boats and calling for air support from the nearby carrier *Ticonderoga*. Minutes later, jet fighters joined the attack, sinking one of the patrol boats and crippling the other two. The *Maddox* withdrew to open waters without damage or casualties, and the jets returned to the carrier.

Coming as it did in the midst of LBJ's 1964 campaign against hawkish Republican Barry Goldwater, President Johnson felt the incident called for a tough response. Johnson had the navy send the *Maddox* and a second destroyer, the *Turner Joy,* back into the Gulf of Tonkin. A radarman on the *Turner Joy* saw some blips, and that boat opened fire. On the *Maddox* there were also reports of incoming torpedoes, and the *Maddox* began to fire. There was never any confirmation that either ship had actually been attacked. Later, the radar blips would be attributed to weather conditions and jittery nerves among the crew.

According to Stanley Karnow's *Vietnam: A History,* "Even Johnson privately expressed doubts only a few days after the second attack supposedly took place, confiding to an aide, 'Hell, those dumb stupid sailors were just shooting at flying fish.'"

But that didn't stop Lyndon Johnson. Without waiting for a review of the situation, he ordered an air strike against North Vietnam in "retaliation" for the "attacks" on the U.S. ships. American jets flew more than sixty sorties against targets in North Vietnam. One bitter result of these air raids was the capture of downed pilot Everett Alvarez, Jr., the first American POW of the Vietnam War. He would remain in Hanoi prisons for eight years.

President Johnson followed up the air strike by calling for passage of the Gulf of Tonkin Resolution. This proposal gave the President the authority to "take all necessary measures" to repel attacks against U.S. forces and to "prevent further aggression." The resolution not only gave Johnson the powers he needed to increase American commitment to Vietnam, but allowed him to blunt Goldwater's accusations that Johnson was "timid before Communism." The Gulf of Tonkin Resolution passed the House unanimously after only forty minutes of debate. In the Senate, there were only two voices in opposition. What Congress did not know was that the resolution had been drafted several months before the Tonkin incident took place.

Congress, which alone possesses the constitutional authority to declare war, had handed that power over to a man who was not a bit reluctant to use it. One of the senators who voted against the Tonkin Resolution, Oregon's Wayne Morse, later said, "I believe that history will record that we have made a great mistake in subverting and circumventing the Constitution." After the vote, Walt Rostow, an adviser to Lyndon Johnson, remarked, "We don't know what happened, but it had the desired result."

Milestones in the Vietnam War

1950

While U.S. troops fight in Korea, President Truman grants military aid to France for its war against Communist rebels in Indochina. The United States will ultimately pay the lion's share—75 to 80 percent—of France's military costs in the war against the Ho Chi Minh–led Viet Minh rebels.

1954

Although the use of an atomic bomb is actively considered, President Eisenhower decides against providing direct military support to the French in their stand at Dienbienphu. Eisenhower instead favors continued aid for France in Indochina, and tells the press in April that Southeast Asia may otherwise fall to Communism. Says Eisenhower, if you "have a row of dominoes set up, you knock over the first one, and what will happen to the last one is the certainty that it will go over very quickly."

May The French stronghold at Dienbienphu is overrun by Vietnamese rebels. The French withdraw from Indochina, and Vietnam is partitioned at a conference in Geneva. A political settlement to the country's division is left to a future election that will never take place. The United States continues its direct involvement in Vietnam by sending $100 million in aid to the anti-Communist Saigon government led by Prime Minister Ngo Dinh Diem.

1955

Direct aid and military training are provided to the Saigon government. Vietnam, Cambodia, and Laos receive more than $200 million in U.S. aid this year.

October The Republic of Vietnam is proclaimed by Prime Minister Diem following a rigged election organized by the United States.

1959

July 8 Two American soldiers, Major Dale Buis and Master Sergeant Chester Ovnard, are killed by Vietcong at Bienhoa. They are the first Americans to die in Vietnam during this era. By year's end, there are some 760 U.S. military personnel in Vietnam.

1961

After touring Vietnam, President Kennedy's advisers, Walt Rostow and General Maxwell Taylor, recommend sending 8,000 U.S. combat troops there. Instead, President Kennedy chooses to send more equipment and advisers. By year's end, there are 3,205 U.S. military personnel in Vietnam.

1962

February 6 The American Military Assistance Command Vietnam (MACV) is formed on February 6, based in Saigon.
May President Kennedy sends 5,000 Marines and fifty jets to Thailand to counter Communist expansion in Laos. The number of American advisers is increased to nearly 12,000.

1963

January The Army of the Republic of South Vietnam suffers a major defeat against a smaller Vietcong force at the Battle of Ap Bac. The performance of the Vietnamese troops and commanders, under American guidance, is disastrous.
May–August Anti-government demonstrations by Buddhist monks provoke violent reprisals. In protest, numerous monks commit suicide by setting themselves afire.
November General Duong Van Minh and other South Viet-

namese officers stage a coup and overthrow the Diem government with U.S. knowledge and CIA assistance. Diem and his brother are murdered. Three weeks later, President Kennedy is assassinated.

December By the end of the year, President Johnson has increased the number of American advisers to 16,300, and the United States has sent $500 million to South Vietnam in this year alone. The CIA begins training South Vietnamese guerrillas as part of an ambitious covert sabotage operation against the North, under American direction.

1964

January Lieutenant General William Westmoreland (b. 1914) is appointed deputy commander of Military Assistance Command Vietnam.

January 30 General Nguyen Khanh seizes power in Saigon; General Minh is retained as a figurehead chief of state.

June Westmoreland is promoted to commander of MACV.

August 2 While conducting electronic surveillance ten miles off North Vietnam, in the Gulf of Tonkin, the American destroyer *Maddox* is pursued by three North Vietnamese torpedo boats. As the patrol boats close in, the *Maddox* opens fire and the patrol boats respond with torpedoes, which miss. The destroyer calls for air support from the nearby carrier *Ticonderoga,* and three United States fighter planes attack the boats. The *Maddox* sinks one patrol boat, cripples the other two, and withdraws. Two days later the *Maddox* and a second destroyer, the *Turner Joy,* are ordered back to Tonkin to "reassert freedom of international waters."

August 4 President Johnson reports to congressional leaders that a second attack has been made on the *Maddox,* although this attack was never confirmed and was later shown not to have taken place.

August 5 U.S. planes bomb North Vietnam in retaliation for the "attacks" on the U.S. ships. The American bombing mission is called "limited in scale," but more than sixty sorties are flown, destroying oil depots and patrol boats. Two American planes are shot down and Everett Alvarez is captured, the first American prisoner of war in Vietnam. He is held for more than eight years.

August 7 By a unanimous vote in the House, and with only two dissenting votes in the Senate, Congress passes the Gulf of Tonkin Resolution, giving President Johnson powers to "take all necessary measures to repel any armed attack against the forces of the United States and to prevent further aggression." Johnson later says the resolution was "like grandma's nightshirt—it covered everything."

August 26 President Johnson is nominated at the Democratic National Convention and chooses Hubert Humphrey as his running mate. Pledging before the election to "seek no wider war," Johnson defeats Republican candidate Barry Goldwater in a landslide, with a plurality of 15.5 million votes.

September UN Secretary General U Thant proposes mediating talks with North Vietnam to avert a war. Withholding some information from Johnson, American officials reject these negotiations.

October 30 In a Vietcong attack on the U.S. airbase at Bien Hoa, six B-57 bombers are destroyed and five Americans are killed.

December 31 The number of American military advisers rises to 23,300.

1965

February 7 Following a Vietcong attack on a U.S. base at Pleiku in which eight Americans are killed, President Johnson orders air raids against North Vietnam and the beginning of a new round of escalation in the war, in what is named Operation Flaming Dart. Communist guerrillas then attack another American base, and Flaming Dart II is ordered in retaliation.

February 24 The United States begins Operation Rolling Thunder, the sustained bombing of North Vietnam.

March 8 Two battalions of American marines land and are assigned to protect the airbase at Danang. They are the first American combat troops in Vietnam.

April 7 President Johnson calls for talks with Hanoi to end the war. The plan is rejected by Hanoi, which says any settlement must be based on their Vietcong program.

April 15 Students for a Democratic Society (SDS) sponsor a large antiwar rally in Washington.

June 11 Air Vice-Marshal Nguyen Cao Ky, a flamboyant young officer, takes over as prime minister of a South Vietnamese military regime.

November 14–16 In the first major conventional clash of the war, U.S. forces defeat North Vietnamese units in the Ia Drang Valley.

December 25 President Johnson suspends bombing in an attempt to get the North to negotiate. By year's end, American troop strength is nearly 200,000, combat losses total 636 Americans killed, and at home, draft quotas have been doubled.

1966

January 31 The bombing of the North is resumed after failure of the "peace offensive" that was designed to promote negotiations.

March 10 In Hue and Danang, Buddhist monks demonstrate against the Saigon regime. Both cities are taken over by government troops.

June 29 American planes bomb oil depots near Haiphong and Hanoi, in response to North Vietnamese infiltration into the South to aid the Vietcong.

September 23 The U.S. military command in Vietnam announces that it is using chemical defoliants, Agent Orange among them, to destroy Communist cover.

October 25 A conference between Johnson and heads of six allied nations involved in Vietnam (Australia, the Philippines, Thailand, New Zealand, South Korea, and South Vietnam) issues a peace plan calling for the end of North Vietnamese aggression. By year's end, American troop strength in Vietnam is nearly 400,000.

1967

January 5 American casualties in Vietnam for 1966 are announced: 5,008 killed and 30,093 wounded. (Totals since 1961 are 6,664 killed, 37,738 wounded.)

January 8 Thirty thousand combined American and South Vietnamese troops begin Operation Cedar Falls, an offensive against enemy positions in the "Iron Triangle." (Among the U.S. battalion commanders in this operation is General Alexander Haig.)

January 28 The North Vietnamese announce that U.S. bombing must stop before there can be peace talks.

July 7 The Joint Economic Committee of Congress reports that the war effort created "havoc" in the U.S. economy during 1966.

August Testifying before Congress, Defense Secretary Robert McNamara says bombing of North Vietnam is ineffective.

September Major Communist offensives begin. General Westmoreland fortifies Khe Sanh.

October 21 Two days of antiwar protests take place in Washington, and are the subject of Norman Mailer's book *Armies of the Night*.

December 8 The wave of antiwar protests becomes more organized and active. In New York, 585 protestors are arrested, including Dr. Benjamin Spock and poet Allen Ginsburg. Spock and four other protesters issue *A Call to Resist Illegitimate Authority*, later used as the basis for Spock's prosecution by the government. In the following days of anti-draft protests, arrests are made in New Haven, Cincinnati, Madison, Wisconsin, and Manchester, New Hampshire. At year's end, U.S. troop strength stands at nearly half a million.

1968

January 21 The Battle of Khe Sanh. A strategic hamlet that General Westmoreland had heavily fortified and stockpiled with ammunition as a future staging point for attacks on the Ho Chi Minh Trail, the Communist supply route from the North, Khe Sanh becomes the scene of one of the war's most controversial sieges. When Vietcong and North Vietnamese regulars begin the siege of American forces at Khe Sanh, it is seen by many Americans, including Westmoreland, President Johnson, and the media as a repeat of the 1954 attack on the French stronghold at Dienbienphu. Westmoreland and Johnson are committed to preventing such a disaster, and Johnson tells one of his senior aides, "I don't want any damn Dinbinphoo." A military catastrophe such as the French suffered is averted as Khe Sanh is heavily reinforced and supported by massive B-52 bombings. But at home, Americans watch the siege unfold like a nightly TV serial. Fought in the midst of the Tet Offensive (see below), the battle for Khe Sanh seems to be one more example of the resolve of the Vietnamese, who ultimately lost some ten to fifteen thousand men at Khesanh against 205 Americans killed. The siege lasts until April. Ironically, the base at Khe Sanh will be abandoned one year later, when a planned strike at the Ho Chi Minh Trail in Laos is cancelled.

January 23 The intelligence vessel USS *Pueblo* is captured by North Korea.

January 31 The Tet Offensive. Although a brief truce is set to celebrate the Vietnamese lunar New Year holiday, the Vietcong launch a major offensive throughout South Vietnam, and the American embassy in Saigon is attacked. Although most of the attacks are eventually repulsed, Tet is seen in the United States as a defeat and a symbol of the Vietcong's ability to strike at will anywhere in the country. It also damages the optimistic views of the war's progress that General Westmoreland and other American military leaders have been bringing back to Congress and the American people.

February 25 After twenty-six days of fighting since the Tet Offensive began, the city of Hue is recaptured by American and South Vietnamese forces. Mass graves reveal that an enormous atrocity was committed by the retreating Vietcong and North Vietnamese who killed thousands of civilians suspected of supporting the Saigon government.

February 29 Defense Secretary Robert McNamara resigns after concluding that the United States cannot win the war. He is replaced by Clark Clifford.

March 12 Senator Eugene McCarthy, an outspoken opponent of the war, nearly defeats President Johnson in the New Hampshire primary, a stunning setback for Johnson.

March 16 Following McCarthy's near upset of Johnson, Senator Robert F. Kennedy announces that he will campaign for the Democratic presidential nomination.

March 31 In an extraordinary television address, President Johnson announces a partial bombing halt, offers peace talks, and stuns the nation by saying he will not run again.

April 4 Martin Luther King, Jr., is assassinated in Memphis, Tennessee.

April 23 At New York's Columbia University, members of Students for a Democratic Society (SDS) seize five buildings in protest of Columbia's involvement in war-related research.

May 10 Peace talks begin in Paris between the United States and North Vietnam.

June 6 Following his victory in the California primary, Robert F. Kennedy is assassinated by Sirhan B. Sirhan.

June 14 Dr. Benjamin Spock is convicted of conspiracy to aid draft evasion. (The conviction is later overturned.)

August 26 The Democratic National Convention opens in Chicago. In the midst of antiwar protests and violent police response, the Democrats nominate Hubert Humphrey.

October 31 President Johnson orders an end to bombing of the North, in an attempt to break the stalemate at Paris. Progress at Paris will presumably help the chances of the Democratic ticket of Humphrey-Muskie.

November 6 In one of the closest presidential elections, Richard Nixon defeats Hubert Humphrey, with third-party candidate George Wallace drawing more than 9 million votes. At year's end, American troop strength is at 540,000.

1969

January Paris peace talks are expanded to include the South Vietnamese and Vietcong.

March 18 President Nixon orders the secret bombing of Cambodia.

May 14 President Nixon calls for the simultaneous withdrawal of American and North Vietnamese forces from the South.

June 8 Nixon announces the withdrawal of 25,000 American troops, the first step in a plan called "Vietnamization," the aim of which is to turn the war over to the South Vietnamese.

September 3 Ho Chi Minh, leader of the North since the 1950s, dies in Hanoi at the age of seventy-nine.

September 25 Congressional opposition to the war grows as ten bills designed to remove all American troops from Vietnam are submitted.

October 15 The first of many large, nationwide protests against the war, the "Moratorium" is designed to expand the peace movement off the campuses and into the cities, drawing broader popular support. Led by Coretta Scott King, 250,000 protesters march on Washington.

November 3 Attempting to defuse protest, Nixon makes his "silent majority" speech, claiming that most of the nation supports his efforts to end the war.

November 15 A second "Moratorium" march on Washington takes place.

November 16 A 1968 massacre of civilians at the Vietnamese hamlet of My Lai is revealed. U.S. Army Lieutenant William L. Calley is tried and convicted for his role in the massacre. The atrocity further discredits the war and adds momentum to the peace movement in America.

December 1 The first draft lottery of the Vietnam era is instituted in an effort to reduce criticism of the draft as unfair. It signals the end of student draft deferments.

1970

February 18 Following a long, theatrical trial highlighted by the courtroom antics of defendants Abbie Hoffman, Jerry Rubin, and others, the "Chicago Seven" are acquitted on charges of conspiring to incite a riot. They are convicted on lesser charges, which are later overturned.

February 20 National Security Adviser Henry Kissinger begins secret Paris negotiations with Le Duc Tho.

April 20 Nixon promises to withdraw another 150,000 men from Vietnam by year's end. The withdrawals are decreasing American casualties.

April 30 Nixon announces that U.S. troops have attacked Communist sanctuaries in Cambodia, following the overthrow of Prince Sihanouk by U.S.-aided Lon Nol.

May 4 As part of the widening campus protests against the war, a demonstration is held at Kent State University in Ohio. When national guardsmen open fire on the demonstrators, four students are killed. Ten days later, two more students are killed, at predominantly black Jackson State College in Mississippi.

October 7 Nixon proposes a "standstill cease fire," and reissues a proposal for mutual withdrawal the next day.

November 23 A raid into North Vietnam, in an attempt to rescue American POWs, comes up empty-handed. Heavy bombing of the North continues. At year's end, U.S. troop strength falls to 280,000.

1971

February 8 The South Vietnamese, with American support, begin attacks on Vietcong supply lines in Laos.

June 13 The *New York Times* begins publication of the "Pentagon Papers," the top-secret history of American involvement in Vietnam, which has been turned over by Pentagon employee Daniel Ellsberg to *Times* reporter Neil Sheehan. Nixon tries to stop publication of the documents, which reveal much of the duplicity within the government surrounding Vietnam. But on June 30 the Supreme Court rules that the *Times* and the *Washington Post* may resume publication. On Nixon's orders to investigate Ellsberg, a group is set up known as the "plumbers," whose purpose is to try to stop "leaks." The "plumbers" soon expand their activities to a campaign aimed at a Nixon "enemies list." Also on their agenda is a break-in at the Democratic National Committee offices at the Watergate Office Building in Washington, D.C.

November 12 President Nixon announces the withdrawal of 45,000 more men, leaving an American force of 139,000 in Vietnam.

1972

January 13 President Nixon announces withdrawal of an additional 70,000 troops.

January 25 President Nixon reveals that Henry Kissinger has been in secret negotiations with the North Vietnamese, and makes public an eight-point peace proposal calling for a ceasefire and release of all U.S. POWs, in exchange for U.S. withdrawal from Vietnam.

March 30 The North Vietnamese launch a massive offensive across the Demilitarized Zone into the South. In five weeks, Hanoi's troops have penetrated deep into the South.

April 15 President Nixon orders resumption of bombing in the North, suspended three years earlier.

May 1 The city of Quang Tri is captured by the North.

May 8 President Nixon announces the mining of Haiphong harbor and stepped-up bombing raids against the North.

June 17 Five men are arrested at the Democratic National Committee offices at the Watergate Office Building. They work for the Committee to Reelect the President. Subsequently, two former intelligence operatives, G. Gordon Liddy and E. Howard Hunt, are arrested for their involvement in the break-in, and the ensuing cover-up by the White House begins to unravel.

October 8 Henry Kissinger and Le Duc Tho achieve a breakthrough in their Paris negotiations. Henry Kissinger returns to the United States to say that peace is "within reach." The announcement is made two weeks before the presidential election, in which Nixon is opposed by the Democratic senator from South Dakota, George McGovern, an outspoken opponent of the war.

November 7 Nixon is reelected in a landslide victory. Following the election, Kissinger's talks with Le Duc Tho break down.

December 18 The United States resumes bombing raids over North Vietnam, which continue for eleven days. Communists agree to resume talks when bombing stops.

1973

January Kissinger resumes talks with the North. A cease-fire agreement is signed and formally announced on January 27. Defense Secretary Melvin Laird announces the end of the draft as the army shifts to an all-volunteer force. During the Vietnam War, 2.2 million American men have been drafted.

March 29 The last American ground troops leave Vietnam.

April 1 All American POWs held in Hanoi are released.

April 30 President Nixon's aides H. R. Haldeman, John Ehrlichman, and John Dean resign amid charges that the White House has obstructed justice in the Watergate investigation. On June 25, Dean accuses Nixon of authorizing a cover-up, and another White House aide reveals the existence of a secret taping system that has recorded conversations in the Oval Office.

July 16 The Senate begins an investigation of the secret air war against Cambodia.

August 14 The U.S. officially halts bombing of Cambodia.

October 10 Vice-President Spiro Agnew resigns after pleading "no contest" to charges of tax evasion. House minority leader Gerald Ford is nominated by Nixon to replace Agnew under the Twenty-fifth Amendment, which allows the President to fill a vacancy in the vice-presidency.

November 7 Over the President's veto, Congress passes the War Powers Act, which restricts the President's power to commit troops to foreign countries without congressional approval.

1974

January South Vietnam's President Thieu announces that war has begun again. Communists proceed to build up troops and supplies in the South.

July 30 The House Judiciary Committee votes to recommend impeachment of President Nixon on three counts of "high crimes and misdemeanors." Nixon resigns on **August 9** and is replaced by Gerald Ford. On **September 8,** Ford pardons Nixon for all crimes he "committed or may have committed."

1975

In an offensive that lasts six months, combined Vietcong and North Vietnamese forces overrun South Vietnam and Cambodia.

April 17 Pnompenh, the capital of Cambodia (renamed Kampuchea), falls to the Khmer Rouge.

April 23 President Ford calls the war "finished."

April 29 The last Americans are evacuated from Saigon, on the same day that the last two American soldiers are killed in Vietnam. On the following day, Communist forces take Saigon.

1976

January 21 President Jimmy Carter unconditionally pardons most of the 10,000 men who evaded the draft.

1982

November 11 The Vietnam Veterans Memorial is unveiled in Washington, D.C. It commemorates the 58,000 American lives lost in Vietnam between 1959 and 1975.

American Voices

From *The Autobiography of Malcolm X* (1965):

> Few white people realize that many black people today dislike and avoid spending any more time than they must around white people. This "integration" image, as it is popularly interpreted, has millions of vain, self-exalted white people convinced that black people want to sleep in bed with them—and that's a lie! Or you can't tell the average white man that the Negro man's prime desire isn't to have a white woman—another lie! Like a black brother recently observed to me, "Look, you ever smell one of them wet?"

If Martin Luther King, Jr., gave J. Edgar Hoover bad dreams, Malcolm X (1925–1965) was his nightmare. Born Malcolm Little, in Omaha, Nebraska, Malcolm joined that vast migration of blacks into the cities, moving to Harlem. While serving prison time, he came under the influence of the black nationalist movement called the Nation of Islam or the Black Muslims. He took the name Malcolm X, renouncing his "slave name," and quickly rose as a charismatic and forceful spokesman for the movement.

After a pilgrimage to Mecca, he returned to the United States and split from the Black Muslims, forming the Organization for Afro-American Unity. Malcolm X seemed to be tilting toward a more conciliatory message. But early in 1965 he was assassinated in a Harlem mosque. Two men, identified as Black Muslims, were arrested for the murder. They were convicted, but, as with other assassinations, the truth behind Malcolm's death remains buried in suspicious circumstances.

What happened in Watts?

In the tumultuous decade after Rosa Parks refused to give up her bus seat (see Chapter 7), the civil-rights movement coalesced behind the leadership of Martin Luther King, Jr., achieved some gains through the courts and legislation, and moved the question of racial equality to the front burner of American life. For most of those ten years, blacks seemed willing to accept King's nonviolent vision of overcoming the hurdles of racism and segregation. But sometimes the front burner gets very hot. Before long, the pot was boiling over.

By 1965 the rhetoric and the actions of the civil-rights movement changed because the country had changed. The war in Vietnam was moving into full swing. The year 1963 brought the assassination of President Kennedy, and Mississippi NAACP leader Medgar Evers (1925–1963) was gunned down in front of his home in Jackson. The nonviolent integration movement was being met by violence and death. A Birmingham church was bombed, with four little girls killed. Goodman, Schwerner, and Chaney (see pages 368–369) were murdered in Mississippi in the summer of 1964. In February 1965, it was Malcolm X who went down. A month later, after thousands of marchers led by Martin Luther King, with U.S. Army protection, walked from Selma to Montgomery, a white civil-rights worker named Viola Liuzzo was murdered. In the car with the klansmen who shot her was an FBI informer.

Once solidly anchored by King's SCLC and the NAACP, with their emphasis on peaceful, court-ordered remedies, the movement was coming under fire. The violence in the air was producing a new generation of activists who lacked King's patience. Men like Floyd McKissick of the Congress for Racial Equality (CORE) and Stokely Carmichael of the Student Nonviolent Coordinating Committee (SNCC) were no longer willing to march to Dr. King's moderate tune. They preferred the martial drumbeat of Malcolm X's aggressive rhetoric. Built on frustration and anger, this basic split in tactics splintered the movement. By the summer of 1965, only days after the Voting Rights Act was signed into law, strengthening protection of black voter registration, the anger no longer just simmered. It boiled over. The scene was a section of Los Angeles called Watts.

This was not the Los Angeles of Hollywood, Malibu, and Bel-Air. Watts was a rundown district of shabby houses built near the highway approaching Los Angeles International Airport. Ninety-eight percent black, Watts was stewing in a California heat wave. In the stewpot were all the ingredients of black anger. Poverty. Overcrowding. High unemployment. Crime everywhere. Drugs widely available. The nearly all-white police force was seen as an occupation army.

On August 11, a policeman pulled over a young black man to check him for drunken driving. A common occurrence for blacks, it seemed to happen all too infrequently to white drivers. When the young man was arrested, a crowd gathered, at first joking and taunting, then growing more restive. Rumors of police brutality started to waft through the summer heat. The crowd grew larger and angrier. Soon the lone policeman called for reinforcements, and when the police arrived, they were met by hurled stones, bottles, and chunks of concrete. Within a few hours the crowds had grown to a mob, and the frustration was no longer simmering in the August heat. it had exploded.

Watts was sealed off, and for a while all was quiet. But the next day the anger returned. By nightfall the small, roving bands had grown to a mob of thousands, hostile, angry, and beyond control. The rocks and bottles were replaced by Molotov cocktails as the riot erupted into a full-blown street rebellion. Black storeowners posted signs that read, "We Own This One." The signs didn't always help. Among the most popular looted items were weapons, and when police and firefighters responded to the violence and fires, they were met with a hail of bullets and gasoline bombs. All of the pent-up rage and helplessness boiled over in white-hot fury. Reason lost out. When Dick Gregory, the well-known stand-up comic and activist, tried to calm the crowds, he was shot in the leg. Mob frenzy had taken over. Watts was in flames.

The battle—for that was what it had become—raged on for days as thousands of national guardsmen poured in to restore order. There was open fighting in the streets as guardsmen set up machine-gun emplacements. Vietnam had seemingly come to L.A. By the sixth day of rioting, Watts was rubble and ashes. One European journalist even commented, "It looks like Germany during the last months of World War II."

The toll from six days of mayhem was thirty-four killed, including rioters and guardsmen; more than 1,000 injured; 4,000 arrested; and total property damage of more than $35 million.

But the aftermath of Watts was more than just a body count, police blotters, and insurance estimates. Something fundamental had occurred. There had been race riots before in America. In Detroit, during World War II, as many people had died as were killed in Watts. There had been smaller riots in other northern cities in previous years. But Watts seemed to signal a sea-change in the civil-rights movement. When Martin Luther King toured the neighborhood, he was heckled. Saddened by the death and destruction, he admonished a local man, who responded, "We won because we made the whole world pay attention to us." The time of King's "soul power" was passing. The new call was for "Black Power."

The Watts summer of 1965 was only the first in a string of long, hot summers that left the cities of the North and Midwest smoldering with racial unrest. In the summer of 1966, several cities saw rioting. But the worst came in 1967, particularly when Newark and Detroit were engulfed in more rebellions. The death due to urban violence toll that year rose to more than eighty.

In the wake of these rebellions, presidential commissions were appointed, studies made, and findings released. They all agreed that the problem was economic at its roots. As Martin Luther King had put it, "I worked to get these people the right to eat hamburgers, and now I've got to do something to help them get the money to buy them." One of these studies, conducted by the National Advisory Commission on Civil Disorders, warned forebodingly that America was "moving toward two societies, one black, one white—separate and unequal."

That was on February 29, 1968. About a month later, Martin

Luther King was killed by James Earl Ray in Memphis. His death set off another wave of riots that left cities smoldering.

Who was Miranda?

No, not Carmen.

For anyone who grew up on a TV diet of Joe Friday and "Dragnet," "Streets of San Francisco," "NYPD," and a hundred other "cop" shows, "Read him his rights" is a familiar bit of requisite dialogue. That is, for any cop shows that came after 1966. To America's lawmen, that was the year that the world started to come unglued.

Ernesto Miranda was hardly the kind of guy who might be expected to change legal history. But he did, in his own savage way. A high school dropout with a criminal record dating to his teen years, Miranda abducted a teenage girl at a Phoenix moviehouse candy counter in 1963, and drove her into the desert, where he raped her. Based on his record, Miranda was soon picked up, and was identified by the victim in a police lineup. After making a written confession in which he stated that he had been informed of his rights, Miranda was convicted and sentenced to prison for forty to fifty-five years. But at the trial, Miranda's court-appointed attorney argued that his client had not been told of his right to legal counsel.

The American Civil Liberties Union took the case of *Miranda v. Arizona* all the way to the Supreme Court, where it was heard by the Warren Court in 1966. The issue was the Fifth Amendment's protection against self-incrimination. On June 13, 1966, the Court announced a five-to-four ruling in favor of Miranda that said a criminal suspect must be told of his right to silence, that his remarks may be used against him, and that he had a right to counsel during interrogation, even if he could not afford one.

Depending on your point of view, it was either a great milestone for civil liberties and the protection of the rights of both the innocent and the criminal, or the beginning of the end of civilization.

As for Miranda, he did not live long enough to see his name become part of American legal textbooks and television culture.

On the basis of new evidence, he was convicted again on the same charges of kidnapping and rape, and imprisoned. He was eventually paroled and ten years after the Court inscribed his name in legal history, Ernesto Miranda died of a knife wound suffered during a bar fight.

What happened at My Lai?

On March 16, 1968, in a small Vietnamese village, "something dark and bloody" took place. With those words, a lone veteran of the war forced the U.S. Army to reluctantly examine a secret that was no secret. America was forced to look at itself in a manner once reserved for enemies who had committed war crimes. With those words, America found out about the massacre of civilians by U.S. soldiers at My Lai.

The GIs of Charlie Company called it Pinkville. That was how it was colored on their maps of Vietnam's Quang Ngai province. Or maybe it was because the village was suspected of being a stronghold for the Vietcong. Under the command of Lieutenant William L. Calley, Charlie Company of the Americal Division's Eleventh Infantry had nebulous orders from its company commander, Captain Ernest Medina, to "clean the village out." In the previous three months, Charlie Company had taken about one hundred casualties without even seeing action. Sniper fire and booby traps were to blame. Frustrated and angry at the hand they had been dealt in a war in which there were no uniforms to separate "good gooks" from "bad gooks," the men of Charlie Company were primed to wreak havoc on a phantom enemy they had never been able to confront in an open battle.

Dropped into the village by helicopter, the men of Charlie Company found only the old men, women, and children of My Lai. There were no Vietcong, and no signs of any. There were no stashed weapons, no rice caches, nothing to suggest that My Lai was a staging base for guerrilla attacks. But under Lieutenant Calley's direct orders, the villagers were forced into the center of the hamlet, where Calley issued the order to shoot them. The defenseless villagers were mowed down by automatic-weapons fire. Then the villagers' huts were grenaded, some of them while still occupied. Finally, small groups of survivors—some of them women and girls who had been raped by the Americans—were rounded up and herded into a drainage ditch, where they too were mercilessly machine-gunned. A few of the soldiers of Charlie Company refused to follow the order; one of them later called it "point-blank murder."

Only one American tried to intervene. A helicopter pilot saw the bodies in the ditch and went down to investigate. Placing his helicopter between the GIs and a band of children, the pilot ordered his crew to shoot any American who tried to stop him. He managed to rescue a handful of children. But that was the day's only heroic deed. Another witness to the massacre was an army photographer who was ordered to turn over his official camera, but kept a second secret camera. With it, he had recorded the mayhem in which more than 560 Vietnamese, mostly women and children, were slaughtered. Those pictures, when they later surfaced, revealed the extent of the carnage at My Lai. But not right away. Although many in the chain of command knew something "dark and bloody" had happened that day, there was no investigation. The mission was reported as a success back at headquarters.

But Ronald Ridenhour, a veteran of Charlie Company who had not been at My Lai, began to hear the rumors from buddies. Piecing together what had happened, he detailed the events in a letter he sent to President Nixon, to key members of Congress, and to officials in the State Department and Pentagon. The dirty little secret of My Lai was out. Within a few weeks the army opened an investigation. More than a year had passed since the day My Lai became a killing ground.

In the immediate aftermath of the investigation, a number of ranking officers of the Americal Division were court-martialed for dereliction of duty. At worst, they were reduced in rank or censured. Thirteen officers and enlisted men were also charged with war crimes. But of these, only Lieutenant Calley was found guilty of war crimes. He was sentenced to life imprisonment, but President Nixon then reduced the sentence and changed it to house arrest in response to the outpouring of public support for Calley, who was seen as a scapegoat. Calley was later paroled. A documentary about My Lai that was broadcast in 1989 showed

Calley, a prosperous businessman, getting into an expensive foreign car and driving off. He refuses to comment on the incident.

To the war's supporters on the right, the atrocity at My Lai was an aberration and Calley a victim of a "leftist" antiwar movement. To the war's opponents, Calley and My Lai epitomized the war's immorality and injustice. In a sense, My Lai was the outcome of forcing young Americans into an unwinnable war. As others have pointed out, this was not the only crime against civilians in Vietnam. It was not uncommon to see GIs use their Zippo lighters to torch an entire village. As one officer said early in the war, after torching a hamlet, "We had to destroy this village to save it." That Alice-in-Wonderland logic perfectly embodied the impossibility of the American position.

Even though the United States would drop 7 *million tons* of bombs—twice the total dropped on Europe and Asia during all of World War II—on an area about the size of Massachusetts, along with Agent Orange and other chemical defoliants, the United States was losing the war. The political and military leadership of this country failed to understand the Vietnamese character, traditions, culture, and history. That failure doomed America to its costly and tragic defeat in Vietnam.

American Voices

Astronaut Neil Armstrong (b. 1930) on July 20, 1969, as he became the first man to walk on the moon:

That was one small step for a man and a great leap for mankind.

Armstrong's words, and the images of him stepping onto the lunar surface, were seen and heard by the entire world. The moment was the culmination of the obsessive push for putting a man on the moon, a challenge that began with the humiliation of Sputnik. (See Chapter 7.) Armstrong and fellow moon-walker Buzz Aldrin planted an American flag on the lunar surface and left a plaque that read, "Here men from the planet Earth first set foot upon the moon July, 1969 A.D. We came in peace for all mankind."

Why did Richard Nixon and Henry Kissinger try to stop the New York Times *from publishing the "Pentagon Papers"?*

In the summer of 1971, President Richard Nixon learned that what you don't know *can* hurt you.

In June 1971, the *New York Times* ran a headline that hardly seemed sensational: "Vietnam Archive: Pentagon Study Traces 3 Decades of Growing U.S. Involvement." What the headline did not say was that the study also traced thirty years of deceit and ineptitude on the part of the United States government.

In page after numbingly detailed page, the *Times* reprinted thousands of documents, cables, position papers, and memos, all referring to the American effort in Vietnam. Officially titled *The History of the U.S. Decision Making Process in Vietnam*, the material quickly became known as the "Pentagon Papers." Richard Nixon was not aware of its existence. But it would shake his administration and the military establishment in America to their toes.

Ordered by Robert McNamara, one of Kennedy's "best and brightest" prior to his resignation as Defense Secretary in 1968, this massive compilation had involved the work of large teams of scholars and analysts. The avalanche of paper ran to some 2 million words. Among the men who had helped put it together was Daniel Ellsberg, a Rand Corporation analyst and onetime hawk who, like McNamara himself, became disillusioned by the war. Working at MIT after his resignation from Rand, which was involved in collecting and analyzing the papers, Ellsberg decided to go public with the information. He turned a copy over to *Times* reporter Neil Sheehan.

When the story broke, the country soon learned how it had been duped. Going back to the Truman administration, the Pentagon Papers revealed a history of deceptions, policy disagreements within several White House administrations, and outright lies. Among the most damaging revelations were cables from the American embassy in Saigon, dating from the weeks before Prime Minister Diem was ousted with CIA encouragement and then executed. There was the discovery that the Tonkin Resolution had been drafted months before the incident occurred from which it took its name. And there were memos showing Lyndon Johnson committing infantry to Vietnam at the same time he was telling the country that he had no long-range plans for a strategy in Vietnam.

The papers did not cover the Nixon years, and White House reaction was at first muted, even gleeful at the prospect of the embarrassment it would create for the Democrats. But Nixon and his National Security Adviser, Henry Kissinger (b. 1923) soon realized that if something this highly classified could be leaked, so could other secrets. Both men were already troubled by leaks within the administration. How could they carry·on the business of national security if documents this sensitive could be photo-copied and handed out to the nation's newspapers like press releases? There was a second concern. The revelations in the Pentagon Papers had fueled the antiwar sentiment that was growing louder and angrier and moving off the campuses and into the halls of Congress.

The administration first tried to bully the *Times* into halting publication. Attorney General John Mitchell threatened the paper with espionage charges. These were ignored. Nixon then tried the courts and received a temporary injunction blocking further publication. But the brush fire started by the *Times* was growing into a forest fire. The *Washington Post* and the *Boston Globe* were also running the documents. A federal court ordered the *Post* to halt publication and the question went to the Supreme Court. On June 30, the Court ruled six to three in favor of the newspapers on First Amendment grounds.

Kissinger and Nixon went nuclear. Said Nixon, "I want to know who is behind this. . . . I want it done, whatever the costs."

When Ellsberg was revealed as the culprit, a new White House unit was formed to investigate him. Their job was to stop leaks, so they were jokingly called "the plumbers." White House assistant Egil Krogh, Nixon Special Counsel Charles Colson, and others in the White House turned to former CIA man E. Howard Hunt and ex-FBI agent G. Gordon Liddy to bring their special clandestine talents to the operation. One of their first jobs was to conduct a break-in at the offices of Daniel Ellsberg's psychiatrist.

As a burglary, it was only marginally more successful than the next break-in planned by the group, at an office complex called Watergate.

Apart from setting into motion some of the events that would mutate into the Watergate affair, the publication of the Pentagon Papers had other important repercussions. From the government's standpoint, American security credibility had been crippled, severely damaging intelligence operations around the world, for better or worse. On the other side, the antiwar movement gained new strength and respectability, increasing the pressure on Nixon to end the U.S. involvement in Vietnam. And the Supreme Court's action in protecting the newspapers from prior restraint established and strengthened First Amendment principles.

But the Pentagon Papers case also reinforced a "bunker mentality" that already existed within the White House "palace guard." There was an us-against-them defensiveness emanating from the Oval Office. Publication of the Pentagon Papers made the Nixon White House far more aggressive in its defense of "national security," an idea that was expanded to include the protection and reelection of Richard Nixon by any means and at any cost.

Why did "Jane Roe" sue Wade?

"To be or not to be." For Shakespeare and the Supreme Court, that was and is the question. There is no other issue more emotionally, politically, or legally divisive in modern America than the future of abortion rights.

Most Americans thought the question was settled on January 22, 1973. That was the day the Supreme Court decided, by a seven-to-two margin, that it was unconstitutional for states to prohibit voluntary abortions before the third month of pregnancy; the decision also limited prohibitions that states might set during the second three months.

The decision grew out of a Texas case involving a woman who, out of desire to protect her privacy, was called "Jane Roe" in court papers. "Roe" was a single woman living in Texas who became pregnant. She desired an abortion, but was unable to obtain one legally in her home state of Texas, and so she gave birth to a child she put up for adoption. Nonetheless, she brought suit against Texas in an attempt to overturn the restrictive Texas abortion codes. The case ultimately reached the Supreme Court, which made the decision in the case known as *Roe v. Wade*.

For sixteen years the *Roe* precedent influenced a series of rulings that liberalized abortion in America. To many Americans, the right to an abortion was a basic matter of private choice, a decision for the woman to make. But to millions of Americans, *Roe* was simply government-sanctioned murder.

The mostly conservative foes of legal abortion—who call their movement "pro-life"—gained strength in the 1980s, coalescing behind Ronald Reagan and contributing to his election. And it will ultimately be Reagan's legacy through his appointments to the Supreme Court who determine the future of *Roe v. Wade*. In the summer of 1989, the Supreme Court decided five-to-four, in the case of *Webster v. Reproductive Health Services,* to give states expanded authority to limit abortion rights. The Court also announced that it would hear a series of cases that would give it the opportunity to completely overturn the *Roe* decision.

American Voices

From Justice Harry A. Blackmun's majority decision in *Roe v. Wade* (January 22, 1973):

> The Constitution does not explicitly mention any right of privacy. In a line of decisions, however . . . the Court has recognized that a right of personal privacy, or a guarantee of certain areas or zones of privacy, does exist under the Constitution. . . . They also make it clear that the right has some extension to activities relating to marriage; procreation; contraception; family relationships; and child rearing and education.
>
> The right of privacy . . . is broad enough to encompass a woman's decision whether or not to terminate her pregnancy. . . . We need not resolve the difficult question of when life

begins. When those trained in the respective disciplines of medicine, philosophy, and theology are unable to arrive at any consensus, the judiciary, at this point in the development of man's knowledge, is not in a position to speculate as to the answer.

How did a botched burglary become a crisis called Watergate and bring down a powerful President?

Break-ins and buggings. Plumbers and perjury. Secret tapes, "smoking guns," and slush funds.

We know now that Watergate wasn't what Nixon press secretary Ron Zeigler called it, "a third-rate burglary." This nationally televised soap opera of corruption, conspiracy, and criminality only began to unravel with a botched break-in at the Watergate office complex. That ludicrous larceny was only a tiny strand in the web of domestic spying, criminal acts, illegal campaign funds, enemies lists, and obstruction of justice that emerged from the darkness as "Watergate." But it ended up with Richard Nixon resigning from the presidency in disgrace and only a few steps ahead of the long arm of the law.

After the Civil War and Vietnam, few episodes in American history have generated as many written words as the Watergate affair. Just about everybody who participated in this extraordinary chapter ended up writing a book about his view of the events. They were joined by the dozens of historians, journalists, and other writers who turned out books. The notoriety of Watergate gave convicted felon E. Howard Hunt a renewed lease on a life as a writer of inferior spy novels, a pursuit in which he was joined by John Ehrlichman and even Spiro Agnew, another of the rats who went down with the sinking ship that was Richard Nixon's second administration. Even the rabidly right-wing former FBI agent G. Gordon Liddy was able to parlay his macho, fanatical, "hand over a lighted candle" image into a lucrative career including playing guest roles on "Miami Vice," founding a "survivalist" camp to teach commando techniques to weekend warriors, and a lecture tour that pitted Liddy in the role of mad-dog conservative against sixties relic Timothy Leary, the onetime high priest of psychedelic drugs.

This ludicrous aftermath has been combined with some of the comical aspects of the bungled break-in and Howard Hunt's notoriously bad CIA-provided disguises to soften the image of Watergate's implications. It seems almost *opéra bouffe*, a light-hearted satire. But that perspective overlooks the seriousness of the crimes committed in the name of national security and Richard Nixon's reelection—two objectives that a large number of high-placed fanatics equated with each other.

American Voices

Richard Nixon, from the Oval Office tapes:

> I don't give a shit what happens, I want you to stonewall it, let them plead the Fifth Amendment, coverup or anything else, if it'll save the plan.

A Watergate Chronology

1972

June 17 At the Watergate Office Building in Washington, D.C., five men are arrested during a pathetically bungled break-in at the offices of the Democratic National Committee (DNC). The men are all carrying cash and documents that show them to be employed by the Committee to Re-elect the President (later given the acronyn CREEP), and the purpose of the burglary is to plant listening devices in the phones of Democratic leaders and obtain political documents regarding the Democrats' campaign strategy. The men arrested include a former FBI agent and four anti-Castro Cubans who have been told that they are looking for material linking Castro to the Democratic Party. Two former White House aides working for CREEP, G. Gordon Liddy and E. Howard Hunt, are also arrested. Hunt, it will be learned, was one of the CIA agents responsible for planning the Bay of Pigs invasion and some of the Cubans arrested also took part in the invasion. The seven men are indicted on September 15. Even though their relationship to the election committee is established, none of the seven men connects the committee or the White House to the break-in.

November 7 After an October Gallup poll shows that less than half of the American people have even heard of the break-in, President Nixon defeats his Democratic challenger Senator George McGovern in a landslide, capturing 60.8 percent of the popular vote and 520 of the 537 electoral votes. McGovern carries only Massachusetts and Washington, D.C.

December 8 The wife of E. Howard Hunt dies in a plane crash in Chicago. She is carrying $10,000 in $100 bills. The money is "hush money" she was ferrying to someone in Chicago.

1973

February 7 Amid swirling rumors of widespread wrongdoing, corrupt financing, and political dirty tricks committed by the Nixon reelection committee, the Senate establishes a Select Committee on Presidential Campaign Activities, chaired by North Carolina senator Sam Ervin (1896–1985).

March 23 Former CIA agent James W. McCord, one of the seven men convicted in the attempted burglary, admits in a letter to Judge John Sirica that he and other defendants have been under pressure to remain silent about the case. McCord reveals that others were involved in the break-in, and he eventually names John Mitchell, the former Attorney General who had become chairman of the Committee to Re-elect the President, as the "overall boss."

April 20 L. Patrick Gray, acting director of the FBI, resigns after admitting he destroyed evidence connected to Watergate, on the advice of Nixon aides in the White House.

April 30 Nixon's chief of staff, H. R. Haldeman, domestic affairs assistant John Ehrlichman, and presidential counsel John Dean III all resign. In a televised speech announcing the shake-up, President Nixon denies any knowledge of a cover-up of White House involvement in the Watergate break-in.

May 11 Charges against Daniel Ellsberg and Anthony J. Russo are dropped for their theft and release of the Pentagon Papers. The judge makes this decision following the revelation that Watergate conspirators E. Howard Hunt and G. Gordon Liddy had burglarized the office of Ellsberg's psychiatrist in an attempt to steal Ellsberg's medical records.

June 25 Testifying before Ervin's Senate committee, John Dean accuses President Nixon of involvement in the Watergate cover-up and says the President authorized payment of "hush money" to the seven men arrested in the break-in.

July 16 In testimony that rocks the nation, White House aide Alexander Butterfield tells the Ervin committee that President Nixon secretly recorded all Oval Office conversations. This startling revelation provides the committee with the means to substantiate testimony implicating the President in the cover-up of the Watergate burglary. It also sets off a constitutional crisis over the President's right to keep the tapes secret under the umbrella of "executive privilege."

October 10 In an unrelated development that further damages White House credibility, Vice-President Spiro Agnew, the chief voice of "law and order" in the Nixon White House, resigns after pleading nolo contendere (no contest) to tax-evasion charges dating from his days as governor of Maryland. Two days later, President Nixon nominates House Minority Leader Gerald Ford to succeed Agnew under the provisions of the Twenty-fifth Amendment, allowing the President to fill a vacancy in the vice-presidency.

October 20 "The Saturday Night Massacre." President Nixon orders Attorney General Elliot Richardson to fire Watergate Special Prosecutor Archibald Cox, who has refused to accept the President's compromise offer to release a "synopsis" of the tapes. Richardson and his assistant, William D. Ruckelshaus, refuse to follow this order and both resign. Solicitor General Robert Bork, third in the Justice Department chain of command, fires Cox. (The Democrats' revenge will come when Ronald Reagan nominates Bork to the Supreme Court in 1988. Bork's nomination will open an acrimonious debate over his legal views, and he will be rejected by the Senate.) The resignations and the firing of Cox raise a storm of protest in Congress, and the House actively begins to consider impeachment of the President.

October 23 The House Judiciary Committee, chaired by Representative Peter Rodino, announces an investigation into impeachment charges against the President. Leon Jaworski is appointed special prosecutor in the Watergate investigation after Archibald Cox's firing.

October 30 After Nixon reluctantly agrees to turn over the Oval Office tapes, investigators learn that two tapes are missing.

November 21 Investigators learn that one of the tapes contains a mysterious eighteen-and-a-half-minute gap. The White House claims that Rosemary Woods, Nixon's secretary, accidentally erased part of the tape while transcribing it, a feat that, owing to the way the recording apparatus was set up, would have required the skills of a contortionist. (In January 1974, analysis of the tape will show that the erasure was deliberate.)

November 9 Six of the Watergate defendants are sentenced for their roles in the break-in. E. Howard Hunt receives a sentence of two and a half to eight years and a $10,000 fine. The others are given lesser sentences. G. Gordon Liddy is sentenced to twenty years, in part because of his refusal to cooperate with investigators.

November 13 Representatives of two oil companies plead guilty to making illegal contributions to the Nixon campaign. The next day, Commerce Secretary Maurice Stans, who was the Nixon campaign treasurer, admits that such contributions were expected from major corporations. Two days later, three more companies—Goodyear, Braniff Airlines, and American Airlines—report similar donations.

November 30 Egil Krogh, Jr., who headed the White House "plumbers" unit, pleads guilty to charges stemming from the break-in at the offices of Daniel Ellsberg's psychiatrist.

December 6 Gerald Ford is sworn in as Vice-President. Besides having been a member of the Warren Commission investigating the death of President Kennedy, Ford is best known for what Lyndon Johnson once said about him: "Shucks, I don't think he can chew gum and walk at the same time. . . . He's a nice fellow, but he spent too much time playing football without a helmet."

1974

January 4 Claiming "executive privilege," President Nixon refuses to surrender five hundred tapes and documents subpoenaed by the Senate Watergate Committee.

March 1 Seven former White House staff members, including Haldeman, Ehrlichman, and former Attorney General John Mitchell, are indicted for conspiring to obstruct the investigation of the Watergate break-in.

April 3 Following months of investigation by a separate congressional committee, President Nixon agrees to pay more than $400,000 in back taxes. Using suspect deductions, the President had paid taxes equivalent to those levied on a salary of $15,000, despite the President's $200,000 salary and other income.

April 29 In another nationally televised address, President Nixon offers a 1,200-page edited transcript of the tapes subpoenaed by the House Judiciary Committee and Special Prosecutor Jaworski. Both Jaworski and the committee reject the transcripts.

May 16 Richard Kleindienst, John Mitchell's successor as Attorney General, pleads guilty to a misdemeanor charge of failing to testify accurately before a Senate committee, Kleindienst is the first Attorney General ever convicted of a crime.

July 24 The Supreme Court rules unanimously that Nixon must turn over the tapes requested by the special prosecutor. Eight hours later, the White House announces it will comply with the order.

July 27 The House Judiciary Committee approves two articles of impeachment against Nixon, charging him with obstructing justice and accusing him of repeatedly violating his oath of office. Three days later the committee will recommend a third charge of unconstitutional defiance of committee subpoenas.

August 5 In another televised address, Nixon releases transcripts of a conversation with chief of staff H. R. Haldeman. The transcript shows that, six days after the break-in, Nixon ordered a halt to the FBI investigation of the affair. Nixon concedes that he failed to include this information in earlier statements, what he calls "a serious omission." This is the "smoking gun" that everybody has been looking for. Following the speech, Nixon's remaining congressional support disappears.

August 8 President Nixon announces his resignation, effective noon the following day. The decision comes in the wake of his revelation three days earlier, after which key Republican congressmen told him he would probably be impeached and convicted.

August 9 President Nixon formally resigns and leaves for California. Vice-President Gerald Ford is sworn in as President.

August 21 President Ford nominates Nelson Rockefeller, the wealthy governor of New York and a three-time candidate for the Republican presidential nomination, as his choice for Vice-President.

September 8 President Ford grants Richard Nixon a "full, free and absolute pardon . . . for all offenses against the United States which he . . . has committed or may have committed or taken part in while President."

1975

January 1 Four of the former White House staffers charged with obstruction are found guilty. They are H. R. Haldeman, John Ehrlichman, John Mitchell, and Robert Mardian. A fifth, Kenneth Parkinson, is acquitted. The Watergate charges against Charles Colson are dropped after he pleads guilty to crimes connected with the Ellsberg-psychiatrist break-in. A seventh defendant, Gordon Strachan, is tried separately.

1976

In the presidential election this year, Jimmy Carter narrowly defeats President Ford. Besides the economic problems facing the country, Carter's victory is widely attributed to the post-Watergate atmosphere of cynicism and a very specific rejection of Ford for his pardon of Nixon.

The final accounting of the Watergate affair produced an impressive list of "high crimes and misdemeanors," as the Constitution labels impeachable offenses. Some of them seem laughably innocuous in retrospect. But others were offenses against the law, against individual citizens, and against the Constitution itself. The Watergate "rap sheet" breaks down into five general categories, as follows:

1. Breaking and Entering/Assault

In the wake of the publication of the Pentagon Papers, Daniel Ellsberg became the prime target of the "plumbers." One of the group's first missions was to break into the office of Ellsberg's psychiatrist and steal Ellsberg's confidential medical records. Although they got in, they were unable to find any incriminating or embarrassing material about Ellsberg.

Some of the same team members later planned the break-in at the Democratic National Committee offices to install listening devices. This job was ordered by White House officials and with the knowledge of some of the President's closest advisers.

One of the Watergate burglars was given orders to "physically harm" Ellsberg when he spoke at a Washington peace rally. This order was not carried out.

2. Illegal Contributions

A secret "slush fund," controlled by Attorney General John Mitchell, was set up to finance a campaign of "dirty tricks" against key Democratic party figures. Some of this money was used to pay the Watergate burglars for the job and later to keep them silent.

The "slush fund" was built out of illegal campaign contributions solicited by Nixon officials from some of the country's largest corporations, who thought they were buying "access" to the President. Other contributions were made to derail criminal investigations or antitrust activities going on in the Justice Department.

Commerce Secretary Maurice Stans took a secret payment of $250,000 from fugitive financier Robert Vesco to kill a Securities and Exchange Commission investigation of Vesco's criminal activities.

3. "Dirty Tricks"

Like the "plumbers," the "Dirty Tricks" team was set up in the White House for the purpose of damaging and embarrassing key Democrats. In fact, the Democrats didn't need any help—they were doing just fine by themselves. The activities ranged from ordering pizzas delivered to Democratic campaign offices to forging letters that were used to discredit and embarrass Democratic leaders like Senators Edmund Muskie and Henry Jackson.

Using material he culled from the Pentagon Papers, E. Howard Hunt forged cables that implied that President John Kennedy ordered the toppling and assassination of Vietnam's Prime Minister Diem in 1963. Hunt then tried unsuccessfully to plant these cables with major news magazines.

An "enemies list" was created, an extensive collection of opposition politicians, entertainers, newsmen, and other prominent public figures deemed disloyal by the White House. The list was used to target the people that the White House wanted to "screw" through the use of selected federal agencies. The list included Jane Fonda, Bill Cosby, and CBS newsman Daniel Schorr.

4. Cover-up/Obstruction of Justice

White House officials, from the President down to lower-echelon staffers, ordered the payment of hush money from the campaign "slush fund" to the Watergate conspirators. These men also orchestrated the cover-up of White House involvement in the conspiracy.

President Nixon secretly pledged clemency to the Watergate burglars in return for their silence.

L. Patrick Gray, acting head of the FBI and in line for appointment to the permanent job of director, turned over FBI files on Watergate to White House staffers.

Nixon ordered ranking CIA officers to dissuade the FBI from investigating Watergate.

Incriminating evidence in E. Howard Hunt's White House safe was removed and destroyed.

Two of the White House tapes subpoenaed by the special prosecutor were discovered to be missing. Another tape contained a crucial eighteen-minute gap, the result of a deliberate erasure.

5. Miscellaneous Offenses and Revelations

Nixon had used more than $10 million in government funds for improvements on his private homes in Florida and California, ostensibly in the name of "security."

Nixon had taken illegal tax deductions on some papers donated to a presidential library.

The illegal secret war against Cambodia was revealed.

What was the real payback for these abuses? President Nixon resigned in disgrace. But he was quickly pardoned, guaranteeing that his pension checks would keep coming. Within a short time,

Nixon was "rehabilitated" by his party and the press, gradually easing his way back into a new role as "elder statesman" and foreign-policy expert. Nixon died in 1994.

Liddy and Hunt both went to prison. Liddy probably used the time to work on his book *Will,* which turned into a television miniseries. Hunt continued to write spy novels. John Mitchell was jailed and disbarred. His book was rejected by its publisher. Mitchell died in 1988.

Haldeman and Ehrlichman, the two aides closest to Nixon, also served brief jail terms. Both wrote successful books. John Dean served four months, but wrote *Blind Ambition,* his memoir of the Watergate affair, a best-seller also turned into a television miniseries.

Many of the other minor characters in Watergate served brief prison terms. A spate of legislation addressing the issues of ethics in government, campaign financing, and presidential powers, all followed in Watergate's wake. The ensuing years brought more investigations that further revealed the extent of the abuses committed by the FBI and the CIA in the name of national security. More laws were passed.

Watergate and those revelations cost the Republicans the White House in 1976, when Gerald Ford, the man who pardoned Nixon, was defeated by Jimmy Carter, who ran as an "outsider" pledged to rid Washington of its corruption. It was assumed that such abuses were now in check and that nobody in the White House could manage such an illegal undertaking again.

Then along came Ronald Reagan's CIA Director, William Casey, and his fire-breathing protégé, Lieutenant Colonel Oliver North. (See pages 413–418.)

How did the Arabs of OPEC cripple America during the 1970s?

The international hot spots during the fifties and sixties were Cold War battles waged in Eastern Europe, Africa, and Asia. But in the late sixties and early seventies, the scene shifted. The Middle East emerged as the world's most significant flashpoint, a political and military battlefield in which superpower rivalries took a backseat to an enmity as old as the Bible. As Arabs and Jews struggled over the existence of Israel and the future of the Palestinian Arabs, the United States got caught "between a rock and a hard place."

Almost from the moment Israel battled the British in a terrorist war of independence in 1948, Israel occupied a singular, untouchable position in American foreign policy. This unique status was based on a tight web of philosophical, religious, social, political, and strategic conditions. After the horrors of the Holocaust, Americans endorsed a homeland for the Jews. Culturally, Americans felt a kinship with Israelis and viewed the remarkable agricultural, industrial, and economic island they had created in the desert with admiration. The Israeli determination to build a nation seemed to mirror the pioneer spirit Americans romantically viewed as their own. The Israelis—many of them transplanted Europeans, along with American Jews—sounded, looked, and acted like Americans.

The Arabs, on the other hand, rode camels, wore funny robes, and carried around mats for praying at odd hours of the day. The typical American view of Arabs as rather backward was seemingly confirmed in a series of brief wars in which Israel easily defeated larger combined Arab armies, expanding its territories with each conquest. While the idea of Israel was widely accepted, the displacement of Palestinians was disregarded.

On the simplistic American scale of good versus bad, Israel was democratic and pro-western. Over the years, a pro-Israeli political lobby, organized for maximum voting impact, kept Israel well armed and well supported. Strategically, Israel was a reliable client-state in the midst of unstable Arab lands. For years, while these Arab states had remained in the control of western oil companies, the American position was comfortable.

But as time passed, that position was transformed from one of unequivocal alliance with Israel to a more slippery footing, greased by oil diplomacy. Beginning in the 1960s, the Arabs increasingly took control of their valuable resource, and the balance of power began to shift. The seesaw tilting toward the Israelis got its most violent bounce after the October 1973 Yom Kippur War. Again the Israeli army prevailed, but its cloak of invincibility had been torn. While Israel beat back the combined offensive of several Arab states, Egyptian armies crossed the Suez and retook territory in the Sinai held by Israel since the Six-Day War of 1967.

But that was only a small part of the shifting sands of Middle East power politics. In an effort to compel the Israelis to return the lands captured in 1967, the Arab nations cut off oil shipments to the United States, Japan, and Western Europe in a boycott that precipitated the first great "energy crisis" of the 1970s. This boycott was made possible by the enormous reserves of petroleum controlled by the Middle Eastern countries, especially the Saudis, who were members of a group called OPEC (the Organization of Petroleum Exporting Countries). Formed in 1960 by the world's principal oil exporters, including Saudi Arabia, Kuwait, Iran, Iraq, and Venezuela, OPEC lacked economic clout until the 1973 Arab boycott demonstrated their power in a world guzzling oil and dependent on other petroleum-related products. (Besides the obvious gasoline and home heating oil, hundreds of other products, such as plastics, fertilizers, paint, and ink, are petroleum-based.)

In the United States, the boycott caused mayhem. A series of energy-saving measures were instituted, from Sunday closings of gas stations to a rationing system based on license plate numbers (plates having even numbers could buy gas one day; odd-numbered plates could buy it the next). Speed limits were lowered; environmental standards were relaxed; a new generation of gasoline mileage targets was set for automakers. American car companies, which had ignored the market for inexpensive, fuel-efficient cars pioneered by the Europeans and Japanese, soon found their once-imperturbable empire crumbling around their expensive, gas-guzzling showboats. Overnight, a generation unaccustomed to the kind of sacrifices made during the Depression and World War II reacted angrily to the idea that a bunch of Arabs could shackle that great American freedom—owning and driving a car. As gas lines lengthened, frustration boiled over into fistfights and even gas-pump homicides. A bit of the American fabric was unraveling.

After the Arab boycott was lifted in March 1974, the future

was altered. Having tasted power through the boycott, the OPEC members realized the control they actually possessed. Pre-boycott oil prices of about three dollars per barrel rose to nearly twelve dollars in 1974. The end of the boycott did not bring a return to the old pricing system. Oil prices stayed high, controlled by Arabs who could make the oil flow in a gush or just a trickle. The non-Arab OPEC members, such as Venezuela and Nigeria, were quite content to allow the prices to go as high as the Arabs wanted. American oil companies eagerly seized on the perception and reality of higher costs to force their prices up as well, bringing new profits to the oil companies at the expense of the American economy.

The following years of oil shortages and altered economic realities produced by the OPEC domination created the highest rates of unemployment since the Depression and historically high inflation—a combination of low growth and rising prices termed "stagflation"—striking a severe blow to American prestige and confidence. Once built on a bedrock of cheap labor and cheap oil, the American economy no longer enjoyed either.

An inflationary cycle of double-digit dimensions had been set in motion, and it would take Americans through a dizzying decade that seemed beyond the control of the country's leadership. The crisis, begun in Nixon's final days, became Gerald Ford's problem. His inability to "WIN"—"Whip Inflation Now" was his administration's inept, empty economic rallying cry—played a large part, along with post-Watergate disillusionment, in the 1976 election of former Georgia governor Jimmy Carter, the first southern President since Woodrow Wilson.

While America agonizingly transformed itself into a more efficient energy user and adjusted to new economic realities, it also began the search for alternative sources of energy. Congress, under Carter, funded development of wind, solar, and synthetic fuels. The American nuclear industry got a new boost as well. But there were still shocks to come. In 1978, Muhammad Reza Shah Pahlevi (1919–1980), the Shah of Iran, a military dictator established in 1954 through a CIA-backed coup, was overthrown by a fundamentalist Islamic revolution led by Ayatollah Ruhollah Khomeni (1900–1989). Iran cut off oil exports, setting off an other mild oil shortage. A year later, America's energy future was darkened when there was a major accident in the core of a nuclear reactor at Three Mile Island in Pennsylvania, which severely curtailed the planned development of nuclear power in this country. To make matters worse, that year OPEC announced another drastic price increase.

But it was the situation in Iran that would move to the foreground of American life, overshadowing Carter's historical achievement in negotiating a peace treaty between Egypt and Israel in 1978. On November 4, 1979, five hundred Iranians stormed the American embassy in Tehran, capturing ninety American diplomats and beginning a hostage crisis that effectively ended Jimmy Carter's hopes for governing effectively and being reelected. Carter's inability to free the hostages, including a disastrous, abortive rescue mission that ended with eight Americans dead in the Iranian desert, seemed to symbolize American powerlessness.

In 1980, America turned to a man it thought represented old-style American ideals and strength. Ronald Reagan (b. 1911), former movie star and governor of California, soundly defeated Carter in 1980 by promising to restore American prestige, power, and economic health. At the moment of Reagan's inauguration, as a last insult to Jimmy Carter and an omen of the good fortune Reagan would enjoy, the hostages were freed by Iran.

American Voices

From Jimmy Carter's "crisis of confidence" speech (July 15, 1979):

> All the legislation in the world can't fix what's wrong with America. So I want to speak with you first tonight about a subject even more serious than energy or inflation. I want to talk to you right now about a fundamental threat to American democracy. . . .
>
> The threat is nearly invisible in ordinary ways. It is a crisis of confidence. It is a crisis that strikes at the very heart and soul and spirit of our national will. We can see this crisis in the

growing doubt about the meaning of our own lives and in the loss of a unity of purpose for our nation.

The erosion of our confidence in the future is threatening to destroy the social and the political fabric of America.

What was "voodoo economics"?

If there is one thing America does not want from its Presidents, it's a sermon. America wants pep talks. America wants the coach to tell the country that it only has to fear "fear itself." America likes the trumpet sounding a summons. Americans want to be told they're the best. When America thumbed its nose at Jimmy Carter's "crisis of confidence" speech, he belatedly learned that lesson. But Ronald Reagan knew it instinctively. He also understood a basic American political precept: This country, since the pre-Revolutionary days of James Otis back in Boston (see page 106) doesn't like taxes.

When Ronald Reagan campaigned in 1980, he promised to cut taxes, reduce government deficits, reduce inflation, and rebuild America's defenses. One of his Republican primary opponents said it could only be done "with mirrors." Another Republican called Reagan's ideas "voodoo economics." He was George Bush, later to become Reagan's loyal Vice-President and then President himself. Bush got a laugh with that line in 1980.

But Ronald Reagan got the last laugh when he was resoundingly elected, bringing to power a new conservative coalition pledged to reverse what it saw as the damage done by decades of liberal Democratic control of American economic and social policy. The Reagan coalition featured the "neo-conservatives," political theorists who put a new face on old-line anti-Communism; the so-called Moral Majority, the religious right wing led by Reverend Jerry Falwell, whose solutions to America's problems included returning prayer to public schools, outlawing abortion, and reducing government's role in social policy; conservative southerners, who responded to Reagan's call for a strengthened American defense and lower taxes; and, perhaps most importantly but least visibly, a blue-collar majority who saw their paychecks disappearing in taxes and an endless inflationary spiral.

The theoretical underpinning of Reagan's plans was called "supply-side economics." The basic premise was that if taxes were cut, people would produce more goods and spend more money, creating more jobs and broader prosperity, which would lead to higher government revenues. Coupled with deep cuts in "wasteful" government spending, these revenues would provide a balanced budget. Reagan supporters even pointed to the fact that Democratic hero John Kennedy had had a similar idea in 1963, when he promoted a tax cut by saying, "A rising tide lifts all boats."

There certainly was nothing new about this idea. President Carter had proposed tax cuts, smaller government, and tight credit to keep down inflation. Earlier in American history, another Republican administration had used a similar strategy. Herbert Hoover had tried the same things during the Depression; back then the name for supply-side economics was "trickle-down economics."

With strong popular support and the congressional backing of a bloc of southern Democrats known as "boll weevils," Reagan's economic package sailed through Congress in 1981. But there was certainly no immediate relief, and the American economy was soon in the midst of a full-blown and devastating recession.

Unemployment was high, inflation continued, bankruptcies and business failures skyrocketed, and family farms went on the auction block. Committed to purging inflation from the world economic system, the Federal Reserve Board under Carter and Reagan had adopted a policy of high interest rates to put the brakes on the economy. Without easy credit, houses go unbuilt, cars unsold, and businesses and factories contract or fold.

Oil had been at the root of the inflationary pressure, and it was only the eventual tumble in oil prices that relieved that pressure. Brought on by the international recession, the oil shortage became oil glut. Buffeted by new competition from non-OPEC oil producers like Mexico, Norway, and Great Britain, OPEC's chokehold on the western economies began to loosen. Suddenly awash in their unsold oil, the OPEC members saw their clout crippled as they struggled to maintain artificially high prices through production quotas that were routinely broken by OPEC's members.

The beneficiary of this reversal was none other than Ronald Reagan. The slide in oil prices signaled the beginning of the recovery. With oil prices falling, the heart of the inflationary dragon was cut out, and Ronald Reagan looked like Saint George. Other pro-business Reagan policies, such as deregulating industry and ignoring the antitrust laws, fueled the recovery. Employment started to grow, and inflation, which had been running at 12 percent, dropped to less than 5 percent. The tax cuts passed in 1981, to be phased in over three years, fueled a resurgence in the financial markets and would reap a bonanza for the nation's wealthiest, but the poor and the middle class would feel few of its rewards.

The shift in tax policy was accompanied by a new reality in government spending. A succession of Reagan budgets slashed domestic spending in those areas that most affected the poor—the legacy of LBJ's Great Society. Welfare, housing, job training, drug treatment, and mass transportation all fell under the rubric of wasteful government spending. Yet in spite of these cuts and the passage of the tax changes meant to stimulate government revenues, the federal deficits ballooned. Apart from the reductions made by the tax cuts, the chief culprit in the deficits was the expansion of the defense budget. Although pledged publicly to cutting the budget, Reagan was merely overseeing a massive transfer of funds from the domestic sector to the Pentagon. For years, conservatives had complained that liberal social programs had tried to solve problems by "throwing money at them." Now, under President Reagan, the conservatives were going to solve the "weakness" of America's defenses by doing the same thing.

American Voices

Thomas K. Jones, Reagan administration defense official in an interview with *Los Angeles Times* reporter Robert Scheer:

> Dig a hole, cover it with a couple of doors and then throw three feet of dirt on top. It's the dirt that does it. . . . Every-

body's going to make it if there are enough shovels to go around.

According to Robert Scheer's 1982 book, *With Enough Shovels*, T. K. Jones was the man responsible for administering a multi-million-dollar civil defense program, the centerpiece of which seemed to be making sure that America had plenty of doors, dirt, and shovels. This was his plan for saving American lives and putting the country back on its feet within a few years of an all-out nuclear war with the Soviet Union.

Why was Reagan called the "Teflon President"?

Through his eight years in the White House and in the period since President Reagan left office, many views of the Reagan presidency have depicted a detached, disinterested Executive who asked no questions, ignored details, and allowed subordinates to run amok. Almost every memoir by former administration figures—most notably those by David Stockman and Donald Regan—as well as a number of books about Reagan's administration by journalists, such as Hedrick Smith's *The Power Game,* and *The Acting President* by Bob Schieffer and Gary Paul Gates, present an almost frightening picture of Reagan as ill-informed and disengaged.

Yet, through it all, Ronald Reagan held on to extraordinary public approval ratings, if national polls are to be trusted. Reagan's uncanny ability to keep the controversies and problems of his eight years in office from sticking to himself prompted the gently derisive nickname of "Teflon President."

Part of that "Teflon" image was simply a matter of Reagan's extraordinary good luck. The fact that the American embassy hostages held in Tehran were freed at the moment Reagan took office, and through no effort of his own, seemed to give the Reagan years the first blush of serendipity. This image got another boost when Reagan survived an assassination attempt on March 30, 1981, and the country reveled in press reports of how he joked with the emergency-room staff. It was only after George Bush's election that Reagan's onetime White House physician stated that the Twenty-fifth Amendment should have been invoked to transfer presidential powers temporarily to Vice-President Bush while Reagan was under general anesthesia and recovering from emergency surgery.

But he emerged from the shooting unbowed, sitting taller in the saddle than ever in the American estimation. The surge in his approval polls after the shooting helped him ramrod through Congress the tax cuts and Pentagon spending plans he called for. After a generation of failed and disgraced Presidents, Washington observers were marveling at Reagan's considerable power. This gloss of invincibility and his personal affability carried Reagan through scandals at the highest levels of his administration, all of which he was able to shrug off with a chuckle, a wave, and a bemused shrug. Even the public embarrassment of his wife feeding him lines to shout to reporters didn't dent the armor. The revelations of gross corruption by a large number of administration officials—the so-called sleaze factor that bubbled beneath the surface for his eight years—continued after Reagan's departure. In the summer of 1989, a new scandal broke through in revelations of abuses in the Department of Housing and Urban Development (HUD), led by a Cabinet secretary, Samuel Pierce, whom Reagan once failed to recognize at a Rose Garden party.

Even major policy disasters rolled off his back. When a terrorist bombing of a U.S. Marine barracks in Beirut killed 239 marines assigned to an indefensible position with no real justification for their presence other than to assert American interests in the area, Reagan assumed "responsibility" without any damage to his image and popularity. An American air raid on the home of Libyan strongman Muammar Khadaffy left only two American pilots and some civilians dead, including one of the Libyan leader's children. Yet Reagan's popularity soared after what amounted to an attempted assassination.

But Reagan's armor got its most severe test with the series of events that came to be called "Iran-Contra." Although the full story of these events may never be learned, President Reagan personally escaped that controversy unscathed, even if it did serve to cripple his administration's final days.

The "facts" in Iran-Contra are still shrouded in some mystery, obfuscated by denials and silence from some of the key participants, including Director of Central Intelligence William Casey, who died before the extent of his involvement was fully known to the press and the public. The situation went back to a problem that had bedeviled Jimmy Carter right up to Ronald Reagan's inauguration—American hostages held in the Middle East. Unlike the Carter hostage dilemma, in which American diplomatic personnel were held by a surrogate arm of the Iranian government and whose whereabouts were known, the hostage situation facing Reagan involved a number of separate hostages held in the chaotic anarchy of Lebanon by mysterious parties, assumed to be linked to Iranian leadership. In addition, one of these hostages, William Buckley, was the CIA head of station in Beirut, a fact likely known to his kidnappers. Reagan was personally tormented by the plight of the hostages and their families, but publicly stuck to his guns that there would be no yielding to terrorist demands. Such a trade-off, it was stated, would only encourage further hostage-taking.

In the summer of 1985, Reagan's National Security Adviser, Robert McFarlane, was approached by a group of Israelis with a plan for winning release of the hostages. That plan involved a rather dubious Iranian arms merchant who proposed that Tehran would use its influence to free the hostages in return for a few hundred U.S. antitank missiles, which Iran needed to carry on its long war of attrition with neighboring Iraq. To McFarlane, the deal presented not only an opportunity to free the hostages but to establish contacts with so-called moderates within the Iranian government. After returning from surgery to remove a malignancy, President Reagan met with key staffers to discuss the arms-for-hostages deal. Secretary of State George Shultz and Defense Secretary Casper Weinberger both voiced strong opposition. (The two later said George Bush was present; Bush claimed he was not present at any meeting at which Shultz and Weinberger objected to the deal.) No decision was voiced at the meeting, and Shultz and Weinberger left thinking the idea was dead.

But in McFarlane's account, Reagan called him with a go-ahead. Reagan would say he had no recollection of such a call. No formal record of this major decision was ever made. The first shipment of arms went through, and one hostage was released. The Iranian arms dealer withheld the news that CIA man Buckley, the man McFarlane wanted out most, was already dead, tortured before being executed. A second arms shipment, now being handled by one of McFarlane's Security Council deputies, marine lieutenant colonel Oliver North, went awry and no hostages were released.

While "Let's Make a Deal" went on with Iran, the Reagan administration was in the thick of another foreign-policy struggle—the ongoing support of a rebel army known as the Contras, committed to overthrowing the Marxist Sandinista regime in Nicaragua. The Democratic-controlled Congress had taken the upper hand in its power struggle with the White House over Contra aid by passing an amendment that cut off all U.S. funds for the rebel army. But inside the White House, plans were hatched to make an end run around Congress by soliciting foreign money for the Contras, and that was done, first from the Saudis. With money in the till, the problem became one of its disbursement. Even though Reagan was advised that sending such funds might be considered an impeachable offense, the plan went ahead, and that job was turned over to the same man who was in charge of the Iranian situation—Oliver North.

The man Reagan was later to call "a national hero" even as he fired him was seen by some White House staff as a power-grabbing zealot, delusional and willing to lie about his contacts and closeness with the President to advance his cause. A battle veteran of Vietnam and a fire-breathing anti-Communist, North had been involved in planning the military strike on the Caribbean island of Grenada to overthrow a Marxist government there on the pretext of rescuing American medical students.

To help him run his secret war in Nicaragua, North recruited a number of characters with past connections to the CIA and the American military, chief among them former air force general Richard Secord. At about this time, someone—nobody wants to take credit—came up with the idea of using profits being made from the sale of arms to Iran to fund the Contras. Hence the title "Iran-Contra." CIA chief Casey was an enthusiastic supporter of the idea and became North's chief White House patron, soon expanding the idea into what was called a permanent "off-the-shelf" covert enterprise that would circumvent congressional oversight of CIA secret operations.

One of the many ironies in this muddle was that the story was broken by an obscure Middle Eastern magazine, which revealed that McFarlane and North had been to Tehran, where McFarlane had tried to deliver a Bible and a birthday cake to the Ayatollah Khomeini as a goodwill gesture. Within days of this revelation, the strings began to unravel in the White House, and a seemingly befuddled Ronald Reagan issued a stream of conflicting statements and press conferences that were contradicted as soon as he made them.

The immediate outcome of the story was the formation of a presidential commission composed of Senator John Tower, a conservative Republican (later to be rejected by the Senate as George Bush's Defense Secretary, owing to reports of his drinking and womanizing); former Senator Edmund Muskie, Jimmy Carter's Secretary of State; and retired General Brent Scowcroft, a former subordinate of Henry Kissinger. The "Tower Commission" released its report early in 1987, and it was a scathing rebuke of Reagan.

In an introduction to one published version of the report, *New York Times* Washington correspondent R. W. Apple, Jr., wrote of the findings:

> The board painted a picture of Ronald Reagan very different from what the world had become accustomed to in the last six years. No trace here of the lopsided smile, the easy wave, the confident mien that carried him through every past crisis; this portrait is of a man confused, distracted, so remote that he failed utterly to control the implementation of his vision of an initiative that would free American hostages and reestablish American influence in Iran, with all of its present and future strategic importance. At times, in fact, the report makes the President sound like the inhabitant of a never-never land of imaginary policies.

The Tower Commission was followed by a congressional investigation in which all of the deceptions. lies to Congress and the public, and illegality attached to large amounts of money passing through various sticky fingers began to be revealed. Although never taken as seriously by the public as was Watergate, the abuses of Iran-Contra were frightening: a President seemingly out of touch with reality and allowing very junior officers to control major foreign-policy adventures without any oversight; a plan to set up a secret CIA to circumvent the Congress; an attempt to ignore a law by using a technicality, a maneuver that even the President's closest advisers said might be an impeachable offense.

In the aftermath of Iran-Contra, only Oliver North has come to trial to date. Under the rubric of "national security," substantial amounts of evidence were withheld in the case. Oliver North was eventually convicted on a number of the Iran-Contra-related charges brought against him. He avoided conviction, however, on some of the most serious of these. In July 1989, with the judge in the case calling him a "fall guy," North was sentenced to a suspended sentence, community service in a drug program, and a fine that he would presumably pay out of his substantial speaking engagement fees.

Iran-Contra was a potentially dangerous escapade that might have seemed like the work of some novelist forming a scenario for a takeover of the inner workings of American government. Only Oliver North wasn't fiction. It is exactly his brand of zealotry that created the need for the system of checks and balances that exists at every level of the system.

History's long-range judgment of the Reagan years will obviously have to wait. Will ten or twenty years of wear and tear dull the "Teflon" finish? Given the American public's tendency to lionize and romanticize its characters from the past, it seems unlikely.

American Voices

George Bush, accepting the 1988 Republic Presidential nomination:

> The Congress will push me to raise taxes, and I'll say no, and they'll push, and I'll say no, and they'll push again. And all I can say to them is Read My Lips: No New Taxes.

The first Vice-President to be elected President since Martin Van Buren in 1836, George Bush (b. 1924) looked like a sure two-termer. In his first two years as President, Bush had witnessed the stunning unraveling of Communism in Europe. Reversing the old Domino Theory, the Berlin Wall crumbled, East and West Germany united, captive nations embraced democracy and, astonishingly, the Soviet Union disintegrated. Soviet leader Mikhail Gorbachev (b. 1931) attempted to restructure the Soviet economy *("perestroika")* and loosen political restraints *("glasnost")*, but he had let the genie out of the bottle. The Cold War was over.

But Bush's high point came after Iraq's 1990 invasion of oil-rich Kuwait. Mobilizing the United Nations against Saddam Hussein, Bush ordered Operation "Desert Storm," a devastating air war led by American forces, followed by a one-hundred-hour ground offensive. With the victory over Iraq, Bush's ratings soared like a Patriot missile. Before the Gulf War, Bush had already notched one win after U.S. troops swept into Panama and captured dictator Manuel Noriega, who had been indicted in a U.S. court on drug charges. Coupled with the victory in Kuwait, American prestige seemed unmatched in Bush's "New World Order."

But every missile that goes up must come down. The glow of the Reagan–Bush foreign policy coups vanished, dulled by a dizzying slide from post-war euphoria. Unemployment surged as high interest rates mired the economy in recession. Bush was viewed as out-of-touch with average Americans, and publicity stunts such as shopping for socks only made him seem more disconnected.

Americans were cranky and George Bush wasn't the only target. Congress faced intense scrutiny as a series of scandals rocked the House. Speaker Jim Wright and Democratic Whip

Tony Coelho resigned under ethics clouds, and a check-writing scam enraged the public. Congress fiddled while America burned. Mounting budget deficits, a savings and loan debacle costing $400 billion, and deep anxiety over health care magnified these problems. The grim national mood darkened with the bitter debate over legal abortion, which President Bush opposed in a reversal of an earlier position. "Gender Gap" tensions rose with law professor Anita Hill's sexual harassment charges against Clarence Thomas, Bush's choice to succeed civil rights legend Thurgood Marshall (1908–1993) on the Supreme Court.

But the gravest sin was George Bush's broken promise. When Bush agreed to new taxes to reduce the deficit, Desert Storm was worth so much Desert Sand. Since colonial days, Americans have hated taxes and reserved a special hell for politicians who raise them. With the recession millstone around his neck, George Bush plunged in the polls as the 1992 election approached.

Can a man called "Bubba" become President?

It probably won't go down alongside other great presidential pronouncements. Nothing like, "Ask not what your country can do for you; ask what you can do for your country." But it was memorable when candidate Bill Clinton told America, "I tried it once, but I didn't inhale."

When Clinton was asked by reporters about smoking marijuana, his reply left many Americans choking with laughter. A Rhodes scholar who attended Oxford, where he avoided the Vietnam draft, Arkansas Governor Bill Clinton (b. 1946) dodged many uncomfortable questions during the 1992 campaign. But Americans were less interested in pot-smoking, draft-dodging, and womanizing than in solving America's problems. Running as an "agent of change" who promised reforms, "Bubba" Clinton became the first "Baby Boomer" President following a raucous election most notable for the candidacy of H. Ross Perot.

A Texas billionaire, Perot (b. 1930) had built his Electronic Data Systems into a billion-dollar firm with large government contracts. With his deep pockets, the amply financed Perot ran as an independent with a campaign aimed at overhauling government. His folksy style and "can-do" approach appealed to millions, but when he abruptly canceled his unorthodox campaign, Perot was dismissed as a wealthy kook. Then he stunned the political world by rejoining the fray only weeks before Election Day. In a series of three-way televised debates, the most indelible image was of George Bush checking his wristwatch as if the limo were double-parked with the engine running. Garnering nearly 20 million votes (19%), Perot drew disaffected voters from Bush and probably tipped the race, allowing Clinton to win with 43% to Bush's 37%.

American Voices

Former Senator Barry Goldwater (b. 1909), a leading conservative, on homosexuals in the American military:

> You don't need to be "straight" to fight and die for your country. You just need to shoot straight.

It may be called a "honeymoon," but Bill Clinton must have been wondering when the fun would start. Before he unzipped his suitcases, Clinton's "honeymoon" was over. Having pledged to overturn the ban on homosexuals in the military, Clinton found himself walking into a Pentagon Chainsaw Massacre. Accepting a compromise "Don't ask; Don't tell" policy, Clinton retreated from his promise, hinting at the policy and personnel reversals that would plague his first two years. Two potential choices for Attorney General were shot down in what was called "Nanny-gate," the use of illegal aliens as childcare workers and nonpayment of taxes on those workers. A Justice Department nominee was attacked as a "quota queen," and Clinton withdrew her name. A standoff with a cult in Waco, Texas, turned disastrous when an FBI assault led to a deadly fire.

Each of these early setbacks overshadowed the recovering economy and the shrinking deficit. Passage of a trade pact with Mexico and Canada (NAFTA) and a handgun control law—the "Brady Bill"—were also victories. But Clinton's gaffes eclipsed his successes. Some miscues were trivial, such as the criticism over a two-hundred-dollar haircut. Others cut deeper. Clinton was dogged by a woman's suit alleging sexual harassment when Clinton was Governor of Arkansas. And when White House aide Vincent Foster committed suicide, his death was tied into an ongoing investigation of the Clintons' investments and real estate deals known as "Whitewater-gate."

The stumbles culminated in the defeat of Clinton's legislative keystone, the overhaul of the health-care system. Proposing a far-reaching plan that would cover all Americans, Clinton saw his prize project wither, bucked by Congress, the public, and an intense lobbying effort by the health-insurance industry. This sharp rebuttal of Bill Clinton's policy centerpiece was an omen of 1994's historic midterm elections. In a political earthquake, Republicans swept control of both the House and Senate, setting the stage for a struggle between the White House and Congress as America moved toward the final presidential election of the twentieth century.

The great historian Edward Gibbon once called history, "Little more than the register of the crimes, follies, and misfortunes of mankind." Voltaire called it a trick played by the living upon the dead. According to Thomas Carlyle, history is "a distillation of rumor." And Henry Ford said history is "more or less bunk."

This American history is a little bit of these and then some. But one thing history is *not* is boring. History is alive and human—and changing all the time. We need to rewrite it. And we need to learn from it.

America has survived a lot. Revolution. A Civil War. Two World Wars. Depressions and recessions. Presidents and politicians, bad and good. And even a baseball strike. As the country takes uncertain steps toward the next century, remembering America's history becomes all the more important. What's past, after all, *is* prologue.

Appendix 1

Is the Electoral College a Party School? A Presidential Election Primer

Final figures from the presidential election of 1988 showed that 91,602,291 Americans voted. That is 50.16 percent of the eligible American voters. Most Third World countries with no democratic tradition do better than that. With nearly 49 million votes, George Bush won a little more than 53 percent of the vote, but that only equals about 27 percent of the voting population. In other words, about a quarter of the people in America determined who would be President.

For years, people have been troubled by this continuing American trend toward anemic presidential-election turnouts. Many critics of modern American politics point a finger at the numbing banality of presidential campaigns that are all gloss and television image-making but little substance.

Without doubt, there is tremendous apathy in this country when election day rolls around—the sense that it doesn't really matter who gets elected, because nothing changes. This is obviously a dangerous attitude that might produce an unpleasant result somewhere down the line.

Another reason some people don't bother to vote for President is that it is an insufferably long, drawn-out, and confusing process. This brief introduction to presidential politics is meant to take some of the mystery out of the presidential election system.

What is the electoral college?

No aspect of the American system is less understood and more bewildering than the electoral college. Grown men turn weak and stammer when asked who makes up the electoral college. The subject of a once-every-four-years debate over its existence, the institution plods on, an enigma to those average Americans who think the voters decide who will be President.

Like almost every other creation of the American political system, the electoral college was the result of a compromise. When the Founding Fathers sat down to write the Constitution and figure out the rules for electing the President, there was only one certainty: George Washington would be the first President. As Ben Franklin told the delegates, "The first man at the helm will be a good one. Nobody knows what sort may come afterwards."

The obvious answer would have seemed to be direct election by the people. But this was opposed by those among the Founding Fathers who feared that too much democracy was a dangerous thing. To maintain control over the presidential process, they came up with the idea of the electoral college, which gave each state presidential "electors" equal to the number of its senators and representatives in Congress. These "electors," chosen by whatever means the separate states decided, would vote for two men. The candidate with a majority of electoral votes became President and the second-place finisher became Vice-President.

But the real safety valve built into this plan was the agreement that if the electoral vote failed to produce a clear winner, the election would be sent to the House of Representatives, where each state would get a single vote. In an era in which no political parties existed, the common wisdom was that after George Washington, no man could win the votes needed for election and the real decisions would be made by the enlightened men in the Congress.

Within a short time after Washington, two presidential elections failed to produce a victor and were sent to the House of Representatives. In 1800, Thomas Jefferson and Aaron Burr, from the same party, received seventy-three electoral votes each. The election went to the House, which put Jefferson in the White House. After this election, the voting for President and Vice-President was separated under the Twelfth Amendment. Then in 1824, Andrew Jackson led in the popular vote but failed to win a majority of electoral votes. In this case, the House of Representatives bypassed Jackson in favor of John Quincy Adams.

People often ask if a candidate can win the popular vote and lose the election. It has already happened twice in American political history. In 1876, Samuel Tilden beat Rutherford B. Hayes in the popular vote. But in some scandalous post-election politicking, Hayes collected enough tainted electoral votes to steal the victory. Then again in 1888, Grover Cleveland won the popular vote but lost to Benjamin Harrison in the electoral college.

In 1988 the electoral college was equal to the 435 members of the House and 100 members of the Senate, plus three electoral votes for the District of Columbia. And who are the mysterious electors? These people, who cannot be members of Congress, are mostly loyalists, or party hacks, appointed by their state political parties to fulfill the largely ceremonial task of casting the electoral votes that were decided on election day. However, there is no law stating that these electors *must* vote for their party's popularly elected candidate. That antique loophole mostly leads to symbolic protest votes, such as the elector from West Virginia who, in 1988, voted for Lloyd Bentsen for President instead of Michael Dukakis. Tradition and party loyalty have dictated that the electoral college has upheld the people's choice on election day.

It is difficult to justify the existence of the electoral college, but it lives on chiefly because most people believe in that old adage, "If it ain't broke, don't fix it." The electoral-college system has affirmed the popular vote for more than one hundred years. But it serves another purpose that is either good or bad, depending on your point of view: the electoral college makes it almost impossible for a third-party candidate to mount a serious challenge to the major party candidates, providing a built-in constitutional shield for the two major parties. Third-party candidates are then left to either make only symbolic campaigns or, in some cases, affect the outcome by drawing off support from either of the two main-party candidates.

An attempt to amend the Constitution so as to abolish the electoral college and replace it with simple direct election of the President was killed in the Senate in 1979. But the issue raises its head every four years, when people look around and wonder why

America needs this antiquated contraption that was only created in the first place to deprive the electorate of its power.

What is a caucus?

Presumed to be derived from the Algonquain word *caucauasu* ("one who advises"), the earliest political caucuses were meetings of party leaders to choose candidates and discuss other party business. These caucuses were the first "smoke-filled rooms" in which powerful party bosses determined who the presidential candidates would be.

In modern political parlance, the word *caucus* is inseparably linked with Iowa, scene of the first state caucus of the presidential campaign season. In the Iowa caucuses, party members in small towns meet to stand up and declare for a candidate. The process is not binding and doesn't select any actual delegates to the national nominating convention, but it has become an early test of a candidate's strength, and leads to major media visibility. Ever since an obscure Georgia governor named Jimmy Carter won the Iowa caucuses in 1976 and went from "Jimmy who?" to front-runner, the significance of this small group of Iowans has been inflated all out of proportion to its real weight. In the 1988 race, the significance of Iowa dropped a few notches when Representative Richard Gephardt won the Democratic Iowa caucus and then proceeded to disappear from the presidential radar screen. Iowa is really only as significant today as the media makes it.

What is a primary?

Unlike a caucus, which is a public meeting, a primary election is essentially a statewide secret nominating ballot in which candidates vie for a share of their party's delegates to the national convention from that state. The first direct primary was held in Minnesota in 1900, and was soon widely adopted by other states.

The traditional first primary state is New Hampshire, which has made the state a significant testing ground for candidates. Perhaps the most famous New Hampshire primary in recent history occurred in 1968, when Senator Eugene McCarthy lost to President Lyndon B. Johnson, but ran so close a contest that it helped bring about Johnson's decision not to run and brought Senator Robert Kennedy into the race.

But, as with the caucus in Iowa, New Hampshire's significance is entirely out of proportion to its population and the number of delegates it actually produces for the winning candidate.

In a series of recent party reforms by both Democrats and Republicans, primary elections have gathered far more weight than they once had in determining candidates. Unlike the old days, when nominees were selected by party insiders who controlled large blocs of delegates, primaries now provide the majority of delegates, allowing a candidate to lock up the nomination well in advance of the nominating convention.

What is a "delegate count"?

All the caucuses and primaries are aimed at one goal: to accumulate enough delegates to the nominating convention to win the party's bid to run for President. Before the reforms of the late 1960s and 1970s, most of these delegates were merely political hirelings controlled by party regulars, kingmakers who had the most say in picking a candidate. In recent years the shift to direct selection of delegates to the nominating convention through presidential-preference primaries has diluted the strength of power brokers and put far more power into the hands of the electorate.

The delegate count is simply the tally of delegates to the nominating convention committed to a candidate. The candidate with the majority of votes wins the nomination. In past years, few candidates were assured of the party bid before the nominating convention. The drama, suspense, and backroom dealing that accompanied dozens of roll-call votes at the conventions has been replaced by highly choreographed pageants that basically only affirm the candidate who has gathered sufficient delegates to take the nomination during the primary season. Although party rules are flexible and are constantly changing to suit political moods, the ascendancy of the primaries over the old system of political bosses means the days of the deadlocked nominating convention are probably over.

Appendix 2

U.S. Presidents and Their Administrations

Year	President (Party)	Opponent
1. 1789	George Washington V-P: John Adams	—
1792	George Washington V-P: John Adams	—
2. 1796	John Adams (Federalist) V-P: Thomas Jefferson	Thomas Jefferson
3. 1800	Thomas Jefferson (Dem.-Rep.) V-P: Aaron Burr	John Adams/ Aaron Burr

Prior to the evolution of a clear two-party system and separate election of the President and Vice-President, there were often three or four contenders for the presidency, often from the same party. The most famous instance of this came in 1800. Jefferson, who was unofficially his party's candidate for President, and Burr, both Democratic-Republicans, tied with seventy-three electoral votes. The two opposing Federalist candidates, John Adams and Charles C. Pinckney trailed with sixty-five and sixty-four, respectively. The election was decided in the House of Representatives in the so-called Revolution of 1800 (see Chapter 3).

Year	President (Party)	Opponent
3. 1804	Thomas Jefferson (Dem.-Rep.) V-P: George Clinton	Charles Pinckney

4. 1808   James Madison (Dem.-Rep.)   Charles Pinckney
           V-P: George Clinton

   1812   James Madison (Dem.-Rep.)   De Witt Clinton
           V-P: Elbridge Gerry

5. 1816   James Monroe (Dem.-Rep.)   Rufus King
           V-P: Daniel D. Tompkins

   1820   James Monroe (Dem.-Rep.)   John Q. Adams
           V-P: Daniel D. Tompkins

6. 1824   John Quincy Adams (Dem.-   Andrew Jackson
           Rep.)
           V-P: John C. Calhoun

In the 1824 election, there were four legitimate candidates for the presidency: John Quincy Adams, Andrew Jackson, Henry Clay, and William H. Crawford. Jackson won the most popular and electoral votes, but lacked the majority of electoral votes needed. The election was thrown to the House of Representatives, which went for John Quincy Adams when Clay, a powerful House leader, threw his support to the New Englander in the so-called Corrupt Bargain.

Year	*President (Party)*	*Opponent*
7. 1828	Andrew Jackson (Dem.) V-P: John C. Calhoun	John Q. Adams
1832	Andrew Jackson (Dem.) V-P: Martin Van Buren	Henry Clay
8. 1836	Martin Van Buren (Dem.) V-P: Richard M. Johnson	William Harrison
9. 1840	William Henry Harrison (Whig) V-P: John Tyler	Martin Van Buren
10. 1841	John Tyler (Whig)	

On Harrison's death of pneumonia a few months after his inauguration, Tyler became the first Vice-President to succeed to the office due to the death of a sitting President. Tyler kept Harrison's Cabinet, but named no new Vice-President. There was no constitutional provision for replacing a Vice-President until ratification of the Twenty-fifth Amendment in 1967.

Year	President (Party)	Opponent
11. 1844	James K. Polk (Dem.) V-P: George M. Dallas	Henry Clay
12. 1848	Zachary Taylor (Whig) V-P: Millard Fillmore	Lewis Cass
13. 1850	Millard Fillmore (Succeeded Taylor on his death.)	
14. 1852	Franklin Pierce (Dem.) V-P: William R. King	Winfield Scott
15. 1856	James Buchanan (Dem.) V-P: John C. Breckinridge	John C. Fremont
16. 1860	Abraham Lincoln (Rep.) V-P: Hannibal Hamlin	Stephen Douglas
1864	Abraham Lincoln (Rep.) V-P: Andrew Johnson	George McClellan
17. 1865	Andrew Johnson (Succeeded Lincoln follow- ing his assassination.)	
18. 1868	Ulysses S. Grant (Rep.) V-P: Schuyler Colfax	Horatio Seymour
1872	Ulysses S. Grant (Rep.) V-P: Henry Wilson	Horace Greeley
19. 1876	Rutherford B. Hayes (Rep.) V-P: William A. Wheeler	Samuel J. Tilden

Tilden won a small majority in the popular vote and the electoral college, but was one short of the required number of electoral votes. Twenty electoral votes were in dispute. To win, Tilden needed just one of these; Hayes needed all twenty. The chairman of the Republican Party claimed Hayes had won all twenty votes, and the dispute lasted until March 1877. The vote was accompanied by widespread fraud, especially in the South.

Congress was left to decide the issue, and an electoral commission
was established to settle the question. Splitting on straight partisan
lines, the commission gave the election to Hayes, who had promised the South that he would bring an end to Reconstruction and
withdraw federal troops from their states.

Year	President (Party)	Opponent
20. 1880	James A. Garfield (Rep.) V-P: Chester A. Arthur	Winfield Hancock
21. 1881	Chester A. Arthur (Succeeded Garfield follow- ing his assassination.)	
22. 1884	Grover Cleveland (Dem.) V-P: Thomas A. Hendricks	James G. Blaine
23. 1888	Benjamin Harrison (Rep.) V-P: Levi P. Morton	Grover Cleveland

In the election of 1888, Cleveland won the popular vote with
48.6 percent of the votes cast, but lost the election in the electoral
college, where Harrison won 233–168.

Year	President (Party)	Opponent
24. 1892	Grover Cleveland (Dem.) V-P: Adlai E. Stevenson	Benjamin Har- rison
25. 1896	William McKinley (Rep.) V-P: Garret Hobart	William J. Bryan
1900	William McKinley (Rep.) V-P: Theodore Roosevelt	William J. Bryan
26. 1901	Theodore Roosevelt (Rep.) (Succeeded McKinley following his assassina- tion.)	
1904	Theodore Roosevelt (Rep.) V-P: Charles Warren Fair- banks	Alton B. Parker

27. 1908   William H. Taft (Rep.)   William J. Bryan
            V-P: James S. Sherman

28. 1912   Woodrow Wilson (Dem.)   Theodore
            V-P: Thomas R. Marshall   Roosevelt

    1916   Woodrow Wilson (Dem.)   Charles E. Hughes
            V-P: Thomas R. Marshall

29. 1920   Warren G. Harding (Rep.)   James M. Cox
            V-P: Calvin Coolidge

30. 1923   Calvin Coolidge (Rep.)
            (Succeeded Harding, who
                died of a heart attack.)

    1924   Calvin Coolidge (Rep.)   John W. Davis
            V-P: Charles G. Dawes

31. 1928   Herbert C. Hoover (Rep.)   Alfred E. Smith
            V-P: Charles Curtis

32. 1932   Franklin D. Roosevelt   Herbert Hoover
                (Dem.)
            V-P: John Nance Garner

    1936   Franklin D. Roosevelt   Alfred M. Landon
                (Dem.)
            V-P: John Nance Garner

    1940   Franklin D. Roosevelt   Wendell Willkie
                (Dem.)
            V-P: Henry A. Wallace

    1944   Franklin D. Roosevelt   Thomas E. Dewey
                (Dem.)
            V-P: Harry S. Truman

33. 1945   Harry S. Truman (Dem.)
            (Succeeded Roosevelt at his
                death.)

    1948   Harry S. Truman (Dem.)   Thomas E. Dewey
            V-P: Alben W. Barkley

34. 1952   Dwight D. Eisenhower   Adlai Stevenson
                (Rep.)
            V-P: Richard M. Nixon

1956	Dwight D. Eisenhower (Rep.) V-P: Richard M. Nixon	Adlai Stevenson
35. 1960	John F. Kennedy (Dem.) V-P: Lyndon B. Johnson	Richard M. Nixon
36. 1963	Lyndon B. Johnson (Succeeded Kennedy following his assassination.)	
1964	Lyndon B. Johnson (Dem.) V-P: Hubert H. Humphrey	Barry Goldwater
37. 1968	Richard M. Nixon (Rep.) V-P: Spiro T. Agnew	Hubert Humphrey
1972	Richard M. Nixon (Rep.) V-P: Spiro T. Agnew/ Gerald Ford	George McGovern

Nixon's running mate Agnew, the former governor of Maryland, was accused of tax fraud and having taken bribes while a county executive. He later pleaded no-contest to the tax-evasion charge and resigned as Vice-President. Under the Twenty-fifth Amendment, enacted in 1967 to ensure orderly succession in the event of a President's death or resignation, Nixon appointed Representative Gerald Ford as Vice-President, and he was confirmed by Congress.

Year	*President (Party)*	*Opponent*
38. 1974	Gerald Ford (Rep.)	

Ford succeeded Nixon following his resignation in the wake of the Watergate scandal. Governor Nelson Rockefeller of New York was appointed Vice-President by Ford under the 25th Amendment.

Year	*President (Party)*	*Opponent*
39. 1976	Jimmy Carter (Dem.) V-P: Walter Mondale	Gerald Ford
40. 1980	Ronald Reagan (Rep.) V-P: George Bush	Jimmy Carter
1984	Ronald Reagan (Rep.) V-P: George Bush	Walter Mondale
41. 1988	George Bush (Rep.) V-P: J. Danforth Quayle	Michael Dukakis
42. 1992	William Clinton (Dem.) V-P: Albert Gore, Jr.	George Bush

Selected Readings

The following list includes general books and histories that cover broad themes and large sections of American history. This list of general readings is followed by a listing of books keyed by chapter to the present work.

The individual chapter sections also include selected fiction titles that are appropriate to the period covered. Relying on fiction for history can be a tricky business, but the selected novels offer a vivid picture of life in a particular period, or interesting interpretations of, and insights into, historical events or characters. They are recommended for their literary value and not necessarily for their perfect historical accuracy. Novelists are permitted license the historian is denied, but when read in tandem with accurate histories, these historical novels can be quite revealing.

The great breadth and number of sources used in documenting this history would have made standard footnoting cumbersome. For the sake of readability, I have chosen to attribute any direct citations in the text; all other sources used are included in the following annotated listings.

I have attempted to use only those sources that are either still in print or generally available through public libraries. Asterisks (*) denote paperback editions.

Bennett, Lerone, Jr. *Before the Mayflower: A History of Black America* (5th edition). Chicago: Johnson Publishing, 1982; New York: *Penguin, 1984. A standard work that assesses the impact of blacks in America and the course of black American history.

Boller, Paul F., Jr. *Presidential Campaigns.* London: Oxford University Press, 1984; *Oxford University Press, 1985. A refreshingly humorous look at the history of America's curious process of selecting presidents. Anecdotal and entertaining as well as fascinating history.

Brandon, William. *The American Heritage Book of Indians.* New York: American Heritage, 1963; Boston: *Houghton Mifflin, 1985. A lavishly illustrated history with much fascinating detail about Indian life and history.

Burns, James McGregor. *The American Experiment: The Vineyard of Liberty.* New York: Knopf, 1982; New York: *Vintage, 1983.

―――. *The American Experiment: The Workshop of Democracy.* New York: Knopf, 1985; New York: *Vintage, 1986.

―――. *The American Experiment: The Crosswinds of Freedom.* New York: Knopf, 1989. A political scientist and mainly a middle-of-the-roader in terms of interpretation, Burns is always lucid and entertaining. The above three volumes cover the period from the making of the Constitution through the Reagan years.

Cunliffe, Marcus. *The Presidency.* New York: American Heritage, 1968; Boston: *Houghton Mifflin, 1987. A thematic approach rather than a simple chronology, this is the work of a historian who analyzes the men who shaped the office.

Evans, Sara M. *Born for Liberty: A History of Women in America.* New York: Free Press, 1989.

Fitzgerald, Frances. *America Revised: History Schoolbooks in the Twentieth Century.* Boston: Little, Brown, 1979; New York: *Vintage, 1980. A revealing study of the textbooks that shaped American impressions of our history.

Grun, Bernard. *The Timetables of History: A Horizontal Linkage of People and Events.* New York: Simon and Schuster, 1975; New York: *Touchstone, 1982. A chronology of world history, tracing developments in politics, culture, science, and other fields. Useful for seeing American history in the larger context of world events.

Heffner, Richard D. *A Documentary History of the United States.* New York: *New American Library, 1985. American history through major speeches, writings, court decisions, and other written documents.

Hirsch, E. D., Jr. *Cultural Literacy: What Every American Needs to Know.* Boston: Houghton Mifflin, 1987; New York: *Vintage, 1988. What we don't know and why.

―――, Joseph F. Kett, and James Trefil. *The Dictionary of Cultural Literacy.* Boston: Houghton Mifflin, 1988. What we need to know, in bite-sized portions.

Hofstadter, Richard, and Clarence L. Ver Steeg. *Great Issues in American History: From Settlement to Revolution, 1584–1776.* New York: *Vintage,

1958. This and the succeeding volumes in the series are a presentation of history through major writings, speeches, and court decisions, with interpretive essays.

———. *Great Issues in American History: From the Revolution to the Civil War, 1765–1865*. New York: *Vintage, 1958.

———. *Great Issues in American History: From Reconstruction to the Present Day, 1865–1981*. New York: *Vintage, 1958.

Hoyt, Edwin P. *America's Wars and Military Excursions*. New York: McGraw-Hill, 1987. An encyclopedic but entertaining overview of America's battles, large and small, naughty and nice.

Hymowitz, Carol, and Michaele Weissman. *A History of Women in America*. New York: *Bantam, 1978. A useful overview of women's achievements and their role in American history and society.

Lavender, David. *The American Heritage History of the West*. New York: American Heritage, 1965; Boston: *Houghton Mifflin, 1985.

McEvedy, Colin. *The Penguin Atlas of North American History to 1870*. New York: *Penguin, 1988. Using a progressively changing map of North America, the author traces the course of American history from prehistory to the Civil War.

Morison, Samuel Eliot. *The Oxford History of the American People*. London: Oxford University Press, 1965; New York: *Mentor (3 volumes), 1972. This is history pretty much the way you may have learned it in school, a highly traditional approach that tends to skim over the unsavory moments in American history and celebrates the nobility of American progress.

Ravitch, Diane, and Chester Finn. *What Do Our Seventeen-Year-Olds Know?* New York: Harper & Row, 1987; *Harper & Row, 1988. This is the controversial study, funded by the National Endowment for the Humanities, that created a furor when its findings were released showing an astonishing lack of fundamental knowledge of American history and literature among high school juniors.

Ross, Shelley. *Fall From Grace: Sex, Scandal and Corruption in American Politics from 1702 to the Present*. New York: *Ballantine, 1988. An amusing overview of the seamier side of American political life that proves there is nothing modern about corruption in high places.

Schlesinger, Arthur M., general editor. *The Almanac of American History*. New York: Putnam, 1983; New York: *Perigee, 1983. A "day-by-day" chronology of American history, with several interpretive essays by prominent American historians.

Wade, Wyn Craig. *The Fiery Cross: The Ku Klux Klan in America*. New York: Simon and Schuster, 1987; New York: *Touchstone, 1988.

Traces the development of the Klan from post Civil War days to modern times.

Williams, T. Harry. *The History of American Wars: From 1745 to 1918*. New York: Knopf, 1985; Baton Rouge: *Louisiana State University Press, 1985. Unfinished at the time of the author's death, this book presents a solid historical interpretation of events in America's wars.

Whitney, David C. *The American Presidents*. Garden City, N.Y.: Doubleday, 1985. A very basic reference to the American presidents through Reagan, with biographical sketches and a brief overview of events during each administration.

World Almanac. *The Little Red, White and Blue Book*. New York: *Pharos Books, 1987. A brief chronology of American history dating from Columbus.

Zinn, Howard. *A People's History of the United States*. New York: Harper & Row, 1980; New York: *Perennial, 1980. Looking at American history from the view of the "losers" (Indians, women, blacks, the poor, etc.), this is revisionist history at its best, and serves as a useful and necessary corrective to such traditional views as those of Morison and other standard American historians.

Chapter 1. Brave New World

Bailyn, Bernard. *The Peopling of British North America*. Knopf, 1986; New York: *Vintage, 1987.

———. *Voyagers to the West: A Passage in the Peopling of America on the Eve of the Revolution*. New York: Knopf, 1986; New York: *Vintage, 1988.

Boorstin, Daniel J. *The Americans: The Colonial Experience*. New York: Random House, 1958; New York: *Vintage, 1985.

Granzotto, Gianni. *Christopher Columbus*. Garden City, N.Y.: Doubleday, 1985. By an Italian historian, a comprehensive and realistic portrait of America's European discoverer.

Jennings, Francis. *The Invasion of America: Indians, Colonialism and the Cant of Conquest*. Chapel Hill: University of North Carolina, 1975; New York: *Norton, 1976. As the title implies, this book departs from the traditional view of a European "discovery" of America, calling it instead an "invasion."

Klein, Herbert S. *The Middle Passage: Comparative Studies in the Atlantic Slave Trade*. Princeton: Princeton University Press, 1978. A standard history of the slave trade.

Lauber, Patricia. *Who Discovered America*. New York: Random House,

1970. A young-adult book that provides a very adequate introduction to pre-Columbian history of the Americas.

Magnusson, Magnus, and Hermann Palsson. *The Vinland Sagas: The Norse Discovery of America*. New York: *Penguin, 1965.

Morison, Samuel Eliot. *Christopher Columbus, Mariner*. New York: New American Library, 1985.

————. *The European Discovery of America: The Northern Voyages*. London: Oxford University Press, 1971.

————. *The European Discovery of America: The Southern Voyages*. London: Oxford University Press, 1974. These two volumes have been abridged and combined by Morison in *The Great Explorers*. New York: Oxford University Press, 1978; New York: *Oxford University Press, 1986.

Nash, Gary. *Red, White and Black: The Peopling of Early America*. New York: Prentice-Hall, 1974; *Prentice-Hall, 1982.

Parkman, Francis. *France and England in America* (two volumes). New York: Library of America, 1983. Writing for the general public during the mid-nineteenth century, Parkman was one of America's first great historian-writers.

Quinn, David Beers. *England and the Discovery of America: 1481–1620*. New York: Knopf, 1974.

————. *Set Fair for Roanoke: Voyages and Colonies, 1584–1606*. Chapel Hill: University of North Carolina Press, 1985.

Smith, John. *Captain John Smith's History of Virginia*. New York: Bobbs-Merrill, 1970.

Snell, Tee Loftin. *The Wild Shores: America's Beginnings*. Washington: National Geographic Society, 1974.

Selected Fiction:

In most historical fiction, the emphasis is on fiction rather than on history. However, there are some very good novels that bring the two together and can be read to get an honest sense of time and place, as long as the reader remembers they are works of the imagination.

Jennings, Gary. *Aztec*. New York: Atheneum, 1980; New York: *Avon Books, 1981.

Marlowe, Stephen. *The Memoirs of Christopher Columbus*. New York: Scribner's, 1987; New York: *Ballantine, 1989.

Settle, Mary Lee. *Prisons*. New York: Putnam, 1973.

Chapter 2. Say You Want a Revolution

Alden, John R. *George Washington: A Biography*. Baton Rouge: Louisiana State University Press, 1970; New York: *Dell, 1987. A sound and readable one-volume biography.

Butterfield, L. H., Marc Friedlander, and Mary-Jo Kline, eds. *The Book of Abigail and John: Selected Letters of the Adams Family*. Boston: *Harvard University Press, 1975.

Commager, Henry Steele. *The Empire of Reason: How Europe Imagined and America Realized the Enlightenment*. Doubleday/Anchor, 1977; London: *Oxford University Press, 1982.

Cunliffe, Marcus. *George Washington: Man and Monument*. Boston: Little, Brown, 1958; New York: *New American Library, 1984, (revised edition).

Demos, John P. *Entertaining Satan: Witchcraft and the Culture of Early New England*. London: *Oxford University Press, 1982.

Flexner, James Thomas. *Washington: The Indispensable Man*. Boston: Little, Brown, 1969; New York: *New American Library, 1979. This single volume reduces the material found in Flexner's four-volume study, another standard among Washington biographies.

Franklin, Benjamin. *The Autobiography and Other Writings*. New York: *Signet, 1961.

Freeman, Douglas S. *George Washington: A Biography*. New York: *Scribners, 1985. An abridgment of the seven volumes that constitute Freeman's biography, considered to be the standard history of Washington.

Hofstadter, Richard. *America at 1750: A Social History*. New York: Knopf, 1971.

Kerber, Linda K. *Women of the Republic: Intellect and Ideology in Revolutionary America*. Chapel Hill: University of North Carolina Press, 1980; New York: *Norton, 1986.

Kitman, Marvin. *George Washington's Expense Account*. New York: Simon and Schuster, 1970; New York: *Harper Perennial, 1988. A funny and even revealing book that does a line-by-line examination of the account the commander submitted to Congress after the war.

Langguth, A. J. *Patriots: The Men Who Started the American Revolution*. New York: Simon and Schuster, 1988; *Simon and Schuster, 1989. A vividly readable history of the Revolution and the personalities behind it.

Levin, Phyllis Lee. *Abigail Adams: A Biography*. New York: St. Martin's, 1987; New York: *Ballantine, 1988.

Nash, Gary B. *The Urban Crucible: Northern Seaports and the Origins of the American Revolution.* Boston: *Harvard University Press, 1986.

Norton, Mary Beth. *Liberty's Daughters: The Revolutionary Experience of American Women.* Boston: Little, Brown, 1980. A recent book exploring a vastly overlooked segment of American history, the role of women during the War for Independence.

Paine, Thomas. *Common Sense, The Rights of Man and Other Essential Writings.* New York: *Meridian, 1984.

Peterson, Marshall D., ed. *The Portable Thomas Jefferson.* New York: Viking, 1975; *Viking, 1976.

Quarles, Benjamin. *The Negro in the American Revolution.* Chapel Hill: University of North Carolina Press; New York: *Norton, 1973.

Rossiter, Clinton. *The First American Revolution.* New York: *Harcourt Brace World, 1956. This paperback standard contains part one of Rossiter's book *Seedtime of the Republic.*

————, ed. *The Federalist Papers: Hamilton, Madison and Jay.* New York: *Mentor, 1961.

Tuchman, Barbara W. *The First Salute: A View of the American Revolution.* New York: Knopf, 1988. The two-time Pulitzer Prize–winner examines key points in the American Revolution, focusing on the intervention of France and Holland and the war's decisive campaign culminating in the victory at Yorktown.

Wills, Garry, *Inventing America: Jefferson's Declaration of Independence.* Garden City, N.Y.: Doubleday, 1978; New York: *Vintage, 1979.

Selected Fiction:

Fast, Howard. *April Morning.* New York: Crown, 1961.

————. *Citizen Tom Paine.* New York: World Publishing, 1943.

————. *Conceived in Liberty.* New York: Simon and Schuster, 1939.

Settle, Mary Lee. *Beulah Land.* New York: Farrar, Straus & Giroux, 1956.

Chapter 3. Growth of a Nation

Adams, Henry. *History of the U.S.A. During the Administration of Thomas Jefferson, 1801–1805.* New York: Library of America, 1986.

————. *History of the U.S.A. During the Administration of James Madison, 1809–1817.* New York: Library of America, 1986.

Adler, Mortimer J. *We Hold These Truths: Understanding the Ideas and Ideals of the Constitution.* New York: Macmillan, 1987.

Bergon, Frank, ed. *The Journals of Lewis and Clark.* New York: Viking Penguin, 1989; *Penguin, 1989.

Brodie, Fawn. *Thomas Jefferson: An Intimate History.* New York: Norton, 1974; New York: *Bantam, 1975. The controversial "psychobiography" that first raised the issue of Jefferson's relationship with his slave Sally Hemmings.

Dabney, Virginius. *The Jefferson Scandals: A Rebuttal.* New York: Dodd, Mead, 1981; *Dodd, 1988. A Pulitzer prize–winning writer's investigation into the Sally Hemmings case, which denies the relationship existed.

Daniels, Jonathan. *Ordeal of Ambition: Jefferson, Hamilton and Burr.* Garden City, N.Y.: Doubleday, 1970.

Ehle, John. *Trail of Tears: The Rise and Fall of the Cherokee Nation.* Garden City, N.Y.: Doubleday, 1988; New York: *Anchor, 1989.

Gutman, Herbert G. *The Black Family in Slavery and Freedom.* New York: Random House, 1976; New York: *Vintage, 1977.

Hendrickson, Robert A. *The Rise and Fall of Alexander Hamilton.* Van Nostrand Reinhold, 1981. An abridgment of the author's *Hamilton I* and *Hamilton II*.

Jahoda, Gloria. *The Trail of Tears: The Story of the American Indian Removal, 1813–1855.* New York: Holt, Rinehart and Winston, 1975.

Kitman, Marvin. *The Making of the President, 1789.* New York: Harper & Row, 1989.

Lavender, David. *The Way to the Western Sea: Lewis and Clark Across the Continent.* New York: Harper & Row, 1989. An exciting narrative account of the epic expedition undertaken after the Louisiana Purchase.

Lester, Julius. *To Be a Slave.* New York: Dial, 1968; New York: *Scholastic, 1986. An excellent book aimed at young adults recapturing the life of a slave.

Malone, Dumas. *Jefferson and His Times* (six volumes). Boston: Little, Brown; *Little, Brown, 1948–81. This is the widely accepted, standard biography of Jefferson.

Morris, Richard. *The Forging of the Union: 1781–1789.* New York: Harper & Row, 1987; New York: *Harper Perennial, 1988. A basic recounting of the creation of the Constitution.

———. *Witnesses at the Creation: Hamilton, Madison, Jay and the Constitution.* New York: Holt, Rinehart and Winston, 1985; New York: *Plume, 1989; New York: *Mentor, 1989. Examines the impact of these three men on the writing and ratification of the Constitution.

Padover, Saul K. *Jefferson.* New York: Harcourt Brace & World, 1942;

New York: *Mentor (abridged edition), 1952. A sound one-volume biography.

Rogin, Michael P. *Fathers and Children: Andrew Jackson and the Destruction of the American Indian.* New York: Knopf, 1975.

Rossiter, Clinton, ed. *The Federalist Papers: Hamilton, Madison and Jay.* New York: *Mentor, 1961. A collection of the famous essays, with interpretive notes and introduction.

Selected Fiction:

Guthrie, A. B. *The Big Sky.* Boston: Houghton Mifflin, 1947.

Styron, William. *The Confessions of Nat Turner.* New York: Random House, 1967.

Vidal, Gore. *Burr.* New York: Random House, 1973.

Chapter 4. Apocalypse Then

Catton, Bruce. *The American Heritage Picture History of the Civil War.* New York: American Heritage, 1960; Boston: Houghton Mifflin, 1987.

————. *The Coming Fury.* Garden City, N.Y.: Doubleday, 1961. New York: *Washington Square Press, 1967.

————. *Gettysburg, the Final Fury.* Garden City, N.Y.: Doubleday, 1968; New York: *Washington Square Press, 1969.

————. *Never Call Retreat.* Garden City, N.Y.: Doubleday, 1965; New York: *Washington Square Press, 1967.

————. *A Stillness at Appomattox.* Garden City, N.Y.: Doubleday, 1953; New York: *Washington Square Press, 1958.

————. *Terrible Swift Sword.* Garden City, N.Y.: Doubleday, 1963; New York: *Washington Square Press, 1967.

————. *This Hallowed Ground.* Garden City, N.Y.: Doubleday, 1956; New York: *Washington Square Press, 1969.

Douglass, Frederick. *Narrative of the Life of Frederick Douglass.* New York: *Signet, 1968. Originally written and published in 1845, this auto-biography by a self-taught slave is an American classic, perhaps the most eloquent indictment of slavery ever written.

Eisenhower, John S. D. *So Far From God: The U.S. War With Mexico, 1846–1848.* New York: Random House, 1989. The most recent narrative account of the war with Mexico.

Foner, Eric. *Reconstruction: America's Unfinished Revolution.* New York: Harper & Row, 1988; New York: *Harper Perennial, 1989. A massive book that examines the social, political, and economic aspects of this controversial period.

Foote, Shelby. *The Civil War: A Narrative* (3 volumes). New York: Random House, 1958–74. New York: *Vintage, 1986.

Kaplan, Justin. *Walt Whitman: A Life.* New York: Simon and Schuster, 1980; New York: *Touchstone, 1986.

Litwack, Leon F. *Been in the Storm So Long: The Aftermath of Slavery.* New York: Knopf, 1979; New York: *Vintage, 1980.

McFeely, William S. *Grant: A Biography.* New York: Norton, 1981; *Norton, 1982. A recent single-volume life of the soldier and president.

McPherson, James M. *Battle Cry of Freedom: The Civil War Era.* London: Oxford University Press, 1988; New York: *Ballantine Books, 1989. This recent prize-winning book is an indispensable single-volume history of the war and the events leading up to it.

Mellon, James. *Bullwhip Days: The Slaves Remember.* New York: Weidenfeld & Nicolson, 1988. Compiled during the Depression, this volume brings together reminiscences of life by the last surviving slaves.

Mitchell, Lt. Col. Joseph B. *Decisive Battles of the Civil War.* New York: G. P. Putnam's Sons, 1955; New York: *Fawcett, 1983.

Oates, Stephen B. *Fires of Jubilee: Nat Turner's Fierce Rebellion.* New York: Harper & Row, 1975; New York: *New American Library, 1983.

———. *To Purge This Land With Blood: A Biography of John Brown.* New York: Harper & Row, 1970; Amherst: *University of Massachusetts Press, 1984.

———. *With Malice Toward None: The Life of Abraham Lincoln.* New York: Harper & Row, 1977; New York: *Mentor, 1978. This recent biography of Lincoln is probably the best and most balanced single-volume history of Lincoln's life and times.

Rosengarten, Theodore. *Tombee: Portrait of a Cotton Planter.* New York: Morrow, 1986; New York: *McGraw-Hill, 1988. Using diaries, the author recreates a vivid portrait of southern plantation life in this prize-winning best-seller.

Sears, Stephen W. *The Landscape Turned Red: The Battle of Antietam.* New York: Ticknor & Fields, 1983; New York: *Warner Books, 1985. A compelling account of one of the bloodiest battles in American history.

Stampp, Kenneth M. *The Peculiar Institution: Slavery in the Ante-Bellum South.* New York: Knopf, 1956; New York: *Vintage, 1989.

———, ed. *The Causes of the Civil War.* New York: *Spectrum Books/Prentice-Hall, 1974. A collection of scholarly essays that discuss the full range of social, economic, political and moral causes of the war.

Selected Fiction:

Crane, Stephen. *The Red Badge of Courage*. New York. Appleton, 1895.
Kantor, MacKinlay. *Andersonville*. Garden City, N.Y.: Doubleday, 1955.
Keneally, Thomas. *Confederates*. New York: Harper & Row, 1979.
Morrison, Toni. *Beloved*. New York: Knopf, 1987.
Safire, William. *Freedom*. Garden City, N.Y.: Doubleday, 1987.
Shaara, Micheal. *The Killer Angels*. New York: David McKay, 1974.
Stowe, Harriet Beecher. *Uncle Tom's Cabin*. Boston: John P. Jowett, 1852.
Vidal, Gore. *Lincoln*. New York: Random House, 1984.

Chapter 5. When Monopoly Wasn't a Game

Adams, Henry. *The Education of Henry Adams: An Autobiography*. Boston: *Houghton Mifflin, 1988.

Addams, Jane. *Twenty Years at Hull-House*. New York: Macmillan, 1910; New York: *Signet, 1960. The personal account of the remarkable reformer who started one of the nation's first settlement houses in Chicago.

Brady, Kathleen. *Ida Tarbell: Portrait of a Muckraker*. New York: Putnam, 1984.

Brown, Dee. *Bury My Heart at Wounded Knee: An American Indian History of the American West*. New York: Holt, Rinehart and Winston, 1970; New York: *Washington Square Press, 1981.

Collier, Peter, and David Horowitz. *The Rockefellers: An American Dynasty*. New York: *New American Library, 1977. A popular history of the family by a pair of modern "muckraking" journalists, this book covers the rise of John D. Rockefeller.

Connell, Evan S. *Son of the Morning Star: Custer and the Little Bighorn*. Berkeley: North Point Press, 1984; New York: *Harper Perennial, 1985.

Fussell, Paul. *The Great War and Modern Memory*. London: Oxford University Press, 1975; *Oxford University Press, 1977. An award-winning book about the British experience in trench warfare from 1914 to 1918, emphasizing the literature that experience produced.

Hofstadter, Richard. *The Age of Reform: From Bryan to F.D.R., 1890–1940*. New York: Knopf, 1955; New York: *Vintage, 1960.

Jackson, Stanley. *J. P. Morgan*. New York: Stein & Day, 1983.

Josephson, Matthew, *The Politicos*. New York: *Harcourt Brace, 1963.

————. *The Robber Barons*. New York: Harcourt Brace, 1934; New York: *Harvest, 1962.

Kaplan, Justin. *Lincoln Steffens: A Biography*. New York: Simon and Schuster, 1974; New York: *Touchstone, 1988. A life of one of the most prominent of the "muckrakers."

————. *Mr. Clemens and Mark Twain*. New York: Simon and Schuster, 1966; New York: *Touchstone, 1983.

Karnow, Stanley. *In Our Image: America's Experience in the Philippines*. New York: Random House, 1989. A fascinating study of America's long entanglement in the Philippines, dating from the time of the Spanish-American War and the Insurrection, and carrying through to recent events following the overthrow of the Marcos dictatorship by Corazón Aquino.

Manchester, William. *The Arms of Krupp: 1587–1968*. Boston: Little, Brown, 1964; New York: *Bantam, 1983. This history of the German munitions and armament family provides a fascinating account of the rise of militarism in Germany that played prominently in both World Wars.

Marshall, S. L. A. *World War I*. New York: American Heritage, 1964; Boston: *Houghton Mifflin, 1987. A military historian, the author concentrates on the armed confrontations, with far less emphasis on the causes and effects of the war or its long-term consequences.

McCullough, David. *The Great Bridge*. New York: Simon and Schuster, 1972; NewYork: *Touchstone, 1983. The story of the construction of the Brooklyn Bridge.

————. *Mornings on Horseback*. New York: Simon and Schuster, 1981; New York: *Touchstone, 1982. A biography of the young Teddy Roosevelt.

————. *The Path Between the Seas: The Creation of the Panama Canal, 1870–1914*. New York: Simon and Schuster, 1977; New York: *Touchstone, 1978.

Morris, Edmund. *The Rise of Theodore Roosevelt*. New York: Coward, McCann & Geohegan, 1979; New York: *Ballantine, 1980. An admiring yet balanced and excellent account of Roosevelt's life, to his first inauguration.

Painter, Nell Irvin. *Standing at Armageddon: The United States, 1877–1919*. New York: Norton, 1987. A fascinating portrait of the country during this period of transition from minor power to empire.

Tuchman, Barbara. *The Guns of August*. New York: Macmillan, 1962; New York: *Bantam, 1976. The Pulitzer Prize–winning account of

European events leading to World War I and the first fighting at the Battle of the Marne.

————. *The Zimmerman Telegram*. New York: Macmillan, 1966; New York: *Ballantine, 1985. An account of the diplomatic turmoil and conspiracy between Germany and Mexico that helped push America into World War I.

Williams, John Hoyt. *A Great and Shining Road: The Epic Story of the Transcontinental Railroad*. New York: Times Books, 1988.

Woodward, C. Vann. *The Strange Career of Jim Crow*. London: Oxford University Press, 1955; *Oxford University Press (third revised edition), 1974.

Selected Fiction:

Adams, Henry. *Democracy: An American Novel* (1883). New York: Henry Holt, 1908.

Bellamy, Edward. *Looking Backward* (1888). Boston: Tickner, 1888.

Brown, Dee. *Creek Mary's Blood*. New York: Holt, Rinehart and Winston, 1980.

Doctorow, E. L. *Ragtime*. New York: Random House, 1975.

Dos Passos, John. *The U.S.A. Trilogy: The 42nd Parallel* (1930); *1919* (1932); *The Big Money* (1936).

Norris, Frank. *The Octopus*. Garden City, N.Y.: Doubleday, 1901.

Remarque, Erich Maria. *All Quiet on the Western Front*. Boston: Little, Brown, 1929.

Settle, Mary Lee. *The Scapegoat*. New York: Random House, 1980.

Sinclair, Upton. *The Jungle*. Garden City, N.Y.: Doubleday, Page, 1906.

Twain, Mark, and Charles Dudley Warner. *The Gilded Age: A Tale of Today*. Hartford: American Publishing Company, 1873.

Vidal, Gore. *1876*. New York: Random House, 1976.

————. *Empire*. New York: Random House, 1987.

Chapter 6. From Boom to Bust to Big Boom

Allen, Frederick Lewis. *The Big Change: America Transforms Itself: 1900–1950*. New York: Harper & Row, 1952; New York: *Harper Perennial, 1969.

————. *Only Yesterday: An Informal History of the 1920s*. New York: Harper & Row, 1931; New York: *Harper Perennial, 1986.

──────. *Since Yesterday: The 1930s in America*. New York: Harper & Row, 1939; New York: *Harper Perennial, 1972. A social and cultural history of life in the Depression years by one of America's great social historians.

Armor, John, and Peter Wright. *Manzanar: Photographs by Ansel Adams; Commentary by John Hersey*. New York: Times Books, 1988. A detailed chronicle of the Japanese-American internment camp, illustrated by Ansel Adams's photo-documentary of the camp.

Blum, John Morton. *V Was for Victory: Politics and American Culture During World War II*. New York: Harcourt Brace Jovanovich, 1976; New York: *Harvest, 1977.

Brooks, John. *Once in Golconda: A True Drama of Wall Street, 1920–1938*. New York: Norton, 1969.

Collier, Peter, and David Horowitz. *The Fords: An American Epic*. New York: Summit, 1987; *Summit, 1988.

Davis, Kenneth S. *FDR: The New York Years, 1928–1933*. New York: Random House, 1985.

──────. *FDR: The New Deal Years, 1933–1937*. New York: Random House, 1986.

Fest, Joachim C. *Hitler*. New York: Harcourt Brace Jovanovich, 1974; New York: *Vintage, 1975. A thorough single-volume biography of the Nazi leader.

Flood, Charles Bracelen. *Hitler: The Path to Power*. Boston: Houghton Mifflin, 1989. A recent biography that documents Hitler's rise to unquestioned power in the aftermath of World War I and the Depression.

Fussell, Paul. *Wartime: Understanding and Behavior in the Second World War*. London: Oxford University Press, 1989.

Galbraith, John Kenneth. *The Great Crash*. Boston: Houghton Mifflin, 1961; *Houghton Mifflin, 1988.

──────. *A Life in Our Times: Memoirs*. Boston: Houghton Mifflin, 1981. An autobiography by the economist, diplomat, and historian, especially interesting for Galbraith's experiences as a member of the bombing survey team that toured both Germany and Japan after the war and concluded that American saturation bombing was inconclusive in both instances.

Hersey, John. *Hiroshima*. New York: Knopf, 1946; New York: *Vintage, 1989. The classic account of the aftermath of the bombing of Hiroshima.

Kazin, Alfred. *On Native Grounds*. New York: Harcourt Brace & World, 1942; New York: *Harvest, 1983. A fascinating and very readable collection of literary criticism, focusing on major American writers of the 1930s and 1940s.

Lash, Joseph P. *Eleanor and Franklin*. New York: Norton, 1971; New York: *New American Library, 1973.

Leckie, Robert. *Delivered from Evil: The Saga of World War II*. New York: Harper & Row, 1987; New York: *Harper Perennial, 1988. A massive and updated single-volume history of the war.

Manchester, William. *American Caesar: Douglas MacArthur, 1880–1964*. Boston: Little, Brown, 1978; New York: *Dell, 1983. This splendid biography of MacArthur is admiring but not blind to the general's shortcomings. MacArthur's life as a soldier—as well as his father's before him—covers almost every facet of American military involvement from the Spanish-American War to the Korean War.

————. *The Glory and the Dream: A Narrative History of America, 1932–1972*. Boston: Little, Brown, 1974; New York: *Bantam, 1975.

————. *Goodbye, Darkness: A Memoir of the Pacific*. Boston: Little, Brown, 1979; New York: *Dell, 1987. The historian's recreation of the Pacific fighting in which he was a participant as a U.S. Marine.

Mencken, H. L. *A Choice of Days*. New York: *Vintage, 1980. This is a collection of pieces from three autobiographical works by the American journalist and social critic.

Morgan, Ted. *FDR: A Biography*. New York: Simon and Schuster, 1985; New York: *Touchstone, 1986. A sound and accessible popular one-volume biography.

Powers, Richard Gid. *Secrecy and Power: The Life of J. Edgar Hoover*. New York: Free Press, 1987; *Free Press, 1988. A solid and unbiased account of the life of one of America's most powerful men, the Director of the FBI.

Rhodes, Richard. *The Making of the Atomic Bomb*. New York: Simon and Schuster, 1987; New York: *Touchstone, 1988. An award-winning history of the development of the first bomb.

Taylor, A. J. P. *The War Lords*. New York: *Penguin, 1976. A collection of lectures given by a prominent British historian, this book offers a neat capsule biography of the personalities of the five men who conducted the Second World War: Mussolini, Hitler, Churchill, Stalin, and Roosevelt.

Terkel, Studs. *"The Good War": An Oral History of World War II*. New York: Pantheon, 1984; New York: *Ballantine, 1985.

————. *Hard Times: An Oral History of the Great Depression*. New York: Pantheon, 1970; New York: *Pocket Books, 1978. Life in the worst years of the Depression, as told to the journalist.

Toland, John. *Adolf Hitler.* Garden City, N.Y.: Doubleday, 1976; New York: *Ballantine, 1984. A best-selling life of Hitler by a popular historian.

———. *Infamy: Pearl Harbor and Its Aftermath.* Garden City, N.Y.: Doubleday, 1982; New York: *Berkley, 1984.

———. *Rising Sun: The Decline and Fall of the Japanese Empire.* New York: Random House, 1970; New York: *Bantam, 1982.

Watt, Donald Cameron. *How War Came: The Immediate Origins of the Second World War.* New York: Pantheon, 1989.

Wyden, Peter. *Day One: Before Hiroshima and After.* New York: Simon and Schuster, 1984; *Simon and Schuster, 1989.

Selected Fiction:

Fitzgerald, F. Scott. *The Great Gatsby.* New York: Scribner's, 1925.

Hemingway. Ernest. *A Farewell to Arms.* New York: Scribner's, 1929.

———. *For Whom the Bell Tolls.* New York: Scribner's, 1940.

Jones, James. *The Thin Red Line.* New York: Scribner's, 1962.

Mailer, Norman. *The Naked and the Dead.* New York: Holt, Rinehart and Winston, 1948.

Steinbeck, John. *The Grapes of Wrath.* New York: Viking, 1939.

Chapter 7. Commies, Containment, and Cold War

Blair, Clay. *The Forgotten War: America in Korea, 1950–1953.* New York: Times Books, 1987; New York: *Anchor Books, 1989.

Caute, David. *The Great Fear: The Anti-Communist Purge Under Truman and Eisenhower.* New York: Simon and Schuster, 1978.

Garrow, David J. *Bearing the Cross: Martin Luther King, Jr., and the Southern Christian Leadership Conference.* New York: Morrow, 1986; New York: *Vintage, 1988. A balanced and honest award-winning biography of the civil-rights leader and the movement he led.

Kluger, Richard. *Simple Justice: The History of* Brown v. Board of Education *and Black America's Struggle for Equality.* New York: Knopf, 1976; New York: *Vintage, 1977.

Miller, Merle. *Plain Speaking.* New York: Putnam, 1974; New York: *Berkley, 1986. This "oral history" presents a vivid picture of the president who has grown in stature as time has passed.

Newhouse, John. *War and Peace in the Nuclear Age.* New York: Knopf, 1988. A companion to the PBS television series detailing the history of nuclear arms and superpower rivalries.

Oakley, J. Ronald. *God's Country: America in the Fifties*. New York: Dembner Books, 1986.

Radosh, Ronald, and Joyce Milton. *The Rosenberg File: A Search for the Truth*. New York: *Vintage, 1984. A widely accepted investigation into the notorious case.

Schneir, Walter and Miriam. *Invitation to an Inquest*. New York: Pantheon, 1965; *Pantheon, 1983. Another investigation of the Rosenberg case, taking a very sympathetic view of the executed couple.

Selected Fiction:

Doctorow, E. L. *The Book of Daniel*. New York: Random House. 1971.

Chapter 8. The Torch Is Passed

Barrett, Lawrence I. *Gambling with History: Reagan in the White House*. Garden City, N.Y.: Doubleday, 1983; New York: *Penguin, 1984. Written by a *Time* magazine correspondent, this was one of the first books to assess the Reagan years negatively, and it provides a useful history of his earliest days in office.

Belin, David. *Final Disclosure: The Full Truth about the Assassination of President Kennedy*. New York: Scribner's, 1988. Unlike more sensational assassination books, this book, written by a Warren Commission investigator, convincingly negates most of the conspiracy theories surrounding JFK's murder.

Bernstein, Carl, and Bob Woodward. *All the President's Men*. New York: Simon and Schuster, 1974; New York: *Simon and Schuster, 1987.

Carroll, Peter N. *It Seemed Like Nothing Happened: The Tragedy and Promise of America in the 1970s*. New York: Holt, Rinehart and Winston, 1982; New York: *Henry Holt, 1984. A broad historical and cultural overview of the "me decade."

Caute, David. *The Year of the Barricades: A Journey Through 1968*. New York: Harper & Row, 1988; New York: *Harper Perennial, 1988.

Collier, Peter, and David Horowitz. *The Kennedys: An American Drama*. New York: Summit, 1984; New York: *Warner, 1988. Although it takes a tabloid approach, this presents a damning and documented account of the rise of this powerful American regal family. Particularly interesting for its discussion of the Kennedy patriarch, Joseph P. Kennedy, Sr.

Davis, John H. *The Kennedys: Dynasty and Disaster*. New York: McGraw-Hill, 1984; *McGraw-Hill, 1985. Another gossipy look, by a relative of Jacqueline Kennedy Onassis. Includes a lot of rumor and speculation, buttressed by recent documented revelations.

Dickstein, Morris, *Gates of Eden: American Culture in the Sixties*. New York: Basic Books, 1977; New York: *Penguin, 1989. An examination of American politics in the period, through the literature and culture of the era.

Epstein, Edward Jay. *Inquest: The Warren Commission and the Establishment of Truth*. New York: Viking, 1966; New York: *Viking Compass, 1969. One of the first and most influential assaults upon the Warren Commission's findings.

FitzGerald, Frances. *Fire in the Lake: The Vietnamese and the Americans in Vietnam*. Boston: Atlantic–Little, Brown, 1972; New York: *Vintage, 1973. A standard book on understanding the roots of the American involvement and failure in Vietnam.

Friedan, Betty. *The Feminine Mystique*. New York: Norton, 1963; New York: *Dell, 1984. The now-classic document on which the modern American feminist movement was built.

Gitlin, Todd. *The Sixties: Years of Hope, Days of Rage*. New York: Bantam, 1987; *Bantam, 1989.

Hackworth, Col. David H., and Julie Sherman. *About Face: The Odyssey of an American Warrior*. New York: Simon and Schuster, 1989. A fascinating, best-selling account of a soldier who fought in both Korea and Vietnam, becoming something of a renegade in Southeast Asia.

Haing Ngor. *A Cambodian Odyssey*. New York: Macmillan, 1987; New York: Warner 1989. A riveting first-person account of the aftermath of the fall of Cambodia to Communists, by the doctor-turned-actor who portrayed the character of Dith Pran in the film *The Killing Fields*.

Halberstam, David. *The Best and the Brightest*. New York: Random House, 1972; New York: *Penguin, 1983. The classic account of the intellectuals and academics surrounding Kennedy who pushed America into Vietnam.

Hersh, Seymour M. *My Lai 4: A Report on the Massacre and Its Aftermath*. New York: Random House, 1970; New York: *Vintage, 1971.

———. *The Price of Power: Kissinger in the Nixon White House*. New York: Summit Books, 1983; *Summit, 1984.

Karnow, Stanley. *Vietnam: A History*. New York: Viking Penguin, 1983; *Penguin, 1984. An indispensable one-volume overview of the war in Vietnam.

Lukas, J. Anthony. *Nightmare: The Underside of the Nixon Years*. New York: Viking, 1976; New York: *Penguin, 1988. A full and comprehensive account of the entire Watergate years, and the definitive work on the fall of Nixon.

Miller, Merle. *Lyndon: An Oral Biography*. New York: Putnam, 1980; New York: *Ballantine, 1987.

Peers, William R. *The My Lai Inquiry.* New York: Norton/Presidio Press, 1979.

Safire, William. *Before the Fall: An Inside View of the Pre-Watergate White House.* Garden City, N.Y.: Doubleday, 1975; New York: *Da Capo, 1988. Former Nixon speechwriter and current *New York Times* columnist, Safire presents a vivid view of Nixon in power before the fallout from Watergate.

Scheer, Robert. *With Enough Shovels: Reagan, Bush and Nuclear War.* New York: Random House, 1982; New York: *Vintage, 1983. A disturbing examination of the Reagan stance on arms and the "winnability" of a nuclear war.

Schieffer, Bob, and Gary Paul Gates. *The Acting President.* New York: E. P. Dutton, 1989. A television newsman's overview of eight years of Reagan that provides a useful capsule of the period, including the Iran-Contra situation.

Schlesinger, Arthur M. *A Thousand Days: JFK in the White House.* Boston: Houghton Mifflin, 1965; New York: *Fawcett, 1966. A partisan insider, the famed historian writes a fascinating view of the Kennedy presidency.

Smith, Hedrick. *The Power Game: How Washington Works.* New York: Random House, 1988; New York: *Ballantine, 1989. A fascinating portrait of the real reins of power in Washington and how they are manipulated; especially useful in assessing the failures and successes of the Reagan administration.

Sumners, Harry G. *Vietnam War Almanac.* New York: *Facts on File, 1985. An encyclopedic reference guide to the war, complete with maps, historical introduction, and a detailed chronology.

The Tower Commission Report: The Full Text of the President's Special Review Board: Introduction by R. W. Apple, Jr. New York: *Bantam, 1987. The damning examination of Reagan's failures in allowing the Iran-Contra scandal to occur.

White, Theodore. *America in Search of Itself: The Making of the President, 1956–1980.* New York: Harper & Row, 1982; New York: *Warner, 1983. A compilation of the author's "Making of" series, assessing the Presidents of the past thirty-five years.

Wyden, Peter. *Bay of Pigs: The Untold Story.* New York: Simon and Schuster, 1979; New York: *Touchstone, 1980. This compelling narrative account tells the complete story of the disastrous invasion of Castro's Cuba. By the author of *Day One* (See Chapter 6 readings.)

X, Malcolm, with Alex Haley. *The Autobiography of Malcom X.* New York: Grove, 1964; *Grove, 1965.

Index

The Following is Excerpted from

DON'T KNOW MUCH ABOUT® THE BIBLE

Kenneth C. Davis's New Book
Coming Soon in Hardcover from
Eagle Brook, an imprint of
William Morrow and Company

Introduction

When I was in the sixth grade, a building was going up across the street from my school. Like most ten- or eleven-year-old boys, I preferred to watch bulldozers in action and concrete being poured to whatever was being written on the blackboard. I spent a lot of sixth grade gazing out the window. I don't think I learned anything that year.

The red brick structure I watched rising with such absorbed fascination was a church. Unlike the soaring Gothic cathedrals of Europe or the formidable fortress-like stone church my family attended, this was not a typical church. It was being built in the shape of a mighty boat. Presumably, it was Noah's Ark. Most of us have a mental picture of Noah's Ark and we think it looks like a cute tugboat with a little house on top.

Except that Noah's Ark didn't look anything like that. You can look it up yourself. Right there in Genesis, you'll find God's Little Instruction Book, a set of divine plans for building an ark. Unfortunately, like most directions that come with bicycles or appliances, these are a little sketchy, providing little more than the rough dimensions of 300 by 50 by 30 cubits (or roughly 450 feet long, 75 feet wide and 45 feet high). God told Noah to add a roof and put in three decks. Beyond that, God's instructions come without a diagram, unless Noah threw away the blueprints when he finished. So we should count Noah putting this thing together in time to beat the rains as one of the first miracles.

Many years after I gazed out that schoolhouse window, I learned that the original Hebrew word for Ark literally means "box" or "chest" in English. In other words, Noah's ark was a big wooden crate, longer and wider than an American football field. So the architect who designed that church to look like the *Titanic* may have understood buttresses and load-bearing walls. But he didn't know his Bible.

He wasn't alone. Millions of people around the world own a Bible, profess to read it, and follow its dictates. Many say they study it daily. But most of us have never looked at a Bible, despite insisting that it is important. According to one recent survey, nine out of ten Americans own a Bible, but fewer than half ever read it. Why? For most folks, the Bible is hard to understand. It's confusing. It's contradictory. It's boring. In other words, the Bible perfectly fits Mark Twain's definition of a classic: "a book which people praise and don't read."

Not only do we praise the Bible, but we quote it almost daily in public and private. It permeates our language and laws. It is in our courts for administering oaths. Despite the First Amendment to the U.S. Constitution, it is on the Capitol steps when America inaugurates a President. It is cited by politicians and preachers, playwrights and poets, peace lovers and provocateurs.

As its phenomenal sales prove, the Bible holds a special place in nearly every country in the world. The worldwide sales of the Bible are literally uncountable. It is even tough to keep track of all the translations of the Bible, or portions of it, that exist around the world. There are Bibles in more than 40 European languages, 125 Asian and Pacific Island languages, and translations into more than 100 African languages, with an additional 500 African language versions of some portion of the Bible. At least fifteen complete Native-American Bibles have been produced. The first Native-American translation, completed in 1663, was made into the language of the Massachusetts tribe, which the Puritan colonists then promptly wiped out.

In English, there are nearly 3,000 versions of the entire Bible or portions of the Bible. While the King James Version, first produced in 1611, and the Revised Standard Version, are still the most popular, publishers thrive on introducing new translations and "specialty" Bibles every year. The *Living Bible*, one contemporary, paraphrased version, has sold more than 40 million copies since 1971. Around the world, active Bible study classes attract millions of students. So, whether we worship in some formal setting or not, people of nearly every nation remain deeply fascinated by the Bible and its rich treasury of stories and lessons.

To many of them, it is still "The Greatest Story Ever Told." For millions of Christians, the Old and New Testaments make up the "Good Book." For Jews, there are no "Old" and "New" Testaments, only the collection of Hebrew Scriptures that are equivalent to the Christian Old Testament. In spite of these differences, the common chord for Christians and Jews is strong: these books have been the source of inspiration, healing, spiritual guidance and ethical rules for thousands of years.

The Bible is clearly many things to many people. The problem is, most of us don't know much about ® the Bible. Raised in a secular, media-saturated world in which references to God and religion leave us in embarrassed silence, we have wide-ranging reasons for this ignorance. For some, it was simply being bored by the drone of Sunday school or Hebrew class. Others received their Bible basics from the great but factually-flawed Hollywood epics, like *The Ten Commandments, The Greatest Story Ever Told,* and *The Robe.*

But most people simply never learned anything at all about a book that has influenced the course of human history more than any other. Public schools don't dare go near the subject of Religion— perhaps we should be grateful for that, given their track record on the other three Rs. The media generally limits its coverage of religion to the twice-yearly Christmas/Easter stories, unless there is a scandal or a lunatic-fringe disaster, like the Heaven's Gate or Branch Davidian cults. We've stopped sending our children to Sunday school or synagogue, and stopped going ourselves. The ignorance doesn't stop at the churchyard gates. In a 1997 survey, The London *Sunday Times* found that only 34 percent of 220 Anglican priests could recite all of the Ten Commandments without help! All of them remembered the parts about not "killing" and not committing adultery. But things got a little fuzzy after that. In fact, 19 percent of these priests thought that the eighth commandment is, "Life is a journey. Enjoy the ride."

At least they didn't think it was "Just do it."

Even those who *think* they know the Bible are surprised when they learn that their "facts" are often half-truths, misinformation, or dimly-remembered stories cleaned up for synagogue and Sunday school. For centuries, Jews and Christians have heard sanitized versions of Scripture that left out the awkward, uncomfortable, and racier Bible stories. Sure, most people have some recollections of Noah, Abraham, and Jesus. But they are less likely to know about the tales of rape, impaling, and "ethnic cleansing" routinely found in the Bible. These are timeless stories with timeless themes: justice and morality; vengeance and murder; sin and redemption. *Pulp Fiction* and *NYPD Blue* have nothing on the Bible!

There was Cain knocking off Abel. Noah's son cursed for seeing his drunken father naked. Abraham willing to sacrifice the son he desired all his life. The population of Sodom and Gomorrah destroyed for its wanton ways. Lot sleeping with his daughters. A tent peg driven through a man's head in Judges. King Saul asking young David to bring him a hundred Philistine foreskins as a bride price to marry his daughter. King David sending a soldier into the front lines so he could sleep with the man's wife. Then there is that ever-popular tale of wise Solomon threatening to cut a baby in half. But did you know that the two women who brought King Solomon that baby were prostitutes?

Raised in a traditional, Protestant church with a full menu of Christmas pageants and confirmation classes, I thought I possessed a fairly solid biblical education. In the annual Christmas pageant, I rose from angel to shepherd to Joseph—a non-speaking role; Jesus's earthly father stood mutely behind Mary with nothing to say. I never made it to the plum roles—one of the "Three Kings" who call on the infant Jesus. They had the coolest costumes. Three very tall brothers in my church always got those parts. I didn't know until much later that they weren't "Three Kings" at all, but magicians from Iran.

While attending a Lutheran college and later, Jesuit Fordham University, I continued to study the history and literature of the Bible. But then, in writing an earlier book called *Don't Know Much About Geography,* I posed a few simple questions related to the Bible:

"Where was the Garden of Eden?"

"What is the world's oldest city?"

"Did Moses really cross the Red Sea?"

That's when I got some surprises. In researching the world's oldest city, for instance, I learned that Joshua's Jericho is one of the oldest of human settlements. It also lies on a major earthquake zone. Could that simple fact of geology have had anything to do with those famous walls tumbling down? Then I discovered that Moses and the tribes of Israel never crossed the Red Sea but escaped from Pharaoh and his chariots across the *Sea of Reeds,* an uncertain designation which might be one of several lakes in Egypt or a marshy section of the Nile Delta. This mistranslation crept into the Greek Septuagint version and was uncovered by modern scholars with access to old Hebrew manuscripts. While it would not have been as cinematically dazzling for C.B. DeMille to have Charlton Heston herd all those movie extras across a soggy bog, this linguistic correction made the escape from Egypt far more plausible.

To me, the fact that one of the key stories in the Bible was garbled by a mistranslation was a striking revelation. And it set me to thinking. How many other glitches are there in the Bible? How many other "little" mistakes in translation have blurred our understanding of the real story? After all, the Bible has been through an awful lot of translations during the past 2,000 years, including, only in fairly recent times, into English and other modern languages. Moses and Jesus never said "thee" and "thou." In fact, even the name "Jesus" is a muddled translation of the Hebrew name Joshua. In the words of one politician, "Mistakes were made." They were compounded over time. What if one of those medieval monks had slipped a bit with his quill when he was illuminating a manuscript? Or perhaps one of King James's scribes had too much sacramental wine the day he worked on Deuteronomy.

My questions about the Bible took a more troubling turn when I wrote *Don't Know Much About the Civil War.* I discovered that Christian abolitionists and defenders of slavery both turned to the Bible to support their positions. Slaveholders pointed to the existence of slavery in the Bible, as well as laws and biblical commands requiring slaves to be obedient, to justify America's "Peculiar Institution." Abolitionists cited Jewish laws for emancipating slaves and sheltering runaway slaves, New Testament verses that suggested freeing slaves, and Jesus's commandment to "Do unto others as you would have them do unto you." How could the Bible be right for both of them? The moral quandary pitting slavery against abolition marked a turning point in American history: for the first time, doubt was cast on the Bible's authority.

My own curiosity about biblical authority and accuracy come at a time when new discoveries and scholarship are challenging many accepted notions about the Bible. For instance, there have been startling discoveries drawn from the Dead Sea Scrolls, the ancient Hebrew Bible texts unearthed fifty years ago in some caves in the desert near the Dead Sea. These scrolls, the oldest known versions of the Hebrew Scriptures that make up the Old Testament, have added immensely to an understanding of Bible texts and life at the time Jesus lived. Even more dramatic and controversial are questions raised in *The Gnostic Gospels,* a book which explores a cache of 1,500-year-old Christian documents very much at odds with the traditional New Testament stories of Jesus. Discoveries such as these are prompting serious scholars to reexamine very fundamental questions: Who wrote the Bible? Did Jesus say everything we were taught he said? Did he say more?

Questions like these resonate deeply with many people, whether well-schooled in the Bible or embarrassed by their lack of Biblical knowledge. *Don't Know Much About the Bible* is aimed at answering these questions for an audience that still considers the Bible sacred and important, but just doesn't know what it says. For instance, most people are astonished to learn that Genesis contains not one but two Creation stories, significantly different in details and meaning. In the first of these Creations, men and women are created simultaneously in "God's image." This is followed by a second Garden of Eden surprise—there was no apple! A few of the other widely-held Bible misconceptions are equally remarkable. David didn't slay Goliath. Jonah wasn't in a whale. And King David and Jesus were both descended from prostitutes.

To clear away the cobwebs of misconception surrounding the Bible, this book traces the history of the Bible itself and how it came to be as we know it. Many of the events described in the Bible, such as the 50-year captivity of the Jewish people in Babylon or New Testament events occurring during the heights of the Roman Empire, can be matched to recorded history. While the ancient Israelites existed as a fairly small group of nomadic herders, the Egyptians built one of the most extraordinary civilizations in human history.

(Do you find it curious that the Bible never mentions the Pyramids?) Jesus lived and preached in a small outpost of the mighty Roman empire, whose language and laws continue to influence our lives.

By examining the Bible historically, one aim of this book is to show which Biblical teachings may have been just fine for an ancient, semi-nomadic world, and which may still apply to life at the dawn of the 21st century. There are many Biblical laws that modern Jews and Christian no longer accept. For instance, even the most hardcore fundamentalists would probably agree that it is no longer necessary for a father to prove his daughter's virginity by displaying a bloody sheet in the town square. It is safe to say that most of us no longer believe that a mother must make a burnt offering after bearing a child or that a woman is "unclean" while menstruating. All these are drawn from the Laws of Moses.

Have you let your animals breed with a different kind? Sown your fields with two kinds of seed? Have you put on a garment made of two different materials? Well, then, you've broken some of God's statutes as laid out by Moses in Leviticus.

How many still think that adultery should be punished by stoning, as Jewish law provides? (Probably quite a few in the "First Wives Club"!) Anyone who wants a sense of biblical justice in the modern world might look at Afghanistan in 1997 under the control of the Taliban, Islamic fundamentalists whose ideas of appropriate behavior and punishment are not too different from those of the ancient Israelites.

The questions I raise in *Don't Know Much About the Bible*, whether profound or irreverent, are aimed at dusting off some time-worn misimpressions and refreshing rusty recollections. Often these questions address "household" names and events from the Bible, such as what the Exodus was or who the "Good Samaritan" was, and what the Sermon on the Mount says. We know they're important, but we can't put our finger on exactly what they are and why we should know about them. But going beyond those, I pry open some bigger cans of worms. Why can't Moses enter the "Promised Land"? Was Jesus born on Christmas? Was Mary Magdalene naughty or nice?

Of course, these sorts of questions challenge "traditional" notions about what the Bible says and I suspect my approach will roil people who are possessive about the Bible. On balance, however, this is a book in which historical accuracy, cultural context, and removing confusions about archaic words and mistranslations are all given a place in understanding these ancient texts. I try not to "interpret" the Bible so much as explain what it is actually in it.

As a historian, I know that "tampering" with the Bible is a risky business. In one attempt to make the Bible accessible to common folk who didn't understand Hebrew, Latin or Greek, John Wycliffe, a renegade English priest, produced one of the first English Bible translations before his death in 1384. The authorities were not amused. Denounced as a heretic after his death, Wycliffe couldn't be executed. Church officials did the next best thing: they exhumed his corpse and burned it.

Another English priest, William Tyndale, didn't fare much better. Upset by the corruption he witnessed among his fellow clergymen, Tyndale (1492–1536) believed the Bible should be read by everyone, not just the few who understood Latin, the language of the Church. He set out to translate the Bible into English. Accused of perverting the Scriptures, Tyndale was forced to leave England, and his New Testament was ordered burned as "untrue translations." Arrested and imprisoned as a heretic, Tyndale was executed in Antwerp by strangling. His body was then burned at the stake in October 1536 for good measure.

In other words, you go into a job like this with your eyes open. There are plenty of people who feel that the Bible is just fine the way it is, thank you. Whenever a Tyndale comes along with different ideas, the "Powers-That-Be" usually lash out. Sometimes the Powers-That-Be realize they were wrong. It just takes a while. In the case of Galileo (1564–1642), the Italian physicist and astronomer who said the earth revolves around the sun, it took the Vatican three and a half centuries to admit that he was right. In 1992—350 years after Galileo died—the Roman Catholic Church reversed its condemnation of Galileo. William Tyndale is now honored as the "Father of the English Bible." Small compensation, perhaps, for having one's neck wrung and being barbecued.

While I don't expect that anyone will call for my execution or excommunication, I'm sure that some people will not be happy with this book because it challenges "conventional wisdom" by asking questions. Many people have been taught not to question the Bible.

They fear that if you pull one loose thread, the whole thing will unravel like a cheap suit. Ultimately, the Bible is a book of faith, not history, biology, biography, science, or even philosophy. The questions I pose may be an affront to people who still believe that the Bible is the *unquestionable* "Word of God." But for centuries, scholars and thinkers, many of them devout believers, have been raising doubts about the Bible. People of faith shouldn't fear these questions. How strong is a faith that can't stand up to a few honest questions?

After all, some of the boldest questions ever asked by men are explored in Job, a book which has the audacity to challenge a God who has made a bet with Satan. "Why?" a beleaguered Job asks of God again and again, "Why have you made me your target?" One of history's most cynical fellows was called "The Preacher" in the book of Ecclesiastes. In the midst of all the Bible books praising God's wonders, "The Preacher" stops us short by asking, "What's the point if you live and work hard and then just die?"

If my questions upset you, blame Adam and Eve! After all, that Forbidden Fruit was plucked from the Tree of Knowledge. And knowledge is what this is all about. Underlying the *Don't Know Much About* series is the notion that "school" doesn't end when we leave the classroom. I believe it is crucial for people to question the easy assumptions they grow up with—about religion, history or a Ford versus a Chevy. The world is a school, life about learning. In the words of poet William Butler Yeats, "Education is not the filling of a pail, but the lighting of a fire."

Beyond "lighting a fire," *Don't Know Much About the Bible* has more ambitious goals. We live in fascinating but confounding times. Rarely has the world seemed so "corrupt," yet rarely has there been such worldwide interest in religion and spirituality. Whether it is millennial curiosity or the weary rejection of modern life, many people are pondering their lives and searching for "something." Call it family values. Morality. Virtue. Perhaps even faith. For these searchers, *Don't Know Much About the Bible* sets out to offer some help in "attaining wisdom and discipline; for understanding words of insight; for acquiring a disciplined and prudent life, doing what is right and just and fair." [Proverbs]

An ambitious goal? Absolutely. In other words, for the modern spiritual journeyer, this book sets out to provide a readable road map through a Bible that remains morally instructive, vividly alive, and spiritually challenging. Can I bring you "faith"? Can I make you "believe"? I'm not even going to try.

If that is what you find, amen. If you don't find faith in these pages, however, I hope you will at least find wisdom.

SPECIAL $3
CONSUMER REBATE!

Receive $3 with the purchase of one of these three books and Kenneth C. Davis's new hardcover, *Don't Know Much About® the Bible.*

Send in your proof-of-purchase (cash register receipts) for both books and the coupon below, completely filled out.

Offer expires 12/31/98.

Void where prohibited by law.

- -

Mail to: Avon Books, Dept. KD, P.O. Box 767, Dresden, TN 38225

Name _____

Address _____

City _____

State/Zip _____